THE LITTLE RED CLIFF

1946 – 1963

Yeo Hong Eng

First published 2013
This edition published 2014

PARTRIDGE
A Penguin Random House Company

Some parts of my activities in the book were featured in the Singapore Media Corps "Foodage" programmes in OKTO channel in August 2011. Many of my activities in the book were featured in the Singapore Memory Projects.

To order additional copies of this book, contact
Toll Free 800 101 2657 (Singapore)
Toll Free 1 800 81 7340 (Malaysia)
orders.singapore@partridgepublishing.com

www.partridgepublishing.com/singapore

Quotes

"This book has a wealth of information about life in the kampongs, from the conditions during the period to the games that were played. The author not only provides instructions on how to play them but also provides beautiful illustrations on how to make a whistle out of a coconut frond, a turning disc out of a bottle-cap. For creative people who like making their own toys, this book is a gift."

Josephine Chia
Author of *Kampong Spirit Gotong Royong/*
Life in Kampong Potong Pasir.

"Mr Yeo is an amazing story-teller because he makes his experience come alive for his audience. He is authentic and knowledgeable about Singapore, having journeyed with her, through her growth."

Mrs Sabrina James
Principal
Hougang Primary

Acknowledgements

My sincere thanks to all those who contributed to the completion of the book, for without whom it would not have been possible.

Author Josephine Chia for her thought-provoking advice and encouragement.

My brothers, sisters, cousins, relatives and friends for their input in recalling certain events.

All blogger friends who directly or indirectly contributed tips, pointers and details on certain events.

Catherine Lim and Chang Soh Kiak and everyone from Sitting-in-Pictures for their encouragement.

All the known and unknown photographers whose photos enhance the understanding of certain events in this book.

Dedications

To my grandfather, Yeo Teow Teng; my grandmother, Koh Cheo Neo; my father, Yeo Koon Poh and my mother, Tan Ah Choon.

Foreword

I first met Hong Eng over a bottle cap. It was a particular, distinctive Sinalco bottle cap with the striking red surface and white lettering. His fascination with this, and other artefacts of the past, at an event the Singapore Memory Project held in Kolam Ayer, intrigued me.

After that, I began to notice him at many of the events organised by the Singapore Memory Project. Each time I saw him, he would be toting a large camera and capturing all the moments he wished to remember with the same love he holds for the antique cameras, matchboxes and the other memorabilia he collects. And each post he writes of his collections for his blog lovingly chronicles the history and detail behind each moment and artefact.

Hong Eng has applied the same loving care to this first book of a series, devoted to his memories of people, places, flora and fauna in a Singapore of the past. When I was conceptualising the Singapore Memory Project, I was determined that there should not just be one grand narrative of Singapore's history. Instead, there should be a tapestry of lives that is as varied and complex as the minutiae of each of our lives.

Hong Eng's book is a glowing example of that, with its cast that ranges from pirate taxi-drivers, chicken thieves and *bomohs* to the one or two banana ghosts. The narrative is as esoteric. It strikes you that he is someone who notices everything and somehow recalls the details meticulously so many years on. Set against the backdrop of Tanah Merah and just a little beyond, the book even looks at the other inhabitants such as iguanas, small white ants and the occasional monkey. I also love how the story strolls sometimes into almost eccentric territory, such as the eulogies to buses and bus stops of the past.

I have always entertained the notion that one could land in a certain place and know unmistakably where one is. I fear this is becoming more and more difficult as more and more places become increasingly homogenised and move toward becoming unrecognisable from one another.

In Hong Eng's book, I managed to relive that sense of a specific time and place. The smells and sounds of that era have come alive again with his evocation of the celebrations of festivals of the past, such as the sound of fire crackers heralding the start of the Lunar New Year. It is unmistakably Singapore, though of a different time and with a generous serving of the kampong spirit we find so elusive these days.

I hope many more will come forward to be storytellers like Hong Eng. They could add one more piece to the tapestry of lives that will help to connect us as a nation through a pervasive culture of collective remembering. Perhaps then we will acquire a sense of the nation we once were, as distinctively and unmistakably as the Sinalco bottle cap was, as we move forward into the future.

Gene Tan
Director, National Library, Singapore

Introduction

*T*his book traces my memories of life in kampong Tanah Merah Kechil, from as far back as I can remember, since I was three years old in 1948, until the early 1960s.

It describes kampong life—the sounds, sights and smells and the daily challenges faced by those living in it. Struggling to live on the land gave us the fortitude to face the challenges posed by the authorities of that time as well as the natural calamities we were vulnerable to.

During those post war years, life was hard and household essentials were difficult to come by. Hence the members of our family, as well as many other families in Singapore, had to strive and improvise to survive. To do so required energy, initiative, presence of mind and courage.

Then, in the 1960s, the land on which my family had their vegetable farm was bought by Leng Seng Land Development. We were proud to say that as a result of our experiences of life in the kampong, we become more resilient, self-reliant and better adapted to face the challenges of modern society.

At this point, I must state that it is not my intention to cause anyone, dead or alive, any discomfort, should my opinions differ from theirs. My aim is to relate what really happened, as I perceived it. The accounts in this book are only my personal judgments and opinions. If anyone should feel offended by my opinions, I extend my sincere apologies.

To those in Singapore who grew up after that period, I hope that this book not only serves as a reference on how hard we had to struggle *in daily life, but also provides a glimpse of the joys and colour of that time. To my contemporaries, I hope this account may evoke a nostalgic sense of those days gone by, which I treasure as some of my most precious memories and that you may join me in these reminiscences of the past.*

Yeo Hong Eng
April 2014

A Sketch Map of Kampong Tanah Merah Kechil in the 1950s

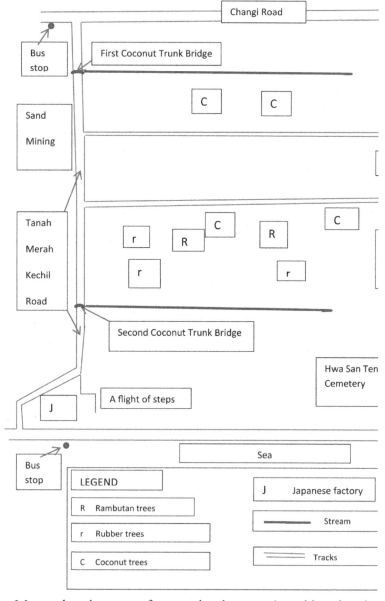

Map and explanation of geographical context/ neighbourhood

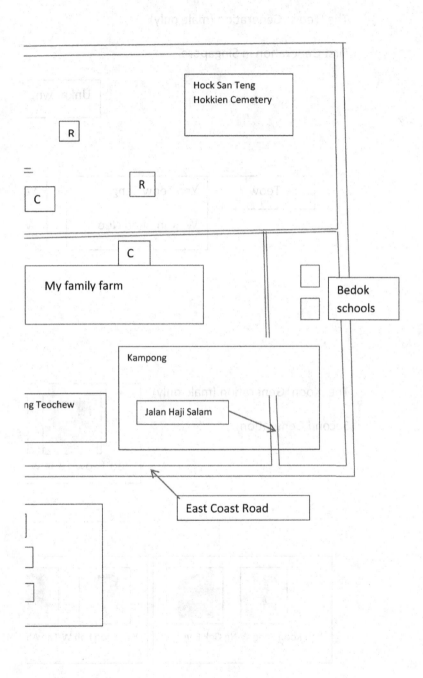

Hock San Teng
Hokkien Cemetery

R

R

C

C

My family farm

Bedok
schools

Kampong

ng Teochew

Jalan Haji Salam

East Coast Road

The 'Teow' Generation (male only)

First Generation in Singapore

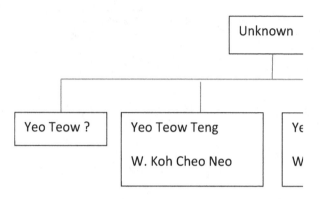

| Unknown |

| Yeo Teow ? | Yeo Teow Teng | Ye |
| | W. Koh Cheo Neo | W |

The 'Koon' Generation (male only)

Second Generation

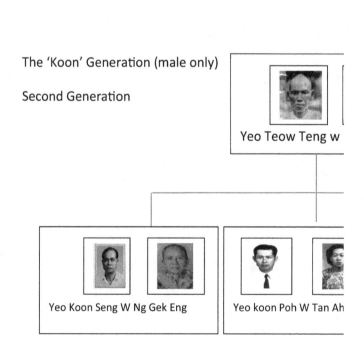

Yeo Teow Teng w

Yeo Koon Seng W Ng Gek Eng | Yeo koon Poh W Tan Ah

ꓶ

Yeo Teow Swee

W. Ho Keok Neo

Yeo Teow Tong

W. Tan Kim Hong

w Koh Cheo Neo

Ah Choon

Yeo Bong Chee

H Chew Hock Seng

The 'Hong' Generation

Third Generation

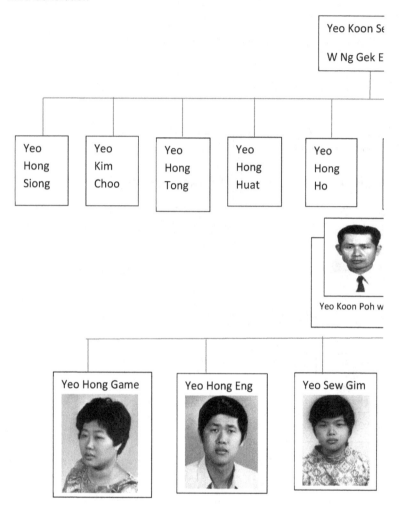

Yeo Koon Se

W Ng Gek E

Yeo
Hong
Siong

Yeo
Kim
Choo

Yeo
Hong
Tong

Yeo
Hong
Huat

Yeo
Hong
Ho

Yeo Koon Poh w

Yeo Hong Game

Yeo Hong Eng

Yeo Sew Gim

Seng

: Eng

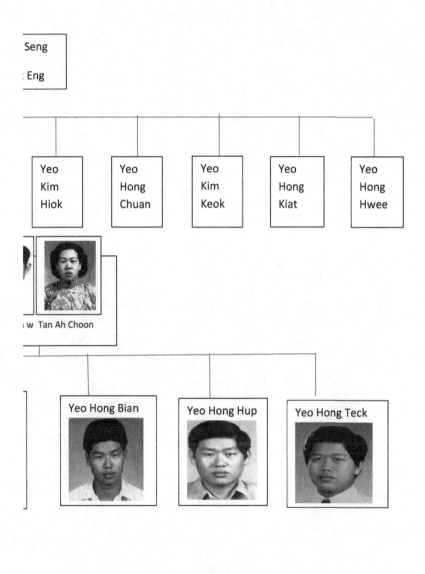

| Yeo Kim Hiok | Yeo Hong Chuan | Yeo Kim Keok | Yeo Hong Kiat | Yeo Hong Hwee |

w Tan Ah Choon

Yeo Hong Bian

Yeo Hong Hup

Yeo Hong Teck

Contents

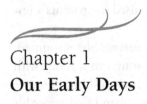

Chapter 1
Our Early Days

O ne day, my grandma decreed that from now onwards, all of us boys had to do one chore in the morning before leaving for school. My job was to clear the dung from the chicken coop. So dutifully, every morning, I took a wicker basket to the chicken coop, swept up the dung, scooped it into the basket and brought it to the farm.

One morning, as usual, I carried my wicker basket to the coop. I unlocked the padlock with the key and pushed open the door. The chickens were unusually quiet. Normally, there would be some cackling noises. But that morning, it was quiet, far too quiet. I looked hard. There were no chickens perching on the roost. I thought I was dreaming. I rubbed my eyes and stared again. The coop was empty. I trembled. How could it be? I was puzzled. I ran as if I were flying to my parents, and in between gasps for air, I told them what I had seen. They hurried to the chicken coop, asking me whether I had locked it the previous night. Obviously, I had. A quick survey revealed that a big hole had been cut through the netting at the rear. My parents stared at each other in despair. The loss was great. Word spread to the neighbours and precautionary measures were taken by everyone.

One day, someone said that a *bomoh* (Malay spirit healer) would be able to help reveal who the thief was. My mum jumped at the opportunity. She was told to prepare two dollars worth of *ang pow* (money in red envelopes) as a service fee. Off they went to the kampong. We children were not allowed to go, as children in those days were not to meddle in adult matters. *"Tua lang cho shi, gi na chau kih,"* they used to say, meaning children should not interfere in adult matters. That might be true as I had caused my parents a few embarrassing moments in my later years.

Well, what did my mum learn from the *bomoh*? She recounted: "The *bomoh*—a man aged about 40—was seated in a room with his legs crossed. He had a basin of water in front of him. He wore a sarong but was without a shirt. He had a headband tied across his forehead. The one who wished to consult him must walk quietly and slowly and sit on the floor facing him. Everyone else outside the room had to keep very quiet. Everyone obeyed, as they did not wish to offend him or to be rude. Then, he asked for the details of the incident. He listened attentively, interrupting only to clear certain doubts. Next, he mumbled some prayers. He then peered into the basin of water."

"Ada dua orang lelaki. Umor-nya dua puloh lebeh tahun. Mereka menchuri duo puloh ekor ayam," he said, informing my mum that two men, of about 20 years old, stole 20 chickens. Then the session was over. The gift of *ang pow* was placed beside the basin. When my mum was walking out, the *bomoh* took the *ang pow* and put in into his cloth bag. He then asked for the next person who had come to see him. My mum left more confused than before.

In those days before there was electricity in the kampongs, the safety match was one of the most important household items. Every household would make the purchase of matches top priority. My parents would purchase matches by the carton. In those days, the more popular brands of matches were the Swedish-made Elephant and Cock brand and the Three Legs brand. Each matchbox and drawer was made of very thin pieces of wood. The wood was then wrapped with a thin piece of paper. A label was pasted on top of the box. Each box contained about 50 matchsticks. Sometimes, my dad would purchase a family-sized box, which I guess must have contained 500 sticks. I remember one evening, Uncle Ah Chiang took us to New World City bazaar and amusement park. Among the stalls was a huge advertisement of a box of House brand matches. Customers queued to purchase these House brand matches as they were on promotion. I remember the matches were produced by George Lee and Co. My dad bought a huge carton. Since then, I have not seen any of George Lee's matches on sale anywhere else.

Besides lighting stoves for cooking and lighting oil lamps, we also needed matches for many other purposes. We needed them to make burnt earth mounds and to burn grass plots for our farming, cook poultry and pig feed, light lamps for the chicken coops and pig pens, make fire brands to destroy bee hives, and to light joss sticks and burn joss paper after prayer. Children loved to play *masak-masak* (make-believe cooking). They needed matches to start a fire to cook a make-believe dish. On New Year's day, we needed matches to light firecrackers. Just imagine the number of matchsticks we used per day! For us, it was the norm to carry a box of matches on our person.

Every provision shop and *mamak* stall was well stocked with matches. I do not know whether the provision shops of other countries in this region had this practice—to have a lighted lamp for people who brought single sticks of cigarettes to light them. Regular smokers would purchase packets of cigarettes together with matches, so they would not bother the vendors for a light. The vendors were obliged to provide a match for such customers. In order to save on matches, each vendor kept a small, lighted oil lamp ready. Small strips cut from empty cigarette boxes were prepared for customers to dip into the flame to light their cigarettes.

Samples of match boxes

My grandparents moved from Lian Teng Hng (otherwise known as Kampong Eunos) just before the Japanese Occupation in the late

1930s to house number 598-21 in Tanah Merah Kechil. Later their house number was changed to 598-29. It was a huge attap house with two big bedrooms, a large hall and a long corridor along the bedrooms. Adjoining the house was a kitchen. There was a large cauldron atop a massive furnace where rice was cooked.

Directly opposite the large cauldron were two smaller stoves on a concrete platform. One stove was for boiling water and the other was for frying vegetables, steaming fish, boiling soup and cooking other dishes. When the water in the kettle had boiled, mum would fill up a hot water flask with a metallic casing that had rusted away. Dad had cushioned a huge empty Milo tin with a rag and put the flask's inner shell within. Mum treasured the old flask and did not have the heart to throw it away as it could still keep water hot better than other flasks. Mum had even engaged a tinsmith once to make a new exterior casing for the flask out of a zinc sheet.

To start a fire, we used dried coconut leaflets as fire starters. We gathered about ten leaves, folded them into halves and set them alight using matches. Once the leaves caught fire, we would tip the burning portion of the leaves lower to allow the fire to spread upwards, creating a fierce fire. Then we put the whole bunch into the stove. Small twigs were added, followed by small branches. When the flame grew more intense, the bigger pieces of wood were added. Smoke from the burning firewood would escape through the chimney at the rear of the stove. My grandma always complimented the mason who constructed such a stove. A badly constructed stove would fill the whole kitchen with smoke. Sometimes, on rainy days, when the roof leaked on the firewood, we had a hard time trying to start a fire. Woe betide us if the matches were wet too. We would desperately try different ways to light the match. One would be trying to strike two or three matches at one go. Another would be putting the matchbox and sticks close to our mouths and blowing our hot breath on them. The last resort would be to get a new box of matches from mum, if she had one. Sometimes, the wood simply could not burn—it only gave off smoke, and the smoke would not escape out the chimney but fill the entire kitchen. Then we would use tongs to remove the pieces of firewood on top and a short metal pipe would be used to blow at the embers. When the twigs started to burn, branches were added. If all failed, we had to call for help. My dad would use a small hoe to remove the accumulated ash from the chimney, allowing fresh air to enter. Then the whole process of lightning the fire would start again.

Our Duties

There was division of duties among us children. Hong Game, being the eldest daughter, had to look after the younger siblings. She was also given kitchen duties—cooking, preparing the ingredients for meals, replenishing firewood, washing as well as ironing.

A charcoal iron
Yeo Hong Eng's collection

Many farming chores such as preparing animal feeds, building troughs and repairing farm tools were done in this corridor.
Photographed by Lu Siang Hee

Before ironing, we had to place few small pieces of charcoal into the base of the iron and light them with a starter. Then, more pieces of charcoal were added. While the iron was being heated, my sister had to moisten the clothes by sprinkling water on them with her fingers or with a sprayer. When the iron was sufficiently heated, she could start ironing. Each piece of clothing was arranged on a table padded with an old folded blanket. Those days, clothing was mostly made of cotton so they were not so sensitive to heat. But one had to put in more effort to iron cotton clothes because they were starched, making the fabric heavy and unwieldy. Sometimes, she had to wax the base of the iron to make the job easier. She would always have to be always mindful of a strong draft because if ash from the iron landed on the piece she was ironing, she had to try to remove it. If she were lucky, a mere flicking of the fingers would suffice. If that failed, she had to wash the piece of clothing again. My younger sister, Siew Gim, was assigned to assist Hong Game with these chores. Later, Hong Game had to help in the field and feed the pigs and poultry, so Siew Gim had to take over Hong Game's kitchen duties.

Washing our clothes was never easy. Because of the
nature of our work and play, clothes were heavily soiled.
Our sisters had to scrub extra hard
using the scrubbing board.

I was delegated to fertilise and water the plants as well as to plough the empty plots. I also had to clear the chicken dung early in the morning from the chicken coop before going to school. In the late afternoons, the boys were to transplant the week-old seedlings from the nursery into neat rows, then water them. The next morning, the newly transplanted seedlings needed constant watering and shading. The shading was mainly done by Hong Bian. It involved knocking Y-shaped stakes into the ground on opposite sides of each bed. A sturdy stick was laid in the middle of the two prongs of each Y-shaped stake. More stakes were driven in, depending on the length of the bed. Then, dry coconut leaves were placed on the sticks to shelter the newly planted seedlings. In the late afternoons, the dried coconut leaves were removed to let dew settle on the vegetables. That process was repeated for several days until the limp seedlings became strong. It was only when the plants became strong and were growing that fertiliser could be added. If it were done before the seedlings had adapted to the transplant, they would either die or their growth would be stunted.

My parents prepared the beds for sowing and transplanting, gathered fruits and vegetables and washed them before transporting them to the market. Vegetables gathered in the afternoons were the hardier ones, such as the brinjals, papayas, long beans, chillies, bitter gourds, snake gourds (snake marrow), *bayam* (spinach), and *kang kong* (water convulvus). Grandma would bring afternoon tea, coffee and biscuits for us. By the time the day's work was done, at about 7pm, it would already be quite dark.

Then, we had to rush home to light our kerosene lamps. We took down the huge kerosene pressure lamp from a hook hanging in the middle of the hall. Then we had to check whether we needed to top up the kerosene oil in the lamp's reservoir. If so, we would use a metal pump to siphon the kerosene from a four-gallon tin into an empty soy sauce bottle. We filled the lamp's reservoir from the bottle using a funnel. Next, we filled a little disc inside the lamp with methylated spirit then lit the disc. The burning methylated spirit heated up the mantle that made the lamp bright. Once the mantle had heated up, we needed to pump air into the reservoir.

The compressed air would force the kerosene to rise up a tube and be sprayed on the mantle, causing it to slowly brighten. The lighted mantle was most delicate. It was in fact made of ash. A jerk of the lamp would damage it. To replace a damaged mantle we had to wait for the parts to cool, then the whole process of lighting the lamp had to be repeated.

We used this metal pump to transfer kerosene from a four-gallon tin to a bottle.

When the lamp showed signs of dimming, we would pump in more air.

One needs experience to light such
pressure lamps.

Folks who could not afford to buy kerosene by the tin would
buy it by the bottle. The standard bottle that was used was
the Gordon's Dry Gin bottle. It was used most likely because
of the volume of liquid it could contain. For each bottle of
kerosene oil the shopkeeper charged 20 cents.

Usually, my dad would come home with our breakfast. He
bought different types of cakes and bread spread with *kaya* (coconut

and egg jam) and margarine every morning. When he reached home, each of us would grab a piece and munch, as we were hungry after our morning farm duties.

Most often, he bought *yu char kway* (*you tiao* in Mandarin), *bey hei chi,* and *ham chin peng,* various types of Chinese fritters. These were from the same hawker. The *yu char kway* was made from a slice of dough with a deep depression lengthwise down the middle. After it was fried, it looked like two pieces joined into one. The *bey hei chi* comprised two cubes of dough joined together, and the *ham chin peng* was a flattened dough ball with a filling of black bean paste or crushed peanuts.

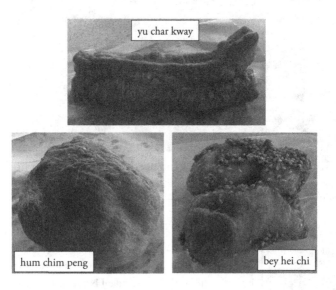

yu char kway

hum chim peng

bey hei chi

My grandma told us how the *yu char kway,* literally translated from Hokkien as 'fried devils', originated. It happened during the Southern Song Dynasty (1127 AD-1279 AD). General Yue Fei was a very patriotic military commander who defended the kingdom from the Jurchen to his utmost capacity. But those close to the emperor thought otherwise and advised the emperor to put Yue Fei to death. The emperor later regretted his action very much when he discovered the truth about Yue Fei's patriotism. A tomb was constructed in remembrance of Yue Fei in Hangzhou. At the entrance leading to his tomb, there were four kneeling statues, two on each side. On the left were Yue Fei's enemies Qui Hui and his wife, and on the right were Qui Hui's two collaborators.

The people were enraged with those four 'devils'. A pastry vendor, in order to remind people of Qui Hui and his wife's evil deeds, joined two elongated lumps of dough and fried them. From that day, *yu char kway* or *yu teow* became a popular Chinese fritter.

With so many brothers and sisters, quarrelling was natural. We would quarrel over the allocation of duties, over name-calling and over not doing our duties well.

One morning, I did not notice my two younger brothers quarrelling. Hong Bian opened his sandwich and slapped Hong Hup, smearing his cheeks with kaya and margarine. Loud cries followed. My dad was most upset. He put down whatever he was doing and caned them at the same time mumbling, "I bought for you to eat, yet you annoy me." My grandma chipped in, "It takes two to fight. If you need to cane, cane both."

My Maternal Family

My maternal grandmother was in Chao Zhou, China. Mum had always wanted to visit her, but at that time in the 1950s, the Peoples' Republic of China had just won the war against the Kuomintang (the Nationalists) and visas were not easy to get, so her trip kept getting postponed. During that chaotic period, her father was repatriated to China and his whereabouts were not known. Mum was raised by her uncle and her second cousin at Kim Keat Road. Her uncle used to visit us, and my mum would entertain us with stories of her childhood experiences with him and her cousins.

My Mum's Ingenuities

My mum, although she had not gone to school, was very resourceful. She was knowledgeable about everyday affairs on the farm and discussed them with my dad and grandma. When my grandma handed the purse strings over to her, she managed the family finances very well. She kept a huge Chinese daily calendar and recorded the household income in secret codes she devised. She also followed in my grandma's footsteps by selling our vegetables herself instead of through a vendor. In that way, she could make a better profit.

Dad would take the vegetables to Chai Chee Market on his bicycle. Mum took the bus there, claimed a place on the ground, and displayed the vegetables for sale. By 12 noon, customers would have already made their purchases and gone home so the vendors were keen to dispose of whatever they had left. Mum bartered her leftovers for pork, fish and other necessities with her fellow vendors. She seldom brought any leftovers home.

Childhood Pains

Once, my dad asked me to fetch a *changkol* (hoe) from the chicken coop, which he had left there earlier. I took a cursory glance and reported to him that the *changkol* was not inside the coop. You can't imagine his expression! He ran to the coop, got the *changkol* from behind the door and came back to the house with it. He hollered, "You couldn't find it and what is this?" He shook the *changkol* and then took out his big thick cane and, with all his might, swished it down on my body repeatedly. I felt excruciating pain on my back, thighs and hands. Well, well, there was no excuse for being lazy. Reflecting back, I think I was feeling lazy that day therefore I was very reluctant to do what he asked. There might also have been some other distractions, so I just wanted to be done with it as quickly as possible.

My parents could be very hot-tempered when they were young. Like most parents of those times, up went their hands and slaps landed on our cheeks at the slightest provocation. The worst feeling was receiving a knock with their knuckles. When those knuckles landed on our head, the pain could be excruciating. One might have to nurse four sore spots on the head from a single episode of knuckle thrashing.

My parents had several canes of various thicknesses and sizes, bent and twisted in the shape of the number nine. They were hung high on the wooden panel of the hall. One look at the canes would send shivers down our spines. Children being children, at times we did things on the spur of the moment without thinking of the consequences.

My mum often nagged the family, especially Hong Game. One day, my eldest sister was helping to cook the food for the pigs and fowl. She did something that annoyed my mum immensely. Seeing that my mum was about to get out of the hearth and get even with her, Hong Game wanted to run off. She threw an empty cooking oil tin at her, followed by a smouldering piece of wood. Then Hong Game screamed. The piece of burning firewood had scalded part of her back. My dad immediately attended to her. Everyone in the house quietened down and did their duties without any fuss. Well! That was discipline. Without discipline, no work could be done efficiently. We had learnt that lesson the hard way.

Madam Ong Ka's Misfortunes

Madam Ong Ka was known for her straightforward, aggressive manner. Her voice was shrill and loud, and she dared to confront anyone who had offended her. She was tall and of a tough build. Despite her age—at that time, she was about 60—she could easily take on any youngster.

As usual, my grandma visited her one afternoon. When Madam Ong Ka heard my grandma's footsteps at her threshold, she huffed and yelled in a muffled voice. We discovered she had been tied up and gagged. It seemed a young man had come to her gate. He pretended that he wanted to talk to her son, Ah Hee, but Ah Hee was not in. Unsuspectingly, she opened the gate and let the stranger in. He immediately tied her up and gagged her. Then he went about ransacking the rooms for cash and jewellery while rattling off curses and expletives on how well she had hidden the money. Although she had not been robbed of much, the incident raised the issue that Madam Ong Ka was living with her son in a big attap house. Her son was not in most of the time. It seemed the robber had surveyed the situation thoroughly before striking. He knew her son's name, he knew when her son was not at home and he knew when my grandma would visit her.

After that incident, her daughters—and sons-in-law visited her more often, deepening their bonds. They brought Ah Beng, Madam Ong Ka's granddaughter, to live with her. As she was the only toddler in the house, naturally Ah Beng was showered with many gifts. As an old lady, Madam Ong Ka did not have the energy to constantly tidy up after her granddaughter and return her toys to their proper place. As such, there would be many toys lying about on the cement floor. One evening, in the semi-darkness lit only by a small kerosene lamp, she stepped on a round toy. Her right foot rolled over it and she fell, twisting her ankle. The pain was so excruciating tears rolled down her cheeks. My grandma then massaged her friend and helped her do some household chores while she was recuperating. The incident happened on the weekend Ah Beng returned home with her parents.

As if she hadn't suffered enough, the worst was yet to come. She was returning home from a trip to Simpang Bedok one afternoon. A car hit her while she was at Pek Kio (the present-day junction of Changi Road and Bedok Road), crossing a small white bridge across a stream between Simpang Bedok and Bedok schools. She was rushed to hospital. The surgeon operated on her immediately but the battle was lost. She had to replace her left eye with a prosthetic one. She received a certain amount of compensation from the vehicle owner's insurance company but everyone knew that money could not replace her healthy eye, nor compensate for all her pain and suffering.

Ah Chiang's Kind Deeds

Ah Chiang, Madam Ong Ka's son-in-law, had always been kind and supportive to us. He had cured our sores and wounds. Not only that, when he saw how hard we had worked and how meagre our meals were, he thought he could help us in many other ways. At

Woodbridge Hospital, where he worked, there was always an excess of meat, bread and vegetables. Instead of leaving them to rot or throwing them away, why not give them to those in need? When he visited us, he would bring loaves of bread, vegetables such as radish—which we did not grow—beef and other food. Although their expiry dates had passed, they were still fit for eating. We removed the slightly mouldy crust of the bread for the pigs and poultry. Then we steamed these loaves. They tasted as fresh as newly baked bread. We had never eaten beef before, due to religious constraints, but nevertheless, beef was still meat. My mum had never cooked beef in her life, and cooking beef the first time was really trying. The beef was as tough as leather. We chewed till our jaws ached.

Making Identity Cards

Our parents were ignorant that we children, upon reaching the age of 12, had to register for identity cards. They were more concerned with daily chores and putting food on the table. When uncle Ah Chiang came to learn about it, he urged Hong Game to register. Early one morning, uncle Ah Chiang arrived in his Morris Minor to drive us to Stamford Road. There, we had to queue up with the other applicants. Uncle Ah Chiang knew one of the clerks there, so he could help us process the application rather quickly but we had to cough up a bit of money. Uncle Ah Chiang inserted $2 between the pages of Hong Game's application form. Queuing in the hot sun was most uncomfortable and made us hungry and thirsty. In the kampong, we had the trees to shade us, but there in town, the air, the fumes, the dust and the hot, tarred ground made us feel sick. Luckily, my sister's turn came quickly, to the surprise of others who were still in the long queue. Then, we went to the coffee stall next to the registration office to get a cup of coffee each. At home, we usually drank sweet black coffee. But that day, uncle Ah Chiang ordered coffee with milk for us. I had never tasted coffee with condensed milk before, and it tasted heavenly. At home, we drank condensed milk only when we were very young or when we were sick.

"Don't you think that we are not fair to others? We get it ahead of others. The rest are still queuing up," I said to uncle Ah Chiang.

"We help him. So he has to help us," came the quick reply.

Next it was my turn to register for an identity card. Our Primary Six teacher announced that we had to go to Bedok Village to register. My dad brought me to Kampong Eunos to take passport-sized photographs. One morning I went alone to Bedok Village to register at a mobile van. I was apprehensive. I had never done this before. All I knew was that my sister had got hers in town. Many people had to accompany her. When I got to Bedok Village, I saw a queue behind a van. A few people were already in the van waiting for the clerk to process their applications. It was my turn next.

The clerk demanded, "Show me your photographs and birth certificate." I showed him the documents.

"Where's the other photo?" He raised his voice.

Oh no. I had brought only one photograph. Feeling very embarrassed, I raced the two miles home and returned to the van with it.

"You're lucky. Just in time! If you'd missed us, you've to come next week." Immediately he set to work. In those days, the identity card was made from blue vanguard paper. My photographs were pasted on each of the two blank cards. Then a stamp was embossed on each half of the two photographs. He transcribed my name and address from my birth certificate onto the two cards. Then he handed me my birth certificate and brand new identity card. My number was S000000 08746 or in short S60 08746. I walked home proudly as if I had wings sprouting from my sides. My dad immediately took a look at the card and kept it in a file for all the important documents in the house for safekeeping.

Our Brush with the Law

In the 1950s, there was one incident that became deeply etched in my mind. One afternoon, two policemen in khaki shorts and grey shirts came to our farm. Our three dogs were barking away ferociously. They usually did that to strangers. Sternly, the policemen demanded dog licences from our dad. He showed them two.

"Dua sahaja? Mana lagi satu?" said one, asking why there were only two and demanding where the other one was.

"Tidak ada. Belum beli, Enche", my dad answered, telling them that he didn't have it because he had not bought it.

Immediately, the man who held the rifle lowered it and threatened to shoot one of our three dogs.

My dad immediately told them to wait, and that they could discuss the matter: *"Nanti! Nanti! Kita boleh seleseh."* Upon hearing that, their stern frowns were replaced with broad smiles.

"Satu anjing kalau tidak lima ringgit, mesti pun mau tiga ringgit," came the quick reply, meaning that if my dad did not have five dollars, three dollars would do.

My dad hesitated and thought about the consequences for a while—to sacrifice the dog or $3. Reluctantly he placed $3 onto the policeman's palm. The man returned his rifle onto his shoulder. The pair proceeded to another family. Well, that day, we only heard barks from our neighbours' homes, no gunshots. I believed their collection must have been quite substantial. In those days, kampong folks like us only wanted to survive. We wanted to live simply. If problems could be solved, we wanted to solve them in the quickest way possible. My dad was one who was always very wary of *cheng hu lang* (translation from which Hokkien: government men). The following day he went to Bedok Police Station to get a third licence for his dog. Upon reaching home he found a piece of wire, shaped it in the form of a dog collar, attached the circular dog licence disc to it and slipped it around the dog's head. A big load was off his mind. He did not want those *cheng hu lang* to trouble him again.

A Mystery

Sometimes, we were so busy at the farm that we had to extend working hours to the evenings. One of the things we had to do in the evenings was to prepare the pigs' feed. We lit carbide lamps as well as the kerosene lamps to brighten the work area. Sharp kitchen choppers as well as chopping boards were laid out. Empty gunnysacks were lined on the floor to catch stray bits of vegetables. We had to chop the water hyacinths, fresh banana trunks and other vegetables into tiny bits and store them in big baskets. The next day, we had to cook the previous night's preparation. While scooping the cut vegetables, we noticed they felt warm. That surprised us. We wondered about it but to this day, we do not know why the vegetables were warm.

The Kampong Band

There were a few occasions when we heard loud banging of different kinds of noises from the kampong on the hill opposite our house (the present-day Kew Gardens). It seemed the noises made some rhythms and tempos. Curious onlookers hurried to where the sounds came from. A group of people were making music from pots, tins, cans and bamboo stems. Some people were dancing to the music. After a few minutes of observing the scene, we decided that it was quite fun. The music went on late into the evening almost every day. Could that have been the forerunner to the modern day garage bands?

Madam Ong Ka's New House

Uncle Ah Chiang's kindness proved to be beyond everyone's imagination. He saw that the attap house that his mother-in-law lived in was in such a dilapidated condition. Furthermore, his daughter was under Madam Ong Ka's care. He contributed money to rebuild the attap house, replacing it with a brick and wood one with a zinc roof. When completed, it was so beautiful. Soon after, the housewarming ceremony followed. A brief prayer was said to thank heaven for having given them the opportunity to live in a new house. Then, guests started arriving. Lunch was not served in the usual style, in which we had to wait until all the guests had arrived so that everyone began eating at the same time. This lunch was conducted on a first-come, first-served basis. Many in the village commented that this was in the Hainanese style. The guests were mainly uncle Ah Chiang's colleagues and friends. As if most of them had the same telepathic idea, they came bearing wall clocks. At the end of the ceremony, the wall was adorned with clocks of different types and sizes. Madam Ong Ka presented us with one. It was indeed a wonderful gift. It was a German Jewel clock with a wooden casing. It chimed every half hour. At every chime, it made a double tone *ti ng to ng*. At 12 noon, the chimes could be quite ear-splitting, as it made 12 *ti ng to ng* chimes. We were so grateful to them, as we had not owned a clock like that before. We had an old Smith table clock, but it was not reliable, so it was left unwound.

The Jewel clock Mdm Ong Kah presented to us about 50 years ago is still ticking away.

The clock became my dad's precious new toy. He was very careful with it and would religiously wind it at exactly the same time every week. Every now and then, he would take it down to oil the gears with Singer oil. The clock is still with me, adorning the wall of my present house.

Before we had the clock, when we attended the morning session at school, we had to estimate the time to leave for school and we were seldom late. When our parents left for the market or when the neighbour's lorry rattled past our house, it was a signal that we should also leave. When we were in the afternoon session, we estimated the time to leave by looking at the shadow of the house.

On cloudy days, it was quite difficult. We would strain our ears to listen to the kampong's radios, as the kampong folks usually turned the volume of their sets quite high. We guessed that certain Malay serial programmes started at the same time as when we had to leave.

Madam Ong Ka's only son, Ah Hee, was a very innovative and enterprising man. After his primary school education, he found a job at a bakery. With the salary he earned, he bought himself a radio, a record player, a bicycle, and later, a Ducati motorbike. He even bought himself a set of carpentry tools to make his own chairs and tables with the wood salvaged from the odds and ends, which the kampong folks usually bought by the lorry load from the sawmills along Rochor River. He was at least ten years older than I. I always admired him for what he did. He had his own room and he had his own writing table, with all the stationery neatly arranged.

One afternoon, he brought a camera to my farm to take pictures of us, our dog and our farm. We were surprised as posing for photographs was something we had never dreamt of. We were very grateful to him for giving us the opportunity to be his subjects.

My First Ride on a Motorbike

One day, I had to meet my grandma at Bedok at Uncle Yam's shop. As Ah Hee would be passing that way, he gave me a lift on his motorbike, my first on a Ducati. It was such an exhilarating experience, but at the time, I was fearful that I might fall off. Along Bedok Road, he sped so fast that I held him tightly around the waist. The breeze whizzing past me was so cool and I could hear the wind whistling past my ears. My eyes were uncomfortable though, and I had to blink incessantly. As he sped and changed gears, I could feel the jerks and vibrations through my buttocks. All too soon, I reached Uncle Yam's shop where my grandma was waiting. It was a most memorable ride.

Opera Programmes on the Radio

Almost every afternoon, my grandma would be at Madam Ong Ka's house to enjoy the Chinese opera programme on her radio.

They listened mainly to the Teochew and Hokkien programmes and would discuss the stories' plots and the characters. In those days, my grandma was very knowledgeable about Chinese plays and mythology. I presumed that my grandpa—he was the most literate in Chinese among his four siblings—had a lot of influence on her. It was a pity that he died in his sixties, if I guess correctly. If he had lived to a ripe old age like my grandma, I believe our lives would have been very much different today.

The Singapore General Elections

In 1955, it was election time. I was in Primary 3. Almost every day, we had visits by candidates of the different political parties. The first was from the Democratic Party. Its symbol was a lion. There was a *rojak* seller whom we saw at almost every *wayang* performance. He urged that we should, like him, support their candidate, Mr Lim Cher Kheng, who was a good man who could do much to help the villagers. The *rojak* seller personally sacrificed a few days of his livelihood and stopped selling *rojak* to campaign for Mr Lim. His famous catchphrase was *"Pang tiow rojak,"* translated from Teochew as to sacrifice *rojak* selling to campaign for Mr Lim. Mr Lim's office was a zinc-roofed house on stilts along Bedok Road, opposite the Bedok schools (the site now houses a church.) At that time, party posters and slogans in blue and red were pasted on coconut tree trunks. Then, another group representing the Peoples' Progressive Party visited. Its symbol was an orchid. Their candidate was Mr S. G. Ghows. Next came the Labour Front. Its symbol was a pickaxe and spade. In Hokkien, it was called *Chiam Kut Sok.* Their candidate was Mr Wong Sau Sheung. Again, after making their introduction to us, pamphlets were distributed and posters pasted on the coconut trees.

My dad and I attended one of the rallies at the kampong Koh Sek Lim. There were shouts, cheers and applause as each speaker was introduced to the constituents. Each speaker spoke with gusto and punched their fists into the air. As for me, I just felt bored. I was too young to understand what was being uttered.

The election date was 2 April 1955. My parents went to Bedok School to cast their votes. We children were not allowed to go. That night, my dad was very eager to know the results. At 9 p.m., he went to Madam Ong Ka's house. Together with Ah Hee, they listened to the results until the wee hours of the morning. The Democratic Party candidate, Lim Cher Kheng, had won for the Changi consistuency. My dad and Ah Hee were elated.

In the countryside, it was the first time the residents had experienced voting for an assemblyman. That election generated a lot of excitement. It was on every adult's lips, and we children picked up a little here and a little there and echoed this in school.

During the 1959 general election, there was another round of campaigning. Mr Soh Heng Chai, who worked for the British Armed Forces, came to campaign for the candidate, Mr Teo Hock Guan. He said the People's Action Party was truly the poor people's party. With Mr Soh around, winning was a sure bet. Mr Soh was an influential man in the kampong. He was one of the few who knew the English language. With him around, the villagers felt some assurance about whom we were casting our votes for. Other candidates also visited, including the past assemblyman, Mr Lim Cher Kheng. He was no longer with the Democratic Party and stood as an independent candidate this time round. UMNO candidate Mr Abdul Raham B. Said and Liberal Socialist Party candidate Mr Wee Tin Teck did not visit. The Liberal Socialist Party cadres pasted their symbol of a torch on coconut trees. Many in the kampong expressed fear that the torch of the LSP could be dangerous. It could be used to torch the attap houses.

It was the first time that voting was compulsory for every person eligible to vote. The Election Department came up with the poster 'Voting is Compulsory', which was pasted alongside the other parties' posters.

The general election was held on 30 May 1959, a Saturday. When the election results were announced, the PAP candidate for Changi, Mr Teo Hock Guan, had won the election.

In 1962, there was a referendum for Singapore to join Malaysia. Singaporeans had to vote for one of three options. If they did not like the three options, the Barisan Socialis party encouraged people to cast blank votes. Every day, repeatedly, Radio Singapore urged the people not to do this, as it would jeopardise the nation. On 1 September 1962, Singaporeans opted to join Malaysia.

In 1963, our then Prime Minister Lee Kuan Yew toured the whole of Singapore. When the news came that he was to pay a visit, a stage was constructed at the junction of the present-day Jalan Limau Kasturi and Tanah Merah Kechil. The kampong folks turned up to hear him speak.

I remember all the pupils of Bedok Boys' and Bedok Girls' schools came to welcome him. Lee Kuan Yew shook hands with the children with both hands. My brother Hong Hup was thrilled because he shook Lee Kuan Yew's hand. I stood at a distance to watch.

Then the secretary of the welcoming committee took the opportunity to propose to the Prime Minister that the muddy track we used daily be upgraded to a road to lead to the Bedok schools. Lee Kuan Yew asked him to make a formal request. A month later the bulldozer came. It broadened the track. In the process of broadening the track, it damaged a portion of my relative's fencing. Yeo Koon Toon, the owner of the land, was hopping mad. The muddy track was a part of his land. Out of goodwill he allowed the public to traverse from Tanah Merah Kechil to Bedok Road. It was illegal to upgrade that muddy track to a public road.

Next, the Prime Minister toured Bedok village. The welcoming committee dressed him up as a Malay dignitary—they put on him a Malay *songkok* and he wore a *sarong songket* and marched under a banner that said '*Selamat Datang Perdana Menteri Lee Kuan Yew*' which translated from Malay as 'Welcome Prime Minister Lee Kuan Yew.' A *kompang* troupe led the procession. The Bedok kampong folks lined the length of Bedok Road to welcome him. I was there too, on my bicycle. I was surprised when I saw the photographs of myself among the crowd in the *Sin Chew Jit Poh* newspaper the next day.

The front and back of a *Sin Chew Jit Poh* matchbox

During the 1963 election, Tanah Merah Kechil was under the Changi constituency. The Barisan Socialis candidate was Mr Siek Shing Min, the PAP candidate was Mr Sim Boon Woo and the Singapore Alliance candidate was Dato Syed Esa bin Almenoar. Mr Sim Boon Woo from the People's Action Party won the election.

On 16 September 1963, Singapore, together with Sabah and Sarawak, became part of Malaysia. There was a celebration at Jalan Besar Stadium. Hong Bian had weeks of practice for the Malaysian parade, a mass display by school children as they held gigantic cards with images of Malaysian lifestyles. His school, Tanjong Katong Technical School, was one of the schools participating.

In and Around Tanah Merah Kechil

I was very curious about the three words '*Tanah Merah Kechil*', which I had seen on old maps. The Malay word '*Tanah*' was sometimes spelt as '*Tannah*', and the word '*Kechil*' was sometimes spelt as '*Ketchil*', or '*Kichi*' but why '*Tanah Merah Kechil*'? '*Tanah Merah*' in English means 'Red Earth' or 'Earth Red' in literal translation. The word '*kechil*' is translated as little or small, but was there a '*Tanah Merah*

Besar' (*'besar'* means *'large'*)? The answer is 'Yes.' The road after the Changi Prison, if you are heading east, is named *Tanah Merah Besar*. I was puzzled as to why the earth here was also red. Was it because the blood of the murdered boy, Nadim, in the legend 'The Swordfish' not only covered Bukit Merah, but also all the hills in Singapore?

The Legend of Bukit Merah

It was said that the land around Bukit Merah was red because it was covered with the blood of a boy named Nadim. Could Bukit Merah in those days have stretched to Tanah Merah? The land at Tanah Merah was also red.

Singapura, according to a legend, was once affected by garfish. The garfish came with the tides, and killed and injured numerous people who lived along the shore. The people appealed to the Bendahara (Prime Minister) and the Sultan. They were at a loss as to how they could fight off the invasion of the garfish.

Up on a hill, there was a little boy named Nadim. He was observing the daily destruction of human lives by the fish. The soldiers sent by the government to check the wanton destruction were mere targets of the garfish. An idea began to form in his mind. He rushed to the Sultan and told him of his plan. He explained that the fish came in together with the tides. He proposed that banana trunks be planted along the shore at low tide when the fish were away. The banana trunks planted along the shore were to fool the fish that they were humans. They would attack the banana trunks and the beak-like jaws of the fish would be trapped in the fibres of the trunks. When the tide had gone away, the fish would be left dangling on the trunks. The soldiers would then be able to slaughter them all.

The Sultan was very receptive to this idea. At once he ordered the Bendahara to do exactly what the boy had told him. At low tide, the soldiers planted banana trunks along the shore. When the tide came, the people saw how the garfish pierced the banana trunks with their saw-blade beaks and were trapped. At low tide, they were struggling to get away. The soldiers were ordered to slaughter each and every one of them.

That went on at every low tide until all the fish were gone. The Sultan was very pleased with the boy but not the Bendahara. The Bendahara thought the boy was a threat to him. He feared the Sultan might one day make the boy Bendahara since he was so intelligent.

One night he told the Sultan that he had foreseen disaster. One day the boy would take over the Sultan's place as he was so capable. The Sultan thought about it for a long time and then asked the Bendahara for his advice. The Bendahara replied happily, "Leave that to me. I will find a solution for you, Tuanku." With that, he hastily dismissed himself.

Immediately he went to Nadim's hut and plunged his *kris* into the boy's heart. Crimson blood gushed out, covering the hills and valleys, making them all red. That is why people called all the hills there, *'Bukit Merah'* or Red Hill.

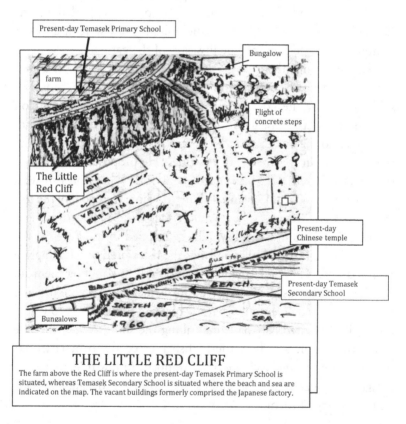

THE LITTLE RED CLIFF

The farm above the Red Cliff is where the present-day Temasek Primary School is situated, whereas Temasek Secondary School is situated where the beach and sea are indicated on the map. The vacant buildings formerly comprised the Japanese factory.

The hills along the east coast just before Bedok were quite high—an average of about 200 feet—and were subject to constant bombardment by the waves. This eroded much of the topsoil, exposing the red laterite soil. From afar, that hill looked red, so that area, according to an early map of Singapore dated 1828, was named 1st Red Cliff. The hill at Ayer Gemuroh was named 2nd Red Cliff. A later map renamed 1st Red Cliff as Little Red Cliff and 2nd Red Cliff as Big Red Cliff. The exposed red laterite soil area of the Big Red Cliff was larger.

The path that led to the Little Red Cliff was also of red laterite soil. My parents, without prior knowledge of the meaning of the name Tanah Merah Kechil, had quite correctly called that track *Ung Tor Lor* in Hokkien, which means 'Red Earth Road'. Tanah Merah Kechil, in the 1950s, stretched from East Coast Road a short distance from Parbury Avenue, went up the incline of the hill to its peak, then sloped down to the valley. A coconut trunk bridge was built across a stream. Then the track went up to the hilltop across Piah Teng's land and down to another valley, where Ban Guan's family lived. There, another coconut trunk bridge was laid across another stream. Then the track continued up an incline to arrive at a ridge where the present 8 ½ Milestone Changi Road is. On rainy days, the earth became soft, and motor vehicles were often caught in the muddy ruts that formed.

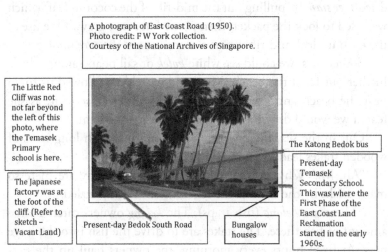

A photograph of East Coast Road (1950).
Photo credit: F W York collection.
Courtesy of the National Archives of Singapore.

The Little Red Cliff was not not far beyond the left of this photo, where the Temasek Primary school is here.

The Japanese factory was at the foot of the cliff. (Refer to sketch – Vacant Land)

The Katong Bedok bus

Present-day Temasek Secondary School. This was where the First Phase of the East Coast Land Reclamation started in the early 1960s.

Present-day Bedok South Road

Bungalow houses

I often went to Bedok with my grandma. Sometimes when we went to uncle Yam's shop, we could get a glimpse of the sea at high tide. As we went nearer, we could see the kampong folks with their children enjoying themselves in the water. The younger children usually bathed naked. Bigger girls and adults had their sarongs on, while the teenage boys had baggy pants on. The pants were usually handed down from their elders.

Some teenagers would ply along the beach selling *otak otak, nasi lemak,* or *mee siam.* Otak otak was fish paste wrapped in coconut leaflets. They would be grilled over a rectangular charcoal rack in neat rows, so the overall effect looked quite like a xylophone. The vendors carried these racks and went about singing, *"Otak! Otak!"* The *nasi lemak* was wrapped with banana leaf. The contents were no different from those of today—*pandan* coconut rice, *ikan kuning*, a small slice of fried egg, some *sambal ikan bilis* and a squarish banana leaf, which separated the chili from the rice. The *mee siam* vendor wrapped their cooked dried *mee siam* with a rectangular banana leaf and formed it into a pyramid. Then the top flap was folded down and pinned to the edge of the opposite sides with a coconut mid-rib. The gravy was contained in a big soy sauce bottle. The vendor went about with a bottle of gravy in one hand and a basket of *mee siam* packets in the other. When making a sale, he unwrapped the packed, dried *mee siam* by pulling out the mid-rib of the coconut leaf, which was used to lock the packet, then poured in some gravy. One use of the coconut leaf mid-rib was as a utensil to eat the *mee siam.*

Sometimes, we could see white *kolek* or sail boats sailing a little further out from the beach. My grandma seldom allowed us to go near the beach and warned us never to wander close to it, as she feared we would drown. We were always very obedient.

Out in the sea, there were many attap huts with long rows of wooden stakes leading into them.

"Ah, Ma! Why are there houses in the sea? Why are there so many sticks by the sides of the sea houses?" I was puzzled.

"These are *kelong* (fish traps). The *kelong* owners catch a large amount of fish there. The stakes are to drive the fish into the huge nets. At fixed hours every morning, the owners haul up the nets and scoop out the trapped fish." My grandma tried to make me understand, but I had no idea what she was saying.

One bright morning, my grandma decided to take me for a walk along the *Ung Tor Lor* (Red Earth Road). It was easy at first, walking past the Malay houses, a *surau* or small mosque, and across a coconut trunk bridge or *ya khong kio*. After crossing the bridge, the walk became tougher. On the left, I could see the tombstones of the Teochew cemetery, Pang Suah Kia. On the right were the farms planted with sweet potatoes and tapioca.

The area straight ahead seemed suddenly devoid of earth and trees—only the blue sky could be seen. I was thrilled at the prospect of what loomed ahead. I laboriously moved higher, step by step, as my legs were aching. Then the light blue horizon came into view. The dark shapes of the islands of Indonesia could be seen. Next were the many *kelong* with their stakes that dotted the sea from left to right, forming an arc. I saw the ripples of the foamy waves advancing towards the coast. And finally, I could see the panoramic view of a whole stretch of the sea and the coast. I was spellbound. No words could describe how I felt. The feeling was accentuated by the cool sea breeze brushing past me. I stood there rooted to the spot, as I had never seen such a wonderful sight at such a height. Later, I realised that I was standing at the Little Red Cliff, which the early cartographer had named.

When I was posted to Dryburgh English School (which later merged with Presbyterian Boys' School), the trip to school via Bedok Boys' School to the junction of East Coast Road and Tembeling Road cost me 15 cents for a student concessionary ticket. In order to save 5 cents, I usually boarded the red Katong Bedok bus at East Coast Road, where the Small Red Cliff was. I used the long flight of concrete steps—about 100 in total—to get to East Coast Road and back. There was a huge bungalow at the highest point of this hill. It was believed to be a storage house for the Singapore Customs, and I often saw big stacks of cigarettes being incinerated at the side of the road. I believed those contraband cigarettes must have been confiscated from smugglers.

At the foot of the hill were the remains of a row of single-storey houses. They looked like they had been looted or had caught fire. I had never been near there as I heard it was haunted. During the Japanese Occupation, my dad said it was used by the Japanese to brew medicine. Others said that the place was an ammunition dump. Some said that it was a chemical experimentation station. Today, the area is in front of Temasek Secondary School. It is fenced up by the Singapore government.

This Japanese factory site is now fenced up by the Singapore government.

Along the coast were bungalows. One particular house nearest to the Katong Bedok bus stop struck me. It had a flat roof with round white lamps around the building. Further down was another bungalow with a gate with a semi-circular sign, 'Wysman Haven', above it. I cannot remember whether the sign had neon lights. As a young boy, I did not discover whose house it was. Only recently did I learn that it was a café belonging to the grandmother of Peter Chan, a Singapore blogger.

Many historic events took place at the site between Temasek Primary and Temasek Secondary Schools. Before the Japanese invasion, the Americans and the British were preparing for the war here—stockpiling war materials and building pillboxes. A factory was built opposite this site. During the Japanese Occupation, the Japanese used the factory to manufacture chemicals. (Now the site is fenced up). In 1963, the Pilot Land Reclamation Scheme was carried out. The hill (the present day Temasek Primary School), which marine cartographers named 'The Little Red Cliff', was levelled. The first lorry load of earth from the hill was dumped at the coast where the present day Temasek Secondary School is. In the 1960s, the bus stop was a metal pole with a plate inscribed 'Bus Stop'.

Further up the coast towards Bedok Village was a huge concrete house. It could have belonged to the Yong family, whose son was my classmate in Bedok Boys' School. But I may be wrong. Today the house has been extended and functions as a Chinese temple. On the left of the house, sheltered by trees and bushes, was a huge Chinese tomb. When we walked past the tomb we felt uneasy, as we had heard a little about its origins.

"A very rich man was buried there. On the day of the burial, slaves carried rice, corn, poultry, salt and sugar and other daily necessities into the cavernous tomb. When the coffin was placed inside, workmen immediately sealed the tomb," a farmer who lived in the area used to say.

"What about the slaves who carried the food supplies?" I enquired.

"They were to be entombed alive with the dead man. They were to serve him after life in the nether world," he quipped.

"Oh no! Poor people!" we moaned, feeling disgusted at such practices.

When the burial ceremony was over, it seemed passers-by heard the wailing of the people inside. They opened up the tomb and released those entombed with the corpse. Was the story true or not? Nobody could provide evidence either way.

Further up the slope, there was an obscure, narrow dirt road named Hwa San Road. It led to the Teochew Cemetery Hwa San Teng. It was mainly used by vehicles during funerals and celebrations of the temple deity's birthday, when *wayangs* (Chinese street operas) were staged. On other days, it was as silent as a graveyard.

As one proceeded further along East Coast Road, there was a pillbox built by the British for the defence of Singapore. We children loved to play hide and seek around it. We played police and thief and 'bang bang bang' around it.

The author on the pillbox.
Photographed by Nancy Lim

My siblings and I then headed towards Kew Drive. We heard that something had happened there during the Japanese Occupation. "When Singapore was in Japanese hands, lorry loads of people were brought here," said my dad. "Their hands and legs were bound. They sat around a pit in the ground. Then a command by the Japanese leader sounded. Rifles exploded. With cries, the victims collapsed into the hole.

When it was all over, the Japanese soldiers kicked the bodies that were at the rim of the hole so they rolled in. Then, to make sure they were really dead, the soldiers poked at the bodies randomly with their bayonets. Earth was thrown in to bury them. Then the soldiers went away." As my dad described it, a look of disgust came over his face.

When we came to the area, silence fell upon us. We feared that the spirits of those who had died might still be lurking around. With our heads bowed, we walked briskly away, heading towards Jalan Haji Salam.

The mass graves were exhumed in 1962. There were several mass graves around the area, as each Japanese commander had his own execution site.

At the junction of Parbury Avenue and East Coast Road, there was a row of Peranakan houses, numbered 495 to 507. They were used as a government maternity and child clinic. My mum brought us there for medical check-ups. At peak hours, it was very crowded. It was made worse with the shrill cries of babies and toddlers. Across the road was a coffee shop.

"With the sea breeze and shade of the trees, here is definitely more comfortable than inside the clinic," my mum used to say in between sips of her *kopi-o* (black coffee).

It was 1954. Most of the kampong womenfolk preferred to have their babies delivered at home. My grandma noticed the discomfort of my pregnant mum. At once she summoned my dad, who was in the vegetable garden tending his crops.

"Ah Sin is in labour. Quick! Go and fetch Ah Leng."

Immediately, my dad stopped what he was doing, changed his shirt and shorts and pedaled to the Changi 8½ milestone. There was a row of attap houses along the road. Outside one of the houses was a black-and-white sign in Chinese and English: 'Ah Leng—Midwife'.

After what it seemed like hours, my dad returned with a middle-aged lady in white sitting on the carrier at the rear of his huge bicycle meant for carrying goods. The bicycle was also known as a gentleman bicycle. She had a large rattan bag in her hand.

Immediately, she went into the bedroom where my mum and grandma were. Then my grandma went into the kitchen to prepare a kettle of lukewarm water. Soon, the fierce cries of a baby were heard. One of my brothers, Hong Teck, was born. My dad took Ah Leng back to her office using the same bicycle.

Over the next three days, the midwife instructed my mum on how to take care of the newborn baby. After the third day, she was to bring my baby brother to the Child and Maternal Clinic at Parbury Road.

In the 1950s, this place used to be the Child and Maternity clinic.

Filming

At times, we saw trucks with 'Cathay Keris Film Studio' painted on their sides. Then the actors and actresses, cameramen, directors and other stagehands took up their positions and got ready for film shooting. Others took down the large rectangular reflectors from the truck and positioned themselves strategically. We, the kampong folks, would stay at a distance to watch the proceedings.

Once, I saw the workers build a huge fire out of the dry twigs and grass, and an actress went behind the fire, struggling and screaming and then 'fainted' while the camera crew was shooting in front of the fire. After that scene was over, the actress changed her dress to a torn and tattered one. The crew then put patches of red paint all over her to simulate blood. Then the shooting continued. On other occasions, other shows were shot. We really had enjoyable times watching those shoots. Well, the next time you watch old Malay films about the myths, legends and heroes of bygone eras by Rose Yatimah, Ummi Kalthoum, Roomai Noor, Maria Menado and Wahid Satay, chances are that some scenes were shot at the hills of Tanah Merah Kechil.

Cathay Keris Film Studio operated at East Coast Road behind Ocean Park Hotel just before the Siglap Canal. At present, in 2013, it is the Ocean Park condominium.

A matchbox from
Ocean Park Hotel
From Yeo Hong Eng's collection

In the 1960s, Datok Loke Wan Tho developed the land at Jalan Buloh Perindu to build Seaside Park, a private housing estate. The roads in Seaside Park were all named after the legends of the Malay era.

Some examples are Jalan Keris, Jalan Selandang Delima, Jalan Puteri Jula Juli, Jalan Negara Ku, Jalan Dondang Sayang and Jalan Azam.

Jalan Keris.
The Ocean Park Condominium can be
seen behind the terrace houses.

Scares
The Tiger

Those days, rumours abounded. There was once a rumour that a tiger was lurking around the neighbourhood. When the sun went down, every household would stay indoors and latch their doors. Everyone was all ears for any unusual sounds. If there were, the entire household would grab whatever they could lay their hands on, be they broomsticks, *parangs, changkols,* spades or metal rods. The able-bodied males would use their powerful torchlights and search high and low in every nook and corner—up the trees, in the pigsties, chicken coops and wood piles. There was a landowner named Mr Gan Cheng Huat. In those days, landowners were allowed to own rifles. One Sunday, he took out his rifle and started shooting at waterfowl and other birds while hunting for the tiger.

When a bird was shot, we would rush to where the bird had fallen and retrieve it.

"This is a mynah, uncle. It's got a yellow beak and a patch of white on its wings," I said, holding the dead bird proudly.

We crossed many hills, from Kampong Tanah Merah Kechil to Siglap, then to Chai Chee. We returned without sighting any tiger but with a handful of dead birds.

"You and your brother, where'd you go the whole afternoon? Have you forgotten your duties? Hurry up! Water the *kangkong* before the sun goes down!" my mum yelled. "The next time if you wish to go anywhere, you'd better inform us. You are living with your parents and your parents are responsible for you . . ." We could not say anything for fear we would provoke her further. We bent our heads in shame and proceeded immediately to do our duties.

The Oily Man

Then there was the oily man scare. It was reported that a naked man whose entire body was smeared with oil was seen loitering around the kampong committing thefts as well as molesting women.

"*Saya takut. Say tidak mahu keluar rumah lagi. Pachik tu chakap dia dapat tangkap orang minyak itu, tetapi fasal badan nya lichen. Pachik tidak kuat tahan dia,*" an old Malay lady was heard saying (translation from Malay: I am scared. I do not want to go out of the house again. That uncle had caught hold of the oily man, but his body was slippery. Uncle had no strength to hold him).

The adults of the whole kampong would light kerosene lamps outside their houses and stay awake to keep watch. There were instances of mistaken identity. The victims were roughed up.

As days went by, no one had any brushes with the oily man again. The scare was soon erased from our minds.

The Missing Pregnant Women

When Chin Shih Huang (Qin Shih Huang), the first emperor of the Chin dynasty (Qin Dynasty), built the Great Wall of China, it was believed that its success was due to the sacrifice of human lives. In the early 1920s, the causeway linking Singapore and Johore was being built. It was also believed that for the construction of the causeway to be a success, human lives had to be sacrificed. The rumours took the kampong by storm. Any new faces that came into the kampongs were carefully watched and sometimes abused. Everybody was on the alert for any eventuality. It was also rumoured that when the Lim Yew Hock government was building Merdeka Bridge between the eastern part of Singapore and the city in the 1950s, pregnant women were needed as a sacrifice. The pregnant women of the kampong made themselves scarce. Madam Ong Ka's daughter, Ong Poh Chu, told us a very convincing story. A lady whose daughter was kidnapped pleaded every day in tears with an inspector whom she knew was involved in such kidnapping cases. The inspector took pity on her. He promised to help but told her not to divulge anything to anyone, as it was a state secret. Naturally, she promised. It was told that she was brought to a tunnel where all the kidnapped pregnant women were drugged and shaved bald. She went to everyone, calling her daughter's name, but in vain. She came out of the tunnel feeling disappointed but related her experiences to everyone she met.

Pontianak

There was also the scare of the *pontianak*, a type of Malay ghost. A *pontianak* was believed to be the wandering spirit of a pregnant Malay pregnant woman who died during childbirth. This spirit supposedly roamed the earth to take revenge on men, since she only attacked males. It was believed she had long hair and always appeared in white, with a stream of blood flowing down one side of her mouth.

Preceding her appearance, there would be a strong breeze. Then she would perch on a sturdy tree and emanate a very strong scent. Should there be a man nearby, she would give a loud, eerie cry, "*Ka! Ka! Ka! Ka!*" and swoop down on him. My grandma gathered us together one afternoon and told us to take precautions. It seemed she floated from tree to tree from dusk to dawn. The whole kampong was very frightened. Nobody dared to venture out at night.

Those who had brushes with her hinted that she was afraid of one thing—the needle. It was advised that whenever any man was attacked, the best defence was to poke her eyes with a needle. My grandma advised every one of us to carry a needle in our wallets. I dutifully did so. With the passing months, as nobody was attacked, the *pontianak* scare gradually faded.

The Unusual Passenger

Then there was also a story of a taxi passenger who took a taxi along Changi Road late one night. She alighted at the Changi 8 Milestone Hokkien Cemetery, paid her fare and walked into the cemetery. When the driver scrutinised the fare, it turned out to be joss paper. He sped home and was sick for days.

The Figurine

One afternoon, I was walking back from school alone. Half hidden in a clump of dwarf bamboos was an unusual object. Being curious, I inched nearer. I had never expected to see such a hideous sight. It was a birdcage, but not the regular birdcage that we saw everyday. There was neither a container for bird food or water nor a rod for a bird to perch on. There was only a small, pale human figure, lying face up on the base of the cage. The most hideous part was the face, with its two bulging eyes with thick black eye brows staring right into me. I had heard of *bomohs* making figures of humans but never expected to experience it first hand. Fearing for my life, I fled home. I had heard that when someone approached a *bomoh* to exact revenge on an enemy, he would cast a spell on a dough figure simulating the victim. When the *bomoh* disfigured any part of the figurine, it would physically affect the victim, inflicting him with pain. For many days, I dared not walk alone along that stretch of road.

Whenever we walked along Jalan Haji Salam, we sometimes encountered an elderly man without a shirt, clad only with a *sarong*, carrying a pot of *kemuyan* (incense), moving around his house, mumbling something we did not understand. The smell of the incense was quite unlike Chinese joss sticks. It was overpowering. I felt as if my head were splitting. We walked briskly away, fearing that he might be a *bomoh* and cast a spell on us.

Films from the Ministry of Culture

In 1959, there were a few occasions when we watched free black and white films screened at an open space in the kampong. At about 6pm, a Ministry of Culture van would show up. A cloth screen was hung between two coconut trees. Then the projector covers were detached to reveal loud speakers. The speakers were then placed at a comfortable distance from the makeshift screen. Loud music was played. The music attracted many of the kampong folks. We siblings were there too. The films were in Malay and we thoroughly enjoyed them. One film that I remember was about a man who fell in love with a mermaid. After the show, there was a brief talk on current affairs in Singapore.

It was really very exciting experiencing the thrills and spills of Malay kampong life. Such experiences enriched us so much that whenever we siblings met in later years, we would recall those days.

The Destruction of the Little Red Cliff

One fine morning, the drone of vehicles was heard in the distance. I was preparing to go to school. When I reached the headland where the flight of steps were near to the rows of dilapidated single-storeyed buildings, there were bulldozers clearing the vegetation away and they were heaving buckets full of earth onto the waiting lorries. The lorries then moved along the laterite Tanah Merah Kechil Road to East Coast Road, turned left, and dumped the earth near the bus stop where I took the Katong Bedok bus. Oh no! It was as if a dagger had pierced into my heart. They were destroying the very icon of Tanah Merah—the Little Red Cliff. "Tanah Merah! Oh Tanah Merah! How the ancient shipfarers viewed you proudly. You're one of the two very beacons that those seafaring people looked out for as they reached Singapore. Yet now these bulldozers are destroying you."

Till today, the memory of the destruction of Tanah Merah Kechil (Little Red Cliff as mentioned in ancient maps) is still vividly etched in my mind. It reminds me of the agony of Munshi Abdullah, Sir Stamford Raffles' teacher, who lamented "What you can't make, don't break", when the British blew up the rock at the mouth of the Singapore River.

When trade in Singapore grew, the Singapore River became busier with each passing day so that eventually, the rock at the mouth of Singapore River became an obstacle. It was said that the rock was carved with ancient inscriptions that no one could decipher at that time. A British engineer then blew up the rock. With the rock destroyed, what was inscribed on the rock was gone. A small part of the rock was preserved at our National Museum.

Today, the site where the Little Red Cliff used to be is the grounds of Temasek Primary School. The first lorry load of earth carted from the Little Red Cliff was dumped at the site where the present day Temasek Secondary School is. If this story is not made known, the residents and later generations of Tanah Merah Kechil might not know how this beloved place got its name.

Kampong Bedok

Once every month, my grandma would take us siblings to Kampong Bedok for haircuts. Sometimes, we took the red Katong Bedok Bus, but often we walked, from Bedok Boys' and Girls' schools to Kampong Bedok. It was only about a mile. We walked past a sign: 'Kampong Bedok'. Directly opposite the Bedok schools' field was a wooden house on stilts. Not far on the right was the Katong Bedok Bus depot. After walking past the bus depot was Jalan Gereja, which led to Bedok Methodist Church.

On the right of the Bedok schools' field was a huge double-storeyed concrete house. The front was very imposing. The owner used to rear a lot of geese in the huge compound behind it. During recess, we sometimes ran to the Bedok Boys' School fence to watch the owner feeding them. Later when I was much older, I learnt that that house belonged to one of the relatives of my uncle's wife.

Sometimes, my grandma would stop by a long attap house. There were people busy pounding fish paste (*belacan*) and packing it in little baskets woven out of coconut leaves. It was a *belacan* factory. I believed a girl, whom I had gotten acquainted with at a tutor's house, named Lim Poh Chu stayed there, as I had seen her playing skipping rope with a group of other girls. My grandma would buy some of the *belacan* from there. Further down the road was a red and yellow Shell Petrol kiosk. I remember there was a big scallop shell atop each petrol pump. Later, the petrol kiosk was demolished. I did not know why.

A Shell petrol pump of the time (without the lamp in the shape of a shell).

My grandma always carried a small rattan basket and a huge lacquered paper umbrella. The bamboo spokes of the umbrella were green. When new, the umbrella exuded a strong, strange smell. The smell most likely came from the lacquer applied on the paper to make it waterproof. Upon reaching a row of attap houses, she would stop to survey the two barbershops—one Indian and the other Chinese (Hainanese), to determine which was less crowded. The Indian barbershop had a small plank painted with three colours—red, blue and white—nailed on to the side of the shop. On the right was a Chinese Hainanese barbershop. The owner of the shop initially rented half of it to a tailor then later to a goldsmith. Whichever barbershop had fewer clients, we would join its queue. Sometimes, we siblings would split up and some of us would join the Indian barber's queue and some join the Chinese barber's queue, as we did not want to waste time waiting for one another.

An Indian barbershop
Photo: Yeo Hong Eng's collection
Photograher: Anon.

My Experiences with the barber

I detested going to any barber. When it was my turn to have my hair cut, the barber would take a well-seasoned plank and put it on the armrests of the barber chair. He would then lift me to sit on the plank.

A barber's chair
with a plank on
the armrests.

That would raise my height so that he need not bend down to cut my hair. A piece of white cloth was draped in front of me. From the two mirrors, one in front of me and the other behind me, I could see my many successions of reflected images, shown alternately front and back. I was very fascinated by that. At that time, I still did not know the principles of reflection of light. Next, he took out a palm-sized container and brought it near to my hair. He took out a powder puff and dusted the hairline. Next, he used a shiny manual shearer and slowly sheared my hair from the nape of my neck upwards. As he pressed the two handles, it made a shearing sound, *Tick! Tick! Tick!* I could not keep still. I had never been asked to keep still in my life. He would hold my head hard with one hand and shear with the other. How I hated that! Next, he combed my hair downwards several times. I did not like that feeling either. My eyes were nearly brought to tears whenever he did that. Then he took a pair of shiny, sharp-pointed scissors and snipped off a chunk of hair in front of my eyes. Then he continuously clicked the scissors, creating a very high-pitched *Tick! Tick!* sound. Then, with a long comb, he combed my hair backwards rather sharply. Again, my head was dragged backwards by the hair caught by the comb. I had to resist being dragged backwards, as my hair was very thick. Then he took another pair of strange instruments with many teeth and a comb. He plunged the instrument into my thick hair and cut with rapid movements. I could hear it snip. Then he combed my hair again. He repeated this many times. After some time, he could do it with ease. He had just thinned my hair with the toothed scissors. In order to complete the job quickly, sometimes he did it so fast that my head pulled back and forth when he combed. The feeling was awful. Next, he would comb my hair forward. With a swift stroke of the comb, he placed it down on to the left side of my hair and gave it a hard part to the left and then parted the other side to the right. He had parted my hair quite neatly. I could see my white scalp in a straight line in between where the hair parted. I thought he had finished the job. But no. He used a small comb and a pair of scissors to snip away the hair that was out of line. He then unclipped the joint that held the white cloth protecting my body from the cut hair. He gathered up the cloth and shook it gently of the cut hair. He put the used cloth into a basket. Then he spread out a white 'Good Morning' towel over my neck.

Next he would take a rectangular object and remove from it a long blade. He went to a corner of his shop, held one end of a dark brown leather strop and stroked the blade against it a few times.

Every time he held that blade near me, I would twitch and squirm. He would shout sternly, "Don't move!" then I would then keep very still. The blade would land on my right sideburn and with a quick stroke, it was

A leather strop

shaved. Then he did the same to the left. It hurt! He ignored me. He continued holding my head firmly and carried on shaving. He proceeded to shave my face, then in between my upper lip and my nose. My throat felt a sensation. I would imagine that one day, should he make a mistake, he would slit my throat. I longed to touch my throat. But the piece of white cloth he tied on my neck was in my way. I had to control myself, full of fear, until he completed the process. When he was done, he would take out a container and pull out a long object. He pulled my ear and pushed a long brass rod with a tiny cup at the end. He brought a lighted tungsten lamp near and peered into my ear. He pushed the ear digger into my delicate ear passage. It gave me a sharp pain. Then he gave it a few twists and scrapes and then pulled it out. He dropped the wax onto a piece of toilet paper. Next, he pushed into my ear a blade that could cut both sides. He gave it a few twists. He then used a small little brush and pushed it into my ear and gave a few turns. This time, the sensation was not bad.

What I liked about the barber was when he took out a bottle of water, aimed the spout at my head, and pushed down a tube with a circular ring as a holder for his finger. I could feel the cool water droplets landing on my face and water seeping down my scalp. The mist also had a sweet fragrance. I can still smell and feel the refreshing coolness trickling down my scalp.

He gave my hair a final comb. This time, it was smooth as silk. He looked at the left of my face then the right. When he was finally satisfied with the cut, he took out the towel, wiped away the remaining bits of hair, then slapped my neck gently a few times with a small towel before carrying me down from the wooden seat. I could see in the mirror that he had given me a new look.

For adults, I noticed the hair cutting process was more complicated. He made the client lie down on the chair. Then he took a brush, dipped it in some sort of liquid, and brushed the sideburns, moustache and goatee. Then he shaved him. Next, he brought a lamp close to the ear. With a pack of long instruments, he began digging out the earwax. He wiped off the wax from the ear-digger with his hands and then washed it. That was not all. He used a pair of sharp, pointed scissors and pushed it into each nostril and made a few snips. The client then blew his nose a few times.

The Indian barber did not provide earwax extraction services but did provide a massage. He would adjust the chair to the sitting position then massage the client's shoulders, neck and back. Following that, he gave the head a hard twist to the left then to the right. Sometimes, a cracking sound could be heard.

Uncle Yam's Shop

After that, I went to uncle Yam's shop, which was named 'Swee Aun', to look for my brothers. They had most likely gone to the barber next door after discovering that their favourite barber had many clients.

Just like any provision shop of those days, uncle Yam's shop was stacked with rice, flour of different types, dried food products, canned food, bottled drinks, stationery and many other items. He usually wore striped pyjama pants and a singlet when conducting business.

On the front row of his shop were huge bottles of preserved fruits such as mangoes, papayas, and peaches. They were preserved with sugar and spices. If one wished to buy a piece of the fruit, he would ladle it up, wrap it with a piece of ready-cut newspaper, and serve the customer.

His rice, beans and other grains were in bags, and the grain at the top of the bags was shaped into peaks. If one wished to purchase some grain, he would detach a triangular bag, usually made of newspaper, and fill it. Then he would use the *daching* (weighing scale) which stood on the peaks of grain and weigh it. He had different lengths of *daching*. The longer the *daching*, the heavier it was meant to weigh. He verified the weight by looking at the pointer at the head of the *daching*, to see if the two pointers aligned. After being weighed, the packet was retrieved from the pan with the apex pointing downwards. He had a particular way of folding the newspaper packets for grain. First he folded down the flap nearest to him, then the right flap, followed by the left and finally folded down the back flap. After that, he pulled a dry reed from a bundle tied to the wooden stand. He tied the packet of conical grains expertly and tucked the ends firmly in between a length of reed and the bag. The excess length of reed was shortened with a sharp tug with his fingernails. For larger quantities of grains, bags made of tough Manila paper, usually meant for packaging cement, were used instead.

A Chinese *daching* Photo: Yeo Hong Eng's collection	A coin till Photo: Yeo Hong Eng's collection

His working desk was right at the back of the shop. He kept his cash in the desk drawer. Above his desk was hung a huge, empty Milkmaid condensed milk tin with a string attached to the bottom. It was just high enough for an adult to reach. Tied on the tin's handle was a string on a system of two pulleys. The string at the end of the second pulley was tied to a counterweight and a small bell. Whenever uncle Yam wished to get some small change, he would reach up and pull down the short string attached to the bottom of the Milkmaid tin. The little bell would ring. After getting his change, he would let the string go. The counterweight at the other end would pull the tin up.

He usually delivered the goods in the afternoon when business was slack. His wife minded the shop when he was away.

An Indian provision shop was so different from a Chinese one. Before one reached an Indian provision shop, from a few yards away, there was the strong, telltale smell of spices. First to greet us were the bags of coloured spices and turmeric powder, shaped into peaks. Behind the bags of spices were the grains in bigger bags. The Indian shopkeeper used a weighing instrument different from the Chinese. He used a weight balance. The accuracy of the weight was read from the pointer at the middle of the set. The two points must align to show accuracy. The weighing balance had two pans—one on each side. One could put the counterweight on either of the pans. Once, I was puzzled when an Indian shopkeeper used a tin of condensed milk as a counterweight. Later, I found out that he wanted to weigh a packet of grain the same weight as the tin of milk.

At most village Indian provision shops, the proprietor would also sell some cooked items, such as *prata* or *mee goreng*. Iced drinks might also be sold. To make shaved ice for the drinks, a block of ice would be removed from a bag of sawdust, which kept it cold, and rinsed off. The ice was put on a block of wood with an upturned blade attached. He would move his ice block to and fro on the blade. The ice shavings were collected from under the block of wood and the remnant of the block of ice would be returned to the bag of sawdust.

At the rear of uncle Yam's shop, there was a little open-air market at a sandy lane. There were no fixed stalls. The vendors would simply lay their goods on the sandy ground, all in a row. A few would spread out old newspapers then arrange their wares on that.

I would help my grandma carry her rattan basket. She would buy fish and meat then take us to a food stall to have *chiok*—rice gruel cooked with pork and egg, seasoned with a little pepper and light sauce added to taste. Using a Chinese spoon, we would slowly skim the surface and eat a little at a time so as not to scald our lips. The dish was usually best eaten when it was steaming hot. After the break, we went back to uncle Yam's shop, where my grandma would sometimes arrange for us to take a bath there, as the wells in our compound were drying up. We felt a great difference in the water. We would tell grandma that the tap water was warmer than the well water. We were thrilled when the water flowed out at the twist of the lever. At home, I used to bathe with well water, regardless of the weather or time. In the morning, well water could be quite chilly. It gave me the shivers. For baths at uncle Yam's store, grandma used a scooper to collect water from the tap and pour it over me. It was a different feeling. I did not feel the chill biting into my skin. After a few scoops, she dried me with a towel borrowed from aunt Yam, then put on my clothes. If you asked me which gave me a better feeling, bathing with well water or tap water, I would choose well water as I liked the feeling of the sudden chill on my skin. Sometimes, we had a bowl of warm noodles cooked by aunt Yam after our bath.

Sometimes, I wandered off to other shops along the row of houses. I went past Bun Siong shop, where my classmate Keong It Leong lived. Further on, there was a sandy path which could lead us to Telok Mata Ikan and Padang Terbakar—the kampongs to the east of Bedok. But instead, I crossed the path to a sandy compound for cars. There was a huge concrete house, with 'Bedok Resthouse' painted on its front wall. I did not know what it was, so I did not venture in.

There were a few times when I went into Kampong Padang Terbakar and kampong Mata Ikan. The residents there were mainly fishermen. Their fishing boats were parked at the shore. Some were kept at home. They dried their fishing nets by the sides of their attap houses. Some were busy repairing their fishing nets.

After the sandy compound, there was a little shack. The owner sold coffee and Malay *kueh mueh* or cakes. He fried *mee goreng* too upon request. We could hear waves lapping the sandy shore. Further up there was a concrete platform with stoves, chairs and tables stacked up neatly along its length. I learnt that this place was busiest when the sun went down. It was known as Bedok Corner.

Bedok corner was just across from our barbershop. Sitting on stools while we waited our turn, we watched the hawkers push their carts with the charcoal stoves burning and bright kerosene lamps. One particular hawker we recognised was a cuttlefish seller. He had a signboard with three large Chinese characters: '*Yue Lai Xiang*' meaning 'When night comes, fragrance appears.' Dried cuttlefish hung from a bar across his cart. Another hawker selling *cheng tng*, or more accurately *ngo bi tng,* (a dessert known as five spice soup) was also busily pushing his cart to the destination. The hawkers, wearing unpainted wooden clogs, were all getting ready to set up their stalls along the beach at Bedok Corner, where one could eat and enjoy the singing of the waves and the caress of the cool sea breeze on one's face.

Today, the Yeh Lai Xiang stall is at Bedok
Corner Cooked Food Center.

Directly across the road was the Bedok Police Station. It was a two-storey concrete building. Whenever a villager wanted to make a birth or death report or apply for a permit for a *wayang* performance or get a dog licence, they had to go there. The policemen wore grey shirts and khaki shorts, with white high socks and black boots. He would write reports and fill up forms in either broken English or Malay.

The front of the police station was decorated with various tropical ornamental plants. In a corner was a red pail filled with sand. I think it was probably used for putting out fires. There was once a black-and-white film screened at the police station compound. It was about road safety. We were thrilled that although the narrators were Europeans, Malays and Indians, they spoke Mandarin. I later learnt that the languages in films could be dubbed.

On the right of the police station there was a laundry shop and a tailoring shop.

My grandma would usually order some provisions from uncle Yam, and after paying for them we would be on our way home with our purchases. It was a long walk in the sun, weaving through the kampong along Jalan Kathi, past Ah Kuei's provision shop, a few Malay policemen's houses, and finally reaching the foot of the ridge where our farm was. Along the way, we recognised policemen's houses by the uniforms, which hung proudly on their verandahs. We knew a few of them. They were Salleh, Jalil, Leng, and Panjang. Finally, we would reach home via the shortcut through the kampong.

Chapter 2
Where We Came From

More about uncle Yam

When he was in China, uncle Yam, whose full name was Yeo Koon Yam, lived in the same 'Yeo's village' as my grandparents, in Chin Kang, Qianzhou, Fujian Province. My grandpa and uncle Yam's father were distant cousins. Uncle Yam and uncle Chai Peng were cousins. The few of us in Singapore were very close, as we had no other relatives here. It was not wrong for latter generations to say that the blood ties of the past generations were thicker, as good friends were few and hard to come by.

Once, my grandma brought me to Teow Swee's shop at Kampong Eunos. It was around 4 p.m. We were waiting for transport. Suddenly, someone lifted me up from behind to a waiting half-tonner truck. I was so shocked, I struggled for dear life and gave out a loud yell. My grandma calmed me down and told me that uncle Yam was taking me home after purchasing some goods to replenish the stock in his shop. That was my first encounter with uncle Yam.

Every New Year's Eve, my parents would bring him gifts of live chickens, ducks and vegetables. In return, he would give us canned food and other dried products.

Uncle Yam had several children by his Singaporean wife. His first wife was in China. His eldest daughter was Hwee Koon, followed by Hwee Sian. His son was Chong Yew. I did not know his other children. The children attended the same school as us. The girls attended Bedok Girls' School, whereas the boys went to Bedok

Boys'. One thing they had in common with us was tortoises. My grandma often brought them tortoises from our pond. They would keep their tortoises in a little enclosure in the bathroom. Every time we met, our conversations centred on the tortoises.

The Kampong Folks

Sometimes, wayward young men from the kampongs nearby would walk around in groups, carrying parangs and slingshots. They would make a lot of noise, joking and laughing as well as challenging each other to commit mischiefs. The noise attracted dogs, which rushed out of their houses growling and barking. Then they would shoot at the dogs with their slingshots. We owners would immediately shoo our dogs back into the houses and plead with them not to disturb the animals. However, there were usually some black sheep among the group. They would continue to shoot at the house, post boxes, and other animals. Once, my brother and I were with a distant cousin, Ah Hock, the son of the eldest daughter of my father's uncle Teow Swee. Ah Hock had the uncanny habit of shooting at birds. He would shoot a bird and smear the blood on his slingshot, believing that his slingshot would find more bird targets. As he was much older than we were, naturally, we respected him as a leader.

One day, he offended some of the youngsters in the Malay kampong. Some of them were most likely from the rowdy group I mentioned earlier. That led to a slingshot war between us and them, lasting over an hour. We were hiding in a clump of bushes. They were outside among the attap huts. We used small pebbles and young guava fruit as ammunition. We traded shot after shot. A few shots hit us but because of the distance between us, by the time these 'bullets' reached us, their force weakened considerably. I was hit once on the ear. The pain was bearable, but it instantly turned red. My brother and cousin were hit too. The 'war' became more intense. At times, we feigned being shot and groaned loudly. I got the impression that the 'groans' infuriated them. We pretended to groan even though the shots went wide.

It stopped only when our parents wanted us to help them in the farm at around 4 p.m. The next morning, my mum discovered that a few of our heavily laden papaya trees had been badly damaged. Some of the unripe fruit had fallen to the ground and was damaged beyond recognition. Most of the other young fruit were dripping white sap. The buds and young leaves were tattered and drooping. We believed the gang whom we offended the previous afternoon was responsible. My mum was furious. We had an earful from her. Of course, all we did was to keep ourselves very quiet and regret what we had done. Then she collected the damaged fruit in a rattan basket and stormed over to the kampong. Swearing, she threw the fruit on the kampong path then yelled for those responsible to come forward. No one did. A few of the adults came to express regret, saying that the children should not have done that. Children's brawls should not lead to destruction of adult property.

In an unrelated incident, once, one of our pigs was stoned to death. Unfortunately, no one took responsibility to bury it. I thought it most likely that our pig fence had been built too near to the perimeter of the kampong. In those days, we built fences around our land using chicken netting as well as odds and ends from the sawmills, so outsiders could gain access to the pigpen easily. As a result, when the carcass rotted, the stench permeated the kampong whenever a slight breeze blew. We believed the elders of those responsible must have given them a shelling.

In 1959, I was going to school at Dryburgh English School. The Katong Bedok bus took me to the bus stop near Bedok Boys' and Girls' schools. Then I walked home via Jalan Langgar Bedok. At 15 cents, the fare was expensive. In order to save five cents, I alighted from the bus stop at Jalan Haji Salam, although the walking distance to school was greater. Along the way, there were people returning from work and from schools and children running errands for their parents. One day along this walk, I met a girl dressed in a white top and a light blue *baju kurong*. She smiled at me and we struck up a conversation. We talked about our school and schoolwork and she showed me where she lived. She lived a few houses away from our immediate neighbour south of our farm. On the weekends, she and her sister brought us their leftover food, which we could use as pigswill, and in return, we gave them some vegetables. That went on for some time. One evening however, a boy came between us and spoke sternly to her as if rebuking her in the Malay. From that time onwards, I never saw her again.

During Hari Raya Puasa, a few families would give us gifts of food arranged on enamel-coated metal trays, wrapped with a piece of cloth, such as *sayur lodeh, ketupat,* chicken, and *kueh-mueh.* We transferred them into our crockery and returned their crockery unwashed, as we did not want to inadvertently contaminate their crockery with pork. We returned the crockery with gifts of red packets, some uncooked rice, and sugar.

The Maria Hertogh Riot

During the Maria Hertogh riots between 11 and 13 December 1950, some representatives of the kampong, Chief Hassan, as well as Fat Night Watcher paid us a visit. Fat Night Watcher was given that name because he was part of the ARP team (Air Raid Precaution) that took care of the security of the kampong during the Japanese Occupation. The people living in the kampong assured us that they would not harm us as it was a matter between the religious leaders and the British government. My parents knew that they would not harm us, as we had cooperated very well during the Japanese Occupation. A few days after that, we saw an aircraft fly past the kampong. Stacks of leaflets were dropped from it. We ran after them and managed to retrieve a few, but they were in Jawi script. Fat Night Watcher translated to us the news that the Maria Hertogh riots had been settled amicably. It seemed during the Japanese Occupation, my parents and the elders in the Malay kampong had developed a very deep understanding and respect towards one another.

Note:
The riot was caused by the British magistrate in Singapore giving the right to Maria, whose foster mother in Indonesia brought her up as a Muslim, to go to Holland to live with her Christian mother. The

three-day riots were sparked by a court decision to award custody of 13-year-old Maria Hertogh to her Dutch-Eurasian Catholic parents. She had been raised as a Muslim by her adopted parents.

Opera

On those nights when there were *wayang* performances at Pang Sua Kia temple, Salleh, a policeman and also my father's friend, would walk back home with us, talking and joking about the villain's character in the performance. In a *wayang*, a villain usually paints his face to look hideous and talks in an outrageous manner. He swears loudly and gestures wildly and imposes his will on others. Some of the more enterprising Malays would set up *satay* stalls among the variety of stalls there to tempt the taste buds of the *wayang* fans.

Kite-Flying

Shorty Bong's son, Pong, was an expert in making *layang bulan* or *wau bulan*. This type of kite was constructed in shapes of animals or objects like the moon. Sometimes it was known as the Kelantan kite as I believe it originated from Kelantan. During the kite-flying season, Pong would fly his kite high up in the sky. Then he would firmly anchor his kite cord somewhere near his house. His kite would remain stationary with the sound vibrator vibrating furiously at a high pitch. Usually from the months of May to July, the weather was dry and the southwest monsoon wind would blow steadily. The kampong folks would make different types of kites with vibrators on. These vibrators were made from a strip of the outer layer of the leaves of sisal commonly found in the kampong. It was stretched taut over a thin bamboo strip so that it looked like a bow. When exposed to a draft, the stretched sisal strip would vibrate to make a sound. The pitch of the sound depended on how taut the strip was stretched. When all the kites were flown at the same time, the sound was fantastic. I remembered a particular poultry feed delivery man from Kampong Chai Chee was very thrilled at hearing the sounds from the kite vibrators, as he had never seen such things in his Chinese village of Chai Chee. Pong, whom we called Ah Pong, would make me a simpler version. I was exhilarated when it ascended into the sky gracefully. Pong limped, most likely due to a polio attack but I remember him for his smiles and easy-going nature.

Bird Catching

Pong was very interested in rearing birds too, especially *merbok*. I was not interested, but Hong Bian was. Pong would teach Hong Bian how to tell the age of a *merbok* by counting the scales on its legs and how to prepare the sticky gum used for the decoy to trap wild *merbok*. Hong Bian would search for discarded Japanese slippers, slice the rubber soles and put them in an empty milk tin. Then he would build a fire on the open ground, and heat the tin. The rubber would melt and catch fire. Then he would blow out the fire and stir the contents. He would smear the sticky liquid rubber onto foot-long twigs. He would place a decoy bulbul up among some bushes with his newly made trap to entice unwary 'suitors'.

Youth to the Rescue

My mum once dropped her purse into a well. Her money and identity card were in it. She used a hooked *gala* (bamboo pole) to try to hook it, but did not succeed after many tries. She was panic-stricken. My dad hurried to the kampong to get help. A young man, whom we had never seen before, immediately volunteered to help. He gingerly climbed over the enclosure of the well and dived in headfirst. As we had never seen a man diving into the water before, we held our breath. We were afraid he might not come up alive. Within minutes, he came up with the purse in his hand. We were so grateful for his assistance we rewarded him with five dollars.

Kampong Marriages

Marriages, Hari Raya Puasa celebrations, and circumcisions were elaborate affairs in the kampong. If someone were getting married, relatives and neighbours would chip in. Tents were erected. Planks were put over the ground inside the tents so that dancers would not soil their feet and their outfits. Decorations of streamers and flowers made from crisp paper were hung up by enthusiastic children. Coconut fronds were split symmetrically and tied up at the main posts of the tent. Colourful balloons were added to the fronds to enhance the beauty of the set-ups. Flags of some nations were hoisted up onto some coconut trees in front of the house of the bride and bridegroom. As the bride and bridegroom would be king and queen for a day, a pair of thrones was set up. A band was hired. Men, women, and children dressed in their best to attend the wedding. A *kompang* (Malay drum) procession was ready to welcome the 'king and queen'. Artificial flowers on sticks were prepared and prayers were said. Cases of large bottles of popular F&N orange squash were ordered and delivered. Three coconut stems cut to a certain length were sunk into the ground. When the day came, a huge pot was heaved onto the three stumps. Rice was washed, spices, turmeric, sauces, and chillies were seasoned and poured into the pot followed by water. Chickens were slaughtered, plucked and washed after a prayer was said. The fire was lit using firewood gathered days before. *Nasi berani* was cooked. Other dishes were cooked in smaller stoves, in smaller volumes.

Guests in their finest apparel, often with intricate embroidery, arrived in droves. Men in *songkoks*, collarless shirts and pants worn under sarongs led their wives and children who were also in matching embroidered *baju kurongs* and *sarongs,* elaborate jewellery and shoes to congratulate the bride and bridegroom. *Assamulaikum* greetings and handshakes were exchanged and hearts were touched. Loud *joget* music filled the air. In between the feasting, dance numbers were played, and men who loved to dance would invite the *joget* girls (hired professional dancers) to dance.

There was no fixed time to start eating. The guests would eat as soon as they arrived. It was not necessary to wait for the bride and bridegroom to be seated on the throne before eating. In the distance the sound of *kompang* music were heard.

"The bride and groom will soon arrive," said an old Mak Cik in her sixties. Those who were eating would hurry up and washed their hands in the aluminium pots and used water chamber prepared for them at a corner. They joined those who were already there along the route where the procession was. A troupe of *kompang* players accompanied the bride and bridegroom. They chanted and sang according to the drumbeat. There were also youths dressed in their best, carrying crisp paper flowers glued onto thick wires. Each 'bloom' was poked into a banana core attached on to a long bamboo pole. There was a group carrying spears and *krises*. They paraded alongside the drummers. Guests, curious onlookers like us, shuffled nearer to watch. Then the newlyweds ascended the throne prepared for them. Well-wishers shook and kissed the couple's hands and wished them *"tahniah atas perkahwinan anda"* (congratulations on your wedding). The revelry continued until late in the evening.

Rounds and rounds of food were served. The leftovers were poured into prepared bins meant for the purpose. After the revelry was over, we collected them to cook with other ingredients for our farm animals.

Kampong Past Times

The kampong folks were always seen gathered together playing, singing, practicing the *kompang*, chatting, playing games such as football and rattan ball *(sepak takraw)*, bird watching, *silat* demonstrating, kite-flying or reciting the Koran before marriages and circumcisions.

One day, a medicine peddler visited the kampong. He spread out his ground sheet and said his prayers, then laid out his medicine and bottles of F&N orange squash. Then he lit his carbide lamps, and did some rounds of silat with *krises* (curved Malay weapons). My dad and us boys also joined the curious gathering. At the end of each performance, he treated his wound (supposedly hurt with his *kris*) with his medicine. Some of the kampong folks would purchase the medicine. On one such occasion, my dad pushed me forward to buy a bottle too. This peddler stared at me and refused to sell me anything. Feeling slighted, we walked away. "Most likely, the medicine does not work on people like us who eat pork," my dad reassured me, who had many Malay friends. How far was that true? I did not know.

House on fire? No, the folks were most probably preparing a meal using firewood.
Photo: Charles Yap's collection.

A Sweet and Sour Relationship

There was one particular Boyanese family, the Borhands, who were the last to move into the land, which had the same owner as mine. We became their nearest neighbour. We were living at the mid-ridge of the hill. They lived at the summit. At first, the father was a chauffeur of one of the rich *towkays* (business proprietors). Later, he became a taxi driver. He had several children. The eldest one was Jalil, the second, Mariam, the third, Ahmad, who was the same age as me, and there were two younger daughters.

At first, our relationship was very cordial. Ahmad and I played together and went to school together. We shared the same food. He would say never mind about *halal* or not—nobody's around. He was a brilliant boy. In Primary 4, he got a double promotion to get into Primary 6. But at that time, there were no more vacancies in our Primary 6 classes. He and three other boys had to join the girls in the girls' school. Having skipped Primary 5, his mathematics was weak, he approached me for help and we practised mathematics together. But later when he got to know the other families living in the area, our relationship began to change.

In 1957, public water standpipes were installed at the border of Piah Teng's and Kim Eng's land. The cemented wash area was very small, able to accommodate four kerosene tins only. Someone took the initiative to go around collecting donations to enlarge the wash area. The area became big enough to accommodate many people washing their clothes there simultaneously. We had to carry water to our homes—a good 300 to 400 metres away. At first, each of us carried two kerosene tins of water using a carrying pole on the shoulder. Then we made our own pushcart. Of course, it always broke down, as it was only made from basic materials—planks nailed together with two bulky axles from the wheels of grandpa's bullock cart. The dirt track was uneven and waterlogged. The cart could not withstand the weight of three or four kerosene tins of water. Ahmad's father also made a pushcart out of a bicycle and his also suffered the same fate. At times, when he got the chance to drive his boss's car home, he would use it to transport the water. He taught Ahmad to drive the car when he was 13. Ahmad would drive along the dirt tracks around the kampong, showing off to everybody.

One evening, I was at the standpipe waiting to fill my watering cans. Ahmad became too impatient to wait. Then, another boy of the same age turned up. He instigated the boy to punch me. *'Tumbok dia! Tumbok dia!'* (translation from Malay: Punch him! Punch him!) The boy really did. Of course, I had to retaliate. While I was struggling with that boy, Ahmad kicked away one of my cans and put his in my place for the water. With the can damaged and outnumbered two to one, I had to admit defeat. I went home feeling very indignant over the incident. My mum, upon learning of my predicament, was furious. Just like the incident with the papaya trees, she went up to Ahmad's house and yelled at him for being *'kurang ajar'* (someone who's had a lack of guidance). Low mumblings could be heard inside the house. It must have been

Ahmad's mother having a word with him. Was she berating him or not? I did not know.

Piped Water

Then, good news came. My dad's cousin was willing to pay for his water, so he would be having a pipe connected to his home, for which he also had to pay. There would be no more squabbling over free water with Ahmad. My dad asked his cousin to extend the pipeline to our house and we would pay him a fixed monthly amount for sharing his meter. When the pipes arrived, we were so excited. Everyone in the house helped to carry the pipes, clear the undergrowth, and dig a channel in the ground where the pipes would lie. Machines for cutting the pipe threads were set up. Then the pipes were clamped down and the threads were cut by turning a thread cutter. The pipes were laid into the channel then buried. The ladies prepared coffee, tea, cakes, and fried *meehoon* for tea. Within an afternoon, the whole project was completed. We were told to wait for the city council to install the water meter. After a week, the water meter was installed, and hey presto, we had pipe water at last. Goodbye to queuing to fill our cans. Goodbye to building and repairing carts. Goodbye to troublemakers.

Ghosts

After giving up being a chauffeur, Ahmad's father became a taxi driver. He had to drive late into the night. One night, he rushed home feeling sick. He stayed in bed for a few days. He claimed that the road beside the Bedok schools was haunted (the present-day Jalan Langgar Bedok). At that time, the dirt road was riddled with potholes and strewn with pebbles and was very dark at night. Both sides of the road were overgrown with dwarf bamboo bushes. On the left side, behind the bushes, was a cowshed. He claimed to have seen a white apparition waving at him. With hair on end, he did an abrupt three-point turn and sped to Bedok Changi Road junction, then to Tanah Merah Kechil Road and reached home. Witnesses said he drove like a flying arrow. I remember hearing a speeding car, followed by a loud dragging of tyres on sandy ground, then the loud bang of a car door. A commotion was heard inside the house. By and by, he recovered from his shock and began driving his taxi again.

After a period of time, it was my turn to experience what he had gone through. One evening in 1960, I arrived home very late after attending a concert at the Victoria Memorial Hall. It must have been around 11 p.m. I got off the bus at the bus stop beside the Bedok schools. I walked up that stretch of track Ahmad's father had used (the present-day Jalan Langgar Bedok). Looking up the pitch-dark path, I saw nothing. I did not have a torch with me. I could not walk fast for fear of kicking pieces of rock or getting caught in a rut or pothole. At the same time, I thought of what Ahmad's father had encountered. With my heart in my mouth, I ascended the path up to the ridge. Then I saw something white moving up and down. I was so fearful that I could not move. My heart was beating very fast and I felt very cold and shivered all over. My hair stood up. I must have stayed in that state for a pretty long time. In my mind, I thought of my grandmother's saying, "You have done nothing to harm others, so you need not be afraid." She told us that every time we were in the dark. In those days, we often walked in the dark and alone too.

Then came the sweetest sound I ever heard. '*Moo!*' All my tension and apprehension evaporated. It had come from either a cow or a bull. Why didn't you 'moo' earlier so that I need not have been so tensed up, I thought. I heaved a very deep sigh of relief and I walked home with a light heart.

At home, my parents and siblings asked me whether I had encountered any ghosts. I told them, "Positively. It was a 'cow ghost'."

The Call of the Faithful

Every morning, my parents woke up at about 4.30 a.m. to gather vegetables from the farm. They washed them in the pond and laid them in the courtyard of the house. By that time, it was about 5.30 a.m. We, the children would lay out the screening boards in the courtyard. All the vegetables were inspected for fungi, worms and freshness. Those heavily infested with fungi or worms would be discarded. Some only needed to be trimmed. Some needed only to have their roots cut off, leaving just the leaves. After all this was done, the vegetables were packed into huge rattan baskets then loaded onto the bicycle. My father would pedal with the load to Chai Chee Market. I would ferry my mother on my bicycle along Tanah Merah Kechil Road to the junction of Changi Road, where she waited for the Changi bus to take her to Chai Chee Market.

I accompanied my parents a few times when they went about their tasks at 4.30 a.m. Being up and about so early in the cold morning, especially when one was alone among the trellises, wooden supports and huts was something not to joke about. Furthermore, the dew and morning fog, the croaking of frogs in the water, and the cacophony of sounds made by the insects and night birds created an eerie atmosphere. No doubt my parents had torches, but how much could the torchlights help when faced with dangers such as thieves, snakes, poisonous caterpillars and other vermin? They needed to gather the vegetables and they didn't have their hands free to tackle unexpected eventualities. One thing was for sure, my mother told us. The morning call for prayers by the *imam* through the loudspeakers of the mosque made them feel reassured that at least there was a human voice around. Furthermore, it was a wake-up call.

In the evenings, we would not put down tools until the evening prayers were called. Before the speakers were installed on the kampong mosque, the *iman* would knock successively a few times on a huge log (*bedok*) suspended from the roof of the mosque, followed by three knocks from a suspended gigantic wood knocker on a huge drum. Then prayers were said.

Mutual Help

In 1955, Yeo Teow Swee's son-in-law, Soh Ah Chew, built a house on the southwest corner of the land which Teow Swee was contracted to manage. His was the nearest to the Hassans' land. His children were very close to us. Ah Hock was the eldest, followed by Ah Lim and the daughters, Ah Erm and Him Tee. Another boy had been given up for adoption. Ah Hock was much older than us, so he was looked upon as a leader. We went about making slingshots, shooting birds, building bird traps, catching and rearing fighting fish and catching spiders. Ah Hock went to Sin Min Public School on East Coast Road. Later, he got married to a girl of the same kampong and his name was changed to Salim.

Soh Ah Chew was very fortunate, as this piece of land was very undulating. Some lived on the ridge and some in the valley. The well he dug was constantly filled with clear refreshing water. Whenever the water from the well was scooped up, the next moment, it would be filled again. Before the standpipe, we had to rely on the rain to fill our wells. If the rain did not come for a few weeks, our wells would all dry up. When our wells dried up, we would go to his well to ferry water home for our cooking and washing.

On the way to the well, we had to walk past Teow Swee's son, Koon Toon's house. His children were very young then. They were Hong Keng, Kok Beng, Bee Choo and Hong Tian. Our family was big, and being older, we extended our help to fill the raised huge water jar with a capacity of 24 gallons for him. A pipe was connected from the jar to the kitchen. So every time when we were ferrying water, we would also fill up his huge jar.

This huge jar has survived after having exchanged hands numerous times. It has given its various owners many memories.

Yeo Teow Swee, although not very literate, was a very capable and ambitious man. He was made the supervisor of the land by landowner Kim Eng. In 1954, he decided to rear white chickens for their eggs. Chicken coops with compartments were built. White chicks were bought and reared. The cockerels were sold while the hens were put into the compartments and fed. Every day, the eggs were collected and transported away, most likely for export, as Singaporeans did not like to eat white chicken eggs. People claimed that white eggs were not as delicious as brown eggs. That claim exists even today.

After breeding a few generations of hens, Teow Swee ventured into pig farming. The chicken coops were converted into a storehouse for pig food. Pig pens and fencing were constructed. At that time I was about ten. I remember volunteering to help carry the timber for the carpenter to build the fencing. Teow Swee was a taskmaster. He was there helping to load pieces of timber onto the shoulders of helpers to carry to the construction site. When it was my turn, I felt that he loaded onto my shoulders much more than I could carry. I could hardly balance the load while traversing along the undulating path. I did not protest as I did not want him to perceive me as lazy.

The fencing enclosed nearly the whole parcel of land, about five acres. Then piglets were bought. They were left to roam the whole area freely—in the bushes, under the coconut and rambutan trees. With their snouts, they made little holes where they could lie down to sleep. Teow Swee summoned his second son and third daughter to manage it. Being inexperienced in pig farming, he sought my father's help. Our whole family was always ready to lend a hand and pitched in with tasks such as repairing the fencing, running after stray pigs, preparing pig feed and topping up the water in the water holes. He reared more than a hundred pigs and a few sows. Teow Swee had connections with the restaurants and coffee shops in town. To impregnate the sows, money was needed to engage the services of the *kan ti ko* (stud breeder). But with so many sows, it did not make economic sense to do so. Instead, the men picked the best boar in the pen. The rest of the male pigs were neutered. That boar grew fast and impregnated all the sows there. Later, it became so big and strong that it presented a problem. It could climb over the enclosure, break through the wooden pen, and go about destroying our vegetables. A very high enclosure of thick, strong timber was built to contain it. But that would not stop its pranks. Whenever anyone went near it, it would fling itself at the fence and grunt at them fiercely, scaring them.

Teow Swee's style of pig farming was known as free running. His pigs were left to roam freely all over the land in the enclosure. They dug for worms and other edible creatures or plants in the soil, rested and took shelter under shady bushes. The person in charge needed to see that the troughs were full and there was enough water in the watering holes for them to wallow in.

As for the meat products, consumers preferred to eat meat from free running pigs, as there was less fat.

Animal Husbandry

On our farm, there were chickens, ducks, pigs, a few rabbits, one or two caged myna birds and several dogs. Once a sow, which we called '*Ti Bu*' or Mother Pig, was in heat and my dad got excited.

"I need to hurry to get the services of '*kan ti ko*'" (the stud breeder)."

Dad hopped onto his bicycle and sped to the neighbouring farm, where boars or '*ti ko*' were reared. The owner of the boars would select one of them, tie a rope around its neck, and walk with it along the road to our house. Then, the boar would climb onto the back of the sow to mate. After a few minutes, the boar's job was done, and my dad had to pay the owner a service fee. That farmer reared several choice boars to perform these services. Sometimes, a boar would not take heed of his command. Once, I heard an anecdote of a man pulled by his sow into a patch of muddy water. When a boar saw a patch of muddy water, the temptation of wallowing in it was greater than providing impregnating services. The boar dragged itself and its owner to the mud pool and stayed there until it was satisfied. The owner could not bear to let the rope go for fear he might lose the boar.

A kan-ti-ko (studbreeder).
Photo credit: People's Association First 20 years Page 58

When the sow gave birth, my parents had to keep vigil through the night. Usually a kerosene lamp would be lit in the sty where the sow was giving birth. Powerful torchlights were always prepared. Once, I stayed up to watch the sow giving birth. With a grunt from the sow, a little limp piglet was pushed out of the vagina. The wet piglet lay down for a little while, before struggling to stand up. After a few struggles, it stood up and tried to walk. After a few attempts, it could walk and went in search for a teat to suck. Sometimes, a sow gave birth to as many as 20 piglets. But a sow has only 14 to 16 teats. During mealtime, some piglets would not have the chance to feed. How did we know that the sow had completely given birth to all the piglets? Well, after the last piglet was born, the sow would pass out the placenta. To prevent the sow from eating the placenta, we took it away to be buried for fear that viruses in the placenta would infect the piglets. We would make sure that when the sow shifted its position to feed the babies, they were safely out of harm's way. (There were instances when the sow smothered the babies to death.) My dad would sell the runts of the litter to the chefs in the market, to make roasted piglets, which was a delicacy to the Chinese. There was a time when we did not have the heart to sell the runts. We filled soft drinks bottles with condensed milk, fixed rubber nipples on their mouths, and let them suck.

After about two months or so when the piglets were big enough to eat solid food, they were weaned then put into the pens. Our huge cemented pen was partitioned into three enclosures. The youngest pigs were released into the enclosure on the right of the pens. The medium ones were driven from the right enclosure through a small gate to the middle enclosure. The grown-up pigs were driven to the extreme right of the enclosure to take the place of the adult pigs, which had already been sold.

When the young pigs were first put into the enclosure, my father would toilet train them. He would wet a corner, which would be where they should urinate and defecate. The first few days were difficult; the younger pigs would treat every place as a toilet. Whenever any one of them strayed away from the wet area to answer the call of nature, my father would immediately drive it back to the wet area. As days went by, they acquired the habit of defecating at the designated place.

Every day after a meal, the pigs had to be bathed. The well was just in front of the sty. My dad would hoist up water with a pail and expertly splash it onto them, taking care not to splash any directly into their ears. From the way they behaved, the pigs seemed to quite enjoy their baths.

Swill for the pigs was always cooked using a huge cauldron. We did it once every few days. On the day of the cooking, we would harvest water hyacinth and water lettuce from our pond. Insect-infested vegetables and other edible plant matter were chopped into pieces and emptied into a container. Sometimes, my dad would go to the kampongs to gather freshly cut banana stems or leftover food. More leftovers were collected after celebrations like weddings or circumcisions. We even collected dumb cane, which we didn't have on our farm, from Kampong Eunos and the remnants of the sago flour after processing. Then each of us would take a corner of the kitchen and chop these vegetables and roots. Then they were scooped up and mixed together with the other leftovers from previous cooking. Then, our own leftovers as well as the kampong residents' were added. Salt, uncooked rice, copra, or dried coconut kernels, and leftover fish from the market were also added.

When all the ingredients were in, two huge semi-circular lids were placed snugly over the cauldron. More firewood was added. Then, it was left to cook. Often, we had to open the lids and mix the food thoroughly using a huge wooden ladle to make sure that the food was well cooked. Cooking for our pigs was a serious matter, unlike what critics at large thought. Sometimes, stray pieces of dried bamboo trunk found their way into the giant stove. A loud explosion would send us scrambling to the stove. The explosion which came from the bamboo trunk was most probably due to sudden expansion of gas present. We had to find out if the cauldron was damaged, and checked for burning splinters which flew out from the stove, which could inadvertently cause fires in the kitchen.

At every meal, the cooked animal food was mixed with water and thoroughly inspected for stray matter such as pieces of metal, wood or fish bones. Lumpy rice balls were smoothed out. Sometimes the food was hot off the stove. We were afraid the animals would get scalded so we had to mix it with cold water. Then, the troughs which usually taken out of the pen after each meal, were put back in place and the food was ladled out with a scooper. Every hungry pig would gobble up the food with haste. No wonder the 'Prodigal Son' we often read about raced home after seeing how the pigs he cared for enjoyed their meals.

Every morning, my father would dutifully use a dung pusher (a long wooden spade) to push the dung out of the sty. While doing this, he would look for any signs of diarrhoea, strange coloured stools or other abnormalities. If there were, he had to identify and isolate the affected animals.

When the pigs began showing signs of being in heat, a date would be set to castrate the boars. My father would prepare the antiseptic. He scraped out some ash from the kitchen pots and woks. He then added camphor (*cheor lor* in the Hokkien dialect) bought from one of the shops in Chai Chee. He mixed the ash and camphor with kerosene oil and stirred thoroughly. The antiseptic preparation was ready.

Many people questioned why our boars and gilts (young females) needed to be neutered. Well, it was the consumers' preference. Consumers claimed that the meat of boars and gilts that were not neutered tasted awful compared to the neutered ones. To the pig breeders, neutered pigs were docile. They ate, slept and grew fat. When they were not in heat, they would not miss their meals or sleep, therefore gaining weight faster.

The day for castration arrived. My father would get hold of a boar and drape it with a gunnysack. He lifted its two hind legs up. He then sat on a stool with his thighs gripping the boar's torso. He spread the hind legs apart to reveal the two testicles. My grandma would wash the testicles thoroughly, then press one of them tight. She took out a NACET razor blade and made a slit on the skin covering the testicle. The boar would squeal and struggle. With the gunnysack over its head though, there was no danger it would bite my father or wriggle away. After making the slit on the skin, grandma pressed out the dissected testicle and detached it. Then she did the same for the second one. After both the testicles were removed, she skilfully stitched up the laceration. The antiseptic preparation was applied onto the wound. The operation was done. My father returned the neutered boar to its fold. This was done for all the boars from the batch.

As for the gilts, an appointment had to be made with an animal ligation specialist. This specialist would tie up all the sows on a long stout pole on the ground revealing the underside of their bellies, where the ovaries were. Then, he washed the skin where the laceration would be. With his surgical knife, he made a skilful slit and punctured a hole in the abdomen. It was horrendous to see how the gilt squealed and struggled with pain. We, and some of the children from the kampong looked on with horror and hid our faces in between our palms as if we could feel the pain. The specialist washed away the blood. He then pushed his finger into the puncture to feel for one of the two ovaries. Then he used the hook on the other end of the surgical knife to remove the first ovary. He did the same with the second ovary. When both were done, he stitched up the laceration. Antiseptic preparation was applied. The sow was then untied from the pole and moved to join the others in the sty. The specialist proceeded to neuter the second one and so on until all the sows were done. He was paid for the number of sows he neutered.

Once, Singapore was struck with swine fever. My father's pigs were not spared. Some of the pigs lost their appetite and became weak and motionless. My father dug a hole in the farm and with much sorrow and reluctance, buried them. Then, more exhibited similar symptoms. Instead of letting these pigs die, my father wanted to recoup part of his losses. A butcher from the Chai Chee Market was summoned. The butcher's response was prompt. It was a race against time. The butcher would not want to buy dead pigs. Since the swine fever was very contagious among pigs but did not affect humans at that time, my father sold all of them to the butcher for a tuppence. He suffered great losses. He had gotten the ingredients for the pig feed on credit from a supplier in Chai Chee. Now he had insufficient money to repay him. It was the first time my father had incurred a debt. Usually, he would pay the supplier when the pigs had come of age and were sold.

Self-Reliance

The earth tracks around that area developed potholes after a period of heavy monsoon rain. Motorised vehicles were often caught in the ruts. Whoever wished to drive through the tracks had to patch up the holes. Sin Min Public School was situated on the cliff of East Road not far from Tanah Merah Kechil. The principal's house was at the rear perimeter of the Bedok schools. He had to gain access to Bedok Road via the dirt track (the present-day Jalan Langgar Bedok). Some kind vehicle owners had contributed stone debris to fill up the holes but still there was more to be done. On Sundays, the principal and his son were seen busily filling the larger holes so his Morris Minor could give them a smoother ride.

But what happened when vehicles got caught in the ruts? The kampong folk usually came forward to provide a helping hand, whether the vehicle owners were strangers or fellow residents. Living in areas where the population was sparse, people tended to be more trusting, more sociable and helpful. Whenever something happened, be it positive or negative, the whole kampong would like to know and if help were needed, they would render whatever was within their means.

A Lift on a Bicycle

In 1960, there was a resident whom we called 'The Secretary'— as he was the secretary of the Citizenship Consultative Committee— who lived on Piah Teng's land. His son had just married a lady from the city. She was not used to walk with high-heeled shoes along country roads. One afternoon, I was about to cycle to Bedok. She approached me and asked if I could give her a lift to Bedok Road. I hesitated. My bicycle was so big—it was a goods bicycle—and it was very high too. I could not even reach the pedals if I were to sit on the saddle. However, I obliged, as I was the type who found it difficult to say no in the face of a request. I thought she must also have had confidence in me giving her a ride safely. I held the bicycle tightly and, at the same time, pressed the brake levers. She stepped on the pedal and sat on the middle bar. Then I gripped both ends of the handlebar, pushed the bike and leaned forward. Upon gaining momentum, I put my right leg through the triangle formed by the frame to search for the right pedal. I pedalled hard up the slope, round the tight corners, paying attention to the stones and ruts. When I came to an elevated path, I had to use all my strength and body weight. Then, I came to the top of the ridge. To get to Bedok Road, I had to go down a steep slope parallel to the cowshed (the present-day Jalan Langgar Bedok). It was there that she asked me to let her down. I was relieved. It was a huge load off my mind and physically a huge load off my bicycle. She must have weighed at least 50 kg. If she had not alighted, I would have had to ride with her down the steep slope.

Grandma and Grandpa

Before going any further, let me tell you more about grandma and grandpa. Grandpa and grandma came from Jinjiang (Chinkang in Hokkien) in Fukien, Yang Ting Xiang (Yeo's Village), Pei Men Huai (Periphery of North Gate). Grandma was born in late 1893. I am not sure about Grandpa.

It is a 'Yeo' character in Chinese

They came to Singapore in the early 1930s. That period in China was chaotic. There was a battle between the warlords, Sun Yat-sen's Kuomindang party, and the Communists. Life was hard for the Yeos. My grandpa had several brothers. He had an elder brother; he was the second son. The whereabouts of my grandfather's elder brother was unknown)—the third was Teow Swee, and the fourth was Teow Tong.

In such a chaotic time, grandpa came to Singapore. "I worked as a coolie, sleeping at the coolie quarters—a huge room shared with so many people. I had only just enough room to lay my tired body. By my side was my little cotton bag where I put my tattered clothing. Most of the time, I used the bag as a pillow to prop up my heavy head. I never touched any of the vices—prostitutes, opium smoking, or gambling. I set my mind with one aim—to earn enough money to bring my wife and my brothers to Singapore,' he told his fellow villagers when he returned to his native village. For three years, he worked hard. Besides being a coolie, he doubled up as a bullock cart driver, fruit seller and any other job that could earn him money.

During the three years when grandpa was away, grandma was constantly bullied by the relatives. They instigated each other to taunt her and took away her belongings—whichever were useful. If she had an extra pair of clogs, one of them would openly take it away. Whatever she cooked, they would get a lion's share. The miserable life she led was perpetually etched in her mind. When we—the siblings and grandma—were together, whenever trivial, unpleasant incidents happened, she would bring up these difficult times from her past. When grandpa went back to China after his three years' sojourn in Singapore, he calculated that the amount he had earned could pay for the passages for grandma and grandpa's two brothers to Singapore. Grandma was so upset with those in the village that she brought with her to Singapore all they had, even the ancestral tablets of grandpa's parents. Because these ancestral tablets were no longer there, my grandpa's relatives in China would no longer be obligated to observe the birth and death anniversaries for these deceased ancestors or perform any other yearly remembrance ceremonies, such as *Cheng Beng*, the ceremony of "sweeping" or tidying the ancestors' graves on the fourth moon of the lunar calendar. Their cousins and other relatives in China would now have no excuses to demand money from them to repair the ancestral graves or to perform other ceremonies.

Note:

The Cheng Beng ceremony, (which translates to "clear and bright" in Hokkien) is based on the belief, that "clear and bright", ancestral tombs bode well for the earthly lives of the descendants.

Before they left, they prayed to their ancestors that their migration to Singapore would turn out for the best. My grandparents believed that their ancestors would understand their plight and give blessings to them in a new land. With reverence, they installed the ancestral tablets beside the main deity, *Toa Pek Kong*, the deity of prosperity, in the hall of their house in Singapore at Kampong Eunos.

Their roots in China were entirely cut off. My grandparents would always say, "We have no other close relatives in China." No wonder then that whenever there was a marriage of one of my father's many cousins, they all proceeded to his house in Kampong Eunos to pay respects to the ancestors whose names were carved on the tablets.

"Thanks heaven and thanks to our ancestors," grandpa would always say. "On our journey to Singapore, the crowded junk was caught in a typhoon. The storm was so great that it blew the junk to the shore of Amoy and was grounded. Luckily, it was low tide then. When the tide was up, fortunately, the junk could continue its journey."

According to Chinese tradition, it was the elder brother's and sister's duty to look after the family after the death of their parents. We had no records of grandpa's parents. My grandparents looked after the welfare of my grandpa's younger brothers, Teow Swee and Teow Tong. Grandpa had an elder brother, but his whereabouts were not known. It seemed that Teow Swee was a resourceful person who was economically savvy. To him, study could not bring home the bacon. When they came to settle in kampong Eunos, Teow Swee slogged and did whatever work he could find to earn and save money. After a few years, he built a house along the main road, Changi 5 milestone. It was a long row of a two-storey attap house whitewashed with lime. He then got married. He set up a coffee shop and a provision shop. He rented the rest of the houses. He and his younger brother, Teow Tong, ventured out to build more houses and rented them out. Singapore in the 1930s saw a great influx of immigrants. There was a shortage of accommodation in town. His foresight and sharp business acumen helped him to prosper. He was also involved in subcontracting general supplies such as brooms, rags and other paraphernalia to shipyards.

When the situation demands it, resourcefulness can know no bounds. My grandparents had their own ways of taking advantage of opportunities to earn money. They partitioned their house and constructed more lean-tos and rented them out. At the same time, they reared pigs and chickens. They had a pond from which they got their pigs' food—water hyacinth, water lettuce and dumb cane. The pond was also a source of food for them—fish, shells and waterfowl. A toilet was built into the pond. One had to walk along a narrow wooden bridge before getting to the toilet. The excreta served as food for the fish as well as nutrients for the water plants. My grandfather was also in the transporting business. He also owned a few bulls and a bullock cart. With the bulls and bullock cart, he could earn more money by transporting building materials for the construction supply yard. In those days, they were mainly sand, cement, attap panes and wooden planks. Attap panes were made from the leaves of the nipa palms found in the swamps and used to make roofs. At the time, there was a building boom in Joo Chiat. He was busy every day transporting sand, cement, attap panes, timber and whatever other materials were needed by Mr Chew Joo Chiat to build houses.

They also went scouting around the rambutan and mangosteen plantations nearby. Once they discovered trees that provided bountiful harvests, they would farm them. They did this by paying the landowner a deposit for the fruits of those trees. When the fruits ripened, they would pay the remaining amount and harvest them. Then they either set up a stall and sold the fruit themselves or sold them to fruit vendors. This method of making a deal with the plantation owner carried a risk however. If the trees produced an inferior quality of fruit, the person who had arranged to purchase them could suffer a loss.

My dad tried to follow in the footsteps of my grandpa. He tried the transport business. But my dad did not use the bullock cart. He pulled the cart himself and sometimes with the help of an assistant. He often got the building supplies from Sim Lim (later renamed Sim Seng), a building supply yard in Geylang owned by Mr Soon Peng Yam, the brother of Mr Soon Peng Leong. My grandpa stopped this work only when they shifted to Tanah Merah Kechil.

Dad's uncle, Teow Swee, had several children—Koon Toon, Koon Hor, Koon Sai, Koon Ee, Koon Huat, and Ah Seng, in order of seniority. Teow Swee's wife died after giving birth to Ah Seng. Ah Seng was the raised by Teow Tong as his own son. Koon Huat died after suffering from a tetanus infection of a leg wound at the age of about 16.

Uncle Koon Seng was only three years old when he arrived in Singapore. My dad, Koon Poh and his sister, aunt Bong Chee were born in Singapore. Yeo Koon Seng's children are Kim Choo, Hong Siong, Hong Tong, Hong Huat, Hong Ho, Hong Chuan, Kim Hiok, Kim Keok, Hong Aik, and Hong Wee.

Grandpa's brother, Teow Swee, had been contracted to manage a piece of land at Tanah Merah Kechil on behalf of someone named

Kim Eng. Every month, Teow Swee would pay the landowner a certain sum of money. This entitled him to collect whatever he could get from the land—rent from squatters on the property, the sale of coconuts and other plantation crops such as rambutans and levies on the sale of sand, earth and other products. Few residents lived there so he invited his brother Teow Teng—my grandpa—to live there, leaving the house at Kampong Eunos for his elder son Koon Seng. The place at Kg Eunos was also a little cramped. So that was good news for him.

Tanah Merah Kechil was a Malay kampong. The houses were built in the midst of tall, mature coconut trees. With so many coconut trees around, their by-products were aplenty. Our house became a collecting centre for the mid-ribs of coconut leaves. When tied in a bundle, these became an effective sweeping tool (known as *sapu lidi* in Malay.) My neighbours would bring coconut mid-ribs to us and my father would weigh them using a *daching* and pay for them. We also acted as agents for collecting rags. Once a month, Uncle Teow Swee and his assistants would weigh those we had collected, reimburse us then transport them away.

My earliest memory of myself was that I was living in an attap hut with my parents, my grandma, my sisters and my younger brother Hong Bian. My brothers Hong Hup and Hong Teck had not been born yet. The house was in the middle of the slope of a ridge facing the east. My grandpa was a man steeped in tradition. He had some knowledge of *feng shui*. He also knew how to interpret the *Tung Shu*—a Chinese almanac. He was a calligrapher and also had some knowledge of herbal medicine. When building that house, his knowledge of *feng shui* came in useful. There was a ridge at the back of the house. The front of the house was facing the sun. On the left and right of the house too were ridges. The two ridges on the left and right looked like two arms holding the heart (our house). It was exactly what a good *feng shui* should have. Right down on the valley, a huge pond was dug. A stream ran in the middle of the valley. The farm was in the valley. Beyond that were Kampong Tanah Merah Kechil and Kampong Haji Salam.

My grandpa died about four months after I was born. I was told he must have been around the age of 60 when he died in 1946. My grandma was a staunch Buddhist. After my grandpa's demise, she vowed she would be a vegetarian. At first, she had vegetarian food only for dinner but later became a full-fledged vegetarian. Every day, she would chant, '*Nan mo or ni tor hoot*' in the Hokkien dialect. (English translation: Homage to the Buddha of Boundless Compassion and Wisdom) while her nimble fingers moved along the prayer beads. After each cycle of prayer beads, she would fill an empty dot on a chart with a red pencil. She visited various temples often and, at the same time, picked up tips on how to prepare vegetarian food. There were separate bowls, chopsticks, spoons, cups and other eating utensils for her. My mum was told to strictly observe grandma's wishes. Her crockery had to be washed and kept separate from the rest. Initially, grandma did her own cooking. Later, the job of cooking her vegetarian meals fell on my mum's shoulders. With my two sisters helping her in the kitchen, they soon learnt the ropes of vegetarian cooking.

My grandpa was a kind, understanding and caring man. During his spare time, he would be practicing his calligraphy. He borrowed books on herbal medical and copied them painstakingly, and in doing so, also improved his calligraphy and knowledge of herbal cures. In those days, modern medicine was hard to come by. Ailments were plentiful. Whenever any villager suffered either spiritual or physical ailments, they would come to consult him. He accepted patients at any hour. When those who suffered physical ailments, such as infected wounds and boils, he would go to the garden and gather some herbs, pound them with some cooked rice mixed with a dash of salt, and apply it on to the wound. Grandma was a good assistant. She learnt much from him. Sometimes, for a mentally disturbed person or someone who had a prolonged fever, grandpa consulted the Tong Shu and interceded on the patient's behalf if he had offended a certain spirit. The patient was instructed to offer thanksgiving to the spirit if he got well.

Grandpa stood firmly on matters of religious harmony. He instructed all our family members to be mindful when walking past *suraus* (small Muslim mosques) in the area, and to avoid making any sniggering comments when the *imams* were praying. A Roman Catholic teacher named Yeo Sian Shen was his good friend. My grandpa called him *Lau Sien See* or Old Teacher. Whenever they met, their conversations always touched on the affairs of the day, avoiding mention of their different religions.

On grandpa's deathbed, it seemed those spirits afflicting former patients, whom he had pacified, came for their dues. Most likely, the patients who were cured because of his intervention did not offer thanksgiving to them as he had advised. He shouted horribly, "They're coming after me! Old Teacher! Please help me!" He heaved and struggled violently. The Goddess of Mercy, Kwan Yin, was sought as the mediator. After that, he died peacefully. This episode was related to me by my dad.

What's in a Name

There are some important facts we ought to know about our names. Look at the name of my grandpa, Yeo Teow Teng. His surname or *seh* is Yeo and so are all before him and after him. His middle name is 'Teow'. That is his generation name. All his brothers and paternal cousins in his generation, regardless of age, took that middle name. It was not proper for his nephews or sons to take that middle name. But why regardless of age? It is possible that a brother and a son are of the same age. The brother can have the same generation name as his but his own son needs to take the latter generation name. The generation names are based on the order of the five elements, namely water, fire, wood, metal and earth. My dad and his brother took the generation name 'Koon'. All his other cousins too took the same generation 'Koon' too, be they living in Singapore or elsewhere. Should they meet, they would be able to piece the puzzle easily by the middle name. My middle name is 'Hong'; so are all my brothers and cousins as well as my father's cousins' children. My children took the middle name 'Zhao' in Mandarin or 'Cheow' in Hokkien. The male heirs of my brothers' children take the same middle name 'Zhao' too.

We could be considered fortunate that our grandparents had given us such wonderful names. Some parents had given their childrens names that would make you recoil in horror. The reason for this is that during our time, doctors were not easily accessible. Even if they were, the sick could not afford to pay for their services. So people depended on make-believe cures and superstition. One belief was that the Evil One would take away children with good-sounding names. As a result, names such as Kow Kia (Puppy), Ter Kia (Piglet), Kow Sai (Dog dung), Gu Sai (Cow dung), Lau Kow (Old Monkey), and Tua Ter (Big Pig) were given to children. It was believed that the more revolting their names were, the higher the chances for the children to survive.

From a young age, we were told to call our parents 'uncle' and 'aunt', just like my cousins called them. The same reason applied that in order to have a peaceful, healthy and harmonious relationship, parents and their children should not express their connection too closely. Later on during our adult lives, we felt very uncomfortable calling them 'pa' and 'ma'.

Grandma

In our attap house, there were two rooms and a hall. A big kitchen was attached to the left of my parent's bedroom. A low sliding door led from my parents' room to the kitchen. My grandma and siblings shared the other room to the right of the hall. When I was about eight years old, my brothers, sisters and grandma shared a huge corrugated iron bed. In that humid tropical climate, mosquitoes were well in abundance. At night, it was not possible to sleep without the mosquito net. Our bed had four high bedposts from which to fix mosquito nets. Every night, before we got into bed, my grandma would religiously put down the mosquito net, light a candle and search for mosquitoes trapped in the net. Whenever she spotted one, she would bring the flame near and torch it. The scorched mosquito would fall on the bed. Sometimes, it was not fatally injured and would be struggling to move away. A quick squeeze with our fingers flattened it on the bed mat leaving a stain.

Sometimes, the flame leapt onto the net. As quick as lightning, she would pinch the flame with her fingers. To us, it seemed she was a very brave lady who was not afraid of fire. If the flame proved too much, she would sweep the flame with her hands in double quick time. The flame was wiped out, leaving behind a burnt hole on the net. After 'torching' the mosquitoes, all of us would lie on the bed to sleep. Grandma would lie down last, as she would sleep at the edge. She prevented us from falling off the bed, which was about a metre high. As the bed was crowded, she would protest that we tossed and turned and sometimes kicked her in the midst of our nightmares.

Grandma had two potties under her bed. In the dark of the night, it was inconvenient to go to the toilet which was in the middle of our pond. We relieved ourselves in the potties. Early the next morning she would clear and wash them in the pond.
Photograph: Yeo Hong Eng's collection

Grandma enrolled me in Bedok Boys' School. Before we slept, sometimes, she asked me about my schoolwork. She asked me to recite what I had learnt in school. Even though she did not understand English, I recited to her nursery rhymes, multiplication tables, schoolchildren's songs and the other things we learned. She took interest in what I learnt at school. That was the wonderful thing about grandma.

As I was the eldest boy in the family, naturally I was the first to do many things with my grandma. My other siblings and cousins had their fair share of experiences with her, but those were of a different nature. The adults believed that girls, once they grew up, would marry and belong to another family. Girls were therefore not sent to school. Furthermore, girls at that time were required to pay school fees but not boys. They claimed they did not have the money to send my sisters to school. My parents later regretted this very much.

On rainy days, when there was not much for her to do, my grandma did not remain idle. She invited her old friend Madam Ong Ka over and played a game of Chinese cards known as *sze sek pai* (Chinese play cards). We children asked her to teach us but she refused. She said that children must not learn to gamble.

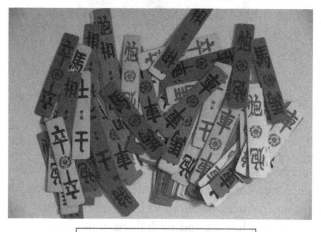

A pack of Chinese play cards

Grandma was a very principled, modest, and thrifty lady. She taught us not to boast of what we had and what we knew. She would tell us to be mindful about conserving things. We must not let things go to waste.

Whenever she saw water gushing out from a public standpipe, she would rush forward to turn it off. When some of the kampong folks were washing their clothes and left the water running, she would chide them for doing so. Usually, the guilty ones would retort, 'It's not your water. Why are you worried?' or 'If I don't waste the water, others will waste it.' Whenever she encountered such people, she would relate it to us and exhort us never to emulate such selfish people.

She would never allow us to spend money unnecessarily. Things that we were not in need of, we shouldn't buy. Things that did not belong to us, we shouldn't take. "Once you have eaten your fill, don't stuff in more. Get away from the table," she always advised after our meals. When it came to spending, she had this to say, "When you need to spend on a necessary thing, even if it costs ten dollars, you need to purchase it. When you need to save, even one cent counts."

On our farm, nothing went to waste. The excreta, urine, and dung were used as fertiliser for the plants. The dried weeds were burnt and the ash was used as a fertiliser too. The discarded vegetables were fed to the pigs and poultry.

One day, she asked my father to prepare a few earthen pots (those used for storing salted vegetables from China). He was to wash and clean them thoroughly. She went to the provision shop in Chai Chee to buy big packets of salt and black beans. Then, she mixed them thoroughly with some water in the earthen pots and closed the lids tightly. They were to be put in a conspicuous place behind our house in the open air. We children were not allowed to go near them. They were placed there for a long time. At times, she would open them up and taste the contents. She gave me a taste of it. It was salty, just like those from the Amoy brand salted black bean can. Not long after that, we had black soy sauce and salted beans to add to our dishes.

We had several jars similar to this one to preserve fruits and vegetables.

When our papaya trees were blown down by storms, we collected the fallen fruit and she salted them too. Sliced preserved papaya became one of our dishes. She did the same with Madam Ong Ka's star fruit.

Sometimes, she added salt to the excess vegetables and dried them in the hot sun. It was used to flavour other dishes.

Once, my grandma and parents bought some glutinous rice, cooked it then mixed it with yeast. After that, they stored the mixture in a jar. They closed the jar tightly for a long time. During the time when they were making it, they told us to keep away and not to say anything as it was taboo. They also kept very silent themselves. About a month after that, they took out the jar and slowly opened it. A very strong smell emanated from it. They said it was fragrance. My grandma dipped her forefinger into the jar and then licked it. She nodded and told my parents, "Successful!" Each of them drank a little of it. I dared not drink. But I took a little of the soft solid at the bottom of the jar. It tasted quite nice, a little sweet and a little sour. After that, they poured the contents of the jar into clean bottles and corked them.

A few days later, Hong Bian complained that his buttock was painful. Upon examining it, true enough, the skin was red with pus and both of the buttocks were affected. My grandma at once said that he must have been drinking the contents of one of the bottles. She took the bottle that was opened, poured out a little of the liquid, and applied it on the affected areas. Slowly, the skin dried up and healed. She said he was allergic to rice wine.

She told us that in whatever we wished to do, we needed to think positive. That was why when the adults were fermenting, baking, salting, cooking and doing other such activities, we needed to keep very quiet and concentrate on our work. Nobody was allowed to say anything inauspicious, or else what they were doing would not be successful. We children did not believe so, but were obligated to agree. Later in adult life, we found that what she said was true.

In those days, almost everything at home was recycled and reused. Discarded metal parts, empty tins and bottles, discarded clothing, and even duck feathers were collected. Someone would come and buy the duck feathers from us, which could be processed into twill cloth. Old clothing was collected and sold to a vendor, who would then supply them to ship repairers for soaking up oil spills. Metal objects were sold to a scrap metal collector, who would arrive in a lorry. He weighed them using a huge *daching*. He paid us according to the weight of the metal we collected.

Sometimes a haberdasher would arrive to sell his wares. He would spread his bolts of cloth, needles, threads, feather dusters, mothballs and other items on a ground sheet for us to pick and choose. The temptation to buy many things from him was great, but it was always controlled by grandma, who 'huah kay shi' ('held the purse strings' in Hokkien).

On certain afternoons, a man named Pek Sian Thoo would come by. He would buy odd farm produce from us such as *galangal* (a species of ginger), turmeric, lemon grass or even *simpoh ayer* leaves (a tropical plant with broad leaves) which could be used for packaging food. When he arrived, we would rush to the hills to collect whatever he wanted. He would then pay us a few cents for our efforts.

My grandma was a very resourceful lady. Once, she rented a place along Changi 8½ Milestone, on the opposite side of the T-junction of Tanah Merah Kechil Road. It was on the fringe of a rambutan estate. On the left of the rambutan estate was a big field of lallang grass. My parents used to call that place 'Pineapple Estate' or *'Ong Lai Hng'* in Hokkien. I did not know why. Most likely, pineapples were planted there before the rambutan trees. I remember once my mum had to pay grandma a visit at that place. It was drizzling. My mum was carrying my brother in her arms, and I was trying to catch up with her to get into the shelter of the umbrella. Then we saw grandma sitting at the doorway of an attap hut. She was weaving little protective sleeves out of lallang leaves. The sleeves were used to cushion wine bottles during transportation, to protect them from damage.

At other times, she and Madam Ong Ka would collect the stiff tough vines of creeping plants. They cut off the twigs and folded the stems with the two ends protruding like a huge writing brush. They used split rattan bark to make regular patterned rattan rings to fasten the handles. The rattan rings were so beautifully done. I always admired their skill in making them. I realised that they were making a brush for washing the large Chinese wok. It was such a waste that I did not learn how they did the weaving.

One afternoon, I saw grandma carrying some pieces of gunny string. Then she sat down on a low stool and rolled up her pants, exposing her right thigh. She placed three pieces of string parallel, each three centimetres apart, on her exposed thigh. Then with her right palm, she pressed down the strings and rolled them forward. Then pulling her palm back quickly, she revealed the three strings now beautifully braided into one. I tried my hand at it. My first attempt was clumsy, but after a few tries, I did it. I really marvelled at how she got the idea to do it. It was braided to make a stronger rope.

Today's women spend a huge sum of money getting professionals to do their facials. In those days, my grandma did that for my mother. Once, I saw my mum sitting on a stool outside the house. My grandma was powdering my mum's face with powder from a colourful square box, two inches by two inches. On the cover of the box was a picture of a beautiful lady. Then she held two lengths of thread taut and with deft fingers, pushed and pulled them over my mum's face. After a few motions, my mum's face looked radiant. My grandma called it *'bun bin mng'* in Hokkein, or 'pulling of facial hair' in literal translation.

I was very impressed with my grandma. Although she had never been to school, by the way she conversed, one would think that she was a highly educated lady. Her knowledge of natural geography, her ability to debate and her moral and social ethics were among the qualities respected by those around her.

Whenever there was any serious conversation between grandma and an adult, we children were always asked not to go near them in case we picked up any wrong information. Furthermore, she considered it rude to eavesdrop. Up till today, I still believe she was right. What do children know? Sometimes adults need to settle a difficult situation amicably, but should a child come in between and spill the beans about certain facts, complications might arise.

Whenever there were visitors, we were told to address and greet them in the proper order of seniority. When drinks or food were served to them, we were taught the proper ways of doing that, by using both hands to serve and receive. When talking to elders, we had to observe the proper etiquette like keeping still and speaking in clear, correct language.

When it came to eating at the table, we were taught the correct way of handling the spoon, chopsticks and bowl. We were taught never to point the chopsticks at anybody or even poke them standing up in a bowl of rice. We must let them rest on the bowl with the tapered end pointing forward. When using a pair of chopsticks, one must not hold it too near the tapered ends nor too far away. We must never use chopsticks for other purpose. After being washed, they must be put in the chopsticks holder with the tapered ends upright.

While eating, proper protocol had to be observed. We were not to talk but concentrate on what we were eating. We had to hold the utensils with care, never letting them knock against each other. We were taught never to take the last piece of food on the dish. We should always leave it for someone who needs it more. After having eaten our fair share, we had to leave the table quietly, carrying the eating utensils with us to be deposited in the appropriate container.

To me, my grandma was always my wise granny. Seeing the healthy children of the 1960s, she had nothing but praise for the health care services of the day. Clinics and government dispensaries were built and their fees were affordable. Such facilities were almost non-existent in the 1950s. Infant mortality rates went down.

It was 1970. Her saddest moment was when she found out my uncle had died. She cried for days and nights, exhorting Buddha to take her away before my only uncle. She went without food or drink. Our whole family kept the sadness in our hearts and did not know what to do. Everyone did his or her share of the farm work in silence, as the farm could not be neglected. By and by, she returned to her normal self, but her body was rather frail. Then she became bedridden for a while, after she fractured one of her legs.

She lived to a ripe old age of 90. She breathed her last on 25 June 1972. While on her deathbed, my sisters and I were with her. She groaned a few times that she was dying. Her breathing became slower and slower, and finally she kept very still. Dr Lee Kim Hwee from Kampong Chai Chee was summoned. He told me that grandma had gone. He put the stethoscope on my ears to hear her heartbeat. There was silence. Although grandma was gone, her spirit still lives in our hearts. Every year, we have an observance ceremony at the Heong Lian See Temple in Koon Seng Road, where her tablet is, and we have a remembrance ceremony on *Cheng Beng* every year at Bright Hill Crematorium.

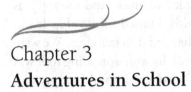

Chapter 3
Adventures in School

My First Day at Bedok Boys' School

It was the year 1953. I was seven years old. Early one cold, rainy morning, my mum woke me up. She had prepared a cup of coffee and a bowl of rice with an egg in the middle. Dark soy sauce was added to taste. She helped me to put on the school uniform, a white shirt and grey pants. She also put on the white shoes for me. I held on to a gigantic oiled paper umbrella. To me, as a small boy, the regular old oiled umbrella seemed very big. Grandma had hers. Grandma and I walked on the wet muddy track to school.

I had no knowledge of what school was like, let alone the huge single-storeyed building. I had never entered such a building before. It was a cavernous white-walled building with wide corridors. I had never seen so many boys, men and women before. A few well-dressed men were calling something out. I could not understand a single word. My grandma led me by the hand and handed me to a tall, fierce man. He pulled me to a spacious room with many pictures on the wall. There were many other boys in the same uniform, all sitting very quietly, looking dazed and shocked. My eyes followed my grandma to the corridor. Whenever she caught me looking out for her, she would wave at me to look away. At times, I could not find her; I began to quiver and tears rolled down my cheeks. To make matters worse, the room was very cold, as it was raining outside. Only the tungsten light bulbs interested me, as I had never seen those before. At home, we used only kerosene or carbide lamps.

Then a loud sound was heard. '*Clang*! *Clang*!' Each of us was given a piece of cake. The smell of it was so strong I wanted to vomit. It was soft, coloured with pink and green, and the top was brown. Some of the boys ate ravenously. I tasted a little of it. It was sweet, but I did not like the smell. I handed it to grandma. We were led to a flight of steps and then to a hall. Its wide-spreading roof was supported by a few thick columns. We queued up. An empty cup was handed to us. Someone was stationed at a shiny tank. He told us to put the cup under the spout before he lifted the lever of the spout. A brown liquid flowed out. The liquid tasted nice. "It is Ovaltine," my grandma said. I had never tasted Ovaltine before. At home, we drank black coffee most of the time. We had it at breakfast, elevenses, lunch, teatime, after dinner, and even for supper.

At the canteen, the children, after getting their drinks from the dispenser, which was placed at the side of a long table, moved to the centre of the hall to find a place to sit and drink. Usually, we stood and drank. Those who had a little cash would buy packets of snacks such as *keropok*, dried cuttlefish, Chinese pancakes, peanuts and *kachang puteh* at five cents each from a small tuckshop (known today as a canteen). My parents seldom gave me extra pocket money to buy snacks. Should I be given five cents, I would buy a crispy Chinese pancake in the hope of getting a five-cent or ten-cent coin encased in it.

Every month, we paid two dollars known as the 'Feeding Fee' to the teacher. Each of us was given a piece of paper with some words printed in green. I did not know how to read those words. Upon reaching home, I immediately gave the paper to my dad. He said that it was the receipt for the payment of the 'Feeding Fee'. That amount entitled us a snack and a drink every school day. The snack and drink combinations were different every day. The different types of snacks were the Indian curry puff, butter cake or even biscuits. The drinks were coffee or tea with milk, Ovaltine, Milo or sometimes soya bean milk.

That first day in school was traumatic for me. I did not know anyone. All the boys looked similar as we were in uniform. The adults sat along the corridor chitchatting. My eyes kept watching for my grandma. Soon, the sound came again. '*Clang*! *Clang*! *Clang*!'

The teacher made us line up in pairs. Then we walked out of the classroom. Grandma pushed through the crowd and reached me. She pulled me aside. All the other parents too did the same, and we walked hand in hand along the bitumen road. It was crowded. Cars, vans, and bicycles would inch past us with the occasional light tooting of their horns if we were too slow to move out of their way.

My grandma pointed out one particular boy to me from the 'A' class. He was Lim Ban Lee, whom I later realised was the son of my father's relative. We had to walk past Bedok Girls' School. More people, bicycles, and cars joined us. Parents were chaperoning the girls. As soon as we walked out of the gate, we had to turn left and walk up a muddy track along the perimeter of the barbed wire fencing. In the 1970s, the track was named Jalan Langgar Bedok.

When we reached home, my mum was waiting for us to have lunch. First, I took off my shoes. She changed me out of the uniform into house clothes then we had lunch.

Without fail, my grandma accompanied me to school every day for a long time, until I was more familiar with the route. Fewer parents also came to wait for their children. One day, a friendly boy came to me and said, "Hong Eng, *ah ma kio*." It means: 'My grandma has called.' That was heard by many others. The others who were not so friendly would echo what he said every time they saw me. I was very annoyed by this. The next day, I decided not to let grandma take me to school. I knew the route. Furthermore, there were other children going to the same school.

Bedok Boys' School 1953-1958

Bedok Boys' School as well as Bedok Girls' School was situated midway along Bedok Road. It was built in the 1950s. The architecture was similar to all Singapore schools built in that era— low single-storey buildings with asbestos roofing and soft board ceilings. Each classroom had four tungsten lamps with translucent lamp shades hanging from the high ceiling. A green chalkboard was fixed at the front of each classroom. Soft boards were on the walls. The teachers pinned their charts on these boards. One thing worth mentioning was that the walls of every classroom had colourful drawings on them. These drawings related to the topics of the school syllabus. I remember in Primary 1, the walls of the classroom had chalk drawings depicting nursery rhymes, such as 'The Cow Jumps over the Moon', 'Baa, Baa, Black Sheep' and 'Little Miss Muffet'. In Primary 5, our history syllabus covered famous personalities like Confucius, Christopher Columbus, and Francis Drake. These personages were illustrated on our classroom walls too. In the geography room there were drawings of the processes of tin mining, rubber growing and fishing, among others. I believed they were drawn with coloured chalk. I do not know whether the drawing was done by one artist or by all the teachers involved. To me, they were all beautifully and tastefully done.

The school comprised several single-storey blocks. However, the number of blocks depended on the demand of the residents of that particular area. Bedok Boys' had two long blocks of classrooms lying parallel to each other. They were separated by a small field. A toilet block lay on the left flank of the second block. The tuck shop was on the right flank. To get to the canteen, we had to climb up a flight of steps. The canteen was shared with the girls' school. Both the boys' and girls' schools were built in the middle of a ridge. To get to the field which ran parallel to Bedok Road, we needed to descend a flight of steps. Behind the second block were bushes of lalang and Singapore rhodenderons. A barbed wire fence ran around the perimeter of both schools. The schools' rubbish dump was outside the right main gate. That was to facilitate easy access for the rubbish truck. On the left flank of the first block was the underground septic tank, where the waste from the toilet was contained and treated. In front of the first block were the basketball court and the unpaved car park. Those facilities were there when I was registered in 1953. Later, servants' quarters were built behind the toilet block.

I can remember vividly that we conducted our natural science experiments behind the second block. We cleared the bushes and planted maize, long beans, bitter gourd, and other vegetables. During recess, we ran all over the bushes behind the school to play hide and seek. Mr Muthu was the school's attendant. When recess time was over, he rang a huge bell which was tied to a beam in front of the office. All of us would race down the hill to line up in pairs in front of our classes. The teachers would arrive, see that we were ready, and then called out "Atten . . . tion! Stand at ease!" several times. When he or she was satisfied we were in order, he or she would let us into the classroom row by row.

Every morning, after Mr Muthu had rung the bell, he would carry all the class registers in his left arm and use the right hand to hand them to the teachers. The teacher marked our attendance by calling our names out loud. When I was in Primary One, I remember that many of us did not respond to the teacher's call. The teacher needed to go to us to read our nametags and tell us our names. Many of us went by our nicknames at home. Some of us attended Chinese schools before coming to Bedok Boys'. So some were familiar with their Mandarin names but not their dialect ones. After the registers had been marked, Mr Muthu would collect them again.

Samples of stamps for pasting on our Schools' Savings Scheme card

Almost all of us chose to participate in the Schools' Savings Scheme. Every school day, as soon as we entered the classroom, after marking the class register, our form teacher collected ten cents from us to buy a ten-cent postage stamp. It was a rectangular-shaped stamp with a portrait of King George VI on it. We licked the back of the stamp, which had dried glue on it, then stuck it on to one of the squares of our savings card. When we had covered the whole card with ten-cent stamps, our teacher collected all of them and posted them to the General Post Office in Kuala Lumpur. Then we would get a Post Office Savings passbook with our names and the amount we had saved recorded on it. Later on, after Queen Elizabeth II's coronation in 1953, our stamps were replaced with a bigger one—a purple stamp with a sailboat and the portrait of Queen Elizabeth II at the top left hand corner. The job became easier for our teacher-in-charge of the Schools Savings Scheme when the mobile post office van came to our school to sell stamps as well as to open and update our accounts.

Our uniform consisted of grey shorts, white shirt, and white shoes. Each of us wore a huge metal badge, which was shaped like a drum. Our motto was *'Tarik megikut gendang!'* which means simply 'Dance to the drumbeat!' During physical training (PT) periods, all of us had to strip off our shirts and remove our shoes. Several boys were appointed to carry whatever PT apparatus was required. When we walked out of the building, we could feel the chill when the morning breeze blew. Then, we proceeded down the slope to the field to do our exercises. The field was jointly used by the girls. During curriculum time, we could use only half of the field. After the PT periods were over, we walked to the lavatory and washed ourselves up before going to our class to put on our shirts and shoes.

Then, there was the fund-raising campaign to build an aviary, an aquarium, and recreational facilities. A letter of appeal was sent to the parents to donate to the fund. My father donated a few dollars. Funds were also collected from the weekend screening of films. Twenty cents was collected from each patron on a Saturday. Two shows were screened. Ten cents was collected on a Sunday as there was only one show. A stage for the cinema projector was constructed in the middle of the little field between the two blocks of building. A huge screen was put up above the left passageway linking the two classroom blocks. The principal (a European) personally brought the films and worked the projector to screen the shows. The shows were mainly about cowboys and Red Indians. One show that struck me deeply was *Black Arrow*. It was about a Red Indian who fought for his tribe against a band of American marauders. There were also Hindustani shows. I saw a Chinese show once. The response was quite poor; not many people went to see the shows.

I got acquainted with a parent by the name of Mr Yang. He seemed to be quite well off. He was always well dressed, with a pressed shirt and matching long pants and leather shoes. He drove a Morris Minor. He was very friendly to the tuck shop vendors from the girls' school. Mr Yang was also seen supplying food to the canteen. I would always help to distribute drinks and collect empty cups from the canteen tables during recess. During the lull period when the pupils were fewer, I helped to wash the cups. Mr Yang saw that, and he always smiled and thanked me. Sometimes when he saw me queuing up to buy a ticket for a Sunday show, he would get me a complimentary one. I was most pleased as I could save ten cents. One day, while on the way to Chai Chee Market with my mother, I saw him driving his signature Morris Minor into a huge concrete house at 6 Milestone Changi Road. I did not know his role in school. I suspected that he must be a member of the PTA (Parents-Teachers Association).

A few months after the appeal for funds was made, an aviary was built near the right passageway of the school. In it were sparrows, mynas, and *burong pipit*. There was a very special swing door. I had never seen such a thing before. When one opened it, the inside panel was closed, preventing birds inside the aviary from escaping. When the inside panel was opened, the outside panel was closed. I could not help but admire such innovation.

This is the site where the aviary and aquarium were when I was a student there. The staircase on the top left led to the canteen.
Photo: Bedok Boys' School Facebook page, courtesy of Dian Suhaimi
'Our last child at the eco garden'. 22 October 2011

Every morning, the school servants fed the birds and cleaned the aviary floor. Outside the aviary was a very long aquarium. One side of it was covered with planks. It was to shade the fish from direct sunlight. Very often, my teacher, Mr Tan Tiong Ghee, asked me to bring water hyacinth from my father's pond for the aquarium. I was very proud to do it. I dutifully got a thick paper bag. (In those days plastic paper bags were not widely used.) I chose the smallest and cutest of the plants. I chose the smallest because the aquarium was quite small as compared to my pond. In the aquarium, goldfish, guppies and mollies were reared. Later on, a bigger aquarium was constructed. It was on the right, just after we climbed the flight of steps to the canteen. I believed the second aquarium was too shallow. We saw very few fish there. Then, a group of senior boys built a model of a *kelong* using bamboo stakes. The whole structure was put in the middle of the aquarium. That *kelong* became a source of attraction for us during recess. I knew that a *kelong* was a fish trap, but I did not know how fish were caught using the *kelong* until very much later in life.

Just before we went down a flight of steps to the school field, many recreational facilities were added. There was a set of four swings. During recess, some of the pupils would race to the swings before everyone else. They could do different types of stunts on the swings, like jumping off a moving swing, standing on the seat to push the swing, or pushing the swing to the highest extreme. That set of swings proved to be the most popular of all the play equipment, but most accidents happened there too. Many children did not realise when a swing was in motion. So they walked into the swing's path and got hit by the sitting board. Others got injured when getting off the swing. To prevent further accidents, the servants immobilised the swings by tying the swinging boards around the supports.

Bedok Boys' and Girls' School Field.
To get to the field we had to descend a flight of steps.
In those days this field had an imaginary line drawn separating the boys'
half of the field and the girls'.
Photo: Bedok Primary School's Facebook page, courtesy of Nur Sakina
Lam. Sports Day 1996.

There were also two sets of monkey bars. One was low and the other was high. Very small pupils, whose arms were not strong enough to hold their bodies, usually fell from the bars and got themselves injured. Some fractured their arms. The monkey bars were good for us to strengthen our arms when used correctly but sad to say, the two sets were often misused as usually, our play was not supervised.

There were also two seesaws. We had a hilarious time playing on the see-saws. Sometimes, we stood on the board and sometimes we sat on it. When no one was around, I loved to stand in the middle and use my legs to tilt the long board one way then the other.

Two long slides were constructed parallel to the flight of steps which led to the football field. The children loved those too. From the top of the slope, they sat on the metal slide and slid down.

"Ah Tong! Don't you know that you have just made two huge eyes on your buttocks?"

"Ha! Ha! Ha!" All the other boys looked at him and roared.

Those who did it successively many times had two holes worn on the back of their pants due to the friction. To prevent pants from wearing out, we squatted on the metal base and tried to slide down. But it didn't work at all. Our shoes refused to move. So someone had a grand idea. He scooped up a handful of sand, walked to the head of the slide, threw the sand on the base, and immediately squatted on it. The sand acted as mini wheels. He came down so fast he screamed with joy. Then everybody imitated him. It was really fun to see everyone screaming their heads off.

One morning when we reached school, we heard loud music. We were totally surprised. Then we traced the source of the sound. It was coming from a huge speaker mounted on the swing. The familiar sounds of the brass bell were gone. We were told to listen to the siren playing on the Public Address (PA) System at recess, before school, and at school dismissal time. During news broadcasts, all speakers in the school were switched on, including those facing the field. Many activities took place using the PA system. Stories accompanied by music were played. Announcements by the principals and teachers were made. Even music lessons were conducted through it.

The news was on every morning at 8 a.m. The teacher would stop whatever he or she was doing, and we were to listen attentively. "Toot! Toot! Toot! This is Radio Malaya broadcasting from Kuala Lumpur . . ." A helpful teacher would immediately scribble the headlines on the board. After the news, he would go through the headlines again. We really learned a lot, especially knowledge of current affairs. We would repeat such names and places like Robert Black, David Marshall, Queen Elizabeth, Mao Tse Tung, and Chiang Kai Shek and Quemoy.

Whenever there were any problems with the sound system, Mr Thumboo, together with a few senior boys, would run around testing the speakers, switches, and even climbed up ladders to the ceilings to find out where the fault lay. Everybody had nothing but praise for Mr Thumboo. For us, whoever was able to handle electrical equipment must be very intelligent. At home, few of us had electrical lines connected, as the main supply had not reached us. There was talk among us boys that Mr Thumboo was able to pinpoint electrical faults just by smelling the cables and equipment. Mr Thumboo could have been right, as we learnt later a little about electricity—that electrical faults could happen when there was a short circuit and the fuse would blow. That emitted a burning smell, which enabled the fault to be detected and rectified.

Mr Tan Tiong Ghee—My First and Final Year Teacher

During those years from 1953 to 1958 (when I was in Primary 1 to Primary 6), Mr Tan Tiong Ghee was involved in so many activities. As a senior assistant of the school, he had to run the school according to the demands of the principal, teachers, non-teaching staff, parents, pupils, as well as the public at large. He was ever so busy. When he walked, he walked fast, always with his head bent with thoughts. If naughty pupils were sent to him, justice was administered fast, with a few grunts from him. The offenders would walk away feeling Mr Tan was one not to be fooled with.

Our textbooks were mostly from England, no matter whether they were for Mathematics or English subjects. The publishers were either the Ginn Brothers or Dean and Sons. I remember that our first reading book was *Old Lob Tom*, about a farmer. For the upper primary levels the textbooks were the *Beacon Study Reader*, *Malayan Geographies*, *The March of Time* (a history text), *Malayan Arithmetics* and *Brighter Grammar*.

Every year, we paid $1 for the loan of all our books. Inside each book cover was stamped: 'This book belongs to Bedok Boys' School and is on loan to . . .'

I remember when I was in Primary 1, on the walls of our classroom, there were beautiful drawings in coloured chalk of characters in the poems we recited. There were pictures of a cow jumping over a full moon or a cat with a fiddle or Old Lob and his farm animals. Every morning, we were to recite nursery rhymes after our teacher: 'Three Little Blackbirds Sitting on the Wall', 'Baa, Baa, Black Sheep', 'Little Bo Peep', 'London Bridge is Falling Down' and many more. I did not understand what it was all about. I just recited them like the rest. The same thing happened with music. I enjoyed the music lessons, but unfortunately, they were only once a week. Prior to those music lessons, I had never heard anyone play the piano. The music from the piano the teacher played was really wonderful. I picked up the tunes very fast, but I did not know the meanings of the lyrics. The mathematics units that we first studied were pounds, shillings and pence, gallons and quarts, miles, furlongs, yards, feet, hands and inches. Later, locals units such as *gantangs* and *chupak*, *pikuls*, *kati* and *taels*, dollars and cents were learnt. As we were not exposed to English units in everyday life, learning to calculate in such units was a chore. All we did was just calculate blindly. As for the learning of multiplication tables, the teachers were very strict about that. In Primary 4, we had to learn not only the multiples of one till 12, we had to know the multiples of 16 too, as it would come handy when we convert *taels* into *katis*—16 *taels* equal one *kati*. Should we not answer the teacher's questions on multiplication tables fast enough, a stroke by the teacher's wooden ruler would come down either on our hand or fingers. Then we had to control our agony in silence.

In Primary 6, the books on loan to us did not include the grammar book *First Aid in English*. We knew of Chua Boon Seng's relative, one Mr Soh Heng Chye, who knew the English language and who worked for the British army. On the evening of his wedding, while my father and I were attending the dinner at his house, I handed the book list to him so he could get a copy for me, as we did not know where to get one.

Another item we had to get was 'The Oxford Mathematical Instruments'. It was not on sale at any shop in Bedok. We were told that it was on sale at one of the shops at Katong. One afternoon, my father and I went to Katong by bus. We stopped at a bus stop in front of the Katong Catholic Church and scouted around the area. In the showcase at one of the Indian shops, we spotted a box with a sleeve printed with 'The Oxford Set Of Mathematical Instruments' and a picture of Oxford University. I was so excited. At home, I took out the mathematical formula, the blue blotter, dividers, compasses, set squares, eraser, a short wooden ruler, and a small yellow pencil.

Then I lined the bottom with cotton wool, as I was afraid there might be scratches. I then closed its lid, which was printed in the same design as the sleeve. It was one of my most precious possessions at that time.

The Oxford Mathematical Instruments, one of my most precious possessions at that time.

I remember when I was in Primary 1, many of my classmates were very much older than I and therefore wiser and more robust. They excelled in whatever the teacher taught them. Two of the classmates who stood out in class Primary 1B were the twins, Teo Ah Tua and Teo Ah Say. The younger one had an earring on his right ear so others could tell the difference between the two. A tall boy, Tan Ah Tu, was always called up to run errands for the teacher. I suspected that he must be very much older than us and therefore more mature. Another classmate was Ang Chuan Nam, who was good at assembling and taking apart fountain pens. There were so many fountain pens in his pencil case. Some of my classmates would bring their fountain pens from home and hand them over to him to take apart. I heard that whenever he discovered a pen was of value, that pen would disappear mysteriously. Of course, our classmates would insinuate that he stole it. He was also a notorious fighter. I had seen him bashing up classmates who were bigger than him.

Then, there were other children who were more sociable and articulate. I was told they had attended Chinese schools before they joined us. Some of them had to hurry to the Chinese schools after our classes were over. They went to either Sin Min Public School or Yeu Nerng School.

One morning, all of us were told to pay 30 cents. It was to purchase a commemorative exercise book for the coronation of

Queen Elizabeth II on 1 June 1953. It was a special book with a white cover and a picture of Queen Elizabeth II.

On the evening of 1 June 1953, it was the coronation of Queen Elizabeth II. The kampong folks lined up along Bedok Road to watch floats lit up by tungsten bulbs, which were fitted very close together. The blinking lights around the huge crown on a float made us think the lights were moving. The applause, the rousing welcome, and the sound of generators added to the highly memorable atmosphere.

One fine morning, the sun was shining brightly. We were asked to go the left side of the building. Benches were arranged in straight rows. Our teacher sized us up and told some of us to stand on the benches. Some were to stand on the grass and some had to sit on the benches. Being quite tall, I stood on the bench in the middle. Then, the teacher in front of the class shouted, "Say cheese and hold your breath!" Then he pressed a button on a black box a few times. Then we were off to our classroom again. I was puzzled about what had just happened. I later learnt that we had had our photographs taken. It was the first time I had a photograph taken. Later, I would have another photograph taken by Ah Hee, Madam Ong Ka's son.

My First School Photograph
Pri 1 B, Bedok Boys' School, 1953.
The author is in the last row, standing 6th from either left or right.

In 1954, I was in Standard I. For reasons I did not understand, after Primary One, we went to Standard One the following year. Then on our third year of school, we went to Primary Three. On the first day, I went to my previous year's classroom, but my classmates were not there. Instead, the room was filled with younger children and their parents. I hurried along the corridor with great apprehension, and suddenly my classmates called me from another classroom. I was surprised. I went in. The teacher was not the same. The room and everything looked and smelt different. It was strange. It was a pretty young lady teacher who taught us. She was very kind, loving, and gentle, with short, well-combed hair. She had a roundish face and small lips. During that year, she never shouted at us or caned us. She left a very good and permanent impression on me.

In 1955, I was in Primary 3. Our form teacher was Mr Raja. Our music teacher was a European lady. She conducted her music lessons through the PA system. We were to follow exactly the instructions given by the announcer. One day, a teacher who was unfamiliar to us came into the room. We stood up. We did not know how to address her.

Miss Isaac said, "When I say 'Good morning, boys,' you must say, 'Good morning, Miss Issac'."

"Good morning, boys."

"Good morning, Miss Issac," the class replied.

We repeated this several times until she was satisfied that the tone and stress sounds were exactly like hers. She said that she was our English teacher. She started off by teaching us grammar using the textbook *Brighter Grammar*. The first grammar lesson was adjectives—demonstrative adjectives.

One day, Mr Raja told us, "We're going to the Johore zoo by train." I had neither any idea what a train was nor a zoo.

"Yeah! I've sat in one before. It is exciting. The train goes *poo poo poo* and my body goes *shake shake shake*. It is a very big and long 'fire car'. It also gives out a lot of smoke through the chimney," said Ah Long, whose father had taken him for a train ride once.

The day came. Everybody was in an uproarious mood. A bus took us to the Tanjong Pagar Railway Station. We were led to a train. The train ride was exciting. As it went, it made rhythmic sounds and we imitated them. It rocked us a little. In the midst of the excitement I felt an urgency to go to the toilet. I asked Mr Raja for permission. He showed me where the toilet was. I entered and closed the door. I was shocked. It was a hole and the urine went splashing directly onto the track. I could not steady myself as the train went. I wet myself. I wanted to wash the urine on my legs but the water from the little tap was so slow. What an experience!

After what seemed like hours, the train finally stopped. We walked for some time. Then we heard a loud screeching, as well as low roaring sounds. That told us that we had reached the zoo. Each of us was asked to pay 30 cents for the entrance fee. To my horror, I realised I had forgotten to ask my mum for it. My thought crumpled and I was nearly in tears. I had only 20 cents, which my mum had given me for buying tidbits. Mr Raja was very kind. He paid on my behalf. Someone from my class whispered that I needed to reimburse my teacher when we returned. I remembered that.

Note:
   The Johore Zoo was opened by Sultan Sir Ahmad Ibrahim in 1928.

In the zoo, we were left to wander by ourselves. The steel cages of the animals were very close together. They looked so pathetic. Most of them cringed in a corner and were half asleep. There were tigers, deer, chimpanzees, monkeys, and a few others I could not remember. The most active were the monkeys. They seemed to be gibbering and swinging from bar to bar in the cages nonstop. I remember that one of the chimpanzees stuck out its right fore limb as if asking us for food. We then made our way to an open space to watch some deer and wild pigs. The deer seemed to be on the alert all the time, watching us with their ears pricked, but the pigs were constantly digging with their snouts, swinging their tails, and munching. They looked smaller than our pigs and each had two short tusks protruding from its mouth. Our domesticated pigs in their pens were very clean, had round bellies, and were very much fatter.

After much wandering, I felt tired and thirsty. Many others also felt the same and were yearning for drinks. Those days nobody carried a water bottle. There was a drink stall. The pupils rushed forward and bought bottles of F&N drinks. They asked for their favourite flavours. I bought a bottle of orange squash which cost 20 cents. I thought that it was very expensive.

A bottle of Red Lion F&N
orange crush

Soon, it was time to go home. The teachers from the various classes did a head count of their charges, and we soon made our way to the railway station. The sights, sounds and smells of that place left a permanent impression on me. The next day, I returned the 30 cents to my teacher. I was grateful to him for helping me pay the entrance fee.

For a few years in succession, at the end of our examinations in November, our teachers made us line up in pairs and walk out of the school compound for excursions in the surrounding neighbourhoods. With several classes walking two abreast, it was an impressive sight to behold. We snaked our way through the kampongs, with dogs barking and half-naked little children running out of their houses. We talked in excitement as we proceeded.

"Teacher, my brother and sister are there," Ah Beng pointed excitedly at the two semi-naked children staring outside their house.

"Hello! Hello!" We waved and shouted. The two smiled showing their toothless gums.

The dogs initially barked ferociously, but after a while, seeing the sheer number of us, they went into hiding.

We walked along Bedok Road towards Simpang Bedok, along Changi Road, past Hiap Seng Leong Building Material Supplies, Yeu Nerng Public School, and crossed a bridge across Sungei Bedok, then went on to Jalan Tiga Ratus. We walked past the *beehoon* factory, chicken farms, rubber and coconut estates. We were feeling hot, but the excitement seemed to override the discomfort. As was the norm then, we did not bring any containers of water along.

At other times, we crossed Bedok Road and went into an unnamed sandy path opposite our school. We walked past the rubber estate and then came to a swamp. Nipa palms were seen crowding the banks. Then we crossed a wooden bridge which spanned the Bedok River. On both sides, the banks were overgrown with ferns and nipa palms. At that time, the Bedok River was very narrow, and at high tide, it flooded its banks.

We came to a huge sandpit. It was Koh Sek Lim's. The sand mounds were piled up so high that they reached almost halfway up the coconut trees. We saw a recent mound where the sand had been removed. The mark on the coconut trunk where the mound's peak had been had roots growing out of it. That reminded me of how Mr Bong, the caretaker of Teow Swee's rambutan estate, marcotted his rambutan trees, with roots growing out of where wet cow dung was packed and tied around the branch of a tree.

From there, we walked seawards along the sandy path. The scenery was different from places such as Jalan Tiga Ratus and Somapah Road. There were attap houses with fishing nets in front of them. There were long poles with floats attached to their ends. There were strange baskets hanging on clotheslines. These bamboo baskets had narrow necks. Each had a lid with thin strips of bamboo sticking inwards. We had no chance to ask our teacher what those containers were for. Soon, we reached the seaside at Mata Ikan, with the cool refreshing breeze blowing past our faces.

Some of us took off our shoes and waded in the sea. Others built sandcastles with their bare hands. After half an hour, it was time to go back to school. We walked past a small market selling more fish than any other items. The dark, elderly, wrinkle-faced vendors had their wares on the wet sandy ground. They folded their sashes and put them over their heads, lifting and adjusting their sarongs before squatting behind their wares to wait for customers.

After wading through the morning crowds, we proceeded past Bedok Rest House, walked along Bedok Road, past Swee Aun Provision Shop (uncle Yam's), and finally arrived back at school. It was a welcome relief to be in the cool classroom. At that time, fans were not installed yet.

Then came the day 5.5.55 (5 May 1955). I was thrilled. I was wondering where I would be and what I would be doing when 6.6.66 or 7.7.77 came. I believed the other children would be thinking the same. When 12.12.12 came, I would be touring Zhengzhou, China.

Every now and then, we were asked to copy ten spelling words from the chalkboard to learn. Sometimes, the teacher would read the words for us, but most often, did not. To me, they were totally strange words. I do not remember whether I knew any of the words. Most often, I got zero for spelling. After receiving the marked paper, I would crush it and throw it out of the open window. In those days, the teachers did not bother to remind us to file our work, or do corrections for answers that were incorrect.

One day, the father-in-law of one of my father's cousins came to visit his daughter. My mum was excited.

"Cheng Kei Kong knows English. Quick! Ask him to teach you your spelling," she urged.

With the list in my hand I approached him respectfully with a bow. He was sitting in the hall. He gave me a toothless grin, and word by word, he taught me how to read. I repeated the words several times until I got them all right. With a wide smile, I bowed and thanked him for his help. The next day, I was anxious for the spelling period to come. The teacher told us to take out pieces of paper to get ready for spelling. We tore out the pages from our blank exercise books, drew the margins, wrote our names, and got ready. The teacher read slowly, word by word. I was excited. I knew how to spell almost all the words. After marking, I found out that I got eight out of ten. I was thrilled beyond description. I scored better than most of my classmates. Some of them insinuated that I cheated. I spelt the words orally to them to prove that I had not. Then they were convinced. That day, I did not crush the paper out of the window. I kept the results carefully in my bag.

As for examinations, I never felt stressed. We were not told what to expect or to revise any work. On examination days, we all sat at our desks. Then a teacher from a neighbouring class appeared. Next, Mr Muthu, the school's office attendant, would go to every class to distribute examination scripts and blank paper. I was thrilled at the cyclostyled, typewritten paper, as it was the first time I had seen it. All along during lessons, notes and questions were written on the green board with a piece of white chalk that came from a box that had 'Made in England' printed on it. When one cleaned the board, the dust would fly about, especially on the front two rows. One thing that was entirely different from the other days was that we could get out of the room when we had finished our examination papers. The atmosphere was so different outside, as there were very few pupils who handed up answer scripts earlier than the others. We would wait and guess who would be the next to come out. Then the bell rang for recess. Those who were slow to finish had to hand in their unfinished papers.

One morning in 1956, when I was in Primary 4, I found out that many of my classmates had gone to another class. They were copying a mathematics problem and its answer from the board as that teacher was the Primary 4 Mathematics examination setter. I was told such a problem would appear in the mid-year examinations. I tried to copy it too, but it was too late. I had to go to our vernacular language class. During the examinations, that problem really appeared. Well! Such things happened in those days.

One incident that stayed vividly in my mind was when my kampong friend Chua Boon Seng was hit in the eye by a wooden chalkboard duster. The teacher could have been aiming at a mischievous boy sitting in front of Boon Seng but missed. Instead, my friend got hit. Blood immediately oozed from his eye. He was immediately sent to the hospital in an ambulance. The doctor said that he was lucky. The eye socket protected the eyeball from being injured. The mischievous boy was given two full lashes of the cane on the buttocks by the enraged teacher, Mr Quintal. Two other classmates whom I remember were Rajagopal and Abdul Rahman. Both were pleasant and I liked their company. During the marking of the daily attendance register, Abdul Rahman's name was the first to be called as his name started with an 'A', whereas mine started with a 'Y' so I was almost the last to be called. I was very anxious as I did not like my name to be called last. No wonder psychologists who had done research on heart attack patients said that people whose names started with letters in the second half of the alphabet most likely suffered from heart attack earlier than those whose names started with letters from the first half of the alphabet.

In Primary 5 in 1957, our form teacher was Mr Anammalay. It was a hectic year for us. Algebra was introduced. So we had three separate papers, namely Arithmetic, Geometry, and Algebra as our Mathematics components. Literature books were also introduced. We had two books—*Moonfleet* and *Thirty-nine Steps*. We enjoyed reading those books together in class. Each of us took turns to read. Each of us had different styles of reading—some fast and some slow. The children's reading enlivened the class. Our teacher went through each turn of events in the stories. After each chapter, there were questionnaires based on it. The teacher would solicit answers from us. It made our understanding of the story better.

History and Geography textbooks were not on loan to us. We copied chunks and chunks of notes from the green chalkboard. For History, we learnt about the famous teachers of mankind. We learnt of Gautama Buddha, Confucius, Jesus, and Muhammad. We also learnt of famous Western explorers like Vasco da Gama, Christopher Columbus, Ferdinand Magellan and Francis Drake. For Geography, we learnt about Malayan produce—rubber and coconut crops, as well as minerals such as tin and their processes. Vernacular languages such as Chinese, Malay, and Tamil were taught for one or two periods a day. The Malays would go to the Malay classes, and the Indians had to go to the girls' school to study Tamil with the Indian girls. The Chinese pupils had to stay put in their room. However, such arrangements were not always the norm.

At that time, some of us who reached school well before school hours would echo what our parents read from the newspapers and heard from the news on the radio.

"Now the Hang Seng is very bad," someone would say.

"China will become rich soon," echoed another.

"Ma Sheow Li (David Marshall) resigns as chief minister," said another.

Although we did not understand what all these things were about, subconsciously, we knew that these happenings would affect our lives.

The barbed wire fencing of the schools stretched from Bedok Road up to the ridge at the periphery of the Malay kampong. The schools occupied only about half of the area. Small plots for science experiments were set aside. The rest were all lalang and rhododenderon bushes. Very often, children would steal inside the fencing by forcing open the lengths of barbed wires nearest the ground. It was easily done by stepping on the bottom length of wire and lifting the one above. The gap would be wide enough for one to pass through. This was at a remote spot where schoolchildren settled their scores after school. Very often, fights did not last long and nobody was seriously injured. Should there be a fight, it usually attracted a big crowd. Often, there would be somebody in the crowd to stop the fight.

112

The Singapore rhodenderon

In 1958, there was a reshuffling of pupils. Many of the pupils were from 5A and 5C. I was in Primary 6B. Our form teacher was Mr Tan Tiong Ghee, who had been my teacher in Primary 1 in 1953. We were surprised that we had so many textbooks on loan to us. Among them were *General Mathematics for Malayan School Volume 1*, *Beacon Study Reader*, *Malayan Geography* and an atlas, *The March of Time* (history text), *Nature Study* and the *Brighter Grammar Book 4*.

That year was the first year that multiple choice questions were introduced in the Secondary Schools Entrance Examinations. Our teacher wrote on the board some sample multiple choice questions for us to copy. We dutifully and painstakingly copied the questions and answered them. The teacher then asked us to exchange books among ourselves to mark on our own whilst he gave us the answers. We had only one commercially produced revision book each for English, Mathematics, Science, History, and Geography. Each of us had a Nature Study exercise book. Every day, we had to measure, record, and draw the growth of our balsam plants along the corridor. For Geography lessons, we had to record the daily maximum temperature and minimum temperature in degrees Fahrenheit. Then we had to shade the weather chart for cloud cover as well as indicate the direction the wind was blowing. We had to study the rooster-shaped weather vane on our school roof. The rain gauge in the school field was uncovered for us to view only a few times.

The following incident is firmly etched in my mind. One morning, I was ready to return to my class after my vernacular language lesson. The doorway was crowded. Half of it was blocked by the huge teacher's table which was covered with the usual tools of teaching—textbooks, storybooks, pencil holder, rulers and other things. As we were inching our way out, a stout, bald-headed teacher, Mr Singh, appeared. He picked up a foot-long wooden ruler and whacked my knuckle. I felt an excruciating pain. It was so painful that tears welled in my eyes. I did not know why he was so angry. I dared not complain to my parents. If I did, surely I would get a thrashing from them. To my parents and grandma, the teacher was always right. In my mind, surely the teacher was a devil. How could he hit me without telling me what I had done wrong?

Another incident was this. It was during one of the afternoons when I was going home by the small side gate on the left of the school perimeter. I walked along the school fence and through the Malay kampong. I saw a tall hefty man carrying a big bundle of grass on his head—most likely to feed his goats. Being young and innocent, I thought he looked quite funny. I pointed at him and smiled. The next day, he was there at exactly the same spot. He mumbled something fiercely and gave me a hard slap on my left cheek. I was nearly flung on to the ground. That time, I really cried all the way home. From that day onwards, I avoided going that way. By pointing, most probably he thought I was jeering at him, but that was not what I intended.

In 1958, I was in Primary 6. It was the first time I attended extra lessons in school. Mr Tan Tiong Ghee volunteered to revise with us a few times during the June school holidays. It was very fun. The whole school was very quiet—the only noise was from our class. After each lesson, he played a game of badminton with us before we went home.

Every morning, the first period of the day was the news. "Toot! Toot! Toot! This is the news from Radio Malaya, Kuala Lumpur." We learnt of the shelling of Quemoy Island by Red China, and that Lim Yew Hock had become our Chief Minister, that Lim Yew Hock had gone to London, what our Governor Sir Robert Black had done and many other things.

Some of my schoolmates in Primary 6 were Gan Teck Chuan, son of landowner Gan Cheng Huat, whose father owned a gun, Quek Teck Meng, Michael Ban, Lim Ban Lee, Toh Thiam Chye, Chua Boon Seng, Prakash, Vu Throng Viet, Chua Peng Cheng, Chia Boon Beng, Sungit and Lim Kim Yew. During recess, we would chant:

"Hey Mambo, Mambo Rock,
Chief Minister, Lim Yew Hock
Go to London . . ."

I did not know how we came to know of a pair of elderly Eurasian sisters staying in the midst of kampong Tanah Merah Kechil. They were Miss E. Mills and her sister. Miss E. Mills was the decision-maker. Her elder sister did whatever she asked her to do. I guess they must have been of mixed Indonesian-Dutch parentage and had come from Indonesia during the Indonesian war of independence, for they spoke Malay very well. They gave tuition to the kampong children for a small monthly fee each. So my classmates Chua Boon Seng, Chia Boon Beng, Sungit, and I enrolled. To our surprise, Lim Poh Chu, whose parents made and sold *belachan* from Bedok, was also there. We learnt English from them. I remember clearly that one of the senior pupils there wrote about the Merdeka Bridge, which was completed in 1956: 'From Merdeka Bridge, the view of Asia Insurance rose like a bird up into the clear blue sky.' Miss E. Mills highlighted to us the beautiful style of writing describing the Merdeka Bridge.

Miss E. Mills was strict with the more physically active pupils. Anyone she found misbehaving would be whacked with a foot-long wooden ruler, followed by a litany of guidelines one should observe.

The elder sister was mild. Slowly, word by word, she would coach the little children to read the English words.

In 1958, I was sitting for the Mathematics paper for the Secondary School Entrance Examination in the hall. The collapsible doors dividing the two rooms were open. Suddenly, in the midst of the examination, someone shouted something to the effect of, "I know the answer already! It's very easy!"

The invigilator rushed to him and asked him how he knew the answer. He said the answer was in his bag. He was told to take it out. There it was. I did not know what followed. All I knew was that boy was my former classmate from Primary 5. He talked at will and loudly too. We knew his ways, so we let him be.

A few weeks later, we were told to retake the Secondary School Entrance Examinations for two papers, English and Mathematics. We later found out that someone in the printing section of the Ministry of Education had sold the papers prior to the examination. Most likely, the boy's teacher could have gotten hold of a copy. The boy's teacher taught me in 1957 when I was in Primary 5. He was a very kind man, slightly bald at the centre of his head. He was always willing to help. In those days, cyclostyling of notes was hard to come by. He used to write notes on the green chalkboard for us to copy. His cursive writing was the easiest to follow. I admired his penmanship greatly. Being elderly, sometimes he talked to himself, shaking his head a little. Sad to say, he was implicated in the leak of the examination papers.

During the December holidays of 1958, we received our results. Many of us were posted to Dryburgh English School in Koon Seng Road. The name 'Dryburgh' did not register in our minds. Then someone said that it was the old Choon Guan School. That sounded familiar to my grandma, who had friends selling food in the canteen.

Bedok Boys' School's Sports Day in the 1950s

In those days, there were few co-curricular activities in the primary schools. The major activities were for track and field. Every afternoon, there were sports practices, dry runs and elimination runs. After each practice, the housemaster would arrange sweet iced drinks to treat the participants. The days of the houses practices were the few occasions when we could use part of the girls' school field. Usually, we had the inkling of an invisible line that divided the boys' side of the field and the girls'. If our sports apparatuses inadvertently went across the invisible line, we would hurriedly retrieve them and return to our side. We did not want the girls to complain that we had intruded into their territory.

In class, our teachers would remind us of the do's and don'ts on Sports Day. Drink coupons were issued to every pupil. The prefect master busily instructed the prefects on their duties, such as showing schoolmates, parents, and VIPs to their allotted seats. Some were appointed to give out the Sports Day programmes. The scouts were also given their duties by the Scoutmaster.

Several days before, the sports secretary instructed the school servant, Yahya, what to do. He, together with the other school servants, was seen busily drawing lines across the field using a small metal-wheeled cart laden with white lime. A few pupils were selected to assist them. Then small, triangular, colorful flags were strung along the tracks. Huge tents were erected at the sides of the field. There were tents for the non-competitors, competitors, parents, and VIPS. Huge loudspeakers were fixed at the top of the tents. Foldable wooden chairs were provided in the parents' and VIPs' tents.

Sports were usually held in the afternoons. Just like in all previous years, a van with a huge Ovaltine drum brought the cold sweet drink. A 'Red Lion' lorry brought crates of the bottled orange drinks and deposited them in the music room. Another lorry brought pots and pans, plates and stoves to set up their kitchen at a small tent reserved for the caterer to cook dinner for the teachers.

An hour before the event, throngs of spectators started arriving and began to occupy the seats at the best vantage points. Children were hurrying here and there, calling out loudly for their friends and parents. They spilled over onto the road as their tents were filled. Loud music blared from the speakers. Then came the principals and teachers, some dressed in their best and with new hairdos, to occupy the seats reserved for them. Among the principals and teachers were some Europeans whom we called *ang mo lang*. Those days, we seldom saw Europeans in the kampong, so we were quite curious. Then the music faded.

A voice rang out. "Will the competitors for Event Number 1 please get ready at the starting point!" Those at the competitors' and non-competitors' tents started cheering loudly for their houses. Their houses were named after the planets—red for Mars, blue for Venus, green for Jupiter, and yellow for Mercury. Loud murmurs could be heard coming from the parents as well as the siblings.

Along the roads, there were Hillman, Morris, and Ford cars, Triumph and BSA motorcyles, and Raleigh and Rudge bicycles. A few ice-cream sellers were also spotted among the crowds.

Sports Day was like a great festival for the people in the kampongs and villages. Each family turned up in full force to witness the day. When the last race ended—usually the parents' race—the scouts formed a circle around the prize table. Prizewinners from the various houses sat behind them. The announcer read the names of the prizewinners for all the events in a clear crisp voice. Loud applause was given to all of them. The loudest applause was for the best winners. At the end of the prize presentation, our principal, who was an Englishman, gave a speech. By that time, it was already quite dark. The photographer's flash went off, followed by a discharge of the spent bulb. Then another was fished from his pocket and fixed on the flash gun, which had a reflector as big as the bowls in our kitchen.

After the speech, a loud voice said, "HIP! HIP! HIP!"

"HOORAY!" went the crowd. This was repeated thrice very proudly. My mind was in a whirl. I did not understand what it was all about as it was the first time I had heard the cheer.

Some mischievous children shouted, *"Kachang puteh!"* to rhyme with 'Hip Hip Horray!' All of us burst into laughter.

Then music—'God Save the Queen'—was played. Everyone stood still. There were hushed voices. We stared at each other, wondering what this was about. In those days we were not very well exposed to the national anthem.

When the music ended, everybody started to leave. A loud cacophony of vehicle and human sounds were heard. The traffic controller at the junction of the road outside the school and Bedok Road had a hard time with so many parents, children, and different types of vehicles. He carried a 'lollipop', a long pole with a red, round disc at the upper end with the words 'Schoolchildren crossing!' When the traffic along Bedok Road was at a lull, he proceeded to the middle with the giant 'lollipop' and shouted in his high-pitched voice at the pedestrians to hurry. He needed to shout, as the prizewinners were concentrating on describing how they won to their parents and siblings, while others were disappointed at not winning anything. Some would walk and admire the shining cups that they had won at the same time.

The principals, teachers and invited guests proceeded to a dinner at the multi-purpose room. The collapsible doors separating the Geography and Music rooms were dragged open, combining the two rooms. Caterers cooked at a shed designated for them. Uniformed waitresses brought the dishes to their tables. Red Lion orange squash drinks were served.

The whole scenario was repeated every year.

A few classmates and I were busily helping the teachers in whichever way we could. There were never dull moments, as every minute, there was something to do. Dinner was provided for us, of course.

Then my Secondary School Entrance Examination came. It was the year 1958. My primary school experiences were to come to an end, but they would always be deeply etched in my mind.

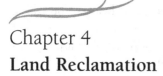

Chapter 4
Land Reclamation

Sand Quarrying at Kampong Tanah Merah Kechil

After WWII, when I was about seven years old, there was a building boom. There was a demand for sand—both non-silty and silty. The non-silty sand was taken from the earth that had been eroded by streams flowing from the hills after sudden, heavy thunderstorms, known as Sumatras, in the afternoons. During the months of November to February, rainwater was in abundance. During the rainy season, the rainwater washed the silt from the surface of the exposed red earth down the stream to the Malay kampong. The water eroded the earth to form gullies and ravines in the upper section and deposited the contents when it came to a flatter part of the areas forming deltas.

By the time the rainwater laden with sand reached the deltas, its flow would slow down and the sand it carried would be deposited at the bottom of the streams. The sand was free of silt, as the silty suspension would have flowed away with the rest of the water. Our whole family would devote ourselves to shovelling this sand from the streams, as nothing much could be done at the vegetable farm. We collected sand almost every day even in the rain. Swiftly flowing streams would not deposit sand. They eroded the soil and carried it down to the valley in the kampong. So we created dams across some streams to slow down the flow of the water thereby forcing it to deposit its load. We would hurriedly shovel the sand out of the 'little lakes' we had created. The sand was shovelled into mounds. After deciding where the mound would be, we would clear the patch

120

of any grass, twigs, pebbles and other objects. When the water from the newly collected mound of sand had seeped to the bottom, we had to sieve the sand for stones, twigs, mud balls and other debris.

Dad was full of imagination and innovation. One day, he was sawing a few timber pieces and cutting a piece of chicken wire netting.

"What are you making this time, Ah Chek?" I enquired, calling him 'Ah Chek', which means 'Uncle'. Our siblings used to call our parents 'Uncle' and 'Auntie', based on the geomancer's advice that our relationship should not appear to be too close, otherwise disaster would erupt.

"Well, you observe. You can help me by bringing the tools and holding the pieces while I nail them," he requested. I did, helping him with whatever was necessary.

The end product was a huge rectangular sieve, which measured one metre by 2.5 metres. Then he made the sieve lean at an angle on a sturdy stick. With a spade, we scooped up the unfiltered sand and spread it out on to the net. Particles like stones and pebbles, which could not pass through the holes of the netting, rolled down and were collected to fill potholes and deep vehicle tracks. The stones and pebbles were big and rough and thus gave much traction to the tyres of the three-ton lorries that came to collect our sand.

Silty sand was dug from the ground. This type of sand was sticky with red silt. That type of sand was meant for a specific purpose— plastering walls. Workmen found it easier to work with a mixture of silty sand and cement. Concrete made of non-silty sand was harder than silty sand, therefore it lasted longer. The value of non-silty sand could be as high as twice the value of silty sand.

Two lorry drivers whom we were acquainted with were Teck Cheong and Geok Huat. Those days, the lorries were Bedfords and Chevrolets. They belonged to the Housing Supplies Companies. We children would sit on the dry ground and watch how the skilful drivers maneuvered their lorries to exactly where they should be. My parents would help shovel the sand into each lorry after its side panel was lowered. After filling the lorry till it was almost half way to the brim, the heavy panel was raised and latched. Then a piece of timber with a huge metal hook bolted on each end was hooked across the middle of the panels. That was to prevent the panels from bulging in the middle when the lorry was fully loaded. Then more sand was shovelled in until it reached the brim. The sand was measured in cubic yards. A lorry load could contain three to six cubic yards of sand. The payment for each lorry of sand varied from $7 to $11 depending on demand. After the day's sale, my father would record the number of lorries of sand into the same sort of notebook used by shopkeepers to record credit in those days, with '555' printed on the cover. At the end of the month, he would pay for the sand collected from the land to the estate manager Teow Swee at $3 per lorry.

Midway along Tanah Merah Kechil Road (the present-day Bedok Court), there was a large area of a rubber estate. Large commercial companies would invest in huge motor pumps. They pumped water into the hills so that it would carry the silty sand from the hills as it flowed down. When the sand-laden water moved along a raised slotted *palong* (compartment), the sand would be trapped in each slot. Lorries then moved under the slots. Trapdoors under the compartments were opened and the sand flowed into the lorries. The remaining water with silt suspended in it rushed down the rest of the *palong* and ended up in a pond. The silty water was left in the pond until the silty suspension sank to the bottom. The clear water near the surface was then pumped up the hill again to flush out more sand from the hill.

During the northeast monsoon season, it sometimes rained continuously every day. That posed a problem to the motorised traffic using the dirt tracks of Tanah Merah Kechil. The rainwater cut deep gullies into the tracks, often leaving pools of water. Road users would have to be prepared for their vehicles to likely be caught in the ruts or veer to the side when travelling on these wet slippery tracks. When the lorries that carried our sand got caught in the mud, we were obliged to help the drivers get their vehicles off the tracks. Usually, when a sand-laden lorry had left our quarry, we would listen attentively to the groaning of the lorry. If the groaning tapered off, that indicated the lorry had made its way safely to the main bitumen road, the Changi 8½ Milestone. If the groaning of the lorry became louder for some time, that indicated the lorry had gotten caught in a rut. We would carry our *changkols* (digging hoes) and spades and hurry to the scene. We would help the lorry driver and his assistant clear the mud from the wheels and scatter pebbles and sand in the rut. Sometimes, we needed to jack up the wheels and insert bricks and planks under them. The worst case was when the whole lorry ended up in a mud pool. To solve such a situation, another lorry was needed to tow the grief-stricken lorry out. It was easier said than done.

Almost the whole stretch of the track would be waterlogged. The towing lorry also faced the same situation—danger of the mud pools—except that it was not caught in the rut. At times, the whole day was spent trying to get the lorry out. When night came, they had to abandon the lorry till the next day. In those days, powerful four-wheel-drive truckers were few and far in between. A lot depended on their ingenuity and the brute strength of everyone involved. After the lorry had cleared the rut, we had to fill the potholes with hard core, which comprised bits of broken brick and stone, pieces of sturdy wood and even coconut trunks. A skilful driver would inspect the road first—looking out for likely danger spots, potholes and areas of soft ground. Then he would drive the lorry at a faster speed than usual to gain momentum to pass over the ruts and potholes without falling into them. There was an incident which is firmly etched in my mind. In the middle of the Malay kampong was an Indian provision shop. Suppliers needed to use the road, but the road was in bad condition on rainy days. The provision shop owner paid a few people to repair the road for the suppliers. We also made use of the road to transport the sand. One day, we were glad after our lorry made a successful passage to the main road. However, our happiness was short-lived. A few workmen came to our house to demand money for using the road they had repaired.

My dad was flabbergasted.

"What? That is beyond reason. The road belongs to the government. The road users have a responsibility to move out their vehicles if they get stuck. They have no obligation to fill the potholes for the next road user. These people receive payment from the Indian shop owner for repairing the road for their suppliers. We do not engage them to repair the road for us."

My dad refused to give in to their demand. Well, they walked away empty-handed. It seemed they were instigated by the shop owner to get payment from us for using the road they had repaired.

Disputes like that happened. However, if one was not happy with the outcome of a talk, one could in those days approach the *kampong chu* (village headman). One such man was Peck Hui. He lived at the junction of Simpang Bedok and Changi Road. He was such a fair and amiable man. His decision was usually well accepted by both parties.

Having such an experience in my childhood days, it helped me to understand physical geography lessons better later when I was in secondary school.

My Premonitions

Old people of my time always said children's words, when blurted out without thinking, were often accurate premonitions.

I might have had many premonitions, but this one clearly would not be erased from my mind. I must have been about eight. My parents were collecting sand from a stream away from our farm, at the valley behind the Bedok schools, to be exact. We had to cross over a hill before we came to the stream. That piece of land still belonged to Kim Eng. There was a house that belonged to Lim Hay Er. Literally, it meant 'prawns', as that family mainly caught prawns for their livelihood. From their accent, we knew they came from Chao An, a county in Fukien province in China. Their daughter was Heng Kee. Further down the valley, a few years later, Mr and Mrs Yeo Bak Seok built a zinc house at the far end of my farm on the land which belonged to Mr Gan Cheng Huat. Mr and Mrs Yeo Bak Seok were an actor and an actress of the Towchew Lau Sai Tor Wayang Troupe. Mr Yeo had a mother who looked after the family when they were away for work assignments. The couple had three children. The eldest was named Kow Kia, second was Ter Kia, and there was a daughter named Boon Hong. The two boys attended the same school as us—Bedok Boys' School and the girl—Bedok Girls' School.

As usual, during the wet northeast monsoon months, the rainwater would bring sand and silt from the hills from both sides of the valley. Sand from the upper part of the stream was coarser and grainier. Sand from the middle stream was of smaller particles, and sand from the lower stream was very fine. The stream ended in the lowland ponds and swamps, depositing the fine silt.

We collected sand from the upper and middle sections of the stream and, as usual, collected them in mounds. Every day, many lorries would arrive and transport the sand away. One day, a lorry backed up and stopped near a mound where I was standing. Out jumped the driver. I blurted out, "Your lorry will have a puncture later on."

"Small boy, get away from here. And don't babble nonsense!" he shouted at me rather fiercely. I moved away.

When the sand was loaded, the driver started the engine. He engaged the clutch. Suddenly, there was a loud cranking sound that came from the back of the lorry. He revved the engine hard, and the vehicle belched a huge cloud of black smoke, but it did not budge. He jumped down from the driver's seat, cursing and swearing at me for voicing that premonition.

At that time, there wasn't a telephone around. Someone was sent to get the mechanic. The driver spent the whole afternoon waiting for the mechanic to arrive. It seemed the back shaft had broken. Spare parts were bought and then the vehicle was repaired. I spent time with them, observing them fixing the shaft. The whole load of sand was released onto the ground. The rear of the lorry was jacked up. The wheels were dislodged after the nuts were undone. The gearbox was opened. With much effort, they pulled out the broken shaft. The new one was inserted, and all other parts were put in place. The lorry was serviceable once again.

The lorry driver's assistant then said that children's utterances could predict future events. They gave us the broken shaft. It proved to be of good use on the farm—for compacting soil, smashing empty tins and straightening rolled-up zinc sheets, among other functions.

I had other premonitions, but they were too insignificant to be recorded.

Land Reclamation

In the 1950s, our house was situated in the middle of the ridge presently known as Jalan Limau Bali. The ridge branched out to the front of our house (the present-day Jalan Limau Manis), and then tapered off at the fringe of the Malay kampong (the present-day Kew Gardens). A track ran along the ridge. The kampong folks traversed along the track to get to either Bedok Road or Changi Road to visit friends or relatives living in Tanah Merah Kechil. At night, lights from the torches of passers-by could be seen moving along the track. Sometimes, kampong folks used the bushes by the sides of the track as latrines. In the kampong, the latrines were built away from their houses. They were little raised huts made of wood and covered by attap roofing. In each latrine, a few planks were laid parallel to one another, leaving an eight-to-ten-inch gap in between. Below the gap was a bucket. When the bucket was filled with excrement, the smell could be overpowering and the houseflies buzzing about and resting on the users could be deplorable. When things reached such a state, the owners had to stop using the latrines. It made practical sense to ease oneself among the bushes if no one was around. Some would use a *changkol* to dig a hole before defecating into it and cover the hole after it was done. Others did not. That activity gave rise to a Malay saying, *"Hendak berak, baru mahu buka jamban"* (Will dig a latrine only when about to defecate). That means that one must be prepared before nature calls. The kampong folks usually did that at night and at a ridge behind their houses. They usually carried torchlights with them.

In 1954-1955, lorries and workers came with *changkols*, wicker baskets with big handles, and long steel spikes. They started to dig the earth at the ridge and shift it to the lorries. The *samsui* women, with their signature red headgear and black outfits, were especially tough. They tirelessly dug the loose earth, and with a heave and a flip, they emptied the earth from their baskets into the lorry. The men used the long steel spikes to poke at the earth and levered it loose for the *samsui* women to scoop into the wicker baskets.

Usually, there would be a person on high ground who loosened and levered the earth so that the workmen below could shovel it into the lorry. One day, there was a commotion. Someone had been caught unawares and knocked down by a huge clump of earth from above. It happened to be Madam Ong Ka's son Ah Hee, who was working to get some extra income. Madam Ong Ka was informed. As she was rushing to the site, tears were streaming from her eyes. Luckily, the injury was not serious. It could have been more serious if he had been directly hit. To avoid accidents like that, I often heard the men who were levering and loosening chunks of the earth from the top of the ridge giving warnings to those working below them.

"*Siam* (move away)!" a man would shout if a chunk of earth bigger than usual were about to roll down. Those below would then look up and if they thought it could pose a danger to them, they would move away. The chunk of earth would then roll down harmlessly.

The workers, especially the *samsui* women, brought along their own drinks and lunch. Their tea was contained in corked soy sauce bottles. A gunny string loop was tied at each of the slender neck of the bottle so that they could hang them on the branches of the trees while they were working. The lunch was contained in tiffin carriers, which were enamel-coated layered containers. Each layer held a separate dish. At lunchtime, they sat in the shade under the huge mango tree to share the food and rest. Their meals were simple— often they had rice, fried salted fish, stir-fried vegetables and fried tofu. The men got the lorry driver to buy their lunch. They came packed in *oh pe hiok* (Hokkien), the sepal of the palm flower. Their coffee was stored in used condensed milk tins with a string made from dried reed stalk, looped through a hole in the middle of the lid.

Note:
A small section of the lid was not cut so that it could be used as a hinge. After the coffee or tea was poured into the empty milk tin, the cut lid was pushed down into the opening of the tin. Then the tin's rim

was pushed inward, effectively locking it so that it would not pop out when lifted by the loop at the centre. One could then carry the tin of hot beverage using the looped string without being scalded.

Today few people still have takeaways like this.

A tiffin carrier

I was too young to know where they had taken the earth. They flattened the hill, leaving the mango tree and land demarcation stone untouched. As a result, after the digging, the demarcation stones and the mango tree looked very high up on a mesa. The digging went on right to the border of Madam Ong Ka's land.

Parts of the newly flattened area served as a football field. On weekends, the kampong folks played soccer there. During the windy season, they flew kites of different shapes and styles there without fear of them being entangled in tall trees or electric poles.

After several years, shrubs and grass grew over the flattened piece of land until the Leng Seng Land company bought it to build semi-detached houses in 1963.

The flattening of hills did not only happen near our house. It also happened along certain sections of Tanah Merah Kechil.

There was a tar-coated cable with a radius of about two centimetres, which lay buried in the earth. It puzzled everyone working on the hill in the area. At first, everyone worked with caution, as they did not want to get into trouble with the authorities and also because the cable might carry electricity. It was left exposed after the earth was cut away. I had seen that cable stretching from underneath my house, exposed at the stream, then continuing on through the ridge after the earth had been moved away. My grandma told me that she had seen the cable at Mata Ikan too. She also told me that at a certain time of the day, a humming sound could be heard at Mata Ikan, coming from the cable. That cable, of a radius of about two centimetres, was also seen running across Tanah Merah Kechil to Opera Estate. Nobody knew who buried it and for what purpose. It was a mystery. Later, some enterprising scrap dealers cut the cable and sold it.

I also saw some kampong folks melt down the tar covering a small length of the cable. It revealed a wide outer aluminium coil around several lengths of thick aluminium wire, each about a diameter of 0.2 centimetres.

Note:
The cable could have been buried by the British military when they were building the pillboxes for the defence of Singapore during WWII.

One afternoon in 1962, a long line of lorries queued up to be filled with earth by the front-end loader up at the cliff of Tanah Merah Kechil off East Coast Road (Little Red Cliff at the site of the present-day Temasek Primary School). The lorries transported the earth and dumped it at the spot where I usually took my bus (the present-day Temasek Secondary School). Once a laden lorry showed up there, the three panels which enclosed the earth within the lorry were unlatched by a team of workers. The hinged panels fell open with a bang when they hit the mudguards of the rear wheels. Then, an earth rammer with its blade held high, pushed the earth out. The lorry then moved away. The bulldozer pushed the earth to the edge of the shore. The waves moved forward and swallowed up some of it, leaving a muddy trail. That was repeated day after day until the sea was pushed further away from the coast. The East Coast Land Reclamation Project was undertaken by the Japanese company Ombayashi-Gumi for the Singapore government.

What a pity! They had destroyed an iconic part of Singapore, the Little Red Cliff, the cliff that ancient cartographers and seafarers had made reference to.

The first phase of reclamation project took several years. On hot sunny days, the movements of the lorries laden with red earth from the interior of Tanah Merah Kechil kicked up clouds of red dust when they sped past. The drivers, token issuers (every lorry that made an earth-laden trip was given a token for accounting purposes), safety personnel, hawkers, bulldozer drivers and other workers each had a handkerchief tied over their nose and mouth because of the dust.

Yeo Teow Swee's daughter, Bong Poh, was very enterprising. She boiled leaves of the boat lily and sold this drink to the workers and drivers. Business was brisk, as boat lily was known for its cleansing and cooling properties.

Once, I was walking home from the bus stop. I had to go past that stretch of road in order to reach home. When the earth-laden lorries moved past me, they kicked up so much dust. I could hardly open my eyes. I had my handkerchief over my nose and mouth too. When I reached home, I cleared my throat. My phlegm was orange, the colour of the dust.

In the first phase of land reclamation, the Malay kampongs and Kim Eng's land were not affected, so we were not scheduled to move out. But every day, we had to tolerate the noises made by the bulldozer heaving the earth onto the lorries and the motorised ploughs moving across the hard layers of the earth. When the topsoil was removed, the exposed layer beneath was very much harder, so a mechanized plough was needed to loosen it before a bulldozer could move the soil. The rumbling of the long chain of lorries across the now flattened landscape continued unabated. To meet deadlines, the work extended right into the night and large floodlights were installed.

In the second phase of land reclamation, the method used was different. Huge rotating buckets scooped up the earth and loaded them onto conveyor belts. These conveyor belts carried the earth all the way to the sea off Siglap, Katong to Tanjong Rhu to reclaim the land there. By then, we had already shifted to Chai Chee at Peng Ghee Road.

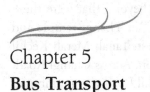

Chapter 5
Bus Transport

" **R** eally? How did they do that?"
We children were very curious. Our dad had just told us that during the Japanese Occupation, from 1942-1945, petrol was scarce. Some local entrepreneurs therefore converted petrol-driven engines into coal-powered engines.

Dad explained, "Before the engine could start, coal had to be loaded and burned. The heat made the boiler produce steam."

"And the steam would force the pistons to move," I excitedly finished the sentence for dad.

"You got it!" he exclaimed.

Before 1935, buses in Singapore were run by a few hundred individual bus operators. Each operator owned a few buses and each bus could carry seven passengers. These buses were called 'mosquito' buses.

In 1925, the Singapore Traction Bus Co. was under the management of the Shanghai Electric Construction Co. It acquired the Singapore Tramways Ltd. In 1935, the Shanghai Electric Construction Co. relinquished its share, and the Singapore Traction Co. management came to its own. The Singapore Traction Co. was to run the city routes and the Chinese bus companies were to run the rural areas.

The Changi Bus

My grandma was the first to take me to Chai Chee Market by the Changi bus. With a rattan basket in hand, we would walk

131

a long stretch along a potholed, water-cut track off Tanah Merah Kechil Road, leading to 8½ Milestone Changi Road. On the right of the track was Hong Cheng's land, and beyond that were the 8 Milestone Hokkien Tua Pek Kong (Hock San Theng) temple and cemetery. On the left was a secondary forest. Tanah Merah Kechil Road and Changi Road formed a T-junction. Across Changi Road, opposite the junction of Tanah Merah Kechil Road was a rambutan estate. A solitary metal pole stood by the roadside. Atop the pole was a red rectangular metal plate and on it was a number 1 painted in white paint. We waited. Then round the corner, a white and red vehicle came groaning. It was the first time I had ever seen a bus. Its front was like a lorry but the body was all covered up. It stopped for us to get on. Its rear served as the entrance and exit. There were no doors, only a flight of steps. The instant we boarded, the bell sounded twice. The bus surged forward. We looked for seats. A man, casually dressed and with a small bag slung over his shoulders, came forward. Without a word, he pressed his empty single hole puncher several times, making rapid *click, click* sounds. My grandma was quick to respond.

"*Chit lei tua lang, chit ley suay kia* (one adult and one child)," she said loudly and clearly in Hokkien, to be heard above the loud groaning of the vehicle up the slope. She handed him a ten-cent coin for an adult fare and a five-cent coin for a child fare. He dropped the five-cent coin into the outer compartment of his pouch and the ten-cent coin in the middle compartment. He took out a pad of tickets from the inner compartment, selected two tickets of the appropriate fare, punched several holes on them and handed them to my grandma. Should anyone wish to alight from the next bus stop, they should signal to him and he would sound the bell once by pressing a red button on the side of the roof of the bus. Around the round chrome frame of the red button were embossed the two words 'Press once.' On the back panel of the driver's seat was information regarding the passenger ratio of adults and children, the number of passengers to be seated, and the number of standing passengers allowed. The words 'Soon Chow Workshop' were prominently displayed on the top left-hand corner of this panel behind the driver on each Changi bus.

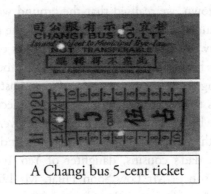

A Changi bus 5-cent ticket

The passengers, especially in the rural areas, carried with them various different types of farm produce. Farmers might carry live fowl like ducks and chickens, or vegetables and fruit. These might be placed along the aisle, obstructing the other passengers. The bus conductor had to wade through the quacking and clucking fowl to get to the passengers who had just boarded.

We found the bus drivers and conductors very impatient and devoid of any human feeling. Usually, the driver would speed so fast along the narrow, winding two-lane Changi Road like a sports car driver and then suddenly hit the brakes for the passengers to alight or to board, throwing everyone forward. But the passengers knew what to expect. They clung tightly to the supports to avoid any accidents. The bus driver was quick to drive off before the last passenger could plant his two feet on the ground. The passengers too learnt that they had to act fast to stay safe.

It was general knowledge that the bus company paid the drivers and conductors according to the number of trips they could make for the day. Therefore they wished to make the most number of trips possible for the day to maximise their earnings.

The Changi Bus Terminus was at Changi Point. It was next to the Changi open-air theatre (the present-day SBS Transit) terminal. The downtown terminus was at Capitol. One of its depots was at 6 Milestone (the present-day Bedok Police Station). The bus I usually took to and from Chai Chee market once had to get into the depot to top up its diesel. Another time, we had to transfer to another bus.

When we got down, we realised that the ground was soaked with black oil and exuded a very strong diesel smell. The passengers had to walk carefully so as not to step in the puddles of black liquid. The Changi bus headquarters and main depot was between Lorong 106 and Lorong 108 (the present-day Great Eastern Assurance Building). I was told, in those days, the coins collected by the bus conductors were by the bucketful, and each day, several people were needed to haul the buckets to the banks to count and deposit them.

One of my dad's cousins, daughter of Yeo Teow Swee, was married to the son of Mr Low Soon Huat. Mr Low was one of several shareholders of Changi Bus Co. Ltd. The main shareholder was Tan Kong Eng. The other shareholders were Guan Thong, Soon Jay Tee and Heng Leong.

The Katong Bedok Bus

We always enjoyed the bus ride to school provided by the Katong Bedok Bus Services. The drivers and bus conductors were caring and patient. On some occasions, I met Hong Siong, my cousin, who served as a bus conductor in this company. He never accepted my fare.

In those days, finding a job was hard. One needed to be recommended for the position. Also, in order not to disappoint the person who had recommended you for the job, the job must be done well. In this way, the loyalty and discipline of the worker was assured, as the person who recommended him also served as a guarantor. Uncle Yeo Koon Seng's sister-in-law's husband owned a substantial, four-wheel share of Katong Bedok Bus Company. In those days the maximum number of wheels a bus had was six. When a person was said to own six wheels, that meant he had 100 percent of the bus company's shares. If he owned one wheel, that meant he owned one sixth of the shares of the company. My cousin, Yeo Hong Siong (who passed away on 7 December 2011 at the age of 77), was given a recommendation to work for the bus company as a bus conductor.

In 1959, I was promoted to Dryburgh English School after passing the Secondary Schools Entrance Examinations in 1958. I had to take a bus from the Bedok schools to Tembeling Road in Katong.

While the bus journey to school was pleasant, the homeward journey was a nightmare. The bus stop at the junction of Tembeling Road and East Coast Road was so crowded at that time as it served the residents of the area, office workers, and students from St Hilda's, Kuo Chuan Girls' as well as Tung Ling schools. By the time the bus reached the bus stop, it was already packed like a sardine can with pupils from Dunman High, Dunman Secondary, Tanjong Katong Girls', Tanjong Katong Technical and Chung Cheng High schools. When that happened, in order to prevent more passengers from boarding, the bus driver had to stop far past the bus stop to let passengers alight. Those of us who were energetic would run after the bus and try to get on. Sometimes we managed to cling onto a metal bar at the entrance of the bus with just one leg on the entrance door step of the moving bus for several stops, alighting at each stop to let passengers to get down and hopping on again before the bus moved off. To take a bus at that hour was definitely not for the weak and the meek.

There was a Katong Bedok bus terminus at Changi Bedok Road junction. The buses stopped in front of the Bedok Post Office. The bus drivers and conductors rested for a while before driving off. The Katong Bedok Bus Service had one of its depots along Bedok Road, diagonally opposite to the field of Bedok Boys' and Girls' Schools. Just like any other bus depot in Singapore, the ground was always oily and smelled of diesel. The other terminus was at Lorong 8 Geylang.

The Singapore Traction Bus Co.

The Singapore Traction Company had the biggest fleet of buses in Singapore. It monopolised the whole of the town area. The bus conductors and drivers were ever so patient and polite. They seldom sped. They wore a light brown uniform. Each had a large badge above the shirt pocket. The bus inspectors were in white. The bus tickets were different from the Chinese bus companies. Each was thicker and shorter and had the amount printed in large hollow letters covering the whole ticket.

One day, my grandma, together with my aunt—Hong Huat's mother—and a few cousins was visiting a relative along Telok Kurau. We boarded a Singapore Traction Bus at Kampong Eunos.

The bus conductor asked us for the fare in Hokkien. *"Long chong kor zee. Lu heng chit kor chiu ho* (The total fare is $1.20. You need to pay only a dollar)." He told us not to breathe a word to anyone. He collected the fare and went to the rear. He did not issue us the tickets. My grandma said that he had given us a concession, therefore no tickets needed to be issued.

Singapore Traction Co. bus tickets

The Trolley Bus

On several occasions, my parents took us to the Balestier Road Chinese Temple via the trolley bus. It was painted green just like other Singapore Traction Co. buses, with the three alphabets 'STC' painted on it. My parents told us that we had boarded the *dian zher* (electric car). The benches were made of wood. I did not know for which occasion, but I remember vividly that it was from Geylang Serai. I was surprised that the bus moved very slowly. It was very silent but hot and stuffy. Only the occasional thumping of the wheels and the cables overhead could be heard. I saw too that in order to switch overhead cables, someone had to use a pole to detach a cable and attach it to another. One could know which way the bus was going by looking at the overhead cables.

Other Buses

During the post-war period, there were 11 bus companies providing transport all over the island. The STC provided transport in the town areas. The others provided transport in the rural areas. Other than the STC, Changi Bus Co. Ltd. and Katong Bedok Bus Co., the other bus companies were namely the Paya Lebar Bus Co., the Keppel Bus, the Tay Koh Yat Bus, the Punggol Bus, the Green Bus, the Hock Lee Amalgamated Bus Company (amalgamation of Ngo Hock and Soo Lee Bus), the Kampong Baru Bus Co., and the Easy Bus Co. I seldom boarded the buses of those companies, so I cannot comment on their services.

Bus tickets

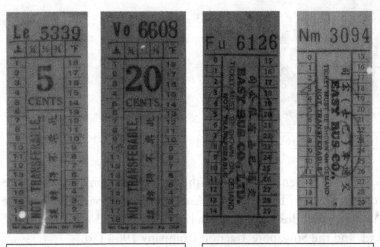

Green Bus tickets
Photo: Peter Chan's collection

Easy Bus tickets
Photo: Peter Chan's collection

Keppel Bus tickets
Photo: Peter Chan's collection

Tay Koh Yat bus tickets

Hock Lee Bus tickets

On 4 November1971, all the buses were amalgamated into four companies. They were the Associated Bus Services Pte Ltd, the Amalgamated Bus Company Pte Ltd, the United Bus Company Pte Ltd, and the Singapore Traction Company 1964 Ltd.

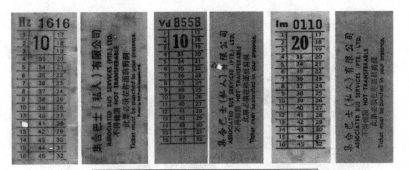

Tickets from Associated Bus Services Pte Ltd

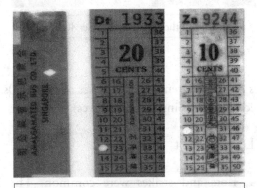

Tickets from the Amalgamated Bus Co. Ltd.

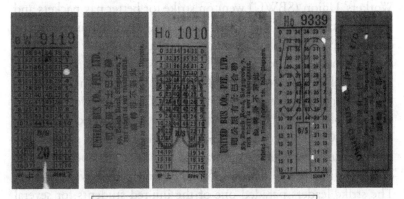

Tickets from the United Bus Co. Pte Ltd

Tickets from the Singapore Bus Service Limited

Note:

(Pictures of the different types of buses of the 1950s and 1960s can be viewed from the Singapore Archives).

The Hock Lee Bus Riot

In 1954, riots and strikes were common. The Hock Lee Bus Riot was the most serious. Bus workers from the Hock Lee Amalgamated Bus Company, who belonged to the Singapore Bus Workers' Union (SBWU) went on strike for better pay packets and working conditions. The Hock Lee Amalgamated Bus Company did not give in to their demands. It hired 200 new workers to replace those on strike as well as forming its own new union known as the Hock Lee Bus Workers' Union (HLBWU). The management had also drawn up a new working roster. Those who were replaced turned violent. The police arrested several of the workers' leaders. Then the Chinese secondary school students went to support the bus workers. The police used batons, tear gas, and opened fire in order to disperse the demonstrators. Several people were injured. The strike leaders paraded one of the injured students for several hours as evidence that the police had treated the people unfairly, to whip up public emotion. The student died on the way to the hospital. As a result of this riot, 31 people were injured and four people were killed—a student, two police officers and a journalist.

Yeo Koon Soon, son of Teow Tong, was a student of Chung Cheng High School. He, together with his schoolmates, went in support of the striking bus workers. He was caught and was jailed. Not long after that, he died. Nobody could throw light on how he was involved in the riot and how he died.

The Bus Stop at the Junction of Tanah Merah Kechil and 8 ½ Milestone Changi Road.

The kampong folks of Tanah Merah Kechil had to board and alight the Changi buses at the bus stop at the junction of Tanah Merah Kechil Road and Changi Road. In the 1950s, that junction was particularly dark and quiet, due to the tall trees and undergrowth on both sides of the road. Changi Road was narrow, with a single lane in the direction of town and another single lane in the direction of Changi Village at 16 Milestone. Traffic was very light. Most often, the vehicles carried produce from the estates and farms around the area. A very frequent sight along this road was the dull green British military trucks with the iconic pair of crossed kukris (the curved Nepali blades used by the Ghurkhas) painted in white on their tailgates. Opposite the junction were tall lalang under the coconut and rambutan trees. On the coconut tree nearest to the junction was a cinema billboard that belonged to the Changi Open air cinema. Every day, a man with a pail of starch and a roll of cinema advertisements would cycle up, brush some starch on the board and stick on an advertisement poster for the film showing at the cinema that evening.

Because the bus stop was remote from the kampongs, there were several cases of robbery, especially in the late afternoon when it was quite dark under the canopies of those tall trees. An enterprising family living nearby, sensing the needs of the bus passengers, set up a stall selling coffee, tea, and *char kuay teow* near the bus stop. The stall expanded to become a mini coffee shop with makeshift tables and chairs. Soft drinks were added to the menu. At first, ice had to be obtained from the supplier at Chai Chee Market, three miles away.

A big wooden box of sawdust was reserved for the blocks of ice that arrived in the supplier's lorry. The ice workers would unload a few blocks of ice then cut them into smaller blocks with a steel saw blade and a mallet. A saw blade placed on the ice block, when hit a few times, created a depression in the ice. Then, with a few blows from the mallet, the block broke up exactly the way the owner intended. The smaller blocks were stored in the wooden box and sawdust was spread over them. If an ice block were needed, the stallholder would extract the piece and wash away the sawdust before making ice shavings.

That shop changed hands several times.

In the 1960s, the Anglican High School was built. The junction became busier. Changi Road was widened and Tanah Merah Kechil Road was paved. The population of that area increased and business flourished. The mini coffee shop became a house as rooms were created on the slope of the road. A staircase was constructed leading from the side of the shop down to the bedroom, kitchen, and a toilet. At the same time, it was stocked with household items so it took on the function of a provision shop as well. Then Yeo Koon Toon bought the shop over and gave up being a Changi bus driver. He became a coffee shop-cum-provision shop owner. He was not new to this line as he had sufficient experience working for his father in a provision shop at Kampong Eunos when he was young.

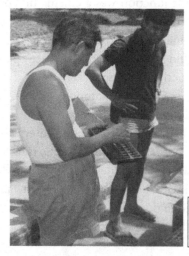

Yeo Koon Toon confirming
the accuracy of his
calculations with an abacus.

A souvenir magazine of
Anglican High School
from 1969.

In the year 1992, the owner repossessed the tiny strip of land adjourning the road. Yeo Koon Toon gave up the provision retail business. Now the strip of land is incorporated into a part of the landowner's house.

The shop at the 8 ½ Milestone Changi Road
bus stop and the junction of Tanah Merah
Kechil Road before it was re-possessed.

Whenever I drove by that bus stop, wonderful memories flashed past my mind. I remember the first time I came to that bus stop was when my grandma was taking me to Chai Chee Market. It was the first time I took a bus. I was thrilled. I took note of the exterior and interior, the bus service personnel, passengers and the landscape that whizzed past me.

It was here one afternoon it was raining heavily. My mum was carrying my youngest brother. I was carrying a huge lacquered paper umbrella to shelter them and, at the same time, watched out for puddles of water on the sandy path.

Then she said rather excitedly, "Ah Ma is there!" I looked up to see my grandma. She was making wine cushions out of lalang grass in an attap hut in the rambutan estate across the road.

I had wonderful experiences with the several successive owners of the shop. Very often I stopped by after alighting from the bus, to buy a drink or just to greet them. In the afternoons I would wait there for my mum to come back from the market to give her a lift on the bicycle home. While waiting a runner would come on a bicycle, brush some glue on the old cinema advertisement on the coconut tree opposite the shop and paste an advertisement for the movie that the Changi 10th milestone Open Air Cinema was showing that night. Usually the shop owner would get one or two complimentary tickets for helping to look after the billboard.

I witnessed how lorries and other vehicles were caught in the ruts during rainy seasons. The drivers and assistants had hard times trying to get their vehicles off the ruts. They often took coffee breaks at the shop and discussed ways of getting their vehicles out.

The treacherous slope of Tanah Merah Kechil before the bus stop evoked several bad memories. One morning I gave my mum a ride on my bicycle. The front fork broke and both of us came crashing down. We sustained some external injuries but nonetheless she still went to the market to do her business. But many days after the incident she still complained of pain on her thigh bone. I suspect she sustained a bone injury.

Few people could have experienced this. One morning I was ferrying my heavy load of vegetables up the slope to where the bus stop was. All of a sudden, several dogs came running after me. I lifted my legs and placed them on the front bicycle bar at the same time staring and shouting at them. My bicycle lost its momentum and fell with a loud crash. Those animals then took off with their tails between their legs. It was most likely the crashing sound of the heavy bicycle that had frightened them off. I had a hard time struggling to get my load of vegetables up from the fallen bicycle.

A few years after achieving self-government from the British, the government had gone all out to help the kampong folks to live decently. The government electrified the kampong and provided free water by means of installing standpipes. It was at this bus stop too that I witnessed the installation of wooden electrical poles and connecting water pipes along Tanah Merah Kechil Road.

During one of the droughts, I remember several of my kampong boys and I clung on to the tailboard of the City Council water tanker lorry to refill water from a hydrant which was opposite the shop. We were thrilled but did not know the danger if it spilt.

Ignorance was bliss. But when facing danger ignorance was not bliss after all. One day after alighting from a bus, I wanted to cross the road. I observed the kerb drill. The road was clear. Half way through I heard a loud screech. The car stopped just in time. I stood rooted to the ground. When I regained my composure the car was gone. One of the reasons I did not spot the speeding car was that there was a double bend. There were several blind spots. An eyewitness reported the incident to my parents. I was given a verbal lashing on road safety.

At that very spot in front of the shop, one of my books fell from a moving bus. I was standing at the doorstep with one hand holding a stack of books and the other holding on to a post. The bus swerved round a corner so fast that I clung for dear life. One of my books fell. When the bus halted, I hurried to retrieve the book. An Indian man had already picked it up. He returned it to me when I told him what had happened.

When Yeo Koon Toon bought over the shop, our relationship had never been closer, especially cousin Yeo Bee Choo, who later became our insurance consultant. That shop was so convenient for every one of our relatives, as it was along the main Changi Road. Whoever came past would stop by. At weekends, sometimes several families would congregate. During Chinese festivals and Chinese New Year the shop was filled with visitors.

Soon unpleasant news came. It was in the early 1990s. The landowner found out that land on which the shop lay was actually his. All the previous shop owners thought that the land belonged to the government. So the owner repossessed the land and the shop had to go.

Chapter 6
Toys

During the lean years of the 1950s, toys, if we could afford to buy them, were few and lacking in variety.

We were very fortunate to have a vast array of tools around. My father needed them to help build or repair the house, chicken coops, pigsties and the fencing around the farm. Tools for knocking ranged from a small hammer to a huge sledgehammer. We had saws—from hacksaws to huge ones that required two people to work. The cutting tools ranged from penknives to parangs. The nails spanned from half an inch to six inches. Of course, there were many other tools. Raw materials, especially from plants, were plentiful. They encompassed soft, twining plants to huge rubber trees. With so many resources available, and a little imagination, we created the toys we saw for sale and others we heard about.

The Piggy Bank

Dead coconuts which were discarded by the owners lay around aplenty. We would select a dead mature nut, which was very light and devoid of water, then husk it and then saw a slit at its weak spot where the shoot would sprout in a healthy nut. We dug out the dried kernel with a thick wire. After that, we gave the nut a thorough rub on sandy ground. The exterior became very smooth and a piggy bank was created.

The Whistle

We made different types of whistles using bamboo stems, coconut leaves, grass blades and other materials. Usually, we cut a leaf blade to a manageable size, folded it into half, then blew through it. We tried this many times until we found the correct angle that provided the best sound.

The Bugle

To make a bugle, we would cut a two-inch green coconut leaf blade and fold it lengthwise into two. Then we would blow through the gap of the fold. It produced a shrill sound. If we wound another green coconut leaf blade around the folded leaf blade then blew through it, a sound with slightly lower resonance was produced. We would continue to wind more leaf blades around the bugle until it got so fat that the leaf blade could not encircle the circumference of the bugle. Then we would get a stout piece of coconut mid-rib and fasten the wound leaf blades in place by poking the coconut mid-rib through the thickness of the circular cone. A bugle was created.

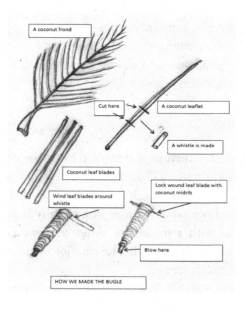

A coconut frond

Cut here → A coconut leaflet

A whistle is made

Coconut leaf blades

Lock wound leaf blade with coconut midrib

Wind leaf blades around whistle

Blow here

HOW WE MADE THE BUGLE

The Flute

We used small bamboo stems as well as the stalks of the papaya leaf to make flutes. We cut holes on the stems to produce different notes. Since we did not have any knowledge of music, we made a cacophony of sounds out of them.

The Lalang Javelin

We used the leaves of lalang grass as javelins. We would cut a stalk of lalang grass then cut off the slack tail end that would prevent the blade from soaring into the air. What remained would be a mid-rib, with blades on either side. From the stalk end, we would peel one side of the blade and discard that. With the other end, we would peel off about three centimetres of the blade. Then using one hand, we would hold the peeled end and throw the stalk in the air. The mid-rib would soar, leaving behind the peeled blade in our hand. We repeated this, trying to outdo our previous throws and also to challenge one another on who could throw their lalang javelin the furthest.

Sometimes, we would play pranks on unsuspecting neighbourhood children. We would pluck a spray of lalang flower then ask one of them to hold the stalk lightly with his lips and close his eyes. We would convince him that he could see the moon in his mind's eyes. As soon as he did that, we would pull the stalk sideways along his lips, leaving him with a mouthful of lalang flowers.

He would spit, trying to get rid of the small flowers sticking to his lips. Fights could ensue if the victim was sensitive. Among friends, we knew who could take such jokes and who could not.

The Yoyo

Different types of yoyos were made. The simplest method was to get a cylindrical piece of wood and cut out the middle section so it became an hourglass shape. Then we tied one end of a piece of gunny string around the narrow middle portion of the wooden piece and wound the string around it. We held the free end of the string and let the wooden piece roll down freely with gravity. When the yoyo had reached the end of the string, we jerked it up. The yoyo would wind itself upward along the string. We repeated this for as long as we liked. Of course, we did not have any other variations like the modern-day yoyo.

We also used rubber seeds to make yoyos. We made two holes on the opposite sides of the seed. We cleared out all the cotyledons (the seed leaves of the plant's embryo) and pushed a short coconut mid-rib about six inches through the seed. Then we made sure the coconut mid-rib could turn freely. We secured it with a rubber seed on each end. The two rubber seeds would act as flywheels. We made a third hole in between the first and second holes, creating a vertical shaft that would meet the inner horizontal shaft between the first and second holes at right angles. With some difficulty, we ran one end of a fairly thick, strong string (no. 20 string at least) through the newly created third hole. We wound the string sufficiently, pulled and released it. The flywheel would turn, freeing the string, and then wind back in the reverse direction. We pulled the string again and repeated the action. We could use other seeds, such as lotus, which had a similar structure, to make this toy.

The Turning Disc

To make this, we flattened a metal bottle cap and punched two holes about three millimetres apart at the middle. We used the metal bottle cap because it had sufficient weight to function as a flywheel. We ran a loop of thick thread through the holes, leaving about a 15-centimetre distance from each end of the disc. We knotted the loose ends and made the thread taut, ensuring they did not get entangled. Then we hooked our middle fingers through each loop end and swung the disc in circles facing us. Both loops on the left and right of the disc would become tightly twisted. When we pulled the strings taut, the disc would spin in one direction, twisting the strings again. We would pull the strings again and the disc would spin in the other direction. We repeated this over and over.

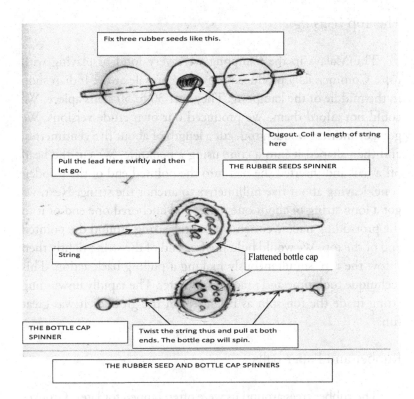

Fix three rubber seeds like this.

Dugout. Coil a length of string here

Pull the lead here swiftly and then let go.

THE RUBBER SEEDS SPINNER

String

Flattened bottle cap

THE BOTTLE CAP SPINNER

Twist the string thus and pull at both ends. The bottle cap will spin.

THE RUBBER SEED AND BOTTLE CAP SPINNERS

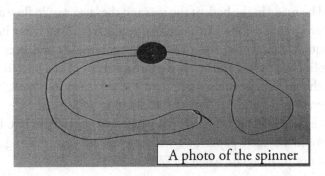

A photo of the spinner

Sometimes, we would hold turning disc challenges among siblings and friends. We would use the turning disc in motion, which had a sharp metal edge, to cut at one another's disc threads. The one whose disc threads snapped was the loser.

The Top (*Gasing*)

The Malays in the kampong were very fond of playing with tops. Commercially produced tops were on sale at the Indian shop in the middle of the kampong. They cost 30 to 50 cents apiece. We could not afford them. We produced our own crude versions. We got a cylindrical wooden rod, cut a length of about five centimetres, and then shaped it into a cone using a penknife. We cut the head off a nail and inserted the nail into the pointed end of the wooden cone, leaving about five millimetres to anchor the string. Next, we got a long string of about one metre and anchored one end of it to the protruding nail. We then wound the string around the pointed end of the top. We would hold the free end of the string tightly then throw the top, simultaneously making a pulling back action. This technique took time and practice to master. The rapidly unwinding string made the top spin as it landed on the ground. It was great fun.

Rubber and Paper Balls

The rubber trees around us were often tapped for latex. Grooves would be made in the bark of the tree and the latex would flow along these grooves and collect in a cup tied to the tree. After a few hours, the liquid latex would coagulate along the grooves and became a soft solid. We pulled and scraped off these strips of coagulated latex from the grooves of rubber trees and shaped them into balls. They had a very good bounce. We played catching with them.

We also collected odd pieces of paper and made them into balls. We would tie each paper ball with a piece of gunny string so it would not disintegrate when kicked.

The Slingshot

Owning and carrying parangs, penknives, sickles, hacksaws and other cutting tools was common in the kampongs. They could be used to chop trees and carve wood into shapes, among other functions. The kampong folks also used them to chop firewood, cut grass for their herds of goats or cows and gather wild fruit and edible herbs. As for us, we needed the kitchen chopper to cut spent banana trunks, as it was much sharper than a parang. We used a parang to cut branches, as it was heavy and thick. A sharp parang would also give the branch a clean cut.

Making a Slingshot

Making a slingshot was not easy. We needed the tools mentioned above.

A slingshot has three parts—two pieces of elastic material, a frame to attach the elastic material and the pocket.

Making the Y-shaped frame depends on the individual's ingenuity. A simple version would be a small, rectangular piece of plank shaped into a Y. Other elaborate versions would be from a stem with two branches growing symmetrically to each other. The main stem should be stout, with a radius of about 1.5 centimetres. One would then shape the two branches into prongs. Wire can be used to force the branches into the desired shape. To make sure the shape stays permanent, heat the prongs with a candle flame. Move the candle to and fro along the branch to get the heat equally distributed. More resourceful people could shape the frame from a cow horn.

Once the shape was fixed, we obtained used bicycle tubing and cut two strips from it, each about 30 centimetres long and one centimetre wide. We did not use motorcycle and motorcar tubes, as they were too hard. A piece of leather, usually from old shoes, was cut to about four centimetres by five centimetres. This would be used as a basket to hurl the projectiles. Then we attached the rubber strips to the prongs of the slingshot with rubber bands.

The projectile or bullet could either be a small pebble or an unripe fruit such as young guava or even a steel ball bearing. We used these slingshots to frighten away birds and other stray animals which wandered into our farm.

Note:

Slingshots are banned in Singapore. Today, Singapore is so crowded that a stray shot from a slingshot may injure a person or damage property. Furthermore, they could be used as weapons. In the early days of Singapore, they were used to shoot wild animals in rural areas.

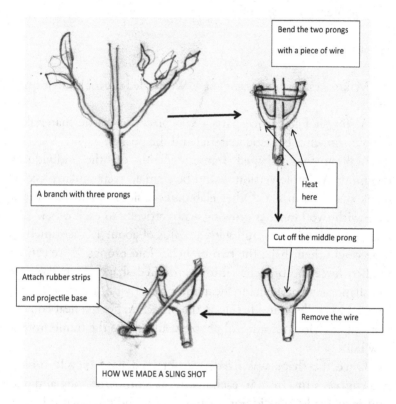

Bend the two prongs with a piece of wire

A branch with three prongs

Heat here

Cut off the middle prong

Attach rubber strips and projectile base

Remove the wire

HOW WE MADE A SLING SHOT

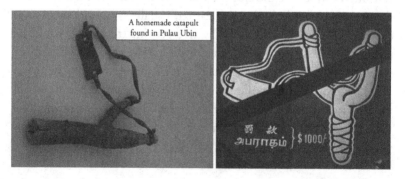

A homemade catapult found in Pulau Ubin

The Tin Can

Different brands of condensed milk were consumed. Milkmaid was the most well known of the brands, but slightly more expensive. It was often dubbed *ang zee* or 'red wording', as it had a few bold Chinese characters printed on the label in red. Images of two coins of an unknown foreign currency were printed on the label too. The coin images were the same size as our local currency ten-cent coin then, which bore the portrait of King George VI. So we often cut out the images of these two foreign coins and pasted them over our local coins and had fun tricking our friends. Next in popularity was the Lifeguard brand with its caricature of an armoured soldier holding a sword. We dubbed it *peng tow* or 'commander'. The Lady General brand was introduced to the Singapore market later.

To extract the milk from a tin, two holes were punctured diametrically opposite to each other at the circumference near the brim. Then we poured the milk out from one end of it. We discovered that it was not possible to pour out the milk if only one hole was punctured. Sometimes, one of the holes was too small and only a small trickle of milk flowed out. One day, Hong Bian had an ingenious idea. He blew in air from one of the holes. Milk gushed out the other hole. We were too young to understand why.

To store the opened can of milk in the larder, we always had half a bowl of water and placed the can in it. Without this set-up, the opened can would be swarming with tiny ants. We thought the milk can standing in a bowl of water was like a castle in ancient times. The water was like a moat protecting the castle from its enemies.

When the milk ran out, the empty can was not thrown away. We opened it with a can opener, lifted the lid and poured hot water into it. There would still be some milk coating the sides. We stirred the water to dissolve the milk and we had another portion of milk to drink.

The empty milk can was still not discarded. We used it for many purposes, one of which was to scoop water or liquid organic fertiliser from pails onto the plants around the courtyard. Another use was as a measure to scoop rice for cooking. My mum would instruct my sister how much rice to cook—"Two cans of rice flush to the brim" or "Two cans of rice tip to the top." My sister would scoop out the rice from a big wooden rice bin and sweep her palm across the brim of the can if she wanted the rice flush with it. She would make a deep scoop with the rice overflowing the brim if she wanted the rice to tip the top.

The empty milk can was also used as a measure for water used to make soup or broth. Sometimes, these cans were used as urns for incense sticks or as candleholders. We removed the label, cut a piece of red paper of equal size to the label and pasted it around the can.

Our lives at that time were never boring. If we had nothing to do, we would puncture a fat nail into the sealed end of two empty tin cans to create two holes. Then we ran a gunny string about two metres long linking one can to the other, and tied each end of the string into a knot under the holes in the centre of the cans. We would set the tin cans with their open ends face down on the ground and we would step onto them. We gripped the string in the centre of each can between our big toe and second toe, so it was just like wearing a Japanese slipper. With our hands, we held the string taut and went clip-clopping about. We were about five or six years old so our feet were small and they remained stable on the cans.

When we got bored of walking on the cans, two of us would each take one of the cans and walk away from each other until the string between us went taut. Then we communicated with each other by speaking through the hole in the centre of the can.

We could play hide and seek with the tin cans too. We put some pebbles inside it, and then hammered the open mouth shut to seal the pebbles inside, thus creating a rattler. Then we identified some players for a game of hide and seek. Someone would shake the rattler and throw it. Then that person would run after the rattler to retrieve it. While this was happening, the others would run and find somewhere to hide. Their time for finding a hiding place was up once the person retrieved the rattler.

Water for poultry was always soiled when poured into open troughs. The chickens would jump in and play with the water. To prevent this, the tin can was put to good use. We removed the lid and punctured some small holes in it, about one centimetre from the rim. Then we filled the can with water and upturned a 10-15 centimetre diameter dish over the can. Then, holding both the can and dish tightly together, we turned them upside down. Water would seep out of the can and fill the dish up to about one centimetre. The chickens would drink the water around the tin can and it would be automatically replenished through the small holes in the can. We would fill the can again when the water ran dry.

On days when the newly planted long bean seeds were germinating, birds, especially the mynahs, were attracted to the shoots. Scarecrows worked only for a short spell to scare them away. We had to gather many empty tin cans of different shapes and sizes to tie into a bundle. We then attached a long rope to the bundle. My dad would hang the bundle in a high, conspicuous place such as a tree or the eave of a hut. We then brought the other end of the rope to a shady spot. When the birds came, we pulled the rope to and fro vigorously. The bundle of different sized cans would produce a variety of tones—jingling, clanking, rattling and rustling. The birds, upon hearing the unfamiliar cacophony, would panic out of their wits and scatter in all directions. We had a good laugh watching their reaction.

Other methods such as using slingshots or dogs to chase them away would harm the seedlings.

What happened to the excess tin cans? They were gathered into a heap. A scrap-metal collector would come and cart them away for a few cents every few months.

The Trundle Wheel

We would get a lid from a big tin of milk powder, punch a hole in the middle then nail it to one end of a stick. In this way, a trundle was made. We would push it around, weaving in and around the house. The purpose was not to measure the distance we covered, as there was no measuring indicator attached. We had a great time.

Later, we even added another wheel. In this second wheel, we punched a hole bigger than the diameter of the stick for the first wheel. We inserted the second wheel horizontally through the stick until it rested flat on the first wheel, which was positioned vertically. When the first wheel turned, its movement made the second wheel resting on top of it move too. We had more fun going around with our toy.

On Chinese New Year, firecrackers could be purchased in abundance. We would light the fuse, upturn a tin can over the lighted cracker, and then move away to a safe distance. When the cracker burst, it forced the tin to shoot up high and then fall. We would challenge each other to see whose tin could shoot up the highest. We experimented with different ways to do this. Sometimes, after waiting for a long time, the cracker did not burst. We discovered that the cracker was a dud. Sometimes, when the explosion was delayed, we would investigate. As soon as we got near it, the cracker exploded. Children frequently got injured that way.

Carts

We cut and nailed pieces of plank together to form a box. Then we got hold of four similar tin covers as wheels. We tied a piece of string to one end of the box, and used it to move sand around the courtyard, at the same time making sounds simulating heavy lorries moving big loads.

We had seen our neighbours pushing around the rims of a bicycle—with the spokes and shafts removed—with a stick. The stick fitted into the groove on the rim, making it easy to control. We did not create that because we did not have a spare bicycle rim.

Pole Vaulting

With a piece of long, sturdy bamboo pole in hand, we pole-vaulted across streams. We felt a great sense of achievement when we made it across. If we failed, we dropped into the water with a splash. We got out of the water and did again and again until we succeeded.

Bows and Arrows

From the toy bows and arrows that we saw at the Indian shops at Bedok as well as from the cowboy films we saw during the School Fund Raising project, we learnt how to make bows and arrows. We got a narrow split bamboo, cut it down to size—about a length of 60 centimetres—and tied one end of it with a gunny string. Then we pulled the string hard until the bamboo bent to a bow shape. We tied the other end of the bamboo tightly with the free end of the string. A bow was made. We used small split bamboos as arrows. Then we went shooting. But that was short-lived. My parents were up in arms about it and explained that it was dangerous because the arrow might hurt somebody. We stopped making and playing with them after that.

Shooting Paper Bullets with Rubber Bands

This was commonly done by every child and still is, even today. But instead of paper bullets, in those days, we used something more lethal—woody twining plant stems. However, these caused too much pain to the victims, so we put a halt to it.

Air Pressure Gun

We used hollow bamboo stems and papaya stalks to make air pressure guns. The piston was made of a small bamboo stick with one end wrapped in wet cloth. To test if it was airtight, we rolled a piece of paper into a tiny ball, wet it and placed it at the firing end of the bamboo stem or papaya stalk. We pushed the piston. The pressure built up in the hollow of the stem pushed out the wet ball of paper with a pop.

The Wooden Clog

Every one of us had a pair of wooden clogs. In those days, every provision shop would sell clogs of different sizes. But one thing in common was its colour. Almost all were red. The plastic piece covering the toes was black. The shopkeepers, as if by common understanding, would string them and hang them either to the left or to the right or on both sides of the shop. A cheaper version—unpainted and with a piece of thick canvas across the toes—was also on sale. But these were very rough. The wearers usually suffered from blisters resulting from the friction between the skin and the canvas.

To make wooden clogs, we cut planks of wood to size and nailed salvaged plastic pieces onto them. But they proved to be uncomfortable and heavy.

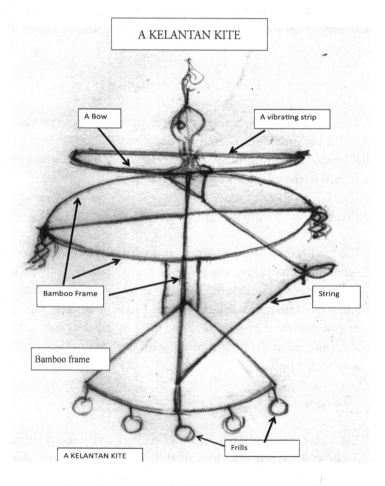

A KELANTAN KITE

A Bow

A vibrating strip

Bamboo Frame

String

Bamboo frame

Frills

A KELANTAN KITE

Paper Folding

We folded paper rockets and aeroplanes, boats, guns and other objects. Many children knew how to make the 'explosive pocket' through a complex series of steps involving folding a piece of tough Manila paper, usually the brown cover of a school exercise book. A few children attempted to make double 'explosive pockets' with 'splinters'. These 'splinters' were small, rolled up pieces of paper. We succeeded in making this if we were patient.

We did not do paper folding much, as we did not have much spare paper around. On religious festivals, we folded coin ingots and boats of different shapes and sizes from joss paper for praying. It was from joss paper that we got a chance to have more practice, because we needed to fold quite a substantial amount for prayers.

Paper-cutting

We did try our hand at paper-cutting, but only on Chinese New Year. We cut characters such as *shi, chun* and *fatt* symmetrically to paste on the sticky cake that mum made. Paper-cutting was not encouraged because it was wasteful.

Shooting Matchsticks

One dangerous toy that we developed was the shooting matchstick. We took four new matchsticks from a box, and wedged two of them—one at each side—at the opposite ends of the box with the match heads pointing upwards. We put the third matchstick horizontally across the ends of these two upright matchsticks, with the match head of the third stick resting on the head of another. We struck the fourth matchstick and lit the two match heads that were resting together. After they burned, the match heads would become ash and the horizontal matchstick would shoot forward.

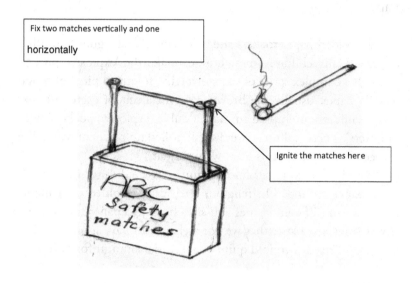

Fix two matches vertically and one horizontally

Ignite the matches here

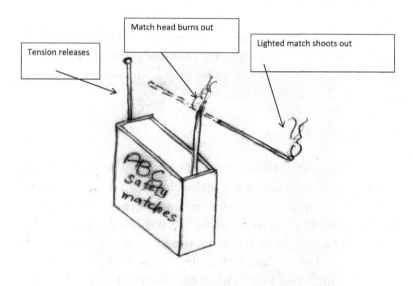

Tension releases

Match head burns out

Lighted match shoots out

How we made the shooting match stick

Masak Masak

My sisters, together with the neighbourhood Malay girls, used to play *masak masak*—make believe cooking—using grass as vegetables and dried grass as fodder for fire to 'cook'.

Rag Dolls

My sisters learnt to sew rag dolls from my mum when she was free. She taught them to cut the rags and stitch them together as dolls with miniature dresses.

The *Chapteh*

Commercially produced *chaptehs* (shuttles) were made from paper and feathers. When wet, they were rendered useless. The paper base disintegrated. We were quick to improvise the making of *chapteh* ourselves. The *chapteh* we made was far more durable. We got punctured rubber tubing from bicycles, motorcycles or cars. Then we cut the tubing into circular discs. We placed one on top of the other. Then we drove a 1.5-inch nail through the centre. On the pointed end of the nail, we tied the stalks of four feathers with a rubber band. We adjusted the four feathers symmetrically, and hey presto! A *chapteh* was created. Later, commercially produced *chapteh* looked much the same as ours except that the rubber base was machine-cut and the feathers were dyed in different colours.

Fads

I did not know how the fads in our day started. Some of them included playing *kuti-kuti* (small plastic animals), homemade toys, cigarette boxes, marbles, rubber bands, tops, kites, *hantam bola*, catching spiders, the guessing game of *ang kong chuah*, which involved numbered picture cards of film scenes, skipping with rubber band ropes, weaving, and braiding using plastic string.

A numbered picture used for the guessing game of *ang kong chuah.*

Some fads could have been started by the manufacturers of the toys involved, such as *kuti-kuti.* When the shops started selling these items, the children would buy them. Then someone would think of how to play with these new toys.

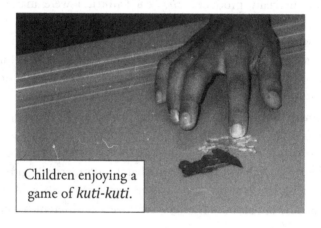

Children enjoying a game of *kuti-kuti.*

The clear plastic animal pieces were named *kuti-kuti* for the flicking action (*kuti* in Malay) involved in a game. The bodies of these animal shapes were usually rounded, so when they lay on a flat surface, one end would tilt upward. To play a game of *kuti-kuti,* each player would select one of their pieces that had a front end tilted higher than the opponent's piece when both pieces were at rest. Then both players would take turns to flick the *kuti-kuti* forward. After each move, the player had to take his finger off the piece. The objective of the game was to flick the piece so that it lands on top of any part of the opponent's piece. If that happened, the opponent's piece belonged to him. Then a new round would start. Those who were not so skilful were the usual losers. Just like with any other fad, all the children in the community would be playing the game. There would be arguments over unfairness, faulty pieces and theft. Parents would lose their tempers because their children would be engrossed in their *kuti-kuti* games and neglect instructions, chores and homework.

If the children had money, they would buy more *kuti-kuti* to play with. In the end, the winners were the shopkeepers and the manufacturers.

Cigarette Boxes

In those days, cigarettes were mostly sold in tens in thin, cardboard boxes just like matchboxes, which had drawers to contain the cigarettes. If a person wished to retrieve a cigarette, he needed to open a flap and push out the drawer. Cigarettes were also sold in tins of fifties. Some brands of cigarettes sold at that time were State Express 555, Torchlight, Player's Navy Cut, Garrick, the Capstan and Craven A—the Black Cat Brand. Children would collect the empty boxes to play with, but adults, especially ladies, would cut them up to make lanterns, baskets and other shapes of different objects, depending on their creativity.

One game that we played using the cigarette boxes was 'First Attack'. This is how we played it:

1. Get a group of players of an indefinite number (too many would be slow and confusing for the players).
2. Get the group to agree on a contribution of cigarette boxes, three, four, five or more per round.
3. Make all the cigarette boxes stand on the sand in a straight row, at intervals of about six inches or more.
4. Draw a home line in front of the row of boxes about five feet away.

5. To determine the order of throws, the players would cast their leads. A lead could be anything that slides or rolls well, such as the base of a glass bottle or a large marble, and is able to knock over a cigarette box. Then, players stand along the home line and cast their leads in the opposite direction to the row of cigarette boxes.

6. The player who casts the lead furthest from the home line gets the first throw at the cigarette boxes, from the position where his lead has stopped. The advantage would be that the player stands to gain all the boxes if he manages to knock over the first box. The disadvantage is that the greater distance between the lead and the boxes decreases the odds of achieving this.

6. If the first player knocks out the first box in position, he gets the rest of the boxes. If he knocks out the second box, he gets all the boxes down the row from the second box onward, and so on for the third and subsequent boxes hit.

7. Next, the player whose lead has stopped second furthest from the home line would get his chance to throw if any cigarette boxes are left standing.

   If there are no boxes left standing, the game is over. If no one knocks over any boxes, the last one who prefers to stay at home (meaning not taking a turn to hit the boxes) would get all the boxes left. That player takes a calculated risk. If he sees that everyone's lead is very far away from the boxes and thinks that no one will be able to make a hit, he may think it wise to stay at 'home'.

The number of cigarette boxes we could collect depended on the smokers around the area. If there were more smokers, then we could likely collect more cigarette boxes. One very good source was the coffee shops. If we were willing to part with cash, we could purchase empty boxes from those willing to part with them.

The preparing of the lead was not an easy job. The best lead should be able to slide to where the player wished it to go. Usually, we would choose a standard-sized bottle, then cut out the base and dull the edges until it became a smooth disc. However, it could get very frustrating if the precious lead broke when colliding with the others.

We would usually practise our skills at throwing and sliding the lead or *goondu* (another term for the lead) during our free time. This game could be played using either rubber bands or marbles too.

A collection of glass marbles. The bigger ones are 'goondus'.

Tops

Tops were a popular game in the early 1950s but their popularity has dwindled over the years. Because of the injuries they caused, schools banned games involving tops. When the game was played in crowded places, especially during recess at schools, tops often landed on children's heads, causing injury. In the early days, a really good quality top made of very hard wood like ironwood or *chengal* was very expensive. It would not break easily nor sustain any indents when hit by an opponent's top.

How a Game of Tops Was Played

First we would draw a circle in the sand. The players would try to spin their tops within the circle. If anyone's top strayed out of the circle, his top would need to be hit by the tops of players who had succeeded entering the circle. These players would aim their spinning tops at the stray top. If the stray top was of low quality, it could not withstand being hit much and it would either crack or split. A skilled top spinner would be able to make the metal point of his top land on his opponent's, creating deep indentations.

The force of knocking the opponent's top could be quite great. When two tops collided, both could fly off in different directions, so passers-by got hit. Those at close range could suffer serious injury. This was one of the main reasons why schools banned top games.

Some people collected tops. One collector I knew was Mr Arif. Wherever he went, he looked for tops.

Rubber Band Game (1)

This game was considered to be a form of gambling by some school authorities, but others saw it as an exercise of skill. Still others saw it as a mathematical game to improve our memory of multiplication tables.

A person—usually someone who had a lot of rubber bands— would be the banker. He dictated the terms. He would choose a rubber band with a small circumference and place it on the floor. Then he would determine a spot by drawing a line, usually 10 to 15 feet away, from which the other players would throw their own rubber bands. He would dictate the number of rubber bands he would pay if anyone could land their rubber band on any part of the circumference of his rubber band on the floor. For any rubber band that landed on his, he would pay its owner, according to what was agreed, maybe three, four, or five rubber bands. He could also set a limit on the number of rubber bands he would pay. Rubber bands that landed beyond the circumference of his rubber band became his winnings. Some skilful children could win handsomely.

I once saw someone use a rubber band to tie a big bundle of rubber bands together. He did this to create a heavier weight, which would increase his chances of hitting the rubber band on the floor. He aimed and then threw. The entire bundle landed snugly in the middle of the banker's rubber band. The banker could only pay him the maximum number, as agreed upon earlier. If a banker wished to attract more players, the throwing distance set would have to be shorter, so the chances of hitting the banker's rubber band would be higher. In such a case, his payment would be less.

If the banker set the throwing distance too far away, few players would take up the challenge because of the low odds of hitting the target. In such a case, the banker would set the payment rate higher. If a player lost everything, he could always buy more rubber bands. In this game, the players must be able to calculate the winnings or payment within seconds, otherwise the other players would complain. Hence, we practised multiplication this way. We also needed to practise our skills at hitting a target if we wanted to win. Finally, to be a successful banker required presence of mind and a keen sense of judgement.

Rubber Band Game (2)

Another way of playing with rubber bands was this:

1. Get a team of two to several players. Too many would slow down the game.
2. Agree on the number of rubber bands each person can contribute to the play.
3. Set up a rack using two mini-poles (usually firm twigs) and stretch a rubber across these poles, two inches above the ground.
4. Balance all the rubber bands flat on the rack.
5. Determine the home line, usually three feet away from the rubber bands in play.
6. Standing behind the home line and facing the opposite direction from the rack of rubber bands, determine the

position of play by shooting/throwing your rubber band. If a person wishes to score first, he will try to shoot his rubber band further than the other players. The person whose rubber band falls furthest from the home line will have the opportunity to score first. He will try to shoot down all the rubber bands from the rack. Those that fall are his winnings. The second player shoots those left on the rack. If the first shooter manages to shoot all of them down, the game is over. Each player contributes the same number of rubber bands once again, and the play is repeated. If no one hits the rubber bands on the rack, the person who choses to stay at the home line and not take a turn will collect all the rubber bands on the rack without having to shoot. We had to be wise to make the decision on whether to stay on the home line or to be a shooter.

Rubber Band Game (3)

String the rubber bands like a long rope and use it as a skipping rope.

There are different variants of play.

Marbles

Marbles could be made of glass, clay, cement or ground from granite rock. The cheapest ones were made from clay and they cracked easily.

Marbles could be played in a similar way to playing games with cigarette boxes or rubber bands.

For marbles, we drew a shape like a capital 'I' on its side on the ground, then placed the marbles closely on the long horizontal line. The rest of the play was the same as playing with rubber bands. One would try to shoot as many marbles as possible out of the I-shape. The marbles which were not hit out of the I-shape would be rearranged for the next shooter. When we were playing with marbles made from limestone, we usually used a more expensive marble made of marble rock as a shooter. It was heavier, smoother and less likely to break on collision with other marbles.

Hantam Bola

To play this game (which means 'hit ball' in Malay):

1. A depression, the depth and size of a soup bowl, was dug in sandy ground. Then a line as agreed on by the players, about six feet away from the hole, was drawn on the ground.
2. The players would try to roll their tennis balls into the depression from behind the line.
3. Once a player's ball entered the depression, he would rush forward, grab his ball and throw it forcefully at any player nearby. He could do this repeatedly if he could get a hit at any player who was still nearby. Sometimes, other players would manage to retrieve his ball before he had a chance to and would throw it at him. When a player was hit by his own ball, the game was over.

Then the play was repeated. This game was quite rough, as it could cause injury at close range.

Flying Kites

During the windy season from May to July, kite flyers from the kampong would come out in droves to fly their kites. It started with the simple, commercially produced fighting kites—two pieces of criss-crossed bamboo strips glued on a square piece of very thin and light paper. A simple coloured design was painted on it. It was sold at 10 cents. The owner could control the movement of the kite by tugging at the string. This type of kite could turn and somersault very fast, according to the whims and fancies of the owner.

The homemade versions were sturdier and heavier. They responded to the owner sluggishly. They were good for stationary flight. The main frame was made of stouter pieces of bamboo. We would run a thin piece of thread round the perimeter of the kite. Then tough, rectangular, tissue-like paper was glued to the thread. A tail was attached to it if the kite was not stable in flight. This type of kite required a fairly strong breeze.

A few of us tried attaching a piece of string to a piece of paper and flying it. We had a whale of a time. We got a piece of exercise book paper and folded it lengthwise into three parts. We tied a piece of short string at two corners of the paper and made a looped knot in the middle of the string. We let this knot hang loosely from the paper, and tied the main string to the loop. We got string of the lightest quality, preferably no. 50 and tied a short tail to stabilise the kite. Our paper 'kite' was ready to fly.

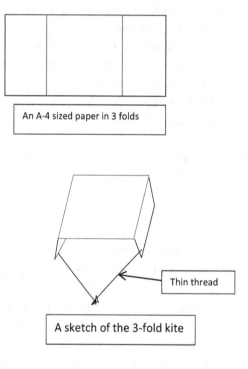

An A-4 sized paper in 3 folds

Thin thread

A sketch of the 3-fold kite

Kite-fighting

In May, the kite-fighting season would start. Kite fighting was different from stationary kite flying. To prepare for kite-fighting, boys would coat their kite strings with glass powder. These were the steps:

1. Get a piece of broken glass.
2. Pound the glass into bits.
3. Sieve the pounded glass.
4. Once there is enough, add starch (usually from cooked rice) to the powder.
5. Mix the mixture thoroughly.
6. Spread out the string by looping it around two poles or trees.
7. Coat the string with the mixture.
8. Wait for the coated string to dry before rolling it around an empty tin (usually a condensed milk tin).

To make the kite, a square piece of paper of 15 by 15 inches was propped up diagonally by a thin bamboo skeleton in the shape of a cross. The intersection of the bamboo pieces was at about the three-quarter point of the vertical piece. Then the skeleton was glued onto very thin rice paper.

Commercially produced kites were painted with simple, standard designs and were on sale at five cents each. This type of kite did not require a stabiliser and could sail, turn and dive according to the wind. It was left to the skill of the flyer to manipulate it using his string. If an opponent's kite was sailing upward, he could make his dive down, until their strings crossed. Both sides would tug at their strings until one of them snapped. This was all part of kite-fighting.

Bystanders would give chase to a stray kite that had escaped its owner. These people carried with them long poles with twigs tied to the top ends. Regardless of danger, with eyes fixed on a stray kite, they climbed across fences, trampled over vegetable beds and carelessly overturned farm tools just to get at the kite. Once the kite was within reach of their poles, they would hit, fight, and pull at the kite until it was in shreds. Then they walked away looking for more strays.

Some children preferred their kites to remain stationary in the air. They fixed a long tail to stabilise it. Kite fighters knew that those were non-competitive kites, so they left them untouched. Such kites could also come in bigger sizes and in various shapes, reinforced with strings at their edges. Such kites needed thicker strings and a stronger, steadier wind. The pulling and releasing of the strings of the kites in flight required much strength and if one was not careful, it might cause burns on the hands due to great friction with the string.

Another type of kite flown at that time was the Kelantan kite or *wau* in Malay. It had its roots in Malacca during the time of the Malacca Sultanate, about six centuries ago. Each kite was huge—from wing tip to wing tip about 1.5 metres and its height was about two metres. When they were all up in the sky, it was a beautiful and exciting sight. Many people from different parts of Singapore who came to my farm always stared at such kites with awe. Such kites produced a sound from a vibrator. The vibrator was shaped from sisal leaves grown in the kampong. A highly taut vibrator would produce a high-pitched sound, whilst a slack one would produce a low *wau* sound.

The making of such kites required skill in trimming the bamboo frames in such a way that it could trap a pocket of air to maintain balance while the kite was in flight. The vibrator and its frame must be light enough so that they would not compromise the flying ability of the kite. The joints must be carefully tied to the grooves so that they would not slip off during flight. The fibrous paper must withstand constant vibrations in the wind. The strings must also be attached in such a way that they can maintain the kite's balance while in flight.

This miniature *wau* kite is owned by the author. The souvenir commemorates the occasion of the 20th APAO Congress held in Kuala Lumpur, 2005.
It was crafted by The World Miniature (M) Sdn.

Other shapes of such types of kites were birds, butterflies, airplanes, boxes and even human figures. Flying the *wau* required a strong and steady wind. At the peak of flying season, there could be about 20 such kites in the sky above the flatland of the newly cut hills overlooking our house. Some kites would sway from left to right and vice versa, producing different tones of sound. Some would remain stationary, making the same monotonous sound— either high or low-pitched. All the sounds combined created an auditory riot that would make us look up at these kites in awe. The kite flyers would sometimes tie their kites at the foot of palm trees or at the pillars of their houses. Sometimes, the kites stayed up in the sky until it turned dark before their owners brought them down. As young children, we would stand, squat, sit or lie on the ground to watch the kites as well as their owners. Among them were Hassan, Said, Panjang, and the popular 'Fat Sentry'.

Occasionally, some of the kites were difficult to fly. The owners would withdraw to make adjustments to them. Some just fell and got entangled among the big trees in front of our house. The owners traced them by following the strings. Once they recovered them, they detached the ends of the string that were fixed to the kite. The ends of the string were left there until the owners reached the kampong. Once home, they reeled in the string.

Watching such activities was one of the most enjoyable parts of my life. After we moved out of Tanah Merah Kechil, up until now, I have not seen such activities.

My brother Hong Bian once made a *wau* kite, but it was not very successful. The children of the kampong folks jeered at him and made sarcastic remarks. Well, kite flying was not everyone's cup of tea.

Other Games

The men in the kampong, when they were not flying kites, organised football games among themselves. The venue was always the same—part of the flattened land next to my farm. It was slightly undulating, with potholes here and there. There were little shrubs with patches of grass. The goalposts were self-made.

We children had our football games too. Hong Bian had accumulated enough money to buy a leather football. Our players included Kow Kiah, Ter Kiah, Ah Lim and the three of us boy siblings.

While the boys were playing their own games and activities, the girls had theirs too. They played hopscotch, five stones, skipping with a rope made of linked rubber bands, *masak-masak* and made dolls from remnants of cloth.

If we saw anybody in school playing with their homemade toys, we would go home and try to make them ourselves.

The Auto Wheel

From the empty wooden thread reel, we could make a wheel that moved by itself.

Method:

1. Get an empty wooden thread reel.
2. Cut grooves into the rims on both sides of the reel.
3. Smear one end of the reel evenly with wax.
4. Put a rubber band through the hole of the reel.
5. Lock the loop with a small pin made from a coconut mid-rib.
6. Pull the rubber band through out other end, which is smeared with wax. Pull it tight, and then tie the rubber band to the end of a thin stick. The other free end of the stick will function as a handle.
7. Rotate the handle to wind up the rubber band.
8. Leave the set-up on the table.
9. Once the handle is released, the set-up will move by itself.

Catching Spiders

Catching spiders was another fad in our days.

The fighting spiders were black, with two long front legs. The brown spiders were not what we wanted. We called them 'devil spiders'.

We would use matchboxes, cigarette boxes and Elastoplast boxes to keep our pet spiders in.

After school, we would go to the bushes to search for leaves that were overlapping. Spiders usually made their nests here.

If we found overlapping leaves, we would gently lift the upper leaf. If there were a spider, we would determine the sex. We determined the sex by looking at the abdomen. If the abdomen was fat, it was a female. If the abdomen was slender, it was a male. If it was female, we would release it.

Then we trained them to fight. We did this simply by releasing one male spider near another. There were practice rounds with our spiders.

Then after gaining confidence that we could win, we let it fight with our friends' spiders. We let them fight on a bigger platform, like the lid of the Elastoplast box.

The loser would run away after a bout. The winner would stay on the surface of the lid, waiting to jump onto his master's finger. The master would then let it hop into its hiding place among the fresh green leaves in his container.

Sometimes an aggressive spider would kill its opponent. If one spider kept winning, he was crowned 'The Spider King'.

We children did not know then if it was cruel or not. We just wanted to have fun.

The Green Beetle

There was one particular type of green beetle, the size of part of our thumb, which lived among the leaves of the star fruit trees. We would search for them and catch them.

Then, we would tie a string on one of the beetle's six legs. Tying a string to its legs was one of the biggest challenges. The beetle would struggle. The claws on its legs would become entangled in our thread. We had to attempt it numerous times before we succeeded in tying the string to one of its legs. Sometimes, we achieved it perhaps by fluke.

Then, we would throw the beetle up to let it fly with the string attached.

We held on to the string and followed it to wherever it flew or until the string fell off.

We tried it with a bigger type of beetle too. There was one particular brown type the size of the whole thumb. We could find it among the taller trees, such as rambutan or jackfuit. This beetle provided a greater challenge, as it was bigger and stronger. The claws on the legs were very sharp. If the claws ever caught on our skin, they were painful to get off. Should we succeed in tying string to its legs, it would fly with such vigour, until the string slipped out of our hands. The beetle would fly to the trees with the string attached to its leg.

We did the same with dragonflies.

Grasshopper Catchers

Do you know that some people caught grasshoppers for a living? There were some people who went around carrying a small container with a netted lid and a small net, looking for grasshoppers. They sold them to the bird shop as food for the birds. We welcomed these people because grasshoppers were pests. Unlike butterflies or the bees, which can pollinate the flowers, the voracious grasshoppers destroyed our crops both during their nymph and adult stages. Grasshoppers looked hideous, with their two huge, bulging eyes and big mandibles. Their two large back legs could give us a painful kick during take off.

One way of having fun with grasshoppers was to catch them and break off their two hind legs. We would watch the reflex actions of the hind legs, twitching after they were detached. Without its hind legs, the grasshopper could not take off, but it could move very quickly away and hide under the leaves. Then we had problems searching for it again. On further investigation, we would realise it had changed its colour. When hiding in green leaves, it was green. When hiding in dead leaves, its colour changed to brown.

Shooting and Catching Birds

With friends around, sometimes we got together to make slingshots (called *lastik* in Malay) and gather unripe guava fruit as bullets. Then we went shooting. The birds, especially the mynahs and the white-headed bulbuls, came hunting not only for worms and grasshoppers; they also ate up the shoots and the buds of flowers and plants. So we went on shooting sprees. But the disadvantage was that we could accidentally damage our plants as we shot at the birds.

Sometimes, we got out of hand and shot at any birds we saw. Once, I shot a tiny bird. It was a mother. It died instantly. The baby bird near it could hardly fly. It was chirping bitterly and was struggling to search for its mother. I walked away feeling very miserable. I had killed an innocent bird, causing a baby bird to be an orphan. I felt very guilty. From that day onward, I refused to kill any birds. We are human but we must not let our desire for fun get the better of us.

Once we caught a baby mynah. It could hardly fly. We got a cage for it and fed it with rice. We filled a little shallow bottle with water and cleared the bird's droppings every day. We taught it how to sing. Most often, it made its own noises, to the delight of everyone. Usually it had fun with its feathers by making them very fluffy.

Catching Fish

As we owned several ponds, we had ample opportunity to catch fish. With a wicker basket in hand, we would go to the bank of our main pond. We shoved the basket underneath the floating weeds and stepped on the weed stems a few times. That would drive the fish out of their hiding places into the basket. Then we raised the basket. Little fish would be leaping up and down. We caught the big ones and put them into a bottle and released the small ones. The fish, which we called *ikan belaga*, were like the size of a fighting fish (four to five centimetres), but they were not as colourful. Other creatures we caught were the tadpoles of frogs and toads, dragonfly nymphs, water spiders, tilapia (also known as Japanese fish and Java fish), baby snakehead, tortoise and catfish.

I was not particularly interested in catching fish, but Hong Bian was. He went out of the way to get separate bottles for each fish, feed them and when they spawned, separate them.

Almost every morning, we could hear the cackle of the kingfishers, the splashing of water by fish, the cry of frogs being caught by snakes, and the calls of water fowl. The sounds of these creatures are forever etched in my mind. As one approached nearer to the pond, there was a hive of activity. The damselfly, the dragonfly and the butterfly were all fluttering about and engaging in their various activities.

Keeping Pets

It was really fun to watch and play with our pets. But we also had to think of their welfare. We had to keep them healthy, keep their surroundings clean and care for them when they were sick. During changes in the weather conditions, we had to see that the temperature of their environment was well regulated. The work was tremendous. Before one decides to keep a pet, one must be prepared to sacrifice money, time and energy.

Chapter 7
My Memories of Kampong Eunos

My grandma was particularly fond of Kampong Eunos. It was where she first settled when she reached *Selat Por* (the word for 'Singapore' in a mixture of Hokkien and Malay) shore from Chinkang, Fukien, China. As soon as my grandparents and my grandpa's siblings reached Kampong Eunos, they cleared the land and attap houses were built. My uncle Yeo Koon Seng was only three years old then. My aunt and my dad were both born here. My dad, Yeo Koon Poh, enrolled in the Telok Kurau Primary School and studied for two years before switching to a Chinese school.

My grandparents built attap houses and pigsties, dug ponds to rear fish and grew water hyacinth as pig food. My grandpa reared cows to pull bullock carts to provide transport services. When Chew Joo Chiat embarked on building attap houses on his coconut and fruit estate, building materials were in great demand. My dad went to work for Sim Seng, a company dealing with building construction materials, whose owner was Soon Peng Leong, the brother of Soon Peng Yam. My grandpa transported building materials on a bullock cart from the timber yard at Geylang to the construction sites. After my dad's marriage, my grandparents and parents moved to Tanah Merah Kechil where we all lived in one house.

In the 1920s, there was a surge in demand for rented rooms, as more immigrants came to Singapore. My grandparents added a room to the left and a room to the right and a few rooms at the rear of their house in Kampong Eunos. Similarly, my other relatives did the same with their houses. Singapore's population grew. The lanes became very small due to the addition of rooms outward from each house. When it rained, the water from the roofs splashed onto the sides of the lanes, making them waterlogged. During heavy rainy weather, they became mini streams. Walking along such lanes on rainy days was a hassle. One had to look out for mud pools, dog poo and pig dung. Cyclists and motorists negotiating the ruts often splashed mud onto unsuspecting pedestrians.

During festivals such as Chinese New Year, Dumpling Festival, Mid-autumn Festival, or the birthday of the deity Seong Teh Kong, grandma would take us to Kampong Eunos. The Seong Teh Kong Temple staged *wayang* shows twice a year. Before the show, a *wayang* stage was put up. It was constructed mainly of attap and logs of mangrove stems. They were tied together with split rattan. The stage floor was laid with planks. Colourful decorations and partitions were made by the *wayang* troupe. The left and right wings were for the musicians as well as for storage for their paraphernalia. Long painting scrolls depicting the theme of the day's performances were held up by pulleys above the stage. The back of the stage was reserved for the actors and actresses to do their make up. The rear, left, and right wings of the stage were boarded up to keep out prying eyes. The electricity supply came from a huge, noisy diesel generator stationed in an obscure corner away from the audience.

Usually, all the temples around Kampong Eunos would stage *wayang* shows for two days successively. If temple devotees wished to give thanks to the gods, they might sponsor another day of *wayang* performance. Every year, the temple committee would appoint a *tow kay* and *lor chu* (committee members) to oversee donations for staging the *wayangs*. The *lor chu* would go around soliciting donations. Receipts were issued to the donors.

My grandma usually took me along with her on visits to Kampong Eunos more often than my other siblings. Most likely, it was because I was older and easier to manage. As we walked along the muddy track to my uncle's house, we could hear the blare of Hokkien and Teochew opera programmes coming from the Rediffusion sets of the residents. Most likely the programmes were scheduled at about 10 a.m. daily—the time we usually reached

Kampong Eunos. On rainy days, we had to be especially careful. One slip of the foot would land one into the muddy stream, which was flanked by water burheads and dumb cane.

In every house, Rediffusion sets provided audio entertainment. The picture above shows some Rediffusion programmes of the 1970s.

My grandma would visit her old neighbours and introduce me to them. As if it was a natural reflex, each neighbour would present me with either a 555 cigarette tin or an empty milk tin containing 12 pieces of rolled up paper, each with a number written on it. They would ask me to pick two numbers, one at a time. The residents of the whole kampongs were playing a game of *chap-ji-ki* lottery. The neighbour would unroll the paper to read the number on it, then throw it back into the can. She would give it a vigorous shake then I would choose a second piece. She would read that then return the can to its place, usually among the joss paper and joss sticks on the altar table. The punter was counting on me to give her luck. She placed her bets through a runner, usually before 5 p.m. The runners brought all the bets to the banker. The banker decided which two numbers to release after calculating his maximum gain of the day.

In the evening, the fans of Ong Toh, the Hokkien storyteller on Rediffusion, would gather at my uncle's house or whomever's house had a Rediffusion set, to listen to the programme. Everyone listened attentively as the storyteller recounted the tales in a very interesting manner. At the end of the programme, he would stop at a very exciting part of the story. This would entice the fans to listen to the upcoming chapter the following evening.

My aunt, whom we called Ah Nia, was Peranakan. She used to get her children to buy coffee from the kampong coffee shop every morning for breakfast. She did the same even for her guests. It seemed to me she had never brewed coffee herself. Unlike where I lived in Kampong Tanah Merah Kechil, Kampong Eunos was a hive of activity. As early as 5 a.m., there were hawkers calling out their wares—the *nasi lemak* sellers, the bakers, *puttu mayam* sellers, and the noodle seller. There was a particular hawker I remember. He rode his tricycle about the kampong. His assistant would carry a piece of wood and a knocker. The curved piece of wood was usually made of bamboo. When knocked, it produced a very clear, loud resonance over a great distance. The attendant would usually knock out a tune different from the other hawkers. Customers would recognise his tune. If they liked his noodles, they would shout for him, *"Hey! Mee!"* or simply *"Mee-ah!"* If they got the attention of the hawker's assistant, the customers would then shout out their orders from where they were, which could be at a neighbour's house. Then the assistant would go to the hawker to place the order. Later the assistant would deliver the food to the customers, then go on knocking his two wooden pieces. After a while, the assistant would return to collect the empty bowls and payment—usually 20 cents per bowl.

There was a particular kampong dweller, as well as a close family friend, named Ah Poh. He was a well-informed man. I think this close affinity must have stretched back to my grandparents' days. He was very jovial and often discussed traditional medicine with my grandma whenever they met. Ah Poh was a multitasker. He was steeped in knowledge of Mandarin, herbal medicine as well as worldly affairs, making him particularly well-liked by the kampong folks. He switched from job to job. Once, he sold stewed duck, carrying it in two baskets slung on a pole across his shoulders. Kampong folks would gamble with him using three dice on a dish. Before gambling, he would discuss the method of play and the wager amount—ten cents for a duck head, 50 cents for a drumstick, $1 for half a duck, or $2 for the whole duck. If the customer lost, they paid for the amount as agreed. If the customer won, Ah Poh would give them the piece of duck agreed upon.

Whenever my dad visited his brother, Koon Seng, he would patronise a noodle stall which was stationed at a corner of my uncle's row of attap houses. It was as if a visit to Kampong Eunos would not be complete without a visit to that stall. That hawker sold only *meepok* noodle soup. One must eat his noodles piping hot; only then could you could enjoy the rich aroma coming from the pork seasoning as well the fried onion oil and soup. The three-layered belly pork was finely chopped and seasoned with a secret recipe. He made the *'kiau'* or *'pian sip'* (similar to *wanton* but stuffed with seasoned pork) himself, occasionally helped by his wife. The thin *pian sip* skin was a three-inch by three-inch square. The chopped pork was spread on to the skin and then folded diagonally into a triangle. His fresh red chilli was sliced by a razor-sharp kitchen knife. His soup had a lasting aftertaste. We never saw how he prepared his soup, but we guessed that he must have done a lot of trial and error before he got it right. When an order was taken, he would first get a handful of uncooked *meepok* noodles. Then he scooped the seasoned chopped pork and a few pieces of *pian sip* into the bowl. Next, he immersed the cooked *meepok* into cold water and boiled it again. After that, he poured the boiling hot soup in the bowl which contained the chopped pork then added the cooked *meepok*. Pepper and a pinch of fried chopped onion leaves were added. It was ready to serve. By the time the bowl of steamy noodles had reached the customer, the pork was already cooked and the temperature was just right for the taste buds. The cooked pork, the steamy soup, coupled with the soft spicy pepper, the sliced chilli and the fried onion oil made the taste heavenly. Words could not describe fully how tasty it was. One could finish the whole bowl within minutes. At peak hours, one had to wait for at least half an hour to get a bowl. The hawker was a tall, slender man from Chao Ann, China. It was not known whether the dish was concocted by him. As he grew older, he hunched so customers used to call his noodle *ku mee* or *kieow ku mee,* meaning 'hunchback noodles'. His descendants now sell his noodles in many coffee shops and hawker centres in Bedok. They name it *bak chor mee.*

Ku mee or *bak chor mee* has many descendants in Bedok. This picture shows the author patronising one of the stalls.

One evening, I visited my cousins Hong Huat and Eng Teng, who invited me out for supper. We walked through the twisting narrow sandy lanes between attap houses. Then we came to a row of houses that formed the shape of a 'U'. In the middle were several rows of crude makeshift tables and benches and a food stall. We waited after ordering. Within a few minutes the dry version of *wanton* noodles with thinly sliced *char siew* arrived. We tucked in. I felt that it was the best *wanton* noodles I had ever eaten. The noodle was springy but not hard. The chilli was tongue-burning but we loved it. The *wanton* was soft, smooth and juicy. They exuded an aftertaste of spiciness and sweetness. We tucked in non-stop, as if by stopping, the delicious flavour would be lost. Soon our porcelain bowls were empty. We proceeded to drink the soup. The mildly salty and spicy soup, sprinkled with a pinch of onion leaves, washed down every morsel. I left the stall with the wonderful aftertaste lingering in my mouth for hours. When the site that this hawker, Mr Ng Ba Eng, operated out of was being redeveloped, he was allocated a stall at Dunman Food Centre. His signboard said 'Eng's Char Siew and Wan Ton Mee'. In 2012, he shifted to Tanjong Katong Road. Mr Ng Ba Eng died on Monday, 17 June, 2013. He was named a Singapore Hawker Master for his *wanton* noodles in 2011. The annual award is given to top hawkers by *The Straits Times* and *Lianhe Zaobao* newspapers.

Unlike my dad's place in Tanah Merah Kechil, the houses in Kampong Eunos were built very close together. A toilet was constructed beside the pond. With so many residents, a single toilet was naturally not enough to cater for everyone. Later, another toilet was constructed on the left of the courtyard under the old mangrove tree. One had to walk up a few steps before going into the toilet. A pungent smell and buzzing houseflies greeted the visitor if he or she went in before the bucket was emptied.

A toilet bucket

Usually, one would either smoke or hold a handkerchief to the nose to dull the smell. A more sensitive person would be kept busy shooing the flies away from the exposed parts of his body. Cleaning was done with either old newspapers or toilet paper. Woe betide the person who forgot to bring his or her toiletries. He or she would shout or scream for a kind soul to get him or her some.

The night soil bucket was emptied once a day by a collector. The owner of the toilet would have to pay him monthly to take the night soil away. The collector carried a shoulder pole with a large metal bin balanced on each end of it. If one bin was heavier than the other, he had to shift his pole so the heavier side was nearer his body. It was not very pleasant if one was inside the toilet when he came along to empty the bucket. When the two metal tins were filled, he carried them to the farms to sell to the farmers. Some people would mention in jest that the night soil carrier earned double wages— owners paid him to clear their toilets, and he got paid by the farmers when he disposed of the night soil.

One incident that is deeply etched in my mind was when some school brats came to learn who the children of the night soil carriers were. They would taunt these children '*Toh Sai Kia! Toh Sai Kia!*' in Hokkien ('Sons of a night soil carrier.') The children were so devastated that they refused to go to school. In those days, some teachers were also not very sensitive. When entering the parents' occupations in the school attendance registers, they literally wrote 'night soil carrier'. I believed many children were emotionally affected by this, as such an occupation, although noble, was not very pleasant. Some considerate teachers recorded this occupation as 'health worker', which I thought was more appropriate.

I must also mention the fruit estate behind the row of shop houses belonging to Yeo Teow Swee. My grandpa, besides rearing fowl and pigs and owning a bullock cart for transport, was also a fruit trader. When the fruit in the estate was in season, he would go scouting for the trees that bore the most number of young, unripe fruit. Then he would farm (reserve) the fruit of that whole tree by making an initial payment to the landowner. When the fruits were ripe, he built a little hut at the estate to keep watch for fruit thieves. He paid the tree owner the rest of the agreed sum once the fruit had been harvested and sold. Some of the fruits were rambutans, mangosteens and durians.

The row of attap houses that Yeo Teow Swee built was exactly opposite the T-junction of Changi Road with Telok Kurau Road.

Whenever we took the Changi bus to Kampong Eunos, my grandma would point to the row of attap houses and say, "We can alight at the bus stop in front of the row of attap houses." So we always did that on subsequent visits. Once, I accompanied my mum there. After alighting from the bus stop, we crossed to the left side of the road. We stopped at the white line in the middle of the road. Suddenly out of nowhere, a motorcyclist with a pillion rider sped by and collided into my mum, who was carrying Hong Hup in her arm. They suffered bruises. The motorcyclist and his pillion rider helped them up and I recognised that they were teachers in Bedok Boys' School. Fortunately, my mum and my brother were not seriously injured.

Yeo Teow Swee had made a name in Kampong Eunos by contracting to supply cleaning materials such as rags and brooms as well as *changkol* handles to the Public Works Department. In this way, we in Tanah Merah Kechil also came to play a part, by acting as a collecting agent for him. That row of houses evoked certain memories in me. There was a coffee shop which was managed by Chew, who lost his leg in an accident. In the coffee shop, there was a huge stove and a big cauldron. Sawdust was used to boil water. Just like any other coffee shop in those days, there were several round marble tables, and around each round table were several wooden chairs. Adjacent to the coffee shop was a provision shop which was managed by Yeo Teow Swee's second son, named Koon Sai. To the left was a tailor. My dad usually got his pants tailored there. I got a few of my pants made there too. Across the road, to the right of Telok Kurau Road, was a bakery. It used charcoal to bake the bread. When the bread was taken out of the oven, the top part of the loaf was usually burnt. The baker would then cut away the burnt part, slice the remaining loaf and wrap it with translucent paper. Coffee shop owners in that area got their bread from that bakery. Whenever we bought bread from him, we would mention the name of the coffee shop and we would get a special discount. It's likely the baker thought we were also retailers so he sold us the bread at a wholesale price. Next to that bakery was a barbershop, which my dad used to patronise.

Yeo Teow Swee, although not literate, had very good business acumen. Besides supplying cleaning materials to the PWD, he built and rented out houses and owned shops; he was also the overseer of the land in Tanah Merah Kechil where we lived. Later, he ventured into rambutan planting as well as fowl and pig rearing. His children, although they had better lives than his nephews and nieces, were not pampered either. They were roped in to help him run his businesses. In 1957, he died after a short illness. The children took over all his businesses.

Describing Kampong Eunos would not be complete if the famed landowner, Chew Joo Chiat, were not mentioned, as he was a major landowner there. His descendants lived in Kampong Eunos, a few doors away from my uncle's house. I had never interacted with them, but my cousins, especially Hong Ho, did as they attended the same school. One of them he mentioned was Chew Peng Hock. Joo Chiat's descendants lived in different areas of Joo Chiat. One of these families—Chew Cheng Chuan's—even lived in Kampong Chai Chee, which my dad often talked about. Many years later, I came in contact with a fellow blogger, Philip Chew, and his cousin Ivan Chew, who are the great grandchildren of Chew Joo Chiat.

In 1968, a row of attap houses near the main road caught fire. Yap Swee Cheng and his wife Teo Beng Khim, the daughter of the maternal granddaughter of Chew Joo Chiat, lived in one of the houses. Their children, Rosalind, Doris, Helen, Richard, Charles and George, who were in their formative years then, later said the fire was so intense that it leapt from one building to another. Several houses were burnt down. It was reported in one of the Chinese newspapers that the then Prime Minister, Mr Lee Kuan Yew, visited the site. Helen's fourth aunt was in the photo in the Chinese newspaper article on the fire too.

As recounted by Yeo Hong Huat, my cousin, the citizens donated cash to build a community centre at the site of the fire. Now the site is rented to the Academy of Fine Arts. In the early 1960s, a developer took over the land fronting Changi Road 5 Milestone, and the row of attap houses was demolished. I remember helping to load some of the timber of the long row of houses onto a lorry and bringing it to Tanah Merah Kechil for firewood. Now, in its place, there is a row of double-storeyed concrete shop houses.

This piece of land, together with the house at Kampong Eunos was acquired by the government in the 1980s, as it encroached on the East West MRT Line.

Activities in Kampong Eunos
Photo credit: Philip Chew

Chapter 8
The Japanese Occupation:
15 February 1942-12 September 1945

I was born in 1946 so I only saw the remnants of the Japanese Occupation legacy—the pillboxes and bunkers, the Japanese factory along East Coast Road, the collapsed air raid shelter, the aluminium shelf with kanji characters, my Japanese birth certificate, Japanese soldiers' caps and helmets, a Japanese doll given to my sister, the Japanese postage stamps and currency notes, and the ration card. I did not experience the atrocities of their rule. What I know of it was told to me by my parents, relatives and friends who had lived through those hellish three and a half years.

Before the War

The Japanese declared war on China after the Marco Polo Bridge Incident on 7 July 1937. There are differing versions of this but the event in Beijing near the Marco Polo Bridge began when a Japanese commander found one of his troops missing and believed the Chinese had kidnapped him. While in search of the missing Japanese soldier, a shot rang out, yet whether it was fired by the Japanese or Chinese and why still remains unclear. It was believed by some to be an excuse for the Japanese to declare all-out war on China. While war was raging in China, emotions ran high in Malaya and Singapore. The Chinese people in Malaya and Singapore began donating money for the China Relief Fund.

My dad sold flowers and sang patriotic songs and played the flute and harmonica in a concert to help raise funds for China. Even when the war was over, many years later, we would often hear him sing the anti-Japanese and Chinese revolutionary songs as well as play music on his favourite instruments, the harmonica and the flute. Then, he would explain the significance of the songs he was singing to us.

There was also a group of people who went around exposing vendors or buyers of Japanese goods. Such people, when caught, were shamed in public.

Two men, who called themselves Abdul and Dollah, were reportedly seen around the vicinity of kampong Tanah Merah Kechil, selling cigarettes and candy on trays suspended from their necks. They did not look like Malays, although they introduced themselves as Malays. My father thought they were more likely Japanese agents trying to collect information about British military installations and anti-Japanese war campaigners who were against the Japanese military. It was also known that Japanese secret agents disguised themselves as photographers, taxi drivers, grass cutters and provision suppliers, among other occupations, to gain entry into the homes of unsuspecting British officers to gather information on British troop movements.

We were told that when the Japanese landed in Kota Baru, every civilian there was making preparations in the event that the Japanese took over. News of the Japanese atrocities in China spread like wildfire to every Chinese household there. The parents of unmarried girls hurriedly betrothed their daughters to any eligible young men. Food was hoarded. Shopkeepers sold their basic necessities at exorbitant prices. Meanwhile, the British army was looking for volunteers to help defend Singapore. Basic military training was provided. Mr Tan Kah Kee, the philanthropist, brought volunteers of the Kuomindang political party founded by Sun Yat-sen and the Communists together under a banner called the Chung Kuo Council. These volunteers were lightly armed by the British, but they were also asked to bring with them whatever weapons they had, such as rifles, knives and swords. In those days, rifles for shooting wild animals were accessible to the public.

Meanwhile, in January 1942, Chinese New Year was coming. The Chinese however, were in no mood to prepare for that occasion. Pillboxes and bunkers were constructed all along the southern coast, from Changi to Telok Blangah, including Pulau Blakang Mati. The British expected the Japanese to attack via the southern coast.

On 31 January 1942, the withdrawing British troops crossed the causeway that connected Johore to Singapore and then destroyed a 50-metre section of it to prevent the Japanese from crossing over. Meanwhile, the British army was ordered to destroy anything that could be of use to the Japanese military. It was their 'Scorch Earth Policy'. Pulau Bukom, the oil refinery, was set ablaze. It kept burning for days. Non-military personnel, wives and children of British officers, and non-combatants were packed on board crowded ships and sent away to Ceylon and India. There were massive traffic jams in town leading to Keppel Road for days.

On 7 February 1942, a small section of Japanese soldiers landed on Pulau Ubin. That offshore island was poorly defended. The British army moved their men at night by trucks to Pulau Ubin. The moving trucks created such a din that the residents could not sleep. My dad recounted that a section of Australian soldiers stopped at his coconut estate, collected the dry coconut fronds, and made a huge bonfire. The reason? It could have been part of the war strategy.

The next day, the trucks returned. It seemed that the attack via Pulau Ubin was a ruse created by the Japanese. Meanwhile, the Japanese bombing missions were kept up—in the docks, airfields, shipyards, as well as residential areas. My parents and those living in the kampong at Tanah Merah Kechil watched the sight from the ridge with heavy hearts. Sounds of sirens could be heard. Every day, they inspected the trenches they had dug. Dry runs were made to see how fast they could get to them should their houses get raided.

On the night of 8 February 1942, the Japanese swum across the Straits of Singapore to Sarimbun Beach in the west of the island. The next day, they gained control of the causeway and immediately set to repair it. The repairs were completed in four days. The Japanese were checked at Bukit Timah by the remnants of the British forces, which consisted of Australians, New Zealanders, Indians, as well as the determined forces of the Chinese volunteers. On 11 February, Bukit Timah fell. The Japanese were furious at the heavy losses they suffered. General Yamashita declared that all Chinese within a five-mile area from Bukit Timah must die. The Japanese soldiers went about shooting every Chinese person—man, woman or child. The residents hid in the jungle by day and moved out by night. The cries of children and the barking of dogs were the giveaway signs. The Japanese promptly moved in and finished them off as soon as they were spotted. Those who escaped from the area found that some of their family members were missing. They lost them while moving in the night.

On 15 February 1942, Singapore surrendered to the Japanese. It was the first day of the Chinese New Year. Lieutenant General Tomoyuki Yamashita insisted that Lieutenant General Arthur Percival, the commander of the Allied forces in Singapore, surrender to him unconditionally at the Ford factory along Bukit Timah Road. The Japanese commander heaved a great sigh of relief as his war resources were depleted. If the British had decided to fight for a few more days, the Japanese might have lost the war.

Singapore was named Syonan-to (昭南島) by the Japanese. It means 'Light of the South'.

For the next three and a half years, it was hell for the remaining British troops and the populace.

The prisoners of war were kept in Changi Prison. Food was scarce. Diseases were widespread and medical treatment was almost non-existent. The majority of them were sent to the Burma-Thailand border at Kanchanaburi to build a railway to connect Burma. Many Chinese, Malays and Indians were also forced to go. Those who refused had their heads chopped off. Tales of horrific treatment at the hands of the commanders there were worse than the stories of life in Changi prison. While at Changi, the POWs were made to do odd-job duties around town. Once some of them were taken to Tanah Merah Kechil to do manual work. They looked so pathetic.

One of them asked my grandma for water. She asked my sister to hand a cup of water to the man when the Japanese commander was not looking. After drinking, he said he was an Australian and was grateful to us.

The members of my family were lucky to escape from *sook ching* (literally meaning 'purge' or 'exterminate' in Chinese). My dad conjectured that farmers were not among the wanted groups of people, as they were the food suppliers. Without the farmers, the whole nation would suffer a worse fate. Chinese aged from 18 to 50 years who lived in the Changi area had to assemble at the Telok Kurau School. Chinese living elsewhere had to report to other centres. At the centre, hooded Chinese informers and Japanese *kempetai* (secret military police) officers would examine each one and determine their fates. Civil servants, anti-Japanese leaders, teachers and people with tattoos were identified by a nod from the Japanese informers and were taken to lorries to be tied up with steel wire. Those who were released were given a stamp—anywhere if there weren't pieces of paper around. The Japanese stamped their hands or palms or any parts of their bodies they wished with the character 'examined'. In order to preserve the stamps on their bodies, the people released had to be careful not to wash them off. If a Japanese soldier demanded to see their stamps and they could not produce them, they could be arrested.

By the time the Japanese enforced *sook ching*, many anti-Japanese insurgents had already escaped by sea and later returned to the Malayan jungles to fight against them.

Meanwhile, the Japanese took no chances. The *kempetai* enlisted Chinese informers to identify anti-Japanese insurgents still present in Singapore. Once a suspect had been named, the Japanese soldiers would go to the address provided to search for him. If the doors were locked, they would kick them open and ransack the whole house. If found hiding at home, he would be taken away for interrogation. Should there be any protests, the soldiers would not hesitate to use rifle butts to subdue them. Should a frightened baby cry incessantly, the soldiers would lift the baby by the arm and toss it in the air. The soldiers would point their bayonets upwards so the baby would land on these blades.

If someone were caught listening to the broadcasts by the Allied forces, a pencil would be forced into the person's ear canal. Other methods of torture including the dunking of head of the victim into water until there was a confession. If a confession was not forthcoming, he would be pushed on to the floor and a soldier would step on his bloated stomach. There were instances where needles were inserted into the victim's fingertips. Many other methods were used by individual soldiers and officers.

During that impoverished time, many opportunists tried to get into the Japanese officers' good books and gain employment. They betrayed their relatives and friends and got rich. As a result, the whole community was nervous trying not to step on each other's toes for fear they would be branded anti-Japanese.

The residents living around the area of Tanah Merah Kechil had uneasy feelings when they heard the Japanese had taken those identified by the Chinese informers as anti-Japanese. They felt horrible when they learnt that these people had been taken to the hills beyond the Hwa San Teng Cemetery (at the present-day Kew Drive and old Jalan Puay Poon) to be shot. The evening after, the residents saw a few movements in their farms. They did not intercept them, as they knew they were obviously victims of the Japanese slaughter. Their hearts were with them and they wished them well. The next morning, my dad and the residents had a hush hush discussion about the events of the evening before and felt that they were lucky to have escaped. They agreed that they must keep what they had seen under wraps. If the Japanese knew about it, surely their lives would be in danger.

The Japanese soldiers often did their exercises around the hills surrounding my dad's farm. Occasionally, the commander would get his men to harvest some tapioca and sweet potatoes for my mum to boil. My grandma would give strict instructions to my sister, who was about three years old then, to hand the boiled food to the commander. If the commander were to give her a small piece of the food to sample to prove that the food was not poisoned, she must eat it and then quickly return home. She carried out her instructions well and she was not harmed.

One day, a group of furious Japanese soldiers came to my dad's house. They were looking for something. They mumbled something that my dad could not understand. Then one of the soldiers (believed to be a Taiwanese) wrote some Chinese characters on the sand. They were looking for a *changkol*. My dad showed them all his *changkols* and assured them that the lost *changkol* was not in his possession. He wrote the reply on the sand too. Feeling satisfied, they went away.

Rice was in short supply. Every member of the family was given a ration card. I asked my dad how it worked. He explained that an adult could buy only 4.8 *katis* of rice, whereas a child could only buy 2.4 *katis* a month. Later, that amount was reduced. The rice supplied was of very low quality. It was powdery and weevil-infested. My mum used to have a huge round rattan tray to separate the good rice from the powder. With several skilful swings of the tray of rice, the good grains were separated from the broken, powdery rice. The weevils were caught and squeezed between the fingers, whereas the powdery rice was used as pig feed. We were told that the fresh rice in the warehouses was kept for the Japanese military. Much of the rice was also sold in the black market. One could buy rice in the black market, but it was very expensive. To supplement rice, we ate yam, tapioca and sweet potato. Out of necessity, the citizens planted sweet potatoes, bamboo shoots, tapioca, *bayam*, *kang kong*, and other vegetables in whatever little plots of land they had. A type of giant-sized *bayam* was also commonly seen planted. Some said that it was introduced from Japan. Others said that it was from India. Anyway, that plant could grow as tall as two metres, and the stems could be as thick as a sugar cane. All parts of the plant could be eaten. Others dug for lalang stems and boiled them for vitamin C. We had chickens, eggs, ducks and pigs. But these were seldom consumed. Mostly they were sold.

As for transport, petrol and diesel were very expensive. Vehicle owners could not afford to buy them. Some had the ingenuity to modify their vehicles to adapt to the circumstances, converting them from petrol—or diesel-driven to steam-driven. They added a boiler and a furnace to the rear of the vehicle and coal was used as a fuel to boil the water to produce steam. The steam forced the pistons to move. To aid in moving the pistons initially, the driver needed to crank the shaft to gather momentum. As the people were hungry and skinny, it was tough for them to start a motor this way.

One day, my dad was pedalling a load of vegetables to the market on his bicycle along Changi Road. A Japanese military truck drove too close to him. The catch of the back panel of the truck grazed his upper right arm and a chunk of his flesh was ripped off. The Japanese officer stopped the truck, came down, and examined his wound. Then he took a bandage from the truck and bandaged the wound. It was such a big and deep cut. It was as big as the area of two 50-cent coins put side by side. When my father returned home, my grandma collected herbs from the garden, pounded them, and applied them on the wound until it healed. Now, during his old age, every now and then when the weather turns bad, he complains of the pain in his right arm.

All schools in Singapore stopped functioning during the Japanese Occupation, except to teach the Japanese language. Japanese soldiers were enlisted as teachers for this purpose. Students in schools and the populace in Singapore had to sing the Japanese national anthem. They had to face Tokyo when singing the anthem, known as *Kamigayo*. Also, all reference to time had to be in Tokyo time, which was two hours ahead of Singapore time.

Everybody had to bow to a Japanese soldier if they encountered one. If anyone disobeyed, they would be slapped or kicked. I read about how our former late President Wee Kim Wee was tortured when he cycled past a guard house one stormy morning without dismounting to bow at the guard standing inside. In the end he described himself as "more dead than alive".

At first, stealing was common during the Occupation. Later, the Japanese caught the thieves and beheaded them. Two heads were put on display at the bridgeheads at Kallang Bridge. Many heads were placed in other areas in town. After that, thieving was reduced to a trickle.

Every now and then, the American B-29s would fly across town. The Japanese Zeros would scramble, trying to intercept them. My dad, who was one of the few who went to the ridge, saw that the Zeros were no match for the B-29s. When the B-29s were unloading their bombs at the Japanese targets, anti-aircraft guns were used on them. He saw that that the smoking missiles from each volley by the Japanese could not reach the B-29s and they would drift downward ineffectually.

The kampong folks were ordered to form ARP (Air Raid Precautions) teams. At night, to prevent the Americans from seeing the targets, all lights had to be extinguished. The ARP team members would walk around the kampongs to enforce the rule. One night, my mum had to cook some food for my brother at a late hour. Not long after the flame was lit, the ARP members arrived and shouted that she had to put out the flame.

After the War

I have mentioned that there were several blocks of disused buildings next to a flight of about 100 steps along East Coast Road near Parbury Avenue. My dad told me that the Japanese brewed medicine there. I have read about a Japanese chemical unit stationed in Singapore during World War II. Could the Japanese have been making chemicals to be tested on the Chinese in Southeast Asia? Today the site, between Temasek Secondary and Temasek Primary schools is still fenced up by the Singapore authorities.

Pillboxes and bunkers were found from Changi coast stretching to Mount Faber and Pulau Blakang Mati. The British had expected the Japanese to attack from the sea south of Singapore. After the war, we children used to play in concrete pillboxes, running in and out of them. In the 1970s, someone put a Chinese-tiled roof over one of the pillboxes at Siglap. It looked quite unique. Those built on the hill behind Ayer Gemuroh stood stoically, whilst those along Telok Paku were tilted due to the erosion by the sea. There was a huge bunker at Loyang, which was overgrown with weeds. It was believed to have been an ammunition store.

When the news came that the Japanese had surrendered, there was an outbreak of looting and revenge killings. At Changi, Japanese and their sympathisers' stores, as well as bomb shelters, were looted. Someone saw a cyclist stop at a roadside store. He went into the store to loot a carton of cigarettes and then tied it on to his bicycle bar. After that, he went in for more. Then another cyclist came by, saw the cigarettes on the stationary bicycle, ripped of the string, and hurried away with the cigarettes. That was the order of the day in that time—looting and being looted.

The Japanese informers were advised to make themselves scarce by their officers. They discarded their usual clothing, shaved, changed their hairstyles and escaped most likely out of Singapore. Those who could not manage to escape were murdered in cold blood. Those whose relatives had been taken away by the Japanese and failed to return took it out on the informers. My dad reported frequent sightings on the periphery of the farm of such men behaving suspiciously. They camouflaged themselves in the bushes to escape being caught by those whom they had betrayed.

While waiting for the Japanese to be repatriated, Singaporeans could engage the soldiers—not the officers for most of them had committed *hara-kiri*—to work for them. My dad engaged some of the Japanese to build pigsties, and do repairs to the chicken coops and the house. Food was supplied to the soldiers. My sister remembers one of them presented her with a rubber doll. It looked like one of Snow White's seven dwarfs.

After the celebrations and excitement of the war's end had subsided, things were bleak. They were no better than during the Japanese Occupation. The British government had their work cut out to clear up the harbour, roads, warehouses and buildings that had been ravaged over the past three and a half years. Raw materials were scarce. Economic activities were negligible. The population was hungry because the price of food skyrocketed and the people had little money.

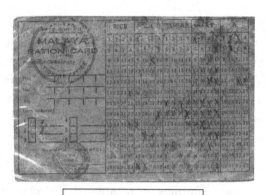

A post-war ration card

Japanese currency was useless and people discarded the notes in bags they left by the roadside. The government set up People's Restaurants, part of their communal feeding programme, to sell food to the people cheaply. Yet some people still went hungry. Family restaurants were set up by the Social Welfare Department to provide subsidised food. The government then set up a few clinics and schools where children below the age of six could receive free milk. Many went to the suburbs in search of cheap accommodation and a piece of land to cultivate vegetables and rear poultry to feed themselves. Essential food items such as rice, sugar and salt were rationed. Such items could be purchased from the black market, but their prices were exorbitant.

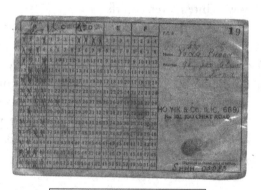

The ration card of 1953.

Despite all the government help, the problems still persisted. The people were very unhappy with the British and thought that they were no longer able to rule Singapore well. Strikes and incidents of labour unrest were common.

We in the kampong felt the effects of this unrest too. Corruption was the norm. My dad was most fearful of *cheng hu lang* ('government officials' in Hokkien). They were the *mata mata* (the Malay word for 'policeman') or *arm pai* (Hokkien for 'policemen'), *tua kow* (literal translation from Hokkien: 'big dogs' or 'police inspectors') and the *tuay goo* or *chin teng* ('land cow' or 'land surveyors'). If any dealings with them were necessary, it was best to do so as quickly as possible and stay far away from them thereafter. We children were warned to be wary of policemen. If we misbehaved our parents would say, "*Mata lai loh! Mata ai liak lu loh!*" (translation from Hokkien: The police have come. The police will catch you!)

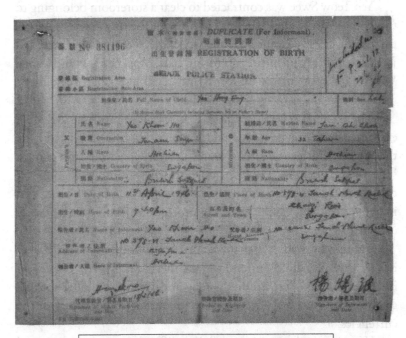

My Japanese birth certificate (front and back)
Up to mid-1946, the British government still used the
Japanese birth certificate.

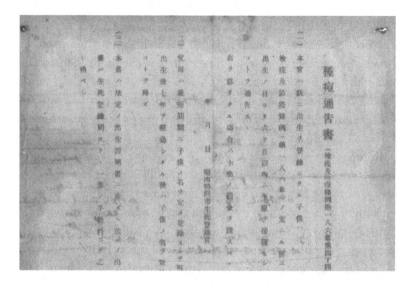

Yeo Teow Swee was contracted to clear a storeroom belonging to the Public Works Department. He brought the unwanted materials to our place in Kampong Tanah Merah Kechil. They included Japanese military furniture, uniforms, hats, caps, helmets and boots. We children put on the uniforms and acted like Japanese soldiers, much to the amusement of the adults.

There were several excavated areas on our farm. My dad explained that they were air raid shelters. He told us that during the war, whenever the sirens sounded, everyone would prepare to hide in the shelters. Those in our farm were simple dugouts on the ground with some timber laid across the opening. I could not imagine how they could offer any protection if bombs were really dropped there.

There were wads of Japanese currency found in a rattan basket in our attic. We children used to take them out to play. They were in denominations of hundreds, tens and fives. My father told us that they were useless. After the war, the British did not honour the currencies.

Very often, the survivors of that difficult period met up and talked about their experiences.

The Civilian War Memorial

The Japanese Cemetery Park
Many of the Japanese soldiers who died
during the war were buried here.

The Japanese Currencies used in Singapore and Malaya during the Japanese Occupation.

Chapter 9
The Tree of a Hundred Uses

In those days, we always lived off the land, whether it was for medicine, food or materials. For my dad, the soil was very precious. He used to say, "Every inch of soil is an inch of gold." Almost every plant was put to good use. One good example was the coconut tree.

Coconut trees thrive well on the slopes of well-drained soil. As a result, coconut trees were planted in abundance in neat rows on the hilly land where we lived. On sunny days, we sat under the shade of the coconut trees to play games. The girls would play *masak masak*, doing their make-believe cooking using coconut leaf blades and weeds as vegetables and the empty coconut shells for cooking utensils. Boys would use coconut fronds as sleighs. Every weekend, playing hide-and-seek among the coconut trees was the norm. When a ripe coconut fell to the ground, we would run to gather it and put it in the pile of coconuts near our house.

When a strong wind blew, the dried coconut leaves detached from the trunk and fell to the ground. Everybody in the village wanted to take the opportunity to gather dried coconut fronds. The leaves would fall from the trees in abundance on stormy days. All of us siblings and parents swung into action. We had no fear of the thunder and lightning or of being injured by a falling coconut. We always believed that a falling coconut would never land on our heads. We had never heard of anyone being injured in such a way. We believed that coconuts had eyes and they knew where to land when they detached from their stalk. Our elders demonstrated to us that a coconut, when husked, would reveal its three 'eyes'. Those 'eyes' would show them where they were heading. How far was it true? We did not know. But none of us had

Coconut buds

ever been hurt by one. Sometimes, we raced with each other to get a fallen frond. Tugs-of-war with neighbours were common. The person who held the stalk of the frond was the winner. But the loser was not at a disadvantage either. He had free hands to get another fallen frond. We did that until we were exhausted. We strung a thick

wire between two coconut trees and then spread out all the fronds we had gathered in neat rows on the ground leaning against the wire, so that they would dry faster in the sun.

The 'eyes' of a coconut

Coconut flowers

A dwarf coconut tree

In the afternoons sometimes, when we were free and when there were sufficient dried coconut fronds, we would strip the leaflets off each frond with a sickle. The stalks that held the leaflets were chopped down to size with a *parang* to be used as firewood. We then sat on homemade stools and removed the mid-rib of each leaflet with a small penknife. That required skill. A person who was not skilful would leave some bits of leaf blade attached to the rib. That would make the mid-rib look untidy as well as hinder the making of a broom. They had to repeat the process, removing the leaf blade that was still attached. Sometimes, they needed to shave off the blade three times. One needed experience to strip the blades from the leaflets. There was always the fear of being poked by the sharp mid-rib or cut by the penknife. When the leaf blade was stripped too fast, the friction between the mid-rib and the finger would cause a thick callus to form. The formation of a callus would not interfere with the work process however. In fact, the stripping process became more efficient, as the callused finger became less sensitive to pain and less likely to get injured by any splinters from the coconut leaflet's mid-rib. A skilful person would strip each leaflet with only one stroke of the penknife. But that was not the end of it.

The mid-rib would then be inspected by the adults, usually my parents and my grandma. If any were not stripped well, the adults would tidy it up for us. Then the mid-ribs were tied together in bundles using gunny strings or ribless coconut leaf blades and stored for sale to my dad's uncle later. The ribless leaf blades were limber. We folded them into halves and tied them up in small bundles to use them as fire starters for our giant stoves.

A broom made of a bundle of coconut frond mid-ribs held together by twine.
My grandma used to make the ties with stripped bark of rattan cane. It held the bundle more neatly and efficiently.

We put the coconut to good use too. The nut had to be husked. A sharp steel spike with a sturdy wooden stump was sunk into the ground. To remove the coconut husk, my dad—he had the skill and the strength to do it—then impaled a nut on to the spike. Then, he deftly pushed the coconut to one side and a small piece of the husk was ripped off. Then he moved on to another area. With time, the pieces of husk that were removed got bigger and bigger, as smaller amounts of strength were required. Within a few strokes, the nut was husked. The husk was dried and used as firewood.

The nut needed to be shelled in order to extract the white kernel. The shell was tough. To break it, we had to use a heavy chopper to hack it off bit by bit until we had the whole, rounded kernel in our hands. The kernel was chopped into two; at the same time, the water inside the kernel was drained away. The broken shell was not wasted either. We dried them to use as firewood. Those cooking in the kitchen preferred to use the shells as firewood as they produced a lot of heat and little smoke.

Heavy chopper

Shelling coconuts

Next came the painful process of grating the white kernel. A homemade grating board was used. A person had to have strength in the fingertips to move the kernel across the grating board. In the process, they had to ensure that the piece of kernel they were holding did not slip away, otherwise they would get nasty cuts on their fingers. Grating the kernel was always done by the adults, especially my mum.

We had a grater produced by the ironsmith, but it was meant for grating a large number of coconuts. It had an iron rod tipped with a disc with saw teeth all round. To grate a coconut, one needed to upturn half a coconut over the saw teeth and push it downward, then bring it up, repeating this until the entire kernel had been scraped.

The shelled coconut

Then water was added to the grated kernel before squeezing out the 'milk', to make extracting the liquid easier. The coconut 'milk' was then sieved using a strainer and poured into a big wok to boil. During the process of boiling, the water evaporated, leaving behind the oil. The coconut oil was bottled for use in cooking and the excess oil was sold to residents in the kampong. Usually, this work took us until midnight.

Different types of lamps were used to light the
area where we worked late into the night.

When darkness fell, different lighting paraphernalia were
used. There were kerosene lamps and candles. Those gave out a
yellowish light. We used carbide lamps too. Carbide lamps could be
purchased off the shelf. Carbide rocks were put into the container
and water was added. This reaction produced acetylene gas. The
gas was channelled through a tiny gas jet. A lighted match was
used to ignite the gas that flowed out of the jet. The carbide lamp
produced a soothing white light, but the smell of the partially burnt
gas could be quite irritating. Because the chemical reaction between
the carbide and water also produced heat independent of the flame,
the container could become quite hot. Furthermore, the slaked
lime that was the result of the reaction needed to be disposed off
properly. Dad had designated a specific location to dispose of it. He
was afraid it could contaminate the soil in which we planted our
vegetables.

Sometimes, when we searched for coconuts, we would come
across a very light nut. We would be sure that the nut was dead,
meaning that the kernel had either dried up or decomposed. We
would saw a small slit in the nut and scrape out the dried kernel.

In this way, we created a moneybox. Or we could cut the nut in half and run a string through the two halves. Then we could step on the overturned shells, slip the string in between our big toes and second toes, and then pull the strings taut. We would walk on these, going *clip clop, clip clop*, just like we did with the condensed milk tins. It was fun to see children go clip clopping about. The older neighbourhood children would make toys of chicken and cat shapes by joining different pieces of coconut shell. After dyeing and polishing the finished products, they looked beautiful. If one of us were to make a whistle out of a small leaf blade of a coconut leaflet, it would trigger a symphony from the kampong children. Some would make 'trumpets' by coiling the whistle with more leaf blades. When all the 'trumpets' were blown simultaneously, it made a cacophony.

On hot, sunny days, we would naturally want some young coconut water to quench our thirst. My brother Hong Bian was good at climbing. He would choose a dwarf tree that was laden with young coconuts. Then he would climb up, hold on to the leaf stalks and give each young nut a hard stamp. Eventually a nut would fall. Using a parang, we would first remove a small little slice of the husk. That would be our 'spoon'. Next, we made several forceful cuts in the nut until a small hole was created. We held the nut up to drink the thirst-quenching water. After drinking, we would split the nut into two halves. Using the 'spoon', we ate the soft tender kernel. We would choose a young nut because the water was sweeter and the kernel was more tender.

To wrap up a young jackfruit to prevent insects from damaging it, coconut fronds were cut and woven into a hood for the fruit.

On the ridge where we lived, there was a low coconut tree. We had fun lowering some fronds of the tree and did acrobatic acts with them. We caught hold of the end of a frond and swung like a pendulum in the air and then let go. We would land on the sandy, grassy slope and then roll down. After we came to a halt, we scrambled up the slope and went swinging from the frond again.

If a coconut tree was in the way while making a house or a chicken coop or had died because of an attack by beetles or it was threatening to fall on a house despite the efforts of securing it with thick, corrugated steel wire, the tree had to be chopped down. If the 'offending' tree were healthy, the kampong folk would take the young green leaflets. They used the leaflets to make *ketupat*—a little woven pouch for cooked rice. Others would go for the bud, also known as the 'heart'. If we stripped off all the leaves of a coconut tree right up to the base, at the base one would find the bud (the 'heart') of the tree that people went after. The bud contained developing young leaflets and baby flowers. The bud, when eaten raw, had a sweet taste. I loved them but unfortunately, each tree only contained one bud. The lucky person who got the bud would often cook it in a tasty curry. It has been so many years since I last tasted coconut 'heart' curry.

Even the coconut trunks were not spared. If a bridge was needed to be built across a stream, the first material that came to mind was the coconut trunk. Before a trunk was used, it was tested by knocking it. If it sounded solid, giving off a long series of vibrations, the trunk could be used. If the trunk gave off only a soft low sound, it was rotting. The selected trunks were cut to size and placed side by side across the stream. To prevent the trunks from moving sideways, huge steel clamps were driven into them to hold them together. If one of them wore out, it could be easily replaced with another trunk.

These trunks were also split to be dried and used as firewood. But a coconut trunk was very difficult to split because it was very fibrous. One had to use an axe, a sledgehammer, and few steel wedges to split it. After splitting, one had to take extra care to remove the chopped pieces of trunk for the stiff fibre could be quite sharp.

I have seen coconut trunks being sawn into planks and made into furniture, but I do not know whether it is popular.

Every year after *puasa*—the month of Ramadan—we would see a familiar sight—Malay men from the kampong would walk among the coconut trees looking for young, yellow coconut leaves. If they found a suitable young frond, one of them would use a short strong rope, tie the two ends together and loop it around his feet.

Then he would climb up the tree rather expertly. Using his parang, which was tied round his waist, he would chop the young leaves and hurl them to his friends below. The womenfolk would make *ketupat* wrappers with the leaves.

Slivers of beef, chicken or mutton were skewed through the mid-ribs of the coconut leaflets and these were then barbecued over a charcoal fire. Cooking oil was smeared on the meat with a stalk of tumeric. When it was cooked, this *satay* was dipped into a thick gravy of coconut, peanuts and spices. A *satay* seller would put his *satay* paraphernalia into two wooden cabinets—one for the meat and coconut skewers and sauce and one for the charcoal, kerosene oil, and a homemade stove. He would balance them with a carrying pole on his shoulder and walk among the houses in the kampong, at the same time calling out in a high-pitched voice: "*Satay!*"

The green leaflets were also used as a wrapper for *otak otak*, which was fish paste cooked with coconut milk and seasoned with *chili belacan*. Large, choice leaflets were cut to size and the fish paste was stuffed between the two blades of each leaflet. Both ends of the *otak* were pinned with a small mid-rib then they were barbecued over a small charcoal fire. Enterprising folks would carefully pin each barbecued leaflet of *otak otak* on to a rack so it looked like a xylophone. They went around selling their *otak otak* from these racks.

Rhinoceros-horned Beetles

Coconut trees thrive in well-drained soil. If the place is waterlogged, the trees will die. But sometimes, they die because they are attacked by a kind of huge beetle called rhinoceros-horned beetle.

Coconut estate managers were fearful of such attacks. Once a beetle had gone inside a living coconut tree, it would drill holes and live in there, feeding on the young bud. Then it laid eggs within the tree. When the eggs hatched into larvae, they fed on the bud too. When the tree died, the larvae would have turned into pupae. The tree would have rotted with the pupae resting comfortably in the decomposed trunk. After several years, when the rotted trunk fell apart, the pupae would already have turned into adults. They would fly to another tree to repeat the cycle.

A wise estate manager would study the fronds of each tree for any sign of withering. If there were, the tree would be brought down and the offending creatures killed.

Harvesting Coconuts

Every month, the estate manager would send a request for them to be harvested. He conveyed the request either through his assistants or personally. Two men would carry long, slender bamboo poles on their shoulders to the estate. The manager would arrive in his lorry, loaded with robust coconut harvesters armed with sharp steel-tipped six-foot rods. The coconut harvesters would fix a crescent-shaped blade on to the tip of the most slender pole. It was joined with a stouter pole at the other end. The joint was tied with thick split cane, and a bamboo wedge was driven in between the coiled cane so that the joint would be tight and firm. It was then hoisted up with the blade to the coconut tree. With his keen judgement—the coconut harvester knew which bunch of coconuts was ripe enough to be harvested—he carefully twisted the blade until it reached the main stalk of the bunch. Then he gave it a sharp tug. This detached the bunch of coconuts and they fell to the ground. The coconuts would scatter in all directions—some would roll down the hill slope, some into the bushes or into a ditch and some simply remained under the tree. The nut pickers, who were a different group of workers from the coconut harvesters, would use their rods to poke at the nuts and gather them into a small heap. Then someone would carry over two huge baskets, balancing them on his shoulders with a tough carrying pole. He would fill the baskets with the coconuts and then carry them to a larger main heap by the main road. A lorry fixed with barricades at the deck would arrive. The lorry owner would usually be the one who bought the coconuts. He and his assistants would pick each nut with a rod, counting as they threw them into the deck of the lorry. At the same time, they would put aside the bad nuts as well those that were too young. We children loved to watch them counting. The two men would poke the coconuts and throw them in an alternating rhythm into the lorry while saying the number of the nut he was counting. For example, A would say, "One," B would say, "Two," then A would say, "Three," and B would say "Four."

The coconut tree owner was paid by the number of coconuts accepted. The harvester was also paid in the same way. So the harvester needed to be very careful not to cut the wrong bunch of nuts. The pickers were paid by the number of hours they worked.

We, who lived in the estate, often gave the pickers a hand. When they left, we collected the leftovers—unwanted nuts, stalks, and the woody spathes and leaves—for use in the stoves and farm.

Sometimes, the purchaser wanted to husk the coconuts in the estate. A very sharp steel-tipped spike was planted firmly into the ground. The 'husker' would put on a thick canvas apron, pick up a nut and impale it on to the upturned spike. He would husk the coconut in exactly the same manner as I have described how my dad did. A skilful 'husker' needed only a few strokes to remove the husk from a coconut. A very skilful one could husk 2,000 coconuts a day. He was paid by the number of nuts he husked. If the coconut husk factory had a demand, the husk was sometimes sold to them be processed and made into ropes, doormats and mattresses.

Husking coconuts
One needed skill
to do this.

Tan Piah Teng, our neighbouring landowner, had a coconut kiln to dry coconut kernels. Many steps had to be taken before the kernel was dried. First, the husked coconuts had to be split.

To split a coconut in two required skill as well as a special blunt, heavy parang. A skilled person would hold a nut with his left hand. Then he made a hard blow on the nut with his parang, at the same time turning over the half-smashed nut, and then he gave it a second blow. The nut was spilt. He was paid by the number of nuts he split.

The split coconuts were arranged on the surface of a rectangular kiln with the kernels facing downward. When the kiln was ready, a fire would start at the bottom of the kiln. The heat would dehydrate the kernels. Once the kernels were dried, they were collected and sent to be detached from the shells. One or two cents was paid for each half coconut kernel detached from the shell.

To detach the kernel from a shell, the person had to use a small, blunt steel scraper. He needed to press the shell down on a board and the scraper was used to scoop out the kernel. It was easier said than done. Sometimes, considerable strength was needed to remove the kernel. Sometimes, if they were lucky, the kernel dropped out by itself. Detaching a few hundred coconut kernels from their shells would earn a fee of a few dollars.

My elder sister, Hong Game, had at one time tried her hand at detaching the kernel from the shell. She even had the shell processed into charcoal. To get her portion of shells turned into charcoal for our use, she was not paid for detaching the kernel.

The shells were not left to waste either. They were used to line the floor of the kiln and burnt to provide the heat needed to dehydrate the kernels. Once the kernels had been dehydrated, the fire at the bottom of the kiln would not be extinguished immediately. All ventilation holes were closed so that no oxygen could enter the kiln. The fire would burn down and finally extinguish itself from the lack of oxygen. The shells would have stopped burning and turned into charcoal. Although the charcoal pieces were very small, they produced much better heat than the charcoal made from mangrove trees.

The dehydrated kernel was then packed into gunnysacks and sold to the factory to be processed into coconut oil or other materials. The residue of processed material, called copra, was dried and pressed into cakes and sold by the bale to the pig farmers as pig feed, as it was very rich in protein and had high nutritional value.

Coconut trees, being very tall, were often struck by lightning. We had experienced thunder and lightning. A person could be traumatised by that. One humid afternoon, the sky was overcast. Suddenly there was a flash of lightning followed by a deafening crack of thunder. The coconut tree not far to our left shook. A leaf immediately fell to the ground. We went nearer. We saw burn marks on the tree trunk. Dead leaves fell from the tree. The healthy leaves drooped and some were twisted beyond recognition. The young leaves had broken and some looked ruffled, like a child's unkempt hair. We children felt a sense of fear mixed with anxiety.

"Would the thunder strike again then? Of all the trees, why would the thunder strike that tree?" we asked one another. There was no answer.

My sister suddenly blurted out, "Maybe the tree was haunted, and the thunder god had to blast the ghost!" With that, we walked away, feeling very uneasy. Every time we walked past the tree after that, we walked with a tinge of fear.

Yeo Teow Swee, a stakeholder of the coconut estate, had a contract with a wood sawmill to supply sawdust to the estate to let it decompose and add nutrients to the soil. Every day, lorry loads of sawdust were dumped under the coconut trees. The whole estate turned red with the dust. On hot, sunny days, the breeze whipped up the dust in spirals and blew it about. We children had our fun playing and somersaulting in the dust heaps. Sometimes, a careless smoker would drop a lighted cigarette butt on a dust heap. That sparked days and days of smouldering embers, with smoke moving in the direction of the breeze. The estate stakeholder was happy. He said the smoke would smoke out and kill the pests in the coconut trees. The embers stopped burning only after a period of heavy rain. After a prolonged period, the heap decomposed. Grasses and weeds grew on them. Coconut roots spread all over them. By and by, the sawdust heaps became a component of the topsoil.

In other estates, young, tender coconut sap was collected and fermented into wine. The sap was also collected and processed into black sugar, also known as *gula Melaka*. However, during our time in Tanah Merah Kechil, the folks did not do that.

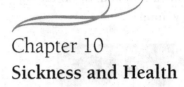

Chapter 10
Sickness and Health

My dad suffered a very serious illness in 1957, after working as a coolie for Chin Guan Company (a dealer in sandalwood) in Jalan Sultan. At first, the income from the farm was not enough to feed us, so he took on additional work so that he could get a regular income. The farm was then managed by my mum and grandma.

Dad came home every weekend. He would buy stationery for us and bring us complimentary postcards and tell us about his work and adventures in town—among them was watching how the Merdeka Bridge was built. Every weekend, we looked forward to his presence. But one afternoon, he staggered home looking very pale. My grandma was the first to notice that something was amiss. Immediately, he went to lie in bed, and there was much discussion between my grandma, my mum and him. We children were not allowed to go near them.

His ill health came to a peak at midnight one night. He vomited blood. I do not know who contacted the ambulance. I remember that two attendants brought a stretcher to my house and put him into an ambulance. He was sent to the *Si Pai Por* (General Hospital) and was warded. In those days, the two words *Si Pai* (corrupted from the word "sepoy") were enough to send shivers down anyone's spine. It could mean a journey of no return. Over the next few days, I accompanied my mum there. Each time, she prepared a pot of nourishing home-cooked food for him. One day, my mum could not make the journey. She felt giddy and vomited into a paper bag that she brought along. I felt worried, but I could not do anything.

When we reached the hospital, we entered through Bowyer's Block and then went to the ward. My dad was sitting on his bed in the hospital gown. I was so tired that I joined him and sat on the soft comfortable bed but was chided by my mum.

This is what is left of the Bowyer's Block at the Singapore General Hospital today.

The next day, the teacher asked me for my feeding fees of $2. I told him, "I no money."

He said, "Get it from your father."

I innocently said, "My father in hospital."

During recess there was a flurry of concerned classmates asking how my dad was. I was so touched that I wanted to cry.

When my dad was discharged, he brought home a lot of medicine. One was a huge bottle of a white, gluey substance. It smelt like mint. (Now I suspect that he must have suffered from a stomach ulcer, either due to irregular meals or skipping meals to save money). His condition became worse. Many *sinsehs* were consulted. One of them, who claimed to have practised curing ailments just by pricking certain veins around the spine, was recommended. He made my dad lie with his face down on the pillow. He used his long needle—I think it must have been about four inches long—and pricked several spots through the skin near my dad's spine.

After that, my dad said he felt much better. The man accepted the red packet my grandma gave him and boasted that he had been handling the needle for the past 30 years. He then went away but the ailment remained.

News of my dad's illness reached another Yeo—a distant relative from Yeo's Village in Qianzhou. We called him Grand Uncle Chew. He had his left leg amputated due to a traffic accident and was fixed with a prosthesis. From Lian Teng Hng (Kampong Eunos), he took a bus to Changi 8½ Milestone and walked all the way along the red laterite road (Tanah Merah Kechil Road) to my house with a stout wooden rod as a walking stick. Seeing my dad in such bad shape, he recommended a famed Chinese physician named Dr Chan Chee Seng. Our direct cousin Hong Huat, who was then working at Moh Siong Huat (a household provision supply), had access to a car on weekends. He was sent to fetch the physician from his home at Geylang. Upon feeling my dad's pulse, he said that he was in a serious condition and had to make several visits. His consultation fee for each house call was $4. House calls would entail payments of several times the consultation fee. We thought he was another of those fly-by-night *sinsehs*. He wrote out the prescription on a piece of white paper. Then he told us to buy the medicine from any Chinese medicine shop. As usual, my mum took the prescription to a Chinese medicine shop in Chai Chee. The dispenser, after collating and calculating the amount with an abacus, totalled it up to only 35 cents. My mum brewed it using a clay pot with its spout constructed at a right angle to the handle. (The spout of a normal teapot is constructed opposite its handle.)

This medicine pot is similar to the one mum used.

After being boiled for the required time, the liquid was poured into a blue eight-sided bowl. The medicine filled 80 per cent of the bowl and it was the right amount. Half an hour after consuming the first dose of medicine, my dad passed a very smelly stool. On his second trip, the medicine Dr Chan prescribed cost only 50 cents. After taking the second dose, my dad felt much better. He could eat a little. After the third visit, he could sit up and talk with us. All these accounts were disclosed by Hong Huat. All the while, cousin Hong Huat provided the transport to fetch the physician, as well as giving us emotional support. On subsequent trips, my dad had to go to the physician's house in Geylang. His health was restored to normal, with many thanks to Dr Chan. Dr Chan explained that he had to make house calls so many times because my dad's health was too weak. He had to find out the suitability of the drugs and the reactions after they were consumed each time.

Dr Chan Chee Seng became our family doctor. Whenever we had any ailments or health complaints, our first thought was Dr Chan. We were indeed grateful to Grand Uncle Chew for having recommended Dr Chan to us.

A few days after that, an Indian man came to our house. My grandma and mother said that he was from the *Hock Lee Por* or Social Welfare. He looked around our house. There was a dilapidated dressing cupboard without doors, an old rusty Smith clock ticking away and an old dining table with unevenly replaced planks covered with a piece of red linoleum. He could see holes like stars in the attap roof. The floor was not properly cemented. Two faded curtains were hanging across the bedroom doorways. He jotted down something and walked quietly away.

A few weeks later, he returned. He said that Social Welfare would initially give us $60 a month but it would get less with each subsequent month. Then I applied for a remission of feeding fees from school. It was approved. We were happy indeed. My dad's health got better. He decided to stay at home to farm, this time with renewed strategy and planning.

The Hong Kong Flu

In 1954, on the first day of the second school term I saw many classmates absent. We were shocked that nearly half of our classmates were absent. A few were complaining of headaches, fever and were coughing away. The teachers too were not spared. Many teachers did not go to school. After that our form teacher told us not to go to school for two weeks.

Our neighbours and relatives too were suffering. We were told not to go near anyone who was sick, as the disease could spread to us. We tried our best but were not spared. We got coughs, headaches and fever too. Then, at one of the Chinese medicine shops at Chai Chee Market, a prescription was issued. That prescription was a cure for the Hong Kong Flu. Immediately, almost every family swarmed the Chinese medicine shops there to buy that medicine. My mum bought a few packets of the prescribed herbs too. She brewed it using the usual spherical clay pot with a spout and a short handle. Its lid was made of clay too. She got my dad to read the instructions. She poured the whole packet of herbs into the pot to brew. Every member of the house was asked to swallow the bitter herbal drink. She brewed it several times for all of us.

Another belief was that drinking the soup of boiled raw olives could treat the disease. The price of raw olives suddenly shot up to $5 per piece overnight.

I did not know if there were any fatalities, but by and by, the disease slowly took its course. Those who suffered eventually recovered. Then school reopened. Just like after any school holidays, the classmates looked a little different—some were paler, others had put on weight and some turned up with new haircuts. We felt strange at first, but at the end of the day, almost everyone became chatty like before.

Poliomyelitis Vaccination

It was the year 1958. Everywhere, there was much talk about vaccination. Very vaguely, the neighbours were talking about bone diseases that could affect children. The best way not to get infected was to get vaccinated.

Early one morning, my grandma rounded up all my brothers and sisters to go to Bedok Clinic opposite a Shell petrol kiosk. When we arrived, a long queue had already formed. We were right at the end. We felt quite cool. But later, as the sun rose higher, we began to feel the heat getting intense. Furthermore, we were sweaty, hungry and thirsty. It was made worse when people jostled here and there, stepping on our toes and weaving in and out of the queue. Our legs went soft like jelly, so we squatted on the sandy ground. After what seemed like eternity, we finally got into the shade of the one-storey building. We caught a glimpse of what we were queuing up for from the opened window. The nurses rolled up the patients' right hand sleeves and rubbed their arms with cotton wool. Then, another nurse scraped the patient's skin at the spot where the other nurse had rubbed it. I could see that some grimaced in pain but some held up bravely. Soon, it was our turn. As soon as the wet cotton wool was applied, I felt a sudden chill on the spot. I wondered what was on the cotton wool. Then I felt a sharp pain. Before I could yell, it was over.

My grandma kept on reminding me that I must inform her should I feel feverish. The next day, I felt feverish. She touched my hands and forehead and said that I should rest. So I rested in bed. Until then, I did not know why I should have undergone that process and suffered. It was only a few years after that I learned that we had been immunised against poliomyelitis.

Windows in Boys' Undergarments

It was usual for small boys in those days to wear a pair of pants with a small hole between the legs to allow their penises to hang out. Their mums were usually busy helping their dads to make ends meet. Often, they wet or soiled themselves. The parents were too busy to change their pants. With a hole where the penis was, a boy could urinate freely without wetting his pants. Our family was no different. One day, one of my brothers (I cannot recall who) was crying and was complaining of pain at the penis. It was swollen and reddish. My grandma took one glance and immediately knew that he had been poisoned by a toad. She took the metal blower (used for blowing air on to a smouldering heap) from the kitchen and started blowing on the affected part. I could not remember whether she inserted any medicine in the pipe before blowing. But anyway, he was cured the next day. My grandma explained that toad's breath was poisonous and therefore, we should avoid any toad if we saw one. However, zoologists beg to differ. Zoologists explain that a toad's poison comes from the warts on its skin.

At the Malay kampong, there was a family that reared a few geese. Sometimes, the whole flock would make such a high-pitched sound, much to our annoyance. One of my brothers who had the windows on his pants walked past the flock and a goose immediately gave chase. He ran as fast as he could, as if he had seen a ghost. Luckily, my elder sister held him up. The goose was after its 'lunch.' From then onwards, we were very wary of the flock.

"Hee! Hee! Hee! Here is my lunch!"
Fearing for his life, my brother ran to my sister. Luckily she was there to lift him up.

Self-medication

Sore throats, headaches due to working in the hot sun, flu and other work-related illnesses were common. My mum would often boil boat lily leaves together with its flowers and the plantaginaceae plant (*gor kuon chow*). She also added rock sugar to it so it had an aromatic taste.

Sometimes, the underground adventitious lalang stems were used. To prepare this drink, the lalang stems were collected. We needed to dig for them. The digging was difficult, as lalang did not grow in the soft alluvial soil. It grew in hard, red laterite soil. The dry scale leaves had to be peeled off. The roots had to be cut off. They were washed and then boiled. Sugar was added to taste. But this was done sparingly, as my grandma said that drinking this to excess would weaken our calves.

If we lost our voices, bamboo buds were boiled with a little salt. It served as the drink of the day. Sometimes, the creeper umbelliferae (scallop shell weed) was boiled to drink.

Sometimes, to cure fever, my grandma would boil some *mee hoon soup* or watery rice and let us eat as fast as we could so that the heat would still be retained in it when we swallowed it. Then she made us put on extra layers of clothing and tucked us into bed. Blankets were put over us. Doors and windows were shut. Soon, we were drenched with perspiration and the fever was gone. She then got us to change into dry clothing. If we did not get changed, we would get a relapse. This method proved to be very effective for me. But today, doctors say that a person can suffer from brain damage, as the temperature is too high for the body.

The Universal Axe Brand oil and the Tiger Balm were two household medicines that the kampong folks could not do without. For headaches, stomachaches, coughs, colds and insect bites, the first medicine that came to mind was either the *por tow peow ku hong you* (Universal Axe Brand oil) or *the hor you* (Tiger oil). I remember when we had a stomachache, my mum rubbed the Axe Brand oil on our stomachs and then sprinkled two drops of it into half a cup of lukewarm water and coaxed us to drink it. It was effective. I saw folks who had stomach troubles put a little of the Tiger Balm into their mouths and then down a lot of water. Today's doctors may say these medicines are for external use only and are not meant to be taken orally.

Boils and Sores

I once had a huge boil as big as a ten-cent coin on my right shin. It was so painful that I could only limp. My grandma examined it when she saw it and immediately went to the grassy patch of a vacant plant bed to search for herbs. After a few minutes, she returned with two or three small plants, one of which was the balsam plant. The leaves were detached from the stems. She upturned a stool, put the leaves on it and started pounding them with a hammer. Then a little salt and a little cooked rice were added. After that, I had to apply the mixture over the boil and bandage it with a shred of rag. It felt very cooling. The pain was instantly relieved. The next morning, the rag was removed. There was white pus on the mixture. The wound was cleaned and another batch of the herbs was prepared and applied. After treating it a few times, the wound was healed.

Everybody had to have their milk teeth extracted. As for us siblings, most of the time, we extracted them ourselves. We constantly agitated the tooth until it came out. If it was too troublesome, our dad helped to pull it with his fingers. He simply pressed it inwards or outwards so that the tooth could dislodge from the gum.

As for caring for our teeth, each of us was given a toothbrush. Every morning, we would simply use a little of the Gibbs Dentifrice toothpaste that came in a cake form and give our teeth a cursory brush, as time was crucial for us. We had to do our household chores, have breakfast and then rush to school. Furthermore, my parents were ignorant of how to take care of our teeth. Dental checkups by a qualified dentist were unheard of.

Mumps

I had seen classmates come to class with a blue patch at the back of their ears. On it would be written the Chinese character 'tiger'. I did not know why so I simply ignored it.

One day, my sister complained that her right ear ached and was swollen. My dad examined it and said, "There is a growth of *ti tou puay* (mumps)." The next day, after returning from the market, he took out what he bought and started to mix some blue powder and a very strong-smelling liquid. I can still remember that I could not stand the smell. Then he dipped a small chicken feather in the mixture and applied it on her swollen cheek. He also wrote the Chinese character 'tiger' on it—exactly the same as the one I saw on my classmates.

One morning, when I woke up, I felt that I could not open my mouth. My cheeks were very painful and swollen. I could neither drink nor eat. How miserable I felt. My dad said that the *ti tou puay* had spread to me. Oh no! He was applying the horrible mixture on my cheeks. He assured me that it would be all right. I covered my nose when he was applying it. He said that the blue powder was indigo and the pungent, smelly liquid was vinegar. The 'tiger' character symbolised a make-believe tiger eating up the *ti tou puay* (literal translation: 'skin of pig head'). The mixture had a very soothing effect, but the swelling did not subside. I had to stay away from school for many days. My teacher did not allow me to go to school either. My dad applied the mixture on my cheeks for several days. Gradually, the swelling went down. I could eat and drink a little. The pain slowly subsided then it was completely cured. How happy I was when I was told that I could go out to school and to play.

German Measles

There were other times when we felt feverish and our bones were aching. Then rashes started to appear on our chest, stomach and the back. My grandma knew what it was. She gave us a white powder to apply and we were given strict orders that we had to put on thick clothing and not come out of the house. We also had to avoid contact with the wind. If we did, there would be serious consequences when we were old. We were so worried. We simply stayed in bed and dared not go out. By and by, the rashes subsided and our skin returned to normal.

Chicken Pox

Our neighbour, Ah Beng, once had chicken pox. She had pockmarks all over her face. My parents, especially my mum, drove us all to play with her. She wanted us to get chicken pox too. A few days after that, we felt pains and aches all over our bodies. We lost our appetite for food, then watery spots began to appear on our skin. It was chicken pox all right. My mum brewed special tea for us. Again, we were confined to our beds. We could only eat, drink and sleep. It was so boring. The reason why she wanted all of us to get chicken pox was that we could get it only once. It was better for us to get chicken pox when we were young. Furthermore, if all of us got it simultaneously, we would all would receive the same treatment and all of us would not get it again. If an adult caught chicken pox, their immune system was not as strong, so the recovery might take a longer time. Furthermore, the illness weakened the body's immune system.

We were told not to have any dark soya sauce as it might cause dark pockmarks to permanently remain on the skin. But this myth has never been proven by modern day doctors.

Anti-tetanus

Uncle Chew had often lamented that Koon Huat would not have died of tetanus if he had been given a drink of green bean seeds soaked in boiling salt water. He always emphasised that even western doctors approved of this remedy. Should anyone in the family happen to step on a nail or a cut, my parents would make us drink that preparation.

In our family, grandma would try to prescribe a herbal drink first for whoever was sick as a first remedy. She had learnt from my grandpa, who had knowledge of traditional herbal Chinese medicine. As I have mentioned, he had tediously copied a number of Chinese medical books and learnt from them. Kampong folks from Lian Teng Hng (Kampong Eunos) often went to him for consultation. Most likely, my grandma at that time was his assistant when he was dealing with the patients. Many years after my grandpa's death, his old neighbours in Kampong Eunos, especially Ah Poh, would visit my grandma. They would discuss Chinese herbs and their uses. They would also tour the farm and identify herbs that I had thought were weeds.

My grandma, Koh Cheo Neo

Should our grandma be unable to treat us, she would bring us to a Chinese physician at Chai Chee Village. I was very sick once. The herbal drinks my grandma prescribed failed to cure me. I was taken to an old Chinese physician at a Chinese medical hall at Chai Chee Village. The medical hall was just at the junction of Changi Road and Peng Ghee Road. We climbed a few steps from the road to the medical hall. There was a row of rattan chairs meant for patients waiting their turn. We sat there, waiting for him to finish his examination of the patient before us. After the examination, the patient handed him a little red packet folded from traditional red paper, which was meant for writing auspicious Chinese characters during Chinese New Year. He then handed the prescription to the pharmacist. The pharmacist laid the prescription on a long table. Two long wooden paperweights were carefully placed—one on the head and one at the end—of the prescription. A huge, pink square Manila paper was placed alongside the prescription with one of the apexes of the Manila paper pointing straight ahead. Then he proceeded to read the prescription and gather the herbs as prescribed. If an herb was too bulky, he had to cut it with his large guillotine. I was curious. I had never seen a guillotine before. He lifted the handle, placed the herb beneath the middle of the huge blade then pressed down the handle. The herb was cut into two. Then when an herb needed to be pounded, he put it inside a brass bowl and pounded it with a pestle with a brass lid attached. As he pounded, the brass lid made a loud, high-pitched, bell-like sound. After he was satisfied with the pounding, he made a few clanging sounds on the brass bowl and returned the pestle-cum-lid rather forcefully onto the empty brass bowl. A final loud clanging sound was made. Perhaps that was to prove that his business was popular. Then he poured the pounded herb on the Manila paper. The smaller items were weighed with a tiny *daching*. That was not all. He took down a long abacus, which was hanging on the wall, and started clacking away. His fingers moved so fast. Sometimes, I wondered whether his calculations were accurate. The final total amount and the instructions to brew the medicine were then written on the prescription. As for the herbs, he brought up the bottom apex of the diamond-shaped paper, first folded it up, then folded at the right apex, followed by the left. Finally, he brought the packet to his eye level, shook it a little so that the herbs would settle, and then he brought down the top fold with the top apex to tuck it in neatly under the left and right folds. A tough twine made from *kiam chow*, a kind of reed, then was tied around the parcel, leaving a loop for the patient to slip his finger in. Several elongated folds were made on the prescription paper then it was tucked tightly into the twine. The patient paid and bowed gratefully before walking away with the parcel swinging from his fingers.

When it was my turn, my grandma introduced me to the physician. He was a slim, elderly, clean-shaven man with sunken eyes and grey hair. He was dressed in a white *magua* (the traditional Chinese gentleman's coat). My grandma called him Lau Sian Shen and told him of my symptoms. On his table was a small red cloth cushion, which was meant for the patient to put his palm on, and a pad of white paper with the name of the medical hall in red at the top. He examined my eyes, my tongue and finally took my pulse. He closed his eyes and concentrated on what my pulse could tell him. Then he told my grandma that I had to abstain from eating certain cooling foods and had to drink more water. With a bow and with both hands, she handed a red packet to him. He accepted the gift with a nod of thanks. Then we waited for the medicine to be dispensed.

At home, my dad would read from the prescription the amount of water needed to brew the herbs and the amount left to be consumed. My mum would bring out her peculiar roundish pot with a clay handle and a tapering spout to prepare the herbal drink.

The herbal brew was usually very bitter. But the Chinese had the saying: 'The more bitter the medicine is, the more effective it is." So that was a little encouragement for us to take the bitter brew. My mum would pour out the brew and wait for it to become lukewarm before letting me drink it in one gulp. Then she would give me a little sweet to suck.

 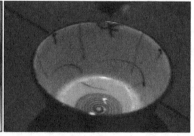

The medicine pot my mum used was similar to this one.	The blue rimmed bowl which mum used to measure out the amount of liquid medicine for us to consume per brew.

We rarely consulted a western doctor. As far as I knew, I had gone to a doctor only once when I had a fever that did not go down. No amount of herbal brew could bring the temperature down. I was brought to an Indian clinic at Siglap and I think the doctor was called Dr Kulkarni. At the clinic, the fan was on full blast. As I had never sat under an electric fan before, I felt so cold that I shivered. But after a while, I felt very much better. Was it because the cool air took away the fever? Anyway, when it was my turn, the doctor examined me. He took a white, flat stick and pressed down my tongue, then he put a stethoscope on my chest. It was over within a few minutes. As for the medicine, it seemed quite costly. I did not know what I suffered from but with the treatment, I got well.

With the working, running, hacking, throwing, dashing, *changkol*-ing, chopping, kicking, knocking, hammering, stamping, stomping, jumping, climbing, paddling, shoving, raking, abseiling, swinging, pulling, biting and digging we did, it was very normal for us to get cuts, boils, insect bites and sores. To our grandma, there was nothing to worry about unless the pain was really serious. All these things caught the attention of Madam Ong Ka's son-in-law, Ah Chiang. Madam Ong Ka had two daughters and a son. The eldest daughter was Ah Kiau, the second, Poh Chu, and the son, Ah Hee. Her daughters, Ah Kiau and Poh Chu, worked as *ayah* (matrons) in the former Woodbridge Mental Hospital at Yio Chu Kang. Ah Kiau's husband, Ah Chiang, worked as a cook there and was most probably quite influential among the workers—the gardeners, the health care workers, the maids, the counsellors, the doctors and the guards. Ah Chiang, being a typical Hainanese, was, without doubt, very friendly, helpful, considerate and thankful to us for treating our closest neighbour—his mother-in-law—like a member of our family. Often they visited us, took a tour round our farm and chatted. One day, Ah Chiang discovered the sores and boils on our legs—large and small. The biggest was the size of a ten-cent coin. He sympathised with us and promised to help us get rid of them. Over the following weeks, he brought us gentian blue, violet lotion, bandages and cotton wool and started to treat us. We sat down on low stools and he swiped, wiped, cleaned the pus and dead cells from our sores. Then he applied the medicine he had brought and bandaged the sores.

He continued to so this for a few weeks and told us to do the treatment ourselves after that, which we did, but of course, not as carefully as he had done. By and by, our sores disappeared. We were indeed very grateful to him and his wife. Whenever they visited us, we accorded them with utmost respect. It was his love and well-intentioned thoughts that were firmly etched in our minds.

Being young, about 12, I took very seriously what my parents would discuss—be it health, politics, history, geography or farming techniques. My siblings' thoughts were similar too. We shared many things, such as the same work, the same type of food and the same bed. When our harvests were poor, we shared the same sorrow. One day, my grandma was chit-chatting with Ong Ka. Ong Ka and grandma were the closest of friends. Each would always be visiting the other. They would discuss child-care and medicine. Well, one might think that Chinese women knew nothing about modern medicine. Not so. Grandma's thinking was progressive for the times. She stated the fact that modern medicine had made children of that day healthier and the mortality rate had gone down. Up to this day, I still hold high respect for grandma.

Mdm Ong Bee Cheng, our nearest neighbour. We called her Madam Ong Ka.
Photographed by Yeo Hong Eng

One of the saddest and most regretful events that I ever experienced was when I accidentally hit my brother Hong Bian on the head with a *changkol*. We were digging for earthworms to feed the brood of ducklings that my parents had bought from Lau Phua, the chick and duckling dealer who lived at Simpang Bedok. We were eager to get as many worms as possible. I was handling the *changkol*. The first few strokes did yield some worms. We got more and more excited. Finally, as I was lowering the *changkol* blade, he bent forward, most likely to get a worm. My blade landed on the right side of the back of his head. Blood immediately spurted out. My other brother shouted that Hong Bian had been injured. My parents raced to the scene. Immediately, they searched for the wound and tried to stop the bleeding. I did not know by what means and where they sent him to get his wound stitched. He had a few stitches and his head was bandaged. I was not sure whether I was caned for the mishap. Anyway, I was glad that his wound healed fast.

There was another time when I was feeling very down after my mum had reprimanded me for doing something wrong. Then, Ah Hock, the son of Soh Chew, saw me in such a state. He taunted me. As he was walking away, I picked up a stone—quite a large piece, about the size of a child's fist—and threw it high in his direction. It was not my intention to hit him. To my misfortune, it landed squarely on top of his head with a *plop* sound. He ran howling to his uncles and aunts. They were there—a distance away from where we were. The uncles and aunts were having a rest most likely after harvesting coconuts as it was coconut harvest time. Cries of horror could be heard. Fear gripped me. I could not run. After making some enquiries, they identified me as the culprit. My dad dragged me to the hall and ordered me to kneel down in front of the image of Tua Pek Kong, our family's patron god. It was of no use trying to reason with the adults in those days. In my mind, I had not intentionally tried to hurt him. I just wanted to threaten him. That was why I threw the stone high. If I had wanted to harm him, I would have thrown it straight at him. It was pure accident that he moved into the path of the falling stone.

Bird Flu

Once, our chickens became infected with bird flu—the disease all chicken farmers dread. All of a sudden, the healthy chicks, hens and cockerels would find their feathers drooping, and then they fell to the ground, struggled weakly and finally lay motionless. Just imagine our sorrow at such a sight. Within days, a few hundred birds could be wiped out. I lamented that I was assigned to keep the coop clean and to lock them up for the night. The next morning, when the door was unlocked and pushed open, there on the floor were lifeless birds. Can you imagine my shock and sorrow? Furthermore, we had to cart them away to bury them in mass graves. The bill for a batch of chicken feed had to be paid but with what? Normally, we paid the suppliers only after the chickens were sold.

Swine Fever

The same thing happened with swine fever. The pigs just fell like ninepins. In order to salvage a few dollars, when signs of swine fever loomed, my dad would rush to the butcher to ask him to slaughter all the remaining pigs. He could sell the meat cheaply, as in those days, swine fever was not known to affect humans. When pigs died in this way, debts owed to the suppliers could not be paid. Nobody could understand the agony of the farmers except the affected farmers themselves.

The people of that time lived simple lives and there were many instances when they had to cooperate with others and rely on themselves to emerge from illness and natural disasters. But if heaven were not so kind, they could perish with them.

Chapter 11
Our Battle with the Elements

Droughts

I will tell you of our experiences in the 1950s and early 1960s. The months from May to July were usually very dry but in some years, they were exceptionally dry. Sometimes, for a month or two, not a drop of rain fell. The grass dried up. The springs in the wells on higher ground, followed by the wells in the valleys, stopped flowing. Our dried up streams and ponds became short-cut routes to the farm. We even sank wells in the middle of the ponds. We took the opportunity to clear the muddy deposits of the ponds. While clearing, we found catfish and snakeheads snuggled in the wet mud. In places where the mud was caked, we could see rotting fish as well as swarms of houseflies feeding on them.

The water lettuce and duckweed perished, but the water hyacinth and water burhead could rehabilitate, adapt themselves and thrive in the muddy patches as they were the hardier plants.

We tried to make do with what little water we got from the spring in the sunken depth of the wells to water the vegetables. We took the opportunity to clear the sunken residue in the wells too. One among us brothers would go down the well with the help of a ladder. Then the ladder was hauled up and a pail was lowered. The one in the well would fill the pail with mud. My parents would haul up the mud and empty it nearby. We tried to deepen the well too, but if the bottom of it had reached a hard layer, then a greater effort was needed. Furthermore, we did not expect to find springs in the hard ground layer.

We could get springs from the well near a stream. We deepened it, but the soft mud gave way and filled up again however deep we dug. A solution was needed. We went to our usual building supplier at Simpang Bedok, Hiap Seng Leong, to order cylindrical concrete retaining walls. These were not much different from huge water concrete pipes, but they were enormous ones, about four feet in diameter. Their height was about three feet. They were lowered into the dugout by means of tough ropes tied to the walls. Extra help was requested from our neighbour, Ah Hee, Madam Ong Ka's son. The person at the bottom of the dugout had to steady the pipes and guide them into place as well as ensure that they were accurately levelled. If each one were not levelled properly, the final one at the top would be skewed at an angle. Then the outer wall was filled with clean sand. Spring water would filter through the layer of sand and into the well through the holes built into the walls for the purpose. Spring water could also seep through the seams of the joints between the cylindrical walls. But if the water quality was not good enough for consumption, it could be used for other purposes—to water the vegetables or feed the farm animals.

For cooking and washing our crockery and clothes, at first we had to channel water from a common well in the Malay kampong. Our parents had often warned us to follow proper Muslim customs and practices when scooping water from the well in a Malay kampong. We had to borrow the scooping pail from a Muslim family, as we did not want them to suspect that we contaminated the water with our non-*halal* containers. On the whole, the kampong folks were very understanding and cooperative. They lent us their pail willingly. Later, we found out that the kampong well showed signs of drying up. We went further to a well at Kampong Jalan Haji Salam, as well as a Chinese well near the perimeter of the Bedok schools. Whichever well we went to, there was always a spirit of cooperation and understanding. We never encountered animosity. Each of us balanced two kerosene tins of water on our shoulders with a carrying pole. The whole family was involved. Usually, we formed three chains—two to get the water from the source, two to take over from them midway and two to carry them up to our storage pots and tanks. When the task was completed, it was already nearly 8 p.m. Then we had our dinner.

A kampong well

In 1962, black and white TV Singapura was introduced. Along the route we traversed to carry water, there lived an Indian family. The father had just bought a television set. Every evening, he would switch on his set to watch Hindustani films. Many of the kampong folks swarmed to his house to watch from the beginning of the show till the end. He was so kind-hearted and good-natured that he allowed them to sit inside his hall while watching. After having filled our water containers, we too joined in the fun. At times, humans are humans; he eventually complained that he could not get enough rest and sleep due to the constant requests from the kampong folks to watch TV. If he wanted a rest, children would knock at his door. If he did not respond to their calls, insults would be hurled at him.

When the water shortage reached a critical point in 1962, the kampong headmen appealed to the City Council for help. The City Council sent tanks of water in their improvised trucks daily to the affected kampong folks. Hours before each truck arrived, we lined up our metallic containers, in various shapes and sizes, by the side of the dirt track. When the truck arrived, the driver filled each container with the hose attached to the bottom of the water tank. When the water in the tank was exhausted, the driver went away to get a fresh tank and the whole process was repeated until we were satisfied. Sometimes, we children clung on to the tailboard of the

241

empty water truck as it moved away to get a fresh supply from the hydrant meant for fire engines a few kilometres away—at Changi 8½ Milestone to be exact. We were too young to know of the danger should the truck suddenly stop or jerk forward.

Then the government installed standpipes in the kampongs. Kampongs Haji Salam and the heart of Kampong Tanah Merah Kechil were the first to get public standpipes. After the standpipes were installed, we got the water from them. The cemented area around each standpipe was small. The kampong folks nearest to the standpipes contributed money to enlarge the area so that the womenfolk could do their washing there and anyone could bathe there without soiling their feet. Well water was only used for washing. In most cases, the wells were closed up, as they were not of use any more.

An example of a typical public standpipe.

When our ponds and wells were all dried up, there was a public standpipe about 50 metres away from our nearest pond. Every day, the kampong womenfolk did their washing at the standpipe. The waste water flowed down into the muddy stream and seeped into the ground. My dad thought he could put the waste water to good use. He created a dam at the stream where the waste water from the standpipe flowed. A big pool of water accumulated. He deepened the stream leading to his pond. The water, although soapy, was better than none. The landlady was apprehensive. She was afraid that the Ministry of Health would not approve of it, as mosquitoes might breed in the water. My dad assured her that by emptying the pond daily, the mosquitoes would not have the chance to breed, as the water was not stagnant. He promised her that once the monsoon period came, he would dismantle the dam. During the onset of the monsoon, the first thing he did was to clear the makeshift dam.

The droughts reached a critical point. The water in the reservoirs in Singapore reached a dangerously low level. There was water rationing. At first, there was no water in standpipes for four hours a day, but as days went on, the water situation did not improve. Water was provided only for six hours a day. Although water was turned on at the official time stated, the standpipes in the kampongs still remained dry. What they heard coming out of the pipe was not water but only air. There was a long queue of water containers. When the water arrived, at first, it was a mere trickle. "It was like a child urinating," some of us would say in jest. Family members took turns to wait for the pails to fill and carried them away. By the time they got the water they needed, it was already way past midnight. Most of them had to get up early to go to work, as their work places were far away.

During those hours of water rationing, every night, we had to wait for the water to fill our containers to use the next day. Our other activities at night had to take a back seat.

Thunder and Lightning

One afternoon, it was raining heavily. My dad wanted to wash away some dirt at the front of the house with the rainwater that was collected earlier. As soon as he splashed the water, it seemed as if a very bright light and a deafening roar resulted. I was nearby. We could feel the heat emanating from the lightning. The flash blinded us temporarily. The pail was flung away. We shook with shock. Then my dad said, "Next time, remember, never splash water on rainy days. The water would conduct the thunder and lightning to us." How far it was true I did not know.

Another incident happened one humid and cloudy day. Out of the blue, there was a deafening thunderclap and lightning flashed almost at the same time. The lalang patch under the coconut trees not far from our house was burning. A light breeze blew. The fire began raging more fiercely. We were afraid it would soon reach our house. Every one of us—no matter how big or small, young or old, anyone who could run—swung into action. My dad took the *changkol*. My mum grabbed pails to fetch water. My grandma had something else. I took the long scythe. The elderly estate manager's workman, Mr Bong, carried a pail filled with water. Other kampong folks carried other things. All of us set out with one aim—to extinguish the fire. We cleared the dry grass nearby, cut away the tall branches, flattened the tall lalang, and splashed water on to the dry grass to act as firebreaks.

Poor old Mr Bong, upon reaching the burning site, discovered that the pail of water that he was carrying had leaked away. *"Chelaka! Ini tong bochor!"* he cursed under his breath and returned to get a new pail of water. The fire died a natural death when it met a firebreak that we made, denying it fuel to consume.

At another time, a fire happened at old Ong Ka's land. The afternoon was very hot. It was about 2 p.m. Suddenly, we heard a sizzling and crackling sound, accompanied with a small explosion, like the sound of firecrackers. Black smoke billowed up into the clear blue sky. We knew it would be dangerous if it were not brought under control. That time, a strong wind was fanning the fire. The fire spread so fast and the smoke was so thick. We tried our best, but with little success. I could feel the intense heat radiating from the leaping fire. I moved away a little. I wanted to get a close-up view of the wall of fire that leapt, swayed, danced and then tapered off into the air. Then someone pulled me away, denying me the chance to watch the fire further. Someone else ran to a public telephone at Bedok Village, which was several kilometres away, to call for the fire engine. When the fire engine—a red Dennis—arrived, it was just in time to see the fire dying. The fire stopped at a well-used sandy path. The firemen did the mopping up—extinguishing little pockets of glowing embers with the knapsack Indian pumps as well as thick flexible swats. Thank heaven the fire had died. If it had spread across the path, it would engulf the pigsties, the heaps of dry coconut leaves and Madam Ong Ka's house. Then it would have gone on to a patch of lalang, and finally to my house.

A few guesses were made as to how the fire had started. Arson was ruled out. Lightning was also ruled out, as the day was hot and no one heard any thunder prior to the fire. It could probably be due to either a smoker carelessly throwing a lighted cigarette butt on a patch of dry grass or sunlight shining on a glass bottle. The concave nature of the glass bottle could focus sunlight onto a patch of dry grass, causing the grass to catch fire.

At the end of the day, we were glad that the fire had not done us much harm; we were mindful that we always had to be on guard not to let it loose, or else one day, a fire would catch us off guard and give us a beating so severe that it would leave us with nothing or could even cause deaths.

I loved cycling around to see places. I wrote that in one of my school essays. One of my cycling experiences was the most fearful and the most unforgettable. While cycling along Changi Road, at the front gate of the Changi Bus depot on the top of a ridge, I saw a huge column of smoke rising far in the distance. I raced to the scene. In the early 1960s traffic was very light. I rode past Paya Lebar Road and then came to Aljunied Road. A huge crowd of people was gathering along the roadside to watch a fire burning a cluster of attap houses among coconut trees. I inched closer to the front. The fire was raging furiously at the dry attap houses and the flames shot up high above it. Suddenly there was a loud explosion. A portable gas tank flew up, reaching a height of about 30 metres and then dropped down on the burning cinders, sending sparks everywhere. There were loud shouts of horror and surprise.

The flame then leapt from the roofs to the coconut leaves above. A strong wind blew, fanning the flames. The raging flames spread and leapt uncontrollably to burn whatever was in its path, leaving a trail of smouldering ash and twisting pipes, clay pots, concrete bases and charred columns in its wake. Soon the policemen and fire-engines arrived. The policemen started to cordon off the area and firemen immediately pumped water onto the burning houses. The victims were sobbing, wailing, fainting and even blaming themselves for causing the disaster while others were consoling and pacifying them. The whole crowd could only watch with mouths agape.

I then cycled away, feeling deep sorrow for the victims. I felt that my energy and strength had been sapped by the burning inferno. With much effort, I pedalled slowly home.

The Rainy Season

Now most people live in flats. The housing estates have interconnecting walkways sheltering them. Rain, no matter how heavy it is, does not cause much bother. People do not hear the pattering of raindrops on their roofs. They do not feel the water under their feet rushing down impatiently to the *longkang* (drains). They do not rush out of their homes with their umbrellas or raincoats to shelter their loved ones returning in the rain.

We who lived in attap houses in the kampongs back then were very much at the mercy of the weather. If it rained, we were very much affected by the noise, the howling wind, the rattling of the windows and doors and the flapping of loose attap leaves on the rooftop and the water that beat and leaked into the house. There was also the constant fear that the storm might rip off the roof. When rainwater leaked into the house, everyone was in a flurry to get containers of any sort—be they washbasins, empty milk tins, pots or pans—to collect the rainwater so that it would not wet the house. Then again, there was the cacophony of sounds coming from the raindrops on the containers. Different containers produced different pitches and tones. My mum would hurry us, or whoever was around, to help to collect the dry laundry from the clotheslines or move the dry firewood into the kitchen.

What about the vegetable beds? Flowing water could erode the embankments, beds and earth shore-ups. If that happened, efforts would be made to minimise the damage or to divert the course of the flowing water. Most often, if possible, my dad himself would do it. But if the damage was great, the whole family had to chip in.

If there were storms, the tall papaya trees, trellises and props for climbers would be brought down. After the storm had subsided, the damage would be assessed and efforts had to be made to clear up the mess and repair work had to be done.

The rainy season greatly hampered our daily chores, such as cooking the animals' food, feeding and cleaning them and looking after their welfare. We could only hope that they would not catch colds or the flu.

My dad, who had so many chicken coops and pigsties, was the busiest on stormy days. He would go from place to place to watch out for floods, the roof being ripped off, and to keep an eye on the more active animals that wished to venture out of their enclosures. They would tear out the stakes, planks and wire netting in order to make their escape. Once discovered, we would round them up, even in the stormy weather. After the rounding-up, there would be repairs. Stakes, planks and netting had to be readied. Tools such as hammers, nails and awls for digging holes, *changkols*, pliers, saws and wires had to be brought. Then, there would be measuring, sawing, digging, nailing and tying. There would be no rest until the repair works were completed. We children sometimes felt the strain and grumbled in silence, but nevertheless, continued. If the job was not completed, could we put down our tools? Definitely not. Sometimes, we had to continue till late in the night. We did not come to regret this. The skills and knowledge we gained proved useful later in our lives. We could not have acquired such experience and skills through books and the Internet.

Chapter 12
Our Festivals and Beliefs

Lunar New Year

In our kampong, the residents' religions were very clear. The Malays were all Muslim. The Chinese were nearly all Buddhist or Taoist (there was no clear distinction between Buddhists and Taoists). The Indian families were Hindu. There may have been a few who were Christian, but they did not openly practise. In my house, there was an image of Toa Pek Kong, the god of prosperity. On either side of the image was a couplet written by my dad, who learned calligraphy from grandpa. Anyone who saw his calligraphy would compliment him on it. Days before Lunar or Chinese New Year, my dad would buy rolls of dark red paper (which was white on the reverse side), brushes and ink stone. Before he wrote, he would get an ink stone out from the drawer of the altar table, pour a little water onto the ink stone and rub the ink stick on it in circular motions. When he was satisfied that the ink was thick enough, he would be ready to write. Sometimes, my mum and us children helped to prepare the ink. He would write a few pairs of couplets, a few sets of four-character verses and a few single characters.

In order to spring clean the house for the Lunar New Year, the *Thong Shu* or the Chinese daily calendar was consulted. It would indicate an auspicious day to start the cleaning. When the day came, my mum would have our roles on a roster. My sisters would clean the kitchen. My brothers and I would clean the windows and sweep the floor, among other chores. My mum would clear the furniture from the hall and kitchen and give them a good scrub. My dad would buy whitewash from Hiap Seng Leong Building Supplies, mix it with water and repaint the outer walls. We helped too. After cleaning and painting, it was time to decorate the house with the characters and couplets my father had written. Tapioca starch was prepared from tapioca flour. A brush was dipped into the starch to smear it on the spot where the calligraphy was to be pasted—one pair of couplets was pasted on the right and left of the deity's image in the hall and one pair by the sides of the main door of the hall and one on the door of the kitchen. Then, a few four-character verses were pasted on the horizontal beams of all the doors and windows. The single characters were pasted on the door and windowpanes as well as the rice bin. Some of the translated verses were: 'Peace be with you when you go in and out of the house', 'Gold and silver fill to the brim' and 'May spring bring you luck'. The character 'spring' can sound like 'sufficient' in Hokkien. Next, a red banner was hung above the doorway. A relative commented, "The whole house looks like new." That was indeed true.

A house with couplets on.
Photo credit: Unknown.
Photo from a street vendor along Sungei Road.

During our younger days, my mum seldom bought our clothing—she sewed them herself. She would buy a long piece of cloth, then she would cut and sew each of us a pair of pyjamas, as it was believed that children sleeping in pajamas on New Year's Eve would prolong the lives of the parents.

My brothers in the New Year
pajamas my mother sewed.
Photographed by Lu Xiang Hee

A few days before the Lunar New Year, a day was chosen to send the kitchen god to heaven to report our doings for the past year. *Nian kao* was made. It was sweet and sticky. It would give the kitchen god a sticky mess in his mouth so he could not give a bad report to heaven on our behaviour for the past year.

Besides *nian kao*, we had to prepare cakes of different types. To grind the flour we had to go to Mr Ong Wah's house. He had a huge grindstone. We would soak rice overnight and carry it to his house to wait for our turn, as many other neighbours were also there. We would help each other turning the huge grindstone manually. Others would help to scoop the soaked rice and feed it into the slot where it would flow onto the grinding surfaces. The ground rice flour, still wet and dripping, had to be carried home in bags made from cotton fabric.

Meanwhile, banana leaves had to be collected, washed and cut into size to line empty tin cans meant for the prepared ingredients for making *nian kao, huat kuay* and other New Year cakes. Flour, sugar, *gula melaka*, eggs, food dye, coconut milk and pandan leaves were readied. Then the ingredients were mixed. We used burning joss sticks as the timing devices for mixing. The huge wok had to be washed and sufficient firewood and water had to be prepared. Everybody was busy in one way or another. One thing my mum was very particular about was negative comments from us. Everybody had to zip up their mouth. In the process of baking, mum would be worried whether the baking would be successful, as she did so only once or twice a year and she might have missed out some steps of the recipe. When the baking time was up, she would be excited to see the outcome. She used her own intuition to estimate the amount of each ingredient, as she was illiterate. Also, there were no measuring scales or written instructions. Every year, she succeeded in making the New Year delicacies which she then proudly distributed to some close relatives and neighbours.

There was a legend on how *nian kao* had helped to overcome famine during the Three Kingdom period in China. During those days, when the harvest was plentiful, the villagers would bake a lot of *nian kao* and store it. Those stored *nian kao* would harden and turn mouldy, but the villagers were not worried. During natural calamities when food was scarce, each family would take out their *nian kao*, brush off the mould, cut them and re-cook it in different ways. They could fry, boil, stir-fry or make soup with it.

Our family seldom ate *nian kao* fresh from the oven, as it was so sticky that it was quite impossible to slice. If one wished to eat freshly baked *nian kao*, they would have to pull a portion from the main cake then struggle to chew it. Their hands would be sticky with it too.

My mum would store the *nian kao* in a big bamboo basket. A few months after that, it would have hardened. She would take a piece and brush away the mould. She sliced it and fried it with flour and beaten eggs. To enjoy the flavour and the aroma, one should eat it when it is warm. The crust was crispy and the *nian kao* inside was still soft. The taste was heavenly. The dish could be prepared in many different ways, depending on one's ingenuity.

Nian kao—the sticky rice cake

On the day before the New Year's Eve, my mum would gather the choice vegetables reserved for that day to sell at the Chai Chee Market. We would also help to distribute them to our neighbours. For very close relatives, we distributed live chickens and vegetables, such as lettuce and *chye sin*. In return, they presented us with different kinds of canned and preserved food as well as homemade New Year delicacies. Uncle Yam, who owned a provision shop, would present us with the branded Mexico abalone besides other items. Teow Swee, who owned a coffee shop and a provision shop, would present us with one or two crates of Framroz and Fraser and Neave aerated water. Of course, that included the F&N bottle opener as well as a Player's ashtray.

On the dawn of New Year's Eve, we woke up as early as 3 a.m. to harvest the vegetables that had been judged to mature on that day. As sales were predicted to be brisk, more than double the amount was harvested. We washed, packed and loaded them onto our bicycles. My dad would pedal a load, and I would pedal another. With the dim light from the bicycle dynamo, we cycled along the unlit and unpaved Tanah Merah Kechil Road. My mum had to reach the market earlier than usual; so would all the other vendors, in order to display their goods. She hurried to catch the first Changi bus in the early morning. Sales were brisk, as that was the festival no one would miss. The Malays and the Indians also joined in the marketing, as they knew that the vendors would take their days off over the next few days. By noon, all business had to stop. Most of the vendors had quick meals at the hawkers before hurrying home to prepare their reunion dinners. The hawkers took this opportunity to raise their prices an extra few cents per serving, with fewer ingredients. By 11 a.m., I cycled to the bus stop to transport my mum and her purchases home. That afternoon, everybody at home had something to do—last minute cleaning or retouching the paintwork. My dad would slaughter a chicken and a duck after mumbling a short prayer. Then, we would defeather them. After that, we would help prepare the ingredients. We pounded chilli, added the *belacan* and the ginger. We also grated the coconuts and squeezed out the coconut milk. We cut and washed the mushrooms, soaked sea cucumbers and prepared the tables for prayer. That evening, joss sticks were lighted. We thanked the heavens for giving us a successful and peaceful year. Then joss paper was burnt.

Dad filled a huge lamp with kerosene. Then it was lit and it brightened the whole house. We had that done only once a year. Of course, the bedrooms and kitchen were also lit, but with smaller lamps. Calendars made from cardboard were easily available from the provision shops. They had pictures of actors and actresses, scenery and scenes from Chinese films. They were arranged in patterns to cover ugly blotches on the wooden wall panels. The whole hall looked new.

Then everybody would chip in to help with the arrangement of seats. Spoons, chopsticks, bowls, cups and dishes were washed thoroughly before arranging them around the huge table. Soft drinks were served too. Everybody, especially the children, was very excited, as it was only during the reunion dinner that such an elaborate and sumptuous meal was served. My mum would bring in the main dish—Mexican deep sea shellfish with 'Red Wheel' brand abalone cooked with pig stomach soup. There was also sea cucumber sautéed with chicken and mushrooms as well as chopped stir-fried chicken, duck and salted vegetable soup, chicken curry, steamed pomfret, mushrooms stewed with three-layered pork, shellfish and leeks fried with fish balls. Sometimes rabbit fish or *paituyi* was also purchased and steamed, but as usual, this dish was always in demand every New Year so the price of the rabbit fish was sky high. This dish was eaten because of the thick fish roe. Once a year, this species of fish would swim south of the China Sea to spawn. Another dish specially prepared by my mother was *or luak*. It was very chewy and tasty. It was prepared from tapioca flour fried with eggs, pounded dried prawns and chilli, strips of brown pork, a touch of celery and onion and a pinch of Buddha's Hand Ve-Tsin Gourmet Powder to taste.

With this mortar and pestle set, many delicious dishes were made possible.

Grandma, who was a vegetarian, had her dishes cooked separately, so her food would not be contaminated with any animal products.

Before dinner started, grandma would want us to count the number of dishes we had. We should have exactly ten dishes. The character ten in Chinese means 'wholesome' and 'completeness', like ten out of ten points. Having ten dishes would mean that the family was intact.

When everyone in the family was present, dinner would commence. Every care was taken not to break anything. Mum would give everyone many refills, especially of the abalone soup, for it was only once a year that we could afford to eat this dish. We tried every dish, as each was a rare treat. That was why we children always looked forward to the New Year.

The leek, in direct translation, sounded like *suan*, which means 'counting'. The seaweed dish sounded like *huat chai*, which means 'prosperous'. The cake *huat kuey* sounded like 'prosperity'. By eating the shellfish, the shell, when put together, made a jingling sound, which sounded like counting coins. Mandarin oranges are always used as a gift, because the word for Mandarin oranges in Hokkien or Cantonese is *kam*, which sounds like 'gold'. We would never offer a gift of Sunkist oranges. These oranges are known as *chiam* in Hokkien and sounded like 'pierce'. On New Year's day, using inauspicious words was a taboo.

After the reunion dinner was over, dad would burn packets of firecrackers. Simultaneously, as if by prior arrangement, the neighbours far and near would also let their crackers off, making a din throughout the whole neighbourhood. The dogs would tuck their tails between their legs and seek a place to hide. The crackers gave off deafening bursts of sound. Mum would carry the babies and cover their ears so they would not get a shock.

Meanwhile, the leftovers from the reunion dinner were boiled and kept in the larder for the next meals, as in those days, we did not have refrigerators. Then the table top was cleared and washed. Chairs were returned to their respective places. Dad would carefully fill each container under the legs of the larder with DDT, so that ants or other pests would not climb up the legs and help themselves to the food.

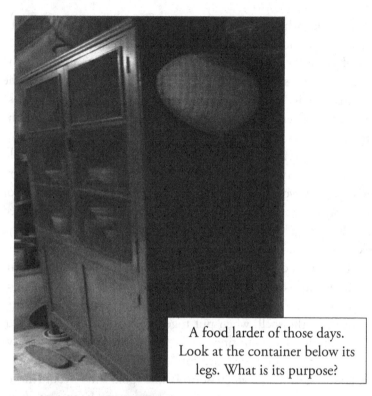

A food larder of those days. Look at the container below its legs. What is its purpose?

After the dinner, the chopsticks were returned to the holder.

The adults would then tell us the dos and don'ts of the Lunar New Year celebrations.

Don'ts

1. No one must sleep before 12 midnight. At 12 midnight, my dad would pray to heaven to welcome the new year, and another round of crackers would be left off. While waiting for midnight, we played card games. It was the only time when we laid aside our books and played till so late. The bright, huge kerosene lamps, table lamps and the candles from the altar made the house look like it was daylight and nobody was in the mood to sleep.
2. For the next three days, the floor must not be swept. If we did that, the wealth would be swept away. We took great care to keep our wooden clogs (*char kiak*) very clean and put them outside the house.
3. No inauspicious words must be used. Dad would give us a stern look if any of us blurted out an inappropriate word.
4. Never to throw tantrums or express anger.
5. Never demand *hongpao*.
6. Never open the *hongpao* in front of the giver.
7. Never eat more than necessary.

Dos

1. We should always be polite to one another.
2. We must obey all elders. We should never argue with them.
3. All bad habits must stop.
4. We must wear pajamas to sleep on New Year's Eve.
5. We must wear red clothing to go visiting. The colour red symbolises good luck.
6. While visiting, we must always carry a gift of Mandarin oranges for the host.
7. The appropriate wishes in Hokkien below must be made when visiting people:

To the old and elderly: *Xinni kian khong* (Be healthy)
To professionals: *Xinni huat chye* (Be prosperous)
To small children: *Xinni gao tua han* (Grow healthily)
To school children: *Xinni gao tak chea* (Study well)

It was believed that whatever one did on the first 15 days of the year would become habitual for the rest of the year.

While waiting for midnight to come, we children would take out cards to play. Play that involved money was never allowed. Dad would be busily cutting red paper into squares to wrap coins in them. The smallest amount I ever got was two twenty-cent coins. We were so happy that we decided to put them in our home-made piggy banks. Neighbours would give two ten-cent coins and some even a ten cent and a one cent. As we grew older and the family income increased, the red packets from our parents were increased to six dollars per person.

The Legend of the Lunar New Year

There was a legend on how the Chinese came to celebrate New Year or *Xin Nian*. In the olden days, in China, during springtime, a hideous monster would come to attack the people, leaving some dead and wounded. Blood would be everywhere. People were saddened at the same time, fighting a losing battle with the monster. Feeling satisfied, the monster went away. This occurrence was repeated year after year. One day, someone suggested that they wear red to simulate blood and make a lot of noise by exploding firecrackers to fool the monster. The idea was accepted unanimously. When the following spring arrived, everybody wore red, hung red banners in front of their houses and stayed at home to let off firecrackers. When the monster showed up, it thought that it saw the blood and that the people were preparing for a fight with him. Immediately, it took flight. So year after year, the Chinese repeated and modified the celebrations for the arrival of spring.

In the 1950s and 1960s, during the New Year celebrations, almost every house had a red banner across its central doorposts. New red couplets and auspicious characters in black were pasted on the doors and windows. The well-to-do had their characters written in gold and they were framed. And everyone was happy about it. For most poor families, the children got a chance to wear new clothes, eat chicken and duck, drink soft drinks, and eat oranges only during this festival. People got the chance to visit relatives, as their Chinese bosses would give them 15 days off. During these 15 days until *Yuan Xiao Jie*, lion and dragon dancers would go from firm to firm to dance and to express good wishes. The bosses would gladly award them with oranges and *hong paos*. It was the same with the cultural singing troupes who went from door to door to sing auspicious songs.

Firecrackers

It was usual for us to scour among the debris of the burnt-out crackers for freaks, unexploded and faulty-fused crackers. We would gather them and try other ways of making them explode. We would open up the unexploded ones and gather the flammable powder. Then we would make bigger firecrackers. If the combinations were correct, these homemade crackers would give a very loud explosion. If the wrapping was too thick, continuous sparks were given off. One particular technique worthy of mention was to cut the unexploded cracker to reveal the flammable black powder. Then, we touched the powder with a lighted joss stick. The sparks would shoot. Immediately after that, we gave the sparkling half cracker a hard stamp with our foot. It emitted a loud report. We still could not explain why it behaved that way. Sometimes, we made a cracker stand on the ground. Then we lit the fuse. While the fuse was still burning, we upturned an empty milk tin and placed it on the cracker. When the cracker burst, it sent the empty milk tin high up about 20 metres. We competed with each other to see who could send the milk tin higher.

I performed a highly dangerous experiment once. I got a very small glass medicine bottle. I inserted a cracker into the opening. Then I touched the fuse with a lighted joss stick. When the cracker burst, it sent tiny glass shards all over. A piece flew on to my arm, causing a small cut. Shivering with fright, I thought I was very lucky to have sustained such a small injury. I shuddered at the thought of losing an eye or two if the shards were to enter my eyes. Fortunately I scooted off to a distance before it exploded. What happened then, I dare not divulge to anybody till today.

Sometimes someone wished to boast that exploding firecrackers could not hurt him. He would hold the lighted crackers with his fingertips. Others followed suit. They did not show any signs of pain either. But I thought they were just pretending.

In the 1950s, two types of firecrackers were popular. The standard ones were about four centimetres long, mainly made in Macau and the wrapper had a picture of a beautiful lady. The other type was the very tiny ones of Kirin Brand. Small children loved to play with them and rarely got hurt. Each was about two centimetres long.

Firecrackers

In the 1960s, more exciting and innovative firecrackers became available. They were mainly made in China.

As for the young and girls, sparklers were popular. They could be dangerous when they were thrown up to the attap rooftops.

Needless to say, during the Chinese New Year period, the fire engine screamed almost non-stop for days. The firefighters were mostly non-Chinese, as the Chinese employees had taken leave. But I thought the firefighters were happy to be on duty, as they were rewarded with *hongpaos*.

On the first day of the New Year, it was customary for the younger generations to visit the elders. The first to visit my grandma were the cousins—Hong Thong, Hong Huat, Hong Ho, Meili, Kim Heok and Kim Kiok. My mum would serve them *mata kuching* or longan tea. Every New Year, my mum brewed a big kettle of it. They had lunch with us and, we let off firecrackers, then they went round the farms and the coconut and rubber estates before going home. As usual, my parents and my grandma would present them with *hongpaos,* as well as exchange oranges. My cousin, Hong Thong, would present my dad with a New Year card. It was a three-by-four-inch, colourful card, serrated at the corners. The envelope was pink and made of Manila paper.

A Chinese New Year
card of the 1950s
From Yeo Hong
Eng's collection

From the first day till the fifteenth day of the lunar month, my dad would religiously burn incense and make offerings of *chian aup* (delicacies which included preserved melon, peanuts preserved with sugar and peanut candy) to heaven early in the morning as well as in the evening. After the prayer, a packet of firecrackers would be let off.

On the eighth day of the New Year, my parents would buy two full-grown sugarcane plants. That night, they prepared the various offerings as well as the various types of paper incense. One outstanding type of incense paper was yellow and it had to be cut several times. The end result looked like very big lanterns. Tied on each side in front of the altar was the fully-grown sugar plant with leaves and roots intact. Each plant was decorated with several red paper bands and yellow incense paper. The Hokkiens believed that they survived a marauding tribe by hiding in a field of sugarcane. Thus, the sugarcane was honoured on this night. At about 12 midnight, my dad would pray to heaven, praising God on his birthday. After that, the paper incense was brought to the courtyard to be burnt. Firecrackers were once again let off.

On the fifteenth day of the New Year, which was *Yuan Siow Jie*, or *Chap Goh Mei*, again there were prayers to mark the end of the celebration of the festival.

Tung Jie

During *Tung Jie, tang yuan* was cooked and offered to heaven. *Tung Jie* is exactly ten days before 1 January of the solar calendar. The *tang yuan* was usually of two colours, one was the original white colour of flour and the other was dyed pink. *Tang yuan* was rolled into round balls about the size of regular fish balls. They were boiled with *gula melaka* (coconut sugar) and ginger.

Dumpling Festival (*Duan Wu Jie*)

During the Dumpling festival on the fifth day of the fifth moon of each lunar year, rice dumplings were boiled and eaten. That festival was celebrated to commemorate the death of the patriotic minister, Qu Yuan, in the ancient state of Chu. Qu Yuan was very disappointed that corrupt ministers around the emperor had undone what he was doing. He felt so miserable that he tied a rock to himself and jumped into the Mi Lou River. The people, fearing that the fish would eat his body, immediately wrapped glutinous rice with bamboo leaves and threw them into the river to distract the fish. Boats also raced to find his body. That gave rise to the Dragon Boat Festival.

Rice dumplings

Zhong Yuan Jie

One of the main Chinese religious festivals is *Zhong Yuan Jie*. The English named it 'Feast of the Hungry Ghost'. Buddhists believe that all souls are allowed to return to earth for one month on the seventh moon of the year. We celebrated this occasion by preparing sumptuous food for all the departed souls who returned. As usual, we slaughtered chicken and ducks, bought roasted pork, baked different types of cakes and offered prayers inviting the returning souls to partake of the food and to receive the gifts we burnt for them. Then, many paper crates of paper money and paper models of the things used while they were on earth were burnt. This festival was different from the others such as the *Zhong Qui Jie* and *Duan Wu Jie* in that a triangular flag with an image of a dragon was placed on each dish of food offering.

At the village level, the temple would organise *wayang* opera performances. Food items were purchased and offered for prayers. Village members who contributed a yearly amount would get a portion of the food. There were also household items put on auction during one of the nights. Before that auction, a grand ten-course dinner would be served. In between the dishes served, the auctioneer would put up items and shout out the reserved price. Those interested would inform the assistants, who in turn alerted the auctioneer. The successful bidder would pay for the item the following year. The most prized item was charcoal, which they called 'black gold'. People would bid thousands of dollars for a small amount of charcoal.

According to Buddhist belief, those who possessed those items which were blessed by the gods would have their lives run smoothly for the rest of the year.

Zhong Qiu Jie or the Mid-autumn Festival

We did not need any reminder about when the Mid-autumn Festival was. My parents, who went to the market every day, would know just by looking at the displays of lanterns and different kinds of mooncake at the Chinese confectionery shops. One such shop was Chop Kian Seng at Chai Chee market.

We did not make mooncakes. We purchased them. On the day of the actual occasion (the fifteenth day of the eighth moon), we offered the mooncakes to heaven. One particular type of mooncake we children loved to eat was a small one that was encased in a colourful plastic cage similar to the rattan one used for trapping and transporting of pigs. Another common type was roundish, rolled up with thick white paper with a very decorative red label describing the confectionery and the content. Each packet contained six pieces or half a dozen. Every piece had the name of the confectionery stamped on it in red. The more expensive ones were packed in decorative cardboard boxes of four pieces to a box.

We got the chance to taste mooncake only during that period. Mum would gather us siblings and she would describe the ingredients inside each piece. Then she would cut it into six equal parts and give each of us one portion. We would relish it, as it was a once-a-year affair. She would then order us to drink a cup of Chinese tea after eating the cakes.

The family had prayers on the fifteenth of the eighth moon with mooncakes as the main offering. My dad would remind us to observe the moon. He would proudly tell us that the full moon was the roundest on that day. True enough, that night, the moon was the roundest and the brightest, as the sky was devoid of clouds. We would stare into the moon and asked our dad about the dark spots on it. Then he would patiently tell us the Legend of the Moon Fairy.

According to ancient Chinese legend, there were ten suns in the universe. Each sun would rule the Earth for a day. One day, the ten suns appeared on Earth. The Earth became so hot that almost everything was drying up. The emperor sent for Houyi, the celestial archer, to shoot down nine of the suns. Houyi had been sent to Earth by the Jade Emperor in heaven. Upon Houyi successfully shooting the nine suns, the emperor decided to reward him with an immortality pill. Houyi however, did not swallow the pill. Instead, he handed it over to his wife for safekeeping.

One day, he was ordered to the emperor's palace. Peng, his assistant archer, pretended to be ill. Houyi excused him and allowed him to go home to rest. Instead of going home, he went to demand the immortality pill from Chang Er, Houyi's wife. Chang Er knew that she was no match to fight Peng so she immediately swallowed the pill. Something strange happened to her. She floated up into the heavens and went to the moon. Houyi, when he learnt of the incident, felt downhearted. He cried for her day and night. The Jade Emperor's wife pitied the couple. She did not want Chang Er to stay in the moon forever. She ordered the Jade Rabbit in the moon to make a pill for Chang Er so that she could descend to Earth to meet her husband. The Jade Rabbit started work immediately. This legend is repeated until today. If you look at the moon, there is a dark patch that resembles a rabbit pounding herbs. Every year on the fifteenth of the eighth moon, Houyi waits for Chang Er to return. On this particular day, the moon is the brightest and the roundest. The Chinese make mooncakes and drink tea while admiring the bright round moon.

Another legend why the *Zhong Qiu Jie* was celebrated was this: During the Yuan Dynasty, the Mongols ruled China. The Chinese were oppressed and tried many times to overthrow the Mongol rulers but failed. Zhu Yuanzhang and his men hatched a plan to drive the

Mongols out of China. It was in the eighth moon. Zhu Yuanzhang and his men baked mooncakes and inserted a note in each piece. They distributed a piece to every household and instructed them to eat it only on the fifteenth. The Mongol soldiers were not suspicious, as it was the custom of the Chinese to distribute mooncakes on this particular date.

On the fifteenth day, the households who cut open the mooncake saw a note urging them to kill any Mongol soldier they saw. The Mongols were caught unprepared. Zhu Yuanzhang rose in rebellion and the Mongol rule came to an end. Zhu Yuanzhang established a new dynasty, the Ming Dynasty, in 1368.

Cheng Beng (Sweeping of the Graves)

Every year, we celebrated the *Cheng Beng* Festival. It is the Chinese version of the Christians' All Souls' Day. It was usually celebrated around April. Descendants of the dead would go to the graves of their ancestors and sweep them and place auspicious joss papers on the tombs. Food such as chicken and duck and the favourite dishes and drinks of the dead were offered. Joss sticks and candles were lit, inviting the souls to that feast. To find out whether the souls had partaken the food, the usual set of *shen pei* (divining cups) was used. Shen Pei are kidney-shaped wooden pieces, ranging in size from a finger to a chalkboard duster. The top of each piece is convex and somewhat cylindrical while the bottom is flat. When the *shen pei* lay with one facing upwards and the other face down, it implied that the souls had satisfactorily feasted. The joss papers and crates of jade bank notes with images of the Jade Emperor were burnt for the departed souls.

Note:

The shen pei or jiao pei is a pair of symmetrical wooden blocks. It is for the gods or the spirits to define whether a job or a task has been done. For example, if the descendants wished to know if the departed souls had partaken of the offering, they would find out using the shen pei. A person would clasp the two pieces in both his hands like in prayer and then toss them lightly. The shen pei would fall on the floor in different combinations.

If both flat-sided blocks fell face upward, it meant the god or spirit was implying that the question was not valid and the seeker was encouraged to think of a valid question.

If the convex side faced upward and the flat side lay face down, it meant the god or spirit had approved or had finished the task requested of them.

If both sides facing upward were convex, it was understood that the gods or spirit could not or were not willing to answer the question.

If a pair of shen pei was not available, a pair of similar coins could be used too.

This practice is common in Chinese temples as well as in private prayers at home.

Today, the significance of this celebration is that relatives and siblings are able to come together and find out how each family is doing. In today's highly competitive society, relatives hardly meet one another during the year.

Other Religious Observances

Most families in those times would offer prayers to heaven on the last day of the moon. Each family would cook a few simple dishes and offer prayers. My dad observed such practices without fail. Every evening, my dad would burn joss sticks and say a simple prayer.

Before my dad went for important tasks or negotiations, he would burn a joss stick and appeal to heaven for a safe and successful journey.

My parents observed the festivals I have mentioned religiously and with reverence, as they practised a mix of Taoism and Buddhism.

Spirits and *Bomohs*

Up until the 1960s, health care in Singapore was still in its infancy. The Singapore government was busy trying to stand on its own feet after taking the helm from the British colonialists. There was so much infighting and distraction that health care took a back seat. The majority of the people of Singapore had to depend on *sin sehs* (Chinese physicians), quack doctors, temple mediums, *bomohs* (Malay medicine men) and other spirit healers. When people were poor and illiterate, they depended very much on spiritual beliefs. Some opportunists were quick to pounce on the ignorant populace.

Some welfare professionals were quick to defend the efforts of such practitioners. These practitioners gave them a ray of hope that their problems could be solved. They would feel positive and would like to get on with their lives.

My dad used to have a *Tong Shu* (Chinese almanac) on the altar table. We were told not to touch it, as it was sacred. We dutifully obeyed.

A Tong Shu (Chinese almanac)

What is *Tong Shu?*

It is the Chinese almanac which was created 2,000 years before Christ. It is a book that records the divination or auspiciousness of the days in the Chinese calendar. The Chinese used this book to predict whether a day is divinely 'good' or 'bad'.

You can find out more information simply by searching for 'Tong Shu' on Google.

He would refer to it to find out the best day to build a shed or to sign a contract for project. He said that his dad had taught him to do this. As I have mentioned, my grandpa, Yeo Teow Teng, was a learned man, a herbalist as well as a *Tong Thu* practitioner. In the 1930s and 1940s, he was well sought after in Kampong Eunos to give medical and spiritual advice. He did not dispense dried ready-made herbs, but live herbal plants. My grandma and a fellow kampong resident named Taukwa Poh learnt much from him. Illnesses, which could not be cured by herbs, could be cured by the instructions from the *Tong Shu.*

From the *Tong Shu*, he would tell the patient what negative forces were affecting him and how to counteract them. He would advise the patient to give thanksgiving to a certain deity that had mediated to counteract the negative forces. Different deities would do the mediation for different negative forces.

There were a few other people like him who practised *Tong Shu* readings, the reason being that, at that time, few people could read or write sufficiently well to understand *Tong Shu*. The *I-ching* is another book that is not easily understood. Today, there are groups of scholars doing research on these two books.

There were others who were either ignorant of *Tong Shu* readers or they would rather follow the crowd, as they were not educated or had only some basic education. For these folks, whenever there was a illness that did not seem to go away after a couple of days, the parents would be quick to suspect that the illness was due to spiritual reasons. He would go to the temple medium and seek advice from a deity.

One particular temple that I knew of was actually an attap house on the fringe of Kampong Tanah Merah Kechil. There were no signboards or any decorations that indicated it was a temple. The only sign was a huge joss stick urn and a large black flag overprinted with a *ying yang* symbol in gold. On certain days, the temple medium would sit in front of the altar and invite the spirit of the deity to enter into him. Meanwhile, his assistants would beat on the temple drums, cymbals and bells. Every temple had its own distinct music to indicate the deity the temple was worshipping. The music attracted a large crowd of kampong folks, including some curious Malay residents. When the spirit was entering him, the temple medium would belch and his body would shake and tremble and his head would roll. The spirit who was entering him had been a general in its earthly life. The spirit, speaking through the medium, would ask for his weapons and then prance around the temple ground holding them. Then he would either lacerate his tongue, slash his arms with a razor-sharp sword or swing a steel spiked ball around his body. His assistants would cover his wounds with paper amulets. When he sobered down, he would sit on his chair and invite devotees to air their problems and then give advice using the native tongue of the deity. The assistants, who most probably knew the native tongue, would write down what was said and translate it for the devotees. The devotees would dutifully follow the instructions.

It was very strange. Sometimes, the devotee would bring up a case in which the devotee himself was in the wrong. The spirit would then give him a verbal lashing, and he had to apologise to his 'victims'.

My grandma was a devout Buddhist. As I have said, after the death of grandpa, she devoted herself to being a vegetarian. She was a member of many temples in Singapore. Some of them were the famed Kreta Ayer Mazhu Kong, the Tang Gah Temple in front of St Teresa's Church, the Ho Lim Keng at Outram Road, the Bright Hill Temple, the Heong Lian Sze at Kong Seng Road, the Hong San See at Kembangan and a few others. During the birthdays of the deities, she would bring me and my siblings along. Sometimes, she would bring our clothes—usually shirts and dresses—and get them blessed and a red imprint was made on the back of each piece of clothing directly below the collar. She would also bring small empty bottles to fill with blessed water to drink. After filling each, a piece of paper indicating the name of the temple was pasted on the side of the bottle.

One day, our neighbour Ah Chiang and his mother-in-law, Madam Ong Ka, drove my grandma and I to an attap temple at Kampong Batak. The smell of incense and candles filled the air as we approached. The whole place was a hive of activity. Cars, lorries, goods tricycles and bicycles were haphazardly parked along the sides of the narrow sandy track leading down to the valley where the temple was. Devotees carried food offerings of rice cakes, chickens, ducks, candies and biscuits in their bamboo and cane baskets in one hand and in the other hand, bundles of incense and red candles.

Upon reaching the temple, all the offerings were unwrapped and laid out on enamelled plates. The wrappers were carefully kept aside. Then candles were lit, followed by joss sticks. The devotees had fixed unwritten steps to follow. First, they prayed to heaven, then to the earth god, followed by the deities in the temple. Those who wished to seek the deities' predictions would have to get a container of prediction sticks and kneel and shake them. The deities needed to be told what problems they faced and whether an action to be taken was appropriate. They would have to shake the container of sticks until one fell out. Then they would take a pair of *shen pei*, clasp the flat faces together, and pray to the deity that the prediction stick that fell out was correct. He would then, with both hands, toss gently in an upward motion and let the *shen pei* fall on the floor. If one of the *shen pei* had the flat side face up and the other had the flat side face down, it would be taken as the correct prediction stick. If both had the flat side faced down, he had to replace the stick in the container and shake again, and the whole process was repeated. If both the flat faces of the *shen pei* faced up, it signified that the deity was laughing at him and he should not continue. He might wish to think of an alternate plan and shake the prediction sticks again.

If the prediction stick was the correct one, he would bring it to a monk. The monk would read the number on the stick among the rack for a corresponding slip of paper. The slip of paper (*chiam si*) would foretell what the outcome of his action was. The *chiam si* slips had the titles of folk stories—happy or otherwise—of ancient China. If one read, 'Wosong fought with a tiger', it would mean that his action would be a struggle but that it would be won at the end. If the slip read, 'Meng Chiang-nu cried at the Great Wall', it would mean that his action was futile. The monk would help to explain what the outcome of their action would be. It is left to the person who sought the prediction to decide whether to carry out the plan.

Concurrently, besides what the devotees were doing, on that day, a lady in her forties, all dressed in white with her hair in a bun with a white ribbon, sat in front of the main altar. While the drums and cymbals were banging away in repeated rhythms, she burped and stared right ahead. The temple assistant, named Koon Ee, would know whether the White Robe Hood Cho spirit had already entered the physical body of the lady. If she did, Koon Ee would invite devotees to air their problems to her. Some sought advice; others sought cures to bodily ailments. Some were complicated ones and had to come for further consultations. For the curing of certain ailments, the Buddha would tell Koon Ee of the prescriptions in her own spiritual tongue and Koon Ee would write out the prescription on a temple form. The devotee would then take the prescription to the Chinese medicine shop to dispense the medicine. When the last devotee had had his consultation, she again sat staring ahead motionlessly. By and by, she regained her bodily self again and mingled and chatted with the crowd.

On the far end of the temple grounds, temple drums were sounded very vigorously in unusual rhythms. A man in his fifties, dressed in tattered clothes with a black kidney-shaped hat on, was carrying a broken fan, swaying and singing out loudly and crisply in a tongue we did not understand. Devotees followed him in single file, barefoot. To my horror, he walked across a pit of burning coals. Devotees followed and continued their way into the temple. None of them suffered from burns. Later, I was told that those who walked on burning coals had to abstain from eating certain foods and did certain actions for a certain number of days to have their bodies cleansed of evil spirits. Crowds went near to examine the coal pit. It was indeed burning hot. Some of them expressed admiration for their bravery and devotion to those who participated in the walk.

After the ceremony, we came back armed with the clothes that we brought to get imprinted, the blessed bottles of water and some yellow amulets with characters written in red ink as well as the food offerings. Each amulet had an imprint in Chinese '*Pei Ee Hood Cho*'. In English, it was 'White Robe Buddha Temple'. Grandma would fold the amulets in a *pa-kau* (eight-sided) pattern and gave one to each of us to wear for safety and peace as well as to ward off evil.

In the late 1950s, the temple was shifted to Great Eastern World at Geylang. Great Eastern World paled in comparison to the cinemas-bazaars and amusement parks of New World, Great World or Happy World, therefore few knew about it.

One afternoon, my grandma took me to the temple now at Great Eastern World, and I was surprised to find one of my classmates from Dryburgh English School practising the temple drum rhythm there.

Today, the temple has shifted, and Housing and Development Board flats are built on the piece of land once occupied by Great Eastern World.

Kampong Batak, which was on a high hill, was flattened. The earth was used to reclaim the East Coast area. Today, that area, according to my estimation could be at Kaki Bukit Industrial Park.

There were a few times when we siblings were ill and my grandma would go to a certain temple to seek advice. I was ill once. My grandma, as usual, sought advice in one of the temples. In the dead of the night, when everyone was in bed, she brought me out to a corner, laid out some food offerings, lit two red candles and said some prayers at the same time, unfolding the unusually long joss paper which she brought along.

She rubbed the joss paper from my head down to my toes, at the front, as well as the back, at the same time chanting a prayer. After that, she said that certain spirits had been appeased and I would be well. I was asked to go home, and she would say further prayers and burn the joss paper. True enough, I was up and about as usual the next day. The illness was gone. Grandma said that I had offended certain spirits inadvertently and that the temple deity where she got the unusual joss paper from had interceded on my behalf.

Whenever we were playing, running or working, she would give advice on behaving ourselves. For example, in the rural areas, searching for a toilet was quite problematic. So one needed to do it behind some bushes. My grandma used to advise us, "Before you pee, make sure you disturb the area around you with your feet and whisper, 'I am going to do my work. Get away from here.'"

There were also unusual tales of *bomohs* and spirits in the Malay kampongs. If a certain illness of a child could not be cured, the Malay parents would send him to a *bomoh*. The *bomoh* would burn *kemuyan*—a very strong incense cake in a prayer cup—and he would say a prayer and at the same time blow mouthfuls of water at the head of the child. Then the child was sent home.

At other times, a *bomoh* was sought to take revenge on an enemy or to win the love of a girl. In such a case, the consequence was usually not very healthy. In the case of winning the love of a girl, the *bomoh* would advise the suitor to give him an object from the girl and he would say a prayer on the object. The object would be returned to the girl, and the girl would return his love. However, should the parents of the girl object to their relationship, they would seek advice from another *bomoh*. The other *bomoh* would reveal what the suitor had done. Should the girl's parents wish to pursue the matter further, then there would be a battle between the two *bomohs*. In a battle, the loser had to pay a price.

There were people who sought wealth and fame. They would seek a *bomoh* to rear little imps, called *toyol*. The *bomoh* would trap the spirit of a child who had just passed away, rear it and train it to work, steal or do anything that the owner wished him to do. The *bomoh* would instruct the owner of the *toyol* on how to reward such a spirit.

The following dialogue illustrates what was commonly believed about how a *toyol* was to be employed:

The bomoh said, "If this *toyol* has done a good job, he should be rewarded."

The owner asked, "How much, sir?"

The bomoh answered, "Initially with the minutest amount. It can be a quarter cent. The next time, the reward should be double the amount."

The owner asked, "But, sir, where can I put the money? The *toyol* is a spirit and money is physical."

The bomoh replied, "Prepare a container. Put the reward into the container. But let me warn you. Whoever takes from the container is going to pay a price. The *toyol* will haunt him until he disappears from the face of the earth."

The owner began to get worried and asked, "But . . . but, but . . . it will come to a time when I can't afford to reward him! What must I do?"

The bomoh responded, "The simplest thing for you to do is to bring him to the sea together with the rewards intact. Let him and the reward float on a tiny floating vessel. Nature will take its course. But if someone takes his reward, let me repeat—he will haunt him until . . ."

The owner said, "I understand, sir. I will take care of the *toyol*."

The masters of the *toyol* would always take full advantage of their quality of blind obedience. For example, the owners would get them to steal as much money as possible. Should they fail to do what the masters wanted, they would be punished. A few mumblings of prayer from the master would send them cowering in fear.

To prevent *toyol* from stealing our money, there were ways to distract it as *toyol* love to hear the sound of jingling objects. One method was to gather marbles and saga seeds for the *toyol* to play with, so they would forget about their master's orders. They would play the whole night long then rush home before daybreak.

My grandma used to advise *sinkeh* (new arrivals from China) thus, "Before checking into a hotel, check the room first. If the room is spotlessly clean, you must suspect that something is amiss. You can test it by messing up the room a bit. After a while, check the room again. If the room is back to its former order, don't accept it." We children could only listen but were not allowed to ask questions. My grandma was telling the new arrivals to beware of hotel owners who employed a *toyol* to look after the cleanliness of the room.

I have heard that the rearing of *toyols* is still alive today. One of my friends has claimed that he has even come across *toyols*. But the *toyols* that he saw were afraid of him and upon seeing him, they scurried away. He claims that he can see spirits. Upon entering a place, he can tell us whether that place is 'clean' or otherwise. I cannot refute him, as I have heard of several others who claim they have this sense of seeing spirits.

I used to cycle along East Coast Road to Dryburgh English School, which was situated along Koon Seng Road. One afternoon there was a group of people crowding around a Hindu temple. The whole area was already cleared of trees and brushes and the construction of a new residential housing estate was in progress. I was curious. I decided to find out what was happening. I saw that a huge yellow Caterpillar bulldozer had already removed the walls of the temple leaving only a black statue. The bulldozer then tried to knock down the statue. It failed after many attempts. I then left the place as I was already late for school. As I was moving away, I was wondering why the bulldozer had failed. Was the spirit of the statue unhappy with the demolition work? Or was the statue so well constructed that it could withstand the power of the bulldozer? Nobody could provide me with an answer.

Chapter 13
Food

In those days, cooking and baking were part of our daily chores. Although our mum specified that the kitchen was not a place for boys—most of the cooking was done by our mum and sisters— our help was still needed in preparing the ingredients as well as getting the fire under the stoves burning. We would help pound the dried chillies with *belacan*, onions, garlic and dried prawns, using a granite pestle and mortar. We were needed to scale the fish and prepare the vegetables. Although we were not required to help to cook, we could not take things for granted.

Do you know what I learnt one morning? We usually had coffee and ate hot, watery rice with salted vegetables, salted eggs, fried peanuts and preserved leeks for breakfast. One morning, I woke up the same time as my mum. To my dismay, breakfast was not ready. Then I watched my mum prepare the kettle and build a fire to boil the water. She got the coffee powder ready and put it into the strainer, washed the rice and cooked it. I had to watch over the fire in the stove. It was a long wait for breakfast. I felt rather uncomfortable, as I always ate immediately after I brushed my teeth. I realised that my mum was the one who got everything ready for us every morning and I had taken that for granted.

Breakfast Before School

On school days, every one of the boys in our family had to perform some chores before breakfast. My job was to clear the dung in the chicken coop before cleaning myself up. When we were ready for breakfast, we went into the kitchen. Breakfast on school days was special. There were four bowls, each with an upturned bowl over it to serve as a lid. Mum would put the bowls on the thick rim of the warm stove. We carried the bowls of food to the dining table. Then we lifted the upturned bowl. A whiff of fragrance emanated from it. I believed it was my mum who had the ingenuity to scoop some hot cooked rice from the watery *muey* (rice boiled with a lot of water) into an empty bowl, crack an egg in it then add some fried onion, a little black sauce and a teaspoonful of cooking oil before filling the bowl with more hot rice. It was still warm from the stove when we ate it. Then my parents would be busy with the vegetables before heading to Chai Chee Market. We would mix the rice and the ingredients thoroughly before eating. Some of us preferred to eat the egg last.

My sisters could not predict what dishes to cook before my mum came home from the market in the afternoon. At the market, when business was ending at about noon, she would gather all the leftovers and barter with the fishmongers, butchers, cake sellers and fruit sellers who were just as eager to get rid of their leftovers. When my mum reached home, my sisters would decide what to do with the bartered items. We seldom harvested fresh vegetables from the vegetable beds. We got them from the rejects of the harvest. The best and whole ones were sent to the market. We selected the parts of the rejected vegetables that were edible. For example, a leaf could be worm infested but the stalk was not. We would cut the stalk up and the worm-infested leaf was given to the chickens or the pigs. Nothing was ever left to rot.

When my mum had bartered vegetables for fish, we would have fish for lunch and dinner. When she arrived home with the fish, we would hurriedly scale them, remove the offal and season them immediately with salt. The water from washing the fish was used for watering the plants around the house. Time was precious, especially with fish. The fishmongers bought their fish early in the morning at about 4 a.m. They reached the market at about 6 or 7 a.m. By noon, the fish would almost be stale, as most of the fishmongers at that time did not preserve them in ice. If they were preserved in ice, customers would not buy them because they would say they were frozen fish.

After seasoning, then the decision had to be made by the cook on whether to fry, steam or boil. The amount of fish we consumed was also dependent on how much mum had bartered. Sometimes, we had so much that it was not possible to finish it within one day. Fried fish could still be eaten the next morning without re-heating it, but for other cooking methods, we had to reheat the fish. If the amount of fish bartered was too much, we had to boil them, take out the big bones and mix it with the pig food for the pigs and fowl. Sometimes, my dad would buy all the rejected fish and leave them to decompose in specially constructed jars. After decomposition, the liquid would be used as fertiliser for the vegetables.

Pork was seldom bartered in great amounts, as the supply in the market was limited. Eggs for lunch and dinner were cooked sparingly, as there were frequent supplies of fish and pork. During birthdays, mum would traditionally boil eggs and dye them red. Sometimes, the peeled, hard-boiled eggs were re-boiled in sugary water. There was seldom an elaborate birthday celebration for every sibling and adult.

Other items that were bartered were fish cakes, *towkua*, *towfu* or even bean sprouts. Sometimes, she would barter the vegetables for a light meal of noodle soup or gluey broth for herself.

During Festivals

As I have mentioned, we ate chicken and duck only during festivals and the Lunar New Year. The main festivals were the Seven Moon Festival, Rice Dumpling Festival, *Tung Chie* (Winter Solstice) *and* Tien Kong's birthday. My dad did the slaughtering. He would skilfully hold a chicken by the legs and at the same time grip the head with his left hand. Then he plucked out the feathers in quick succession from the part of the neck he was about to slice. He said a prayer, something to this effect:

> Be a chicken,
> Be a duck,
> Birth and death,
> Cannot be predicted,
> May you be reincarnated henceforth.

Then he speedily lacerated the neck with a few strokes of a sharp penknife. Blood would spurt out and was collected. When the chicken had turned lifeless, its head was tucked in between the wings. Then boiling water was poured over it. Sometimes, the bird was soaked in the boiling water. Then we children had to help pluck it. The fine down feathers were the most difficult to pull out, as they were short and fine. We had to use a pair of tweezers. After it was done, the offal was taken out. The intestines were cleaned and the undigested contents were scraped off with a penknife. Just like the fish water, the water from washing the chicken was used to water the plants. The feathers were collected and used as fertiliser. As for duck feathers, they were dried and sold to a collecting agent. He would then sell it to the main agent, who would pack the feathers in bales and send it to the factory to be processed into twill cloth.

My mum would decide how to cook the chicken or duck— whether to fry, boil, stir fry, sauté or cook with other ingredients such as mushrooms and sea cucumber. She had neither written recipes nor kitchen scales to help her. Every little step or amount of ingredient added was due to her experience and ingenuity.

Mum's Innovations

Despite such a heavy schedule and family responsibilities, my mum tried to find time sometimes to add innovations to her cooking. She would try her hand at making *roti prata*—of course, using whatever ingredients there were in the house. We would lay our hands on anything she tried making.

Sometimes during the school holidays, we had simple breakfasts such as hot broth eaten with cut *chilli padi*, dried prawns, raw onions and garlic, with light or black sauce to taste. Sometimes broth was eaten with preserved mini-snails, salted vegetables and salted black bean seeds.

There was this particular dish that I must mention. It was something akin to *paella* in Spain. Mum cooked rice in a pot, then she added carrots, sweet potatoes, long beans, green chilli, pork, prawns, fried onions, salt and pepper to taste, but no cheese. The whole family usually had their bowls arranged on the table. The pot of cooked rice with mixed ingredients was placed in the middle and we dished out our food from the pot. Then we had the freedom to sit wherever we liked. It was like a break from tradition once in a while and we enjoyed it. If she wanted a watery version of it, she would just add more water to the pot.

Baking

Mum baked the traditional cakes that were used for offering to the god of prosperity as well as the kitchen god. They were *ang ku kueh*, bean pastry, *kueh baolu,* and *fah kueh* among others. We ground the flour with the huge stone grinder of Mr Ong Wah, who lived on the other side of the hill. My mum soaked the rice before carrying it over. During festivals, many other families would be waiting for their turn to grind their flour. We would help one another to grind. After grinding, we had to let the water drip off to become dough. Red dye was added if we wanted to make auspicious cakes. Other preparations such as green beans needed to be soaked and smashed. Sugar and salt would be added too. Then we got some dough and flattened it. We scooped a sufficient amount of bean paste and put it on the flattened dough. The flattened dough was wrapped around the bean paste. Then we pressed the dough that was filled with bean paste into a wooden mould to make auspicious patterns. Next, we had to lay it on pieces of green banana leaf. They were put into a big cauldron for steaming. One or two days earlier, we had to go round the banana groves to select the best leaves, wash them and cut them to use as a base for the cakes so that the cakes would not stick on the bottom of the utensils.

A flour grinder

For the preparation of other cakes that required beating, my mum would improvise a beater by using coconut mid-ribs. To calculate the duration of the beating, she used a lighted joss stick. When the joss stick burnt out, it was time to stop the beating. Almost everyone was involved in one form or another but we seldom grumbled. Work like that was for the good of all. When the baking was done, we would admire how the dough with the added yeast made the cakes rise and the patterns form. It was indeed exciting. Then we would use red dye to dot the surface of the cakes so they looked auspicious. I was told that traditional cakes that were not dotted were meant for offerings to the dead. During baking, my mum was most particular about anyone saying anything negative.

Cooking Long Beans, Sweet Potato and Tapioca Leaves

Many of us had never experienced eating long bean leaves, sweet potato leaves or tapioca leaves. Mum had a way to cook all those.

The Ingredients

Among the main ingredients stored in her kitchen were lard, cooking oil, *ikan bilis, belachan,* dried prawns, preserved beans and vegetables, salt, vinegar, light and heavy sauce, Ve-Tsin, fried onions with oil, *buah keras,* ginger, *langkuas* and turmeric. Rice was ordered in a huge gunnysack—100 *katis* per sack. Whenever a soup or a simple meal was needed, she would whip it up with ease and it was tasty too. Hong Game learnt the ropes of preparing and cooking very fast, and every dish was delicious. Hong Game had once gone to stay at the Heong Lian See temple at Koon Seng Road for a length of time. There she learnt the ropes of cooking vegetarian food of different kinds such as mock *ngoh hiang* (spicy fritter), pig trotters, *char siew* (roasted pork), *wanton* (minced pork wrapped in thin dough) and spring rolls.

If one were to see Hong Game wield the chopper, one would not believe she was only a housewife. The way she chopped and sliced was like an expert chef. It was a pity her talent was not spotted for the benefit of the public.

Our most common drink was black coffee with sugar. Every week, a coffee powder supplier would supply us a packet of coffee powder. Then, we would pay him at the end of the month. It was something like a standard order. We seldom added condensed milk to the coffee. Fresh cow's milk was unheard of. Once in a while, we had Milo, Ovaltine and Horlicks. Chinese tea was made only on hot days or only when we had fever. We had condensed milk only when we were very young or when we were sick. The Milkmaid brand (*ang zee guni* in Hokkien), which had a few Chinese characters in red printed over the English instructions on the label, was more expensive than the others. Other brands included Lifeguard and Blue Cross. We had a tin of Lactogen milk powder but we seldom touched it.

A tin of Nestle Lactogen

Plain crackers from Tai Hong and Siong Hoe were usually bought by the *katis* from a biscuit vendor in Chai Chee Market. We usually had them during coffee breaks. Other types of biscuits were sometimes purchased—namely, cream crackers and cookies of different shapes and colours. Our favourites were the alphabet biscuits and the iced sugar biscuits.

Alphabet biscuits   Iced sugar biscuits

All of us would agree that the food we ate was very organic, as we never used any artificial or inorganic fertiliser on our plants. The pigs and poultry were all fed in the same way.

Itinerant Hawkers

Besides the coffee powder supplier, there was the Indian bread seller who came by on his bicycle. He had a box tied to his bicycle in which he put his loaves of bread, *kaya* and margarine. He came at about 8 a.m. He alerted us to his presence by ringing his bicycle bell. The neighbours would usually get their supplies on credit, but not us. One day, we tried telling him that we wanted to pay on credit too. Surprisingly, he agreed without hesitation. When our mum heard it, she was furious.

"Although we're not rich, we can afford to pay in cash. If we've no cash, then forgo the purchase," she said. She insisted that we must return the amount we owed him the next morning. The next morning, we returned the bread seller his dues and never took anything from him on credit again.

That maxim became so deeply ingrained in us that even up to today, we prefer, if possible, not to purchase anything on credit.

I once observed the bread seller take out his milk tin of *kaya*. On the surface, there was a layer of mould. I wanted to alert him, but he was too quick. He immediately stirred and mixed the content and then spread it on the bread and sold it to unsuspecting buyers. I felt disgusted but dared not voice anything, as I was very young—about eight years old then.

There was yet another Indian bread seller who came by in the afternoon. The man had a huge rattan basket balanced on his head, which was topped with a towel folded neatly into a square. He carried a folding stand with him too. Whenever he stopped to display his wares, he would unfold his stand and remove the basket from his head and place it on the stand. He would open the lid of his tin container to reveal the different products he was selling. He sold triangular-shaped curry puffs, French loaves and *sugi* biscuits (round, sweet Indian pastries). We always admired his neck, which was so strong that it could support the huge heavy basket. As he walked along, he would sing, "*Roti, curry puff!*"

Sometimes, a *puttu mayam* seller would come by. He too balanced his tin container on his head, but it was smaller. His *puttu mayam* was priced at five cents each, and just like today, we could choose to top it up with either ground coconut or brown *gula melaka*. As he moved along, he would shout, if I heard correctly, "*Yam*" or "*M'yam.*"

On rare occasions, an Indian hawker would use a stout piece of wood to balance on his shoulder a box which he put his eating utensils in and in the other, a pot of cooked millet called *bubor terigu*.

There were very few itinerant Chinese hawkers there. The most frequent hawker was the ice-cream man. His ice cream was loaded into a cubical metal box, which was painted yellow with the italicised word '*Coolen*' painted on it. He sold different flavours of ice cream, such as durian, red bean, chocolate and coconut.

I saw this hawker only once. He came by with my uncle, Yeo Koon Seng. I did not know whether he brought him there or met him on the way. He carried two rattan baskets. In each was a huge, thick, circular slab of cream-coloured sticky cake. He called it *kikuey*. He used a *daching* to weigh a slice of it by the *kati* and *tahil*. It was plain and quite tasteless but it tasted different when one fried it with eggs. I have never seen it on sale at any cooked food centre today, but I once saw someone selling it illegally at the Bedok Market.

At the heart of the Malay kampong, there might have been other types of hawkers, but the Malay *nasi lemak* sellers were always there every morning. The *otak otak* and the *mee siam* sellers were there at odd times. Each packet of *nasi lemak* was wrapped with green banana leaf. It contained some rice cooked with coconut milk, a small *ikan kuning*, a piece of cucumber, a thin slice of fried egg and a little *sambal* on a small square-shaped banana leaf. The banana leaf could double up as a spoon for the Chinese. The Malays scooped the food with their fingers. As he moved along, the hawker sang, "*Naaasiii leeeemak.*"

Otak otak was made from fish paste stuffed into coconut leaflets. Each stuffed leaflet was heated over a charcoal fire. After cooking, they were pinned in neat rows on two parallel sticks cut up from a coconut frond. That was to facilitate easy transport and accounting. The sellers would simply shout in quick short syllables, *'Otak'*. Each packet of *mee-siam* was wrapped up with a banana leaf blade. The packets were put into a bamboo basket. The seller also carried a bottle of sauce. He sprinkled the sauce over the *mee-siam* when requested. Some enterprising hawkers would include *mee goreng* for sale.

The satay sellers were seen at fixed spots but sometimes were seen moving from place to place.

Those were the itinerant hawkers we met in our kampong, but I believe different kampongs and villages had hawkers selling their special fare in their various ways.

Chapter 14
Our Entertainment

We never had a dull moment during our childhood. Our house was situated in the middle of a huge coconut estate surrounded by rambutan estates, a Malay kampong and a Chinese village. Furthermore, my parents' farm constantly required us to help in one way or another. It was in such an environment that we always had much interaction with the land, the flora and fauna and people of different races around us.

Chinese *Wayang* Performances

These were the most sought after form of entertainment. They always brought the carnival spirit to the village folks. This was when the village folks found time to say thanks to the village gods and goddesses in the temple, interact with one another and be entertained by the opera performances.

The twice-yearly *wayang* peformances were organised by almost every temple in and around Bedok. Along Changi Road, there were several temples—at 6 Milestone, 8½ Milestone, 9 Milestone and 10 Milestone. Then at East Coast Road (the present-day Kew Drive), where the Teochew cemetery was, there was the Hwa San Ting, or as we called it, Pang Sua Kia. At the New Village at Koh Sek Lim was another temple. Days before the temple celebrations, the *lorchu* (committee member) would go round to collect donations and inform the devotees of the dates of the performances. When the performance days arrived, my parents would prepare food as offerings for the gods who had protected us from harm for the year and to seek their protection from future harm. Each temple would set aside two days and nights for the *wayang* performances, especially during the Seventh Moon Festival and the temple gods' or goddesses' birthdays. Sometimes, someone would sponsor a third day of performance. The performances in the afternoon—2 p.m. to 5 p.m.—would usually involve family themes, folklore and legends for the women and children. At night from 7 p.m. till 12 midnight the performances were geared toward the men. The themes were mainly about historical Chinese wars and heroes. In some cases, when different temples engaged the same performing troupe, they would choose a long story continuing over a few nights at different temples. After each performance at a temple, the audience would be told that the performance would continue at such and such a temple on which nights. Interested audience members would flock in droves to watch the continuation of the episodes. Some popular Hokkien troupes were *Sin Sai Hong* and *Sin Ki Lin*. Some Teochew ones were *Lau Sai Thow* and *Sin Yong Hwa*.

A Chinese opera performance

There were many factors behind why certain troupes were popular with the audience. Firstly, the actors and actresses played the most important part. They had good looks, good dancing skills as well as acrobatic skills, good voice projection, the ability to coordinate with their team and possessed presence of mind. The make-up team had to be able to make the performers look like the original historical characters. I once overheard someone comment negatively about a certain troupe, "The 'Pao Kong' (on stage) doesn't look like Pao Kong. The original Pao Kong had a black face and a crescent on the forehead, but this one doesn't."

Secondly, good musicians were key, who could capture the music of the period of history depicted in the performance to enliven the mood and spirit of the audience so they felt as if they were part of the story. The audience's emotions were evoked and they would want to follow the characters in the story till the end.

Finally, the period costumes, as well as the props such as jewellery the actors and actresses used, should look appealing and authentic. Certain scenes needed appropriate lighting, pyrotechnic displays and sound effects. The audience would be thrilled if they saw effects they had never seen before. The scrolls for the backdrop should also be appropriate. To lend authenticity to the costumes as well as the jewellery they used, the *wayang* troupes got Poh Heng and Million Goldsmiths, both well-known goldsmiths at the time, to sponsor the jewellery the performers were wearing.

After each performance, which lasted for four to five hours, firecrackers were let off to inform the audience that the performance had ended. In the mornings, there were rehearsals as well as practices for certain scenes or acrobatic skills on the stage. For newly recruited actors and actresses, if a mistake was made, the instructor would give them a light caning on the palm. We children often went under the stage and peeped through the gaps to see the actors and actresses practicing for the next show.

An opera actress playing
with her brother

On the days when there were performances, both sides of the road leading to the temples were packed with hawkers selling popular food such as *char kuay teow, chai tow kuay, chengtng, rojak* and *tikam* ice cream.

Tikam was a form of gambling. It was a spinning rod with a pointer balanced on a shaft. The shaft was nailed on to the middle of a board. The board was divided into equal sections. The figures '1' and '2' were written alternately on each section. If a person wished to play *tikam* ice-cream, he could pay five cents and spin the rod once. When the pointer pointed to '1', he got a cup of ice cream. If it pointed to a number '2', he got two cups.

There were others who sold toys, fruits, cakes and balloons. There was a Malay family who frequently sought out such performances to sell *satay*. A hot and cold drinks seller would seek a bigger space for his tables and chairs so his stall was usually at a corner. He would place bottles of popular drinks of the time on his table—Framroz orange, ice-cream soda, Green Spot, Frazer and Neave Red Lion and Sarsarspirilla—likely to tempt the thirsty audience. Hot drinks such as coffee and tea were also served.

There were illegal gambling syndicates, table football games and other fun game operators. One particularly fun game was 'Ring the Cockerels'. The cockerels made from clay were very brightly painted. It was in fact a coin bank. It was popular, as each cockerel was big and attractive and looked easy to ring. But the game master was careful to arrange them in such a way that the rattan ring could not loop the necks of the cockerels so easily.

A cockerel coin bank

Two particular toys that I can never forget on sale at these sites were the wind-up toy cars and the rotor blades. At such a young age, I was fascinated that a toy car could move after winding it a few times. Of course, when it was 'overwound', the spring gave way. Then I would prise open the toy car to find out what was inside. There was only a thick spring and two gears. I would study it and try to fix it, but in vain.

The other toy was the flying rotor blade. I would fix the rotor blade into a twisted rod. Then from a holder, I would push the rotor blade up. The rotor turned and turned out of the rod and into the air. It was such fun, but I did not know why it behaved like that. Later on in life, I learnt that the idea of the helicopter was borrowed from this toy.

There was one occasion when someone exploited the deformity of a child. That child had a very big head. A huge poster was put up: 'Big head, small body, 30 cents.' The boy was enclosed with canvas cloth in a little corner. Those who wanted to take a look had to go past a cashier. He collected 30 cents from each curious viewer. That attracted quite a crowd everywhere when there were *wayang* performances. In those days, there was no awareness of such things as human rights or child abuse.

At certain performance sites, the audience could bring their mats in front of the stage to sit and watch. Those who preferred to stand had to do it at the rear. But at other sites, the audience could only stand to watch. At such sites, the shorter audience members were at a disadvantage. They had to take glimpses through gaps between the moving heads in front of them. When the show got exciting, more so with the loud war drums of the troupe, the place became more packed. One could hardly move. On warm nights, you can imagine the smell of the stale sweat coupled with the cigarette smoke and smoke from the burning joss paper of the huge incense burner in front of the temple. Others who were more innovative climbed to higher ground such as the base of a coconut tree or makeshift wooden platforms away from the main viewing areas. My grandma often said she always had something sharp with her. Whoever tried to make use of such crowded situations to get fresh with her would get a poke.

291

At Changi Road 8½ Milestone Tua Pek Kong temple, one night, a very interesting and exciting performance was on. It must have been around 9 p.m. Suddenly, a loud, brief alarm bell sounded. Police jumped out from several huge Black Marias and sprang into action. They began rounding up those *chakangkong* (tattooed) men and other gang suspects. There was a huge stir in the crowd. Robust young people, in order to escape arrest, squeezed themselves into the crowd, followed by the police and detectives.

My neighbour, whose nickname was 'Hai Lam', was arrested. His mum was very worried about him. He was a weak person, who always wore a jacket wherever he went. Early that morning, he was released. He said, "Luckily, I have my hospital appointment card and medicine with me or else I would be with them *chiak or thau png*" (literal translation: eating black bean rice or prison food).

Every now and then, ice-cream sellers would squeeze into the already packed audience carrying large vacuum flasks, at the same time ringing their bells. Others, like the preserved fruit sellers, would hold up their wares high on a metal tray and shout out the product they was selling.

Making Ice Balls

One very interesting treat sold during *wayang* performances was the ice ball, which we could purchase at five cents each. The ice-ball machine was worked by gears. The vertical rotating action of the hand-turned wheel would be translated into the horizontal rotating action of the base plate. Below the base plate was a slit where a steel blade was attached. A cube of ice was then clamped to sit on the base plate. When the rotating handle was worked, ice shavings would collect below the slit. The shavings were then shaped into a little ice ball. The hawker would make a small depression in the ice ball with his index finger then fill it with cooked red bean paste. Syrup of different colours was splashed over the ice ball. The usual colours were red, black and green. There was one type without colour added to it. One could request for the colour or colours that they wanted or even to cut the ball into halves. The ice ball was then sucked.

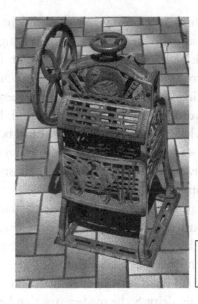

The ice-shaving machine
Yeo Hong Eng's collection

One of the reasons why the eating of ice balls was discontinued was that personal hygiene was compromised. The hawker used his bare hands to collect and shave the ice. The customer used his bare hands to hold the ice ball. At the *wayang* sites, clean water supply was a problem. To wash our hands before handling the ice balls was out of the question so customers had to make do with dirty hands. Sometimes, with our sweaty hands, when we sucked the ice balls, we could taste a mixture of sweet and salty!

At every *wayang* performance there was a giant electric generator to supply electricity to the *wayang* stage, hawkers and paths leading towards the stage. Usually the electric generator was situated away from the site as it was very noisy. It was so loud that I had to cup my ears every time I walked past. The fumes belching from the exhaust pipe coupled with the smell of diesel oil could make me faint.

Festivals like those created opportunities for the kampong folks to get together to interact as well as enjoy some forms of relaxation. The story themes of the *wayang* performances were related to human values like filial piety, kindness, chivalry, courage, determination, loyalty, thrift, compassion and integrity which one ought to emulate.

I remember once after a performance was over at 12 midnight, my parents and siblings, as well as many neighbours, were walking and talking along the pitch dark path. Since I was a fast walker, I walked straight ahead of them from Changi 8 1/2 Milestone to our home. I was the only one walking ahead. I had to walk between tombstones and tall grass. The word 'ghosts' was not in my mind. I kept a steady gait and ignored whatever strange sounds I heard, be they insects or night birds. Fear was not in my mind. My grandma always had this to say, "If you have not harmed anybody, no ghosts will harm you." I hold that maxim to this day.

There was a farmer whose farm was at the periphery of Uncle Kidd's farm (today it is Bedok South Market). He had been suffering from *siechua* (shingles). In those days, doctors were hard to come by. He depended on local quacks and herbalists but could not get it cured. Others suggested that he had the disease because he was not religious and had offended a certain deity. So he made a vow that he would build a temple for the deity and would stage a puppet show in honour of him if his illness were cured. True enough, his shingles were cured so he built a small temple for the deity at the ridge and a puppet show was staged over two days.

After the temple was built, devotees from around the area flocked in droves to worship the deity. My mum and siblings also went. She cooked a few dishes as offerings to the deity. I saw a small stage, very unlike the huge *wayang* stage I had seen. Traditional opera music could be heard. Upon looking closer, I saw small little puppets dressed in traditional Chinese costumes dancing and singing to the music. I was surprised and thrilled, as I had never seen such a show before.

My grandma was quick to explain, "In *Teng Sua* (China) such a show is common. In Selat-por you can see more in *Gu Chia Chwee* (Kreta Ayer, Chinatown). Such a show is known as *bong kachng hee* ('touch buttocks show' a literal translation from Hokkien). The puppeteers manipulate their puppets under their costumes. Watch carefully what each has to do."

I was dumbfounded. The puppeteers manipulated the puppets to perform their roles so realistically, as if they were live actors and actresses. When a scene was over, the music changed. The puppeteers had to quickly switch to another set of puppets that would play new roles. I would never see another puppet troupe like that until very much later in life elsewhere.

On some of the occasions, besides watching the weekend open-air cinema show at Bedok Boys' School, we would go to watch the open-air cinema in other places. The poster of the show of the day was pasted on either lamp posts or coconut trees. Concessionary tickets were given to those who permitted the cinema to paste these posters on their premises. The entry ticket was 20 to 30 cents. It was free seating for all. The hard, bare seats were constructed from timber from the timber yard. When it rained, we had to run to the nearest shelter. If the rain were too heavy, the show would be postponed. There were several such open-air cinemas—at Changi 10 Milestone, at Kampong Chai Chee Road and one at Siglap. To the locals, those open-air cinemas were known as *chuah yiah* (paper image) or *dian yiah* (electrical image).

Hide-and-Seek

Besides chasing away birds from the seedlings in the farm in the afternoons, we sometimes had time to play hide-and-seek with the neighbours. Our hiding places include the coconut trees, bushes, pigsties and chicken sheds. We had to play several rounds of *oh som* or *chiam, chiam, pak,* quite similar to today's 'rock, paper, scissors' to determine who would hide or who was to seek. The odd one would have to play the role of a seeker. The seeker would stand behind a coconut tree and close his eyes. Then he would count slowly and loudly up to ten. While counting, the rest would run to hide, making sure that the seeker would not see them. If someone was caught, the seeker would call out his name and the place he was hiding in and run back to the coconut tree and tag it. If the seeker went too far from the tree, a player could emerge from his hiding place and run to tag the tree. Upon tagging it, the first one being sought out was saved. The seekers had to find as many players as possible to prevent them from being saved by the ones hiding. The first player hiding who was not saved would be the next seeker. If everyone was saved, then the seeker would have to perform that role again. It was degrading to be a seeker. If one was a seeker more than thrice, he was a *pasang lenget*. The game was off when all the players unanimously agreed it was over.

Story-telling by Father

Most evenings, my dad would read stories from books rented from bookstalls in the markets. He would light a candle and read the story aloud in the Hokkien dialect like the storytellers in town. Some titles that he read from included the *Journey to the West*, *Li Mo Pek* and *Sam Kok*.

Shelves of Chinese storybooks for rent.

All of us would listen attentively. We could talk only during toilet or coffee breaks. Usually, he ended at about 10 p.m. Although my dad had only primary school education, his knowledge of Chinese was good enough to read storybooks and newspapers and then translate it into Hokkien. His Standard 2 English education in Telok Kurau Primary School was good enough to see us through our lower primary. He even attempted to teach our sisters who did not enrol in school. From him, we learnt the finer points of the Hokkien dialect. Hokkien spoken today is a mixture of different local languages and dialects mixed with vulgarities and uncouth words. Many people simply do not know the deeper meaning behind the words they utter.

Do you notice the scorch marks on this wooden rice bin lid?
My dad used to light candles and place them on this rice bin lid and read us stories. At times, he concentrated so much on his stories that he did not realize that the candle had burnt itself out and had scorched the lid.
The damaged part was caused by rats trying to get into the bin for rice.

The rice bin and its cover.

297

Chinese Marriage Proposals in the Kampong

Whenever the villagers made proposals for marriage, the most important documents they had to produce were the dates and times of birth, called the *bah zi*, of both parties. Both parties would consult the *tangki* (person in a trance) or fortune-teller. If a fortune-teller was consulted, he would refer to his almanacs and other reference books before coming to a conclusion on whether such a match was compatible. The fortune-teller would use examples of classical stories to predict the future. If he said that a certain marriage would end up like *Hsuan Zhang Chu Jing* (Monk Hsuan Zhang obtaining the Buddhist scripts), it would mean the marriage would be tough. If it were like *Sam Peck Yeng Tai* (the Celestial Bridge), the couple would not be together always—maybe once a year. Or if it was *Tan Sar Ngoh Niu*, the marriage would not last long.

Another way a person could get his fortune told was to go to the temple, pay obeisance to the deity and shake the fortune sticks from a cylindrical bamboo tube. Every fortune stick that dropped out from the tube had a number. He had to take the number to seek a corresponding numbered *chiam si* (fortune slip). The *chiam si* would tell him whether he should take a certain course of action to overcome his problem.

Strange Tales

The following episode I am sure will not go down well with the Teochew people. It involves the play 'Tan Sar and Ngoh Niu'. Tan Sar was a Teochew man who was going to the capital in ancient China to take an examination. He had to pass by Fukien Province, where he fell in love with a lady named Ngoh Niu. Their relationship did not last long. Upon completing his examination successfully, Tan Sar did not return to marry Ngoh Niu. Thus, at that time, people would believe that certain events should not take place or else events would turn out like certain historical episodes. When a Teochew man proposed to a Hokkien lady, the lady's side would definitely not agree. But it was all right for a Hokkien man to marry a Teochew lady.

Here is another tale that will not go down well with the Teochews. It was said that during the opening of Johore State in the nineteenth century, numerous labourers were needed to clear the jungle. The labourers were from different dialect-speaking groups from China. In those days, tigers roaming the jungle were plentiful. At night, they would appear to carry labourers away. Strange as it might sound, the tigers carried away only the Teochews. If there were a Hokkien man among the Teochews, no tigers would appear. So it was said that whenever a new piece of jungle was to be cleared, the Teochew labourers would always request a Hokkien to be with them. It was said that a Hokkien would bring them *hock* or luck. Isn't that a bizarre tale?

Free Films

Aside from the films shown on the weekends at Bedok Boys' School, the Ministry of Culture sometimes turned up with a grey van. Sound speakers were wired up. Music was played and a film show was screened. I remember that one of the shows was *Dugong*—A Mermaid. It was very entertaining. The kampong folks sat on the grass in the open area, with their eyes glued to the screen until the show ended. Then the officer in charge would either make a few announcements or report current events or explain certain government policies before calling it a night.

There was yet another place where free film shows were screened on weekends. It was at the Reformative Training Centre at Jalan Lembah Bedok. It was introduced to us by our close friend, Lim Ban Lee. He gathered another friend, Tok Thiam Chye, who later became his brother-in-law. We would cycle along the semi-dark, winding kampong path. They had their roadsters—Ban Lee had a Rudge and Thiam Chye had a China-Forever. I rode my dad's heavy goods carrier. With the dynamos switched on, at about 8 p.m., we pedalled along the narrow paths under the coconut trees, along wire fencing, vegetable farms and dark village *attap* houses. We rode past Hong Bian's classmates at Geok Chuan's house and then crossed unstable narrow plank bridges over streams. At that time, we did not think of the danger—should we miss the planks over the streams and fall into them or collide with another bicycle when we went round corners. We just pedalled on. We had to pedal at a certain speed in order to get sufficient light from the dynamo. With my heavy-duty carrier, the bicycle rattled. Village dogs growled and barked ferociously inside their flimsy fences. At the quadrangle of the Reformative Training Centre, we, together with many villagers from Jalan Tiga Ratus, parked our bicycles at a corner of the building and watched. One particular film that I remember watching was Robert Stevenson's *Treasure Island*.

The return journey was worse. It was already past nine and most of the lights in the village houses had already been dimmed. Occasionally, we heard the mothers lullabying their children to sleep or calling the bigger children to get to bed or even babies having their nightmares. The barking of dogs was constant. One really had to concentrate hard to cycle in almost pitch darkness. The only visible lights were the ones from our dynamos.

It seemed the superintendent of the Reformative Training Centre was appreciative of the support given by the villagers. That was why he screened the shows on Sundays for them.

Father's Musical Instruments

As I have mentioned, in the pre-WWII days, my dad had been helping out in the China Relief Fund. He had been involved in concerts, selling flags and collecting funds. As a result, the musical instruments he learnt to play in school came to be of good use. After the war, occasionally, he would take out his flute and harmonica. He would play a tune and then he would explain to us what the songs were about. Usually, he played anti-Japanese and Chinese patriotic songs. We children would sit and admire how he played those instruments, but he never attempted to teach any of us how to play.

His Master's Voice Gramophone

"What has happened in the hall?" my elder sister enquired while heaving a load of firewood. "It's music from the Chinese *wayang*."

We rushed into the hall to find out. Dad had a huge black box and music was coming from it. There was a black disc rotating and a head with a needle lying on the disc. On the cover was a picture of a dog facing a funnel. There was a phrase 'His Master's Voice' printed above the picture.

My dad said he had borrowed the record player from his cousin at Lian Teng Hng (Kampong Eunos). He said that the black records were very expensive and fragile. Once dropped, the record would be shattered. So we were extra careful when handling those records. Some of the records were from Victor, others from Decca and Columbia. The records he borrowed were mainly Mandarin songs of the period, as well as Hokkien and Teochew operas.

A Gramophone
Owned and photographed
by Yeo Hong Eng

To operate the gramophone, one needed to wind the spring with a winder provided. A record was lowered onto a felt-coated plate. The brake was released and the turntable would turn. The head with its needle would then rest on the rim of the record and music would then play. If the sound seemed to waver, my dad would use the winder and wind it vigorously a few times so the turntable would pick up speed again. It would play until it came to a halt.

Then the needle was lifted up and the record was turned over to play the other side, which had different songs.

After a few songs, he said the needle was blunt and needed to be replaced. He had a small box of needles hidden inside a slot in the record player.

Once my dad tried to wind the player, but the winding did not seem to work. He said the spring inside the player had broken. So he returned it to his cousin to get it repaired.

There was an incident in school during which my classmate was asked to read a passage. He read so slowly and softly that it annoyed the teacher. The teacher then made a winding action with his hands behind his buttocks. The whole class laughed. I laughed too but did not know why he made that action. After seeing my dad winding the player, I understood what the teacher meant. He was trying to simulate winding a record player.

The Table Tennis Table

There were many thick plywood boards around the house. On days when we were free, we would get a few chairs to prop up the boards and a makeshift table tennis set-up was ready. We cut out pieces of plywood and shaped them in the form of table tennis bats. We used dried rubber latex and shaped it into a small ball. Then we had a fine time playing table tennis. Sometimes, dad joined in too. He would describe the different terms for the actions of the table tennis game to us such as a screwball, a smash and a corner.

These many different types of entertainment I believe, made our lives morally wholesome and healthy and left us better equipped to face any eventuality in life.

Chapter 15
Flora

Plants and Trees in Our Area

In the 1950s and1960s, the standard plantation crops in our area were coconut, rubber and rambutan trees. There was an estate at kampong Haji Salam that had a mangosteen plantation crop. Landowners might plant crops on their estates and harvest the fruit. Tenant residents living on these estates were not entitled to the harvest.

Rambutan Trees

Yi Shih had the largest rambutan estate in our area. The other estates owners who had a considerable number of rambutan trees were Gan Cheng Huat, Tan Piah Teng, as well as Kim Eng, whose land was put under Yeo Teow Swee's charge. Yi Shih's rambutan estate was well known at that time. It stretched from the perimeter of the Bedok schools right up to the Hokkien Cemetery, Hock San Theng. His sprawling house was situated along Bedok Road. He had a very able estate manager named Chui Beng. Chui Beng was a Hock Chia, whilst his wife was a Teochew. They had a son and a daughter. Chui Beng and his wife used to call his son Baby Kia and his daughter Ah Muey. I did not know why they were given those names. Chui Beng was very strict with his son. The way he disciplined him was indescribable. Chui Beng's family, just like any of our neighbours' families, was very friendly and helpful. During the rambutan season from June to September, the estate usually

303

had a bountiful harvest. Many workers were needed to help pluck, count and bundle the fruit into groups of fifties and hundreds. Many kampong folks, including my mum and sister, were recruited to do those jobs. At the end of the day, they received their pay as well as gifts of stray and oddly shaped rambutans.

A bunch of sweet, ripe rambutans

Yi Shih had a very loyal estate worker named Ahmad. He lived with his wife and son in a small attap hut in the rambutan estate. I guessed he must have been Javanese, for he spoke Malay with an accent quite unlike the local Malays. He ate what the Chinese ate. I believe he must have been an animist. He seldom mixed with the Malays in the area. Sometimes, my dad needed help on the farm. We would employ Ahmad. He had the aptitude and the strength to do the work required. I never heard him grumble. I remember only his smiles.

If you were coming up from Bedok Road and turned into Jalan Langgar Bedok to the rear of the perimeter fencing of the Bedok schools, Yi Shih's rambutan estate was on the right. On the left was a little Malay kampong. After the Malay kampong was Gan Cheng Huat's land. Gan Cheng Huat had a very big and imposing estate house made of concrete. It was the norm in those days to have such a house if you owned an estate. He owned several huge dogs and we children were always afraid to go near the house. He also owned a rifle. In those days, estate owners were entitled to own rifles. He had several children. I got acquainted only with Teck Chuan and Teck Ann, who attended Bedok Boys'. I did not know how many girls he had, but I knew they attended Bedok Girls'. It was well known that Teck Chuan always scored best in the school examinations. Coconut and rambutan trees were planted in and around his house. Several tenant residents lived on his land. One of them was the Yeo family (no relation to us). The husband and wife were performers in the Teochew Opera Troupe, *Lau Sai Thow*. While they were away for performances, his mother and two brothers looked after his three children, sons Kow Kiah and Ter Kiah and daughter Boon Hong.

On Kim Eng's land, we did not know who planted the major crops—coconuts and rambutans. The whole estate was put under the charge of Yeo Teow Swee. At that time, it was hard to get people to settle on the estate. I did not know the real reason why my grandparents moved from Kampong Eunos to that area. During the rambutan season, the whole of Teow Swee's family would be up harvesting the bright red, succulent fruit. Out of obligation, my parents would ask us to help pluck and gather the fruit. Teow Swee's trusted estate worker was responsible for the upkeep of the estate, including the marcotting of the rambutan trees, should new saplings be needed to replace the old ones.

We children always liked to observe something new and marcotting was something we seldom saw. We would observe how Mr Bong, the estate caretaker, chose a healthy branch, then made two cuts about an inch apart around the branch and peeled off the bark. Next, he took a coconut husk and filled it with cow dung which had been purchased, and tied the filled husk to the peeled section of the stem. Then, both ends of the husk were secured with sliced rattan cane. He used a makeshift scooper (a condensed milk tin with holes at the bottom) to water the marcot. Watering was done every day. After a few weeks, roots could be seen appearing out of the coconut husk. It was time to cut the marcot and plant it.

Trees planted using the marcotting method were short and they produced fruit very quickly. Sometimes, on the marcot itself, there would be flowers and fruit. Thus, when detached from the parent plant, it continued its process of producing fruit. The quality of the fruit was also the same as the parent plant's. There were great differences between a fruit which came from a marcot, and a fruit which came from a seed. If the rambutan ovules were fertilised by the pollen of a tree which was of a lower quality, the fruit could be of a lower quality. The tree would also be very tall and slender and would take several years to produce fruit.

What constituted good quality rambutan fruit? Firstly, the translucent flesh of the fruit should easily detach from the seed. Secondly, it must be sweet. Thirdly, the hair of the fruit should not be too bushy and must be succulent and bright red when ripe. One must be able to feel the crunchiness of the flesh when the fruit was chewed. It was said that fruits from the Penang species of rambutan were the best. I have eaten the fruits of the trees that were grown from seeds. The fruits from such trees were usually very small and the translucent flesh somewhat fibrous and adhered tightly to the seed. If we forcefully yanked the flesh from the seed, the flesh might get caught in the gaps between our teeth. I have eaten very sour rambutans too. Some of them were very small and some of them were yellowish green when ripe. Usually, the estate workers would chop down trees that produced such inferior fruit, as they considered it a liability to the estate.

Unripe rambutans were green and very hard to peel. The sap was very bitter and sticky. The scent was unpleasant and the taste was horrid. When the sap got onto our clothing, the brown stain it left was permanent. No amount of detergent, no matter how powerful, could wash the stain off. That was how Mother Nature protected the young fruit from being eaten.

The rambutan flowers were pollinated by insects and they grew in bunches. The fruits too grew in bunches. During the ripening season, the estate owners had to be on the alert for unwelcome visitors—fruit bats, birds and squirrels, as well as rambutan thieves. Usually a small hut was built for a watchman to keep a lookout for thieves. An air rifle was used to shoot fruit pests such as bats and *musang* (civet cats).

Behind every succulent rambutan fruit was backbreaking work. Everybody working in the estate had to be on the alert for parasites such as aphids, mealy bugs and other insects. There were strict routines to spray pesticide on the trees and ripening fruit. The mixture of water and concentrated pesticide should not exceed the Ministry of Health regulations.

After the harvest, it was time to spread nutrients on the roots. Holes had to be dug in between the trees away from the main roots for applying fertiliser. These fertilisers could be cow dung, pig dung or even human excreta bought from latrines in town. After the fertiliser was poured into the pit, it was topped with a layer of earth. For this reason, one should not wander about the estate. One could unwittingly step in a hole which had just been filled with fresh fertiliser. The estate workers had to prune the trees, clear the weeds and discard the debris at a designated place.

A luxuriant tree did not equate to a tree that would produce healthy fruit. Such a tree usually did not bear too much fruit. Workers not only pruned weak and diseased branches, they also cut away branches that bore too much foliage.

Often during the flowering season, fruiterers such as my grandpa, as I have described, would show up, make mental calculations and offer to buy the fruit of the desired whole trees when they were ripened. A deal would be struck and the landowner would warn his workers and residents against plucking fruits from these trees.

There were tales from kampong folks who plucked Ee Shih's rambutans. His rambutan tree branches grew outside the fences of the estate. Some were warned against plucking, whilst others, who were luckier, were told to eat them on the spot but not to take away any fruit. There were also stories of rambutan thieves who cut the rambutan branches at random under cover of darkness and ran away.

To learn more about coconut trees, see Chapter 6: The Tree of a Hundred Uses.

Pulasan

There was a species of fruit which looked like the rambutan. Its hair was very much thicker, like thorns. The fruit was very much bigger, heavier and quite elongated. The translucent flesh was sweet like the rambutan but did not detach easily from the seed. So far, in Kim Eng's estate, I only saw one such *pulasan* tree. This fruit was not very popular, so estate owners seldom planted the trees.

Other Fruit

Madam Ong Ka was such a resourceful lady. In and around her house, she planted many different kinds of fruit trees, namely olive, *buah belinjau, chempedak, buah nangka, buah yew kam, jambu batu, jambu ayer*, star fruit, pomelo and soursop as well as curry plants. To prevent insects from damaging the *chempedak* and *nangka* fruit, she wrapped them with hoods made from coconut leaves as well as from old clothing.

Some of the fruit trees we planted included guava, *buah chiku*, soursop, custard apple, cherry, gooseberry, passion fruit—both wild and domesticated—oil palm, betel nut, *sireh* palm, pomegranate, noni, mango, papaya, banana, *belimbing, buah keras*, cashew nut, durian and Buddha's palm (chiffon fruit).

The *Buah Keras* Tree

The *buah keras* (candlenut) tree in front of my house was a very tall tree—about 60 metres high. The flowers were small and white and the fruit had a soft outer covering. The nut—about the size of a rubber seed—was very hard. We had to place it on a stout piece of wood and use a heavy hammer to give it a hard blow. Then the kernel was scraped off using a spoon. The *buah keras* was mixed with chillies and *sambal belacan* and then pounded. A dish of curry tasted different without a few *buah keras*.

The leaves were huge like *cocoyam* leaves and heart-shaped. The tree had soft wood, so it was not advisable to climb or sit on the branches. Visitors were often in awe of the tree, as they had never seen one before.

Buah keras leaves

Buah keras tree

Buah keras flowers

Among the local fruits we ate but did not plant were the *buah sentut, buah langsat, bajang* and *buah rambai.*

The Kapok Tree

The local kapok tree looked very odd. The branches were at right angles to the main stem. The ripe pods hung down from the branch. They looked like bats having their nap so we were quite fearful when walking past a kapok tree. When the pods were mature and dried, the outer coverings dropped off, exposing the kapok (cottony seed). On windy and sunny days, we used to see the white cottony kapok floating off in the wind. Once we collected them and used them for stuffing our pillows.

The Henna Tree

Believe it or not, we had a nail-staining tree—henna. When it flowered, the white flowers seemed to emit a very fragrant scent.

The Malays in our area used to ask us for it to stain their nails. As for us, we used it as for medicine. Whenever we injured our fingers—we often did when we nailed something—we would pluck some of the leaves, pound them with a pinch of salt and apply it to the wound. The following day, the wound would not be so raw, but the surrounding area would be stained. The wound would heal completely after a few days.

A description of our farm would not be complete without mention of the flora and fauna in the ponds and streams. Floating on the water were the water hyacinth, water lettuce, the water-moss ferns and the duckweed. Growing in the water were the elodea and cabomba. Growing from the bed and out of the water were the water burheads and reeds. They were all very healthy and luxuriant. The water hyacinths were as tall as a metre high, as they got their nutrients from the pigsty. Those growing far away from the nutrient source were stunted. Besides being cooked into pig and chicken feed as I have described, the water hyacinth was also fed to the pigs and chicken uncooked. A small part of the pond was fenced up for our ducks. The ducks fed on the duckweed, water lettuce and the buds of the water hyacinth. They often dived into the water for fish.

During lull periods when the pigs and poultry had been sold off, the pond was often overgrown, as few water plants were harvested as animal feed. We would then have to trim them. Unhealthy plants were removed and laid on the banks to dry and healthy ones were spaced out. We children were encouraged to go into the pond to stir up the sunken deposits so that they could be more evenly spread throughout the pond water. The sunken deposits contained many nutrients.

Usually, the pond was teeming with fish. The most abundant were the snakehead, followed by the catfish, the Java fish, the eel and the climbing perch. They were edible and we often caught and cooked them. The water snails were harvested and eaten as well.

There were smaller fish such as fighting fish, mollies, guppies and other unnamed fish we called 'grass fish' or *longkang* fish. We caught them, put them into bottles and admired them.

When the discarded water hyacinth at the bank dried, we had a fine time playing with the dried bulbous stalks. Each one was like a mini balloon. We would press each one hard and a loud *pop* could be heard. That was due to the sudden escape of the compressed air in the fibrous, bulbous stalk.

Ferns

In and around the estates, they were so many different types of ferns. Some grew on the ground and some were saprophytes. Some were edible and others not. Behind our house was a colony of *resam* ferns. Only that particular species of fern grew there. Perhaps other plants had been strangled by them. The stalks and stems of the *resam* were very stiff and hard. Each made a loud snap when broken. The broken ends were sharp. We often got pricked by them.

The staghorn ferns grew very healthily on our rubber trees. Sometimes, the British soldiers would be in the area for military exercises. They were particularly fond of plucking the scraggy fronds and using them as camouflage as they hid themselves in the bushes. We children would then follow them and laugh. They would put their fingers on their lips to bid us not to make noise. We once plucked the fronds and dressed up in them. Our two pet dogs, Black

Our pet dogs
Photographed by Lu Xiang Hee

Mouth and Folded Ears, did not like that one bit. They turned wild, as if they thought we were aliens from space. They ran forward, baring their teeth and growling ferociously at us. Immediately, we tore off the costumes. When they recognised us, they stopped abruptly. After a few seconds they began shaking their legs and bodies, then came near us and licked us. We must have alarmed them quite a bit.

There was one particular fern we loved to play with. It grew mostly in the shade. We would

311

pluck the frond and put it on our arms with the underside facing down and tap it a few times. We could see the silver imprint of the frond on our arms. I believe that the silver imprint could have been the spores.

At times, we plucked the young fronds of *sayor paki* (a type of edible fern) to cook. They were either very light green or reddish in colour and soft to the touch. My mum would separate the leaves from the stalks and cook curry with them.

Small children liked to pluck the leaves of dragon scale ferns, with its thick, disc-shaped fronds that were about the size of standard shirt buttons, and play make-believe buttons with them, as well as *masak-masak*. They were saprophytes and were found growing on dead matter on the host trunks.

Lalang (*Imperata cyclindrica*)

The lalang or blade grass had long, spear-like leaves with tiny thorns at the edges of the leaf blades. It had long, underground adventitious stems, which grew very well in hard laterite soil. Buds grew from the axis of the stems. The buds were very hard and sharp. Its flowers were golden, and when the seeds matured, the hair-like structure around each seed would float away with the slightest breeze. At school, we often saw lalang seeds stray into our classrooms. Then when they moved towards us, we would blow at them and they would shift direction. Such amusements caused much annoyance to our teachers.

We often got cuts from the edges of the leaf blades and got pricked by the buds when we went into *lalang* bushes barefoot to retrieve lost items.

However, the plant had many uses. I have described how my grandma once harvested lalang to roll into bundles to make cushions for wine bottles for a wine-brewing factory. Very often, lalang blades were also used as short twines to tie bundles of vegetables or firewood. We often chewed the stems for its juice. When we had a sore throat, our mum would dig up some of the underground lalang stems, strip off the scale leaves, wash and then boil them to make a cooling drink. But we were warned not to have too much, as it would have an adverse effect on our bodies.

If there were bushes of lalang within pig pens, the pigs would dig and dig for the stems until the bushes were gone.

During our free time, as I described in the chapter on toys, we would use lalang leaves to play 'shooting javelins' or play naughty tricks on our unsuspecting friends with the flowers.

During the Japanese Occupation, medicine was scarce. We have seen how the prisoners of war boiled the underground stems of the lalang as a source of vitamin C.

Fungus

Living in areas with large trees which provided ample shade, naturally we would find fungi growing aplenty. Fungi were classified as non-green plants, but as recently as the 1980s, they stopped being classified as belonging to the plant family and now occupy a class of their own—fungus.

From just a rotting trunk, we could find so many species of fungus. The most notable was the bracket fungus. It was very colourful, in white and red, and it grew out of decomposing trunks. My parents would warn us of its poisonous nature.

"The more colourful a fungus is, the more poisonous it is," my grandma would always warn us. Therefore, we would never dare to touch them. There were small white ones, black ones and some that would release a cloud when disturbed. There was one particular fungus which was very soft and springy to the touch. I guess it must have been Jews' ears.

After a period of rain, we could find lots of fungi springing up from the ground under the trees. The toadstools stood out among them. It had a cap and the hollow, patterned stalk supporting the cap was so fragile that it broke with the lightest touch. There were the puffballs, which we liked to kick. We always tried to avoid the cloud it released as we kicked it. There were also many different types of mushrooms around. They looked like those my mum bought from the market. We were tempted to collect them to cook.

But my grandma always warned, "Before you eat a mushroom, you must know its species." Did we know the species? Of course not.

Luminous Fungus

There was one species of fungi that glowed in the dark. On very dark, cloudy nights, we would go looking for the glowing mushrooms in some corners outside the house. We would gingerly pick them up, place them in our palms and admire their soft glow. I always asked my teachers the name of this species of glowing mushroom during my biology lessons but was reprimanded for trying to annoy them. Most likely, that species had not been classified then.

Char Hiok or *Simpoh Air*

There is a particular species of plant *(simpoh air)* whose leaves were used by the Malays to wrap *tempeh* or fermented beans but I was not able to determine the English equivalent of the plant's name. The food hawkers used either this type of leaf *(char hiok* in Hokkien) or the *oh pei hiok* (palm sheath) to wrap food. They were used most likely because they were large and durable. I remember that once a month, we would receive a visit from a general vegetable collector, whose name was Pei Sian Toh. He would carry two huge baskets slung on a pole across his shoulder. He helped himself to the groves of *langkuas* or turmeric or any herbs he thought he would be able to sell. We children would run to the wooded hills to gather *char hiok.* Usually, those leaves were beyond our reach, as the plants were tall (compared to us then) and the thick undergrowth hampered our gathering of the leaves. We had to race against time to pluck the leaves to sell to him. Ignoring the insects and caterpillars, the lalang shoots and the thorns from the undergrowth, we scrambled and heaved to get to the plants. Then we stretched, climbed, scrambled, tore and scratched to pluck the intact leaves. Very old and insect-eaten leaves were discarded. We siblings would then compare how many leaves we had collected. Uncle Peh Sian

Toh would estimate and pay us a few coins each. With the money earned with our own sweat and muscle, we were on cloud nine.

The *simpoh ayer* plant

We came across many other types of plants, but there were simply too many to list here. Furthermore, we were not familiar with their names.

The Uses of Banana Plants

My dad once asked me to bring a bunch of bananas to one of the Indian provision shops along Bedok Road to sell. I sold it for about $2. Then, wild thoughts began to form in my young mind. I thought of transforming the whole of our estate into a huge banana plantation. When it produced fruit, we could sell the fruit for a lot of money.

Actually, whenever my dad was free, he would go around the estate looking for spaces in between the coconut trees wide enough to plant more banana trees. He would select the choice species such as the red rajah or the *pisang mas*, as these were more popular with the kampong folks. The Philippines species of green horn banana was avoided, because according to Chinese belief, it caused wind in

315

the stomach. The cow horn was popular for making *goreng pisang* (banana fritters). There was also a species of scarlet banana. That species of banana, when ripe, turned completely red. Another species that consumers avoided was the seeded banana. This species had seeds throughout the fruit and tasted sour. The seeds in the fruit were more than the kernel. As a result, one would constantly have to stop munching to remove the seeds in the mouth. This species was actually planted for its leaves, which were commonly used as a food wrapper.

A dwarf banana species

After deciding the plots in which to plant new banana plants, he would dig a hole deep enough to sink the suckers. Then he would choose the more desirable species and dig up the suckers from a big grove on our farm. If the leaves of the suckers were too big, he would remove them. My dad did not tell us why he had to remove almost all the leaves before transplanting. Later, I learnt that removing the leaves prevented water loss through transpiration in the young plants. The plants would take root faster and therefore grow more quickly. After having transplanted them, we would carry large pails to water them every day until they adapted to the new environment.

Although we planted banana trees, we seldom reserved a bunch for our own consumption. We preferred to exchange the fruit for cash. At first, just like any other fruit, my grandma would carry the whole bunch to Simpang Bedok to a fruit and vegetable purchaser to sell. Later, a wholesaler, just like the papaya wholesaler, would come to my house to harvest the fruit himself. He would also harvest the unripe bananas.

Besides selling the fruit for cash, there were many fringe benefits to planting bananas.

Trunks as Pig Food

To add variety to the pig food, besides the water hyacinth and dumb cane, banana trunks were added. After a bunch of bananas was harvested, the trunk could not grow new fruit any more. If it were left in the grove, it would live for some time then die. In the meantime, it shaded the younger plants from getting sunlight and they would not grow healthily. After harvesting the fruit, my dad would cut up the trunk, strip off the dead outer leaves and chop it up into tiny bits. Then he would cook it together with other vegetables and feed it to the pigs. Sometimes, when there was a lack of banana trunks in our estate, we would go to the *kampongs* to purchase them from the owners of banana groves. In most cases, the owners had just harvested the fruit but had not cut away the trunks. They could have been purely ignorant or just too lazy to dispose of them. My dad would pay 20 cents per trunk and we children would help him carry them home.

Banana String

We used to have dried reeds, which we purchased from provision shops, to tie small, elongated items such as sticks. But usually, those were a standard length—about a metre. If we wanted a longer length of tying material, we would get gunny string or coconut rope. However, to tie rice dumplings which were wrapped in bamboo leaves (the fifth day of the fifth moon marked the start of the Rice Dumpling Festival or *Tuan Wu Jie*), the Chinese kampong folks would specifically choose the banana leaf fibre. One reason could be that it was non-poisonous and the other that they were durable, as the rice dumplings would be cooked in a pot of boiling water.

Besides using the banana fibre for tying rice dumplings, we used it for almost everything else that needed tying.

Making Banana String:

1. Choose a healthy banana trunk. Check for signs of worm attack and damaged parts.
2. Peel off the leaf stalk piece by piece.
3. Use a small penknife and run along the fibre of the leaf stalk lengthwise, at about one-centimetre intervals.
4. Hang them up to dry.
5. After drying, bundle them for use.

Processing banana stalks was a whole family affair. We practised division of labour. Someone would peel the stalk, another would shred it lengthwise, and yet another would bring it out to dry in the sun. After drying, we would collectively inspect every strand and bundle it up. The superior bundles were cut into equal lengths and used to tie rice dumplings.

Each strand could also be separated into smaller strands, depending on what we wanted to use it for. If we wanted to control a growing climber on to a specific support, we could use a very small strand to do it, as a big strand might damage the delicate stem.

To tie a bigger bundle of objects, such as a bundle of sticks, we could combine several strands to make a big rope. The string could also be made into bags to support heavy fruit from falling prematurely from trees. So the banana rope had multiple uses.

The Use of Green Banana Leaves

There was once an emperor who heard that a king in India was so rich that the inhabitants, after finishing their meals, would throw their crockery away. So he decided to send a large force to conquer that country. Upon arriving in India, he found that what the inhabitants threw away after eating were the banana leaves.

The use of banana leaves as containers is very practical. They are used in place of plates, as food separators, food container liners and as food packaging. Banana leaves are not poisonous, are waterproof and have a large surface area. After use, they are discarded. They are biodegradable and therefore do not harm the environment.

The use of banana leaves has never lost its practicality, even though today there is competition from artificial materials. Today, banana leaf supply is dwindling because the land for planting such groves is limited.

In our farm, there was a species that was specially grown for their leaves. That species was very tall and the leaves were very broad. The fruit was sour and had many seeds in it. Every now and then, a leaf harvester would come with a knife to gather the leaves for sale.

At every festival, we would bake cakes. We children would wash the banana leaves and then cut them with a pair of scissors to line the baking containers.

As for the green leaf stalks, we would split each halfway and make it into a clapper.

On days when there was a light drizzle, we would each cut a banana leaf, hold it over our heads and walk to school.

The Legend of the Banana Spirit

There were many legends in connection with banana trees. One particular legend was told many times over by gamblers who wanted to strike it rich. It goes like this:

A gambler has to make a choice—to make use of the green banana spirit or the red banana spirit. If a person chooses the red banana spirit, he has to plunge a nail into the banana trunk of a red species, then tie a string on the head of the nail and lead it to the head of his bed. It is important to be alone with all the lights switched off—the room must be pitch dark. He must lie down on the bed, close his eyes and go to sleep. Soon the red banana spirit will come and plead with him to pull out the nail from the trunk. The gambler must use this opportunity to ask the spirit for lottery numbers that will make him rich. If the amount struck were not substantial, he would not pull out the nail but wait for the spirit to come again. He can ask the spirit for the winning numbers until he is satisfied, and then pull out the nail. This will work also on the spirit of the green species of bananas.

Was the legend true or not? I had never heard of anyone trying it. A good piece of advice would be not to try it. If a gambler gets rich in this way, he may be poorer in another. Engaging in such activities could be detrimental to his life.

The Uses of Bamboo Plants

Bamboos grow profusely in the hot, wet climate of the tropical and equatorial forests. There are many different varieties of bamboos, which range from minute, decorative bamboo plants to the tall, huge variety.

Bamboos are well known for their tensile strength and their supple quality, and we could tap on the strength of each variety and make full use of them.

The Chicken Feed Trough

When making a trough for putting chicken feed, a dried, medium-sized bamboo was used. Several lengths of bamboo of equal diameter at both ends were cut from a bamboo tree. Each length was about six feet. They were then each carefully split into two. The nodes were removed, leaving behind one on each end. That was to prevent chicken feed from spilling out. Then two stabilisers (made from split bamboo too) were nailed at the two ends to prevent the bamboo piece from rolling about. Lo and behold, we had a bamboo trough.

The Fruit Picker

If we wanted to pluck some fruit, such as guava or mangosteen, we needed a fruit picker. To make a fruit picker, a long and slender bamboo pole was chosen. At one end of the bamboo pole, several small splits were made so that the strips fanned outward. Then either a small stone or a hard unripe fruit was used as a wedge to make the split open like claws. To pick the fruit from the tree, we pushed the picker on to the ripe fruit, caged the fruit and gave it a light twist. The ripe fruit would be held within the picker. We then lowered the picker and retrieved the fruit. If it was too short, we could always get another pole to join to it.

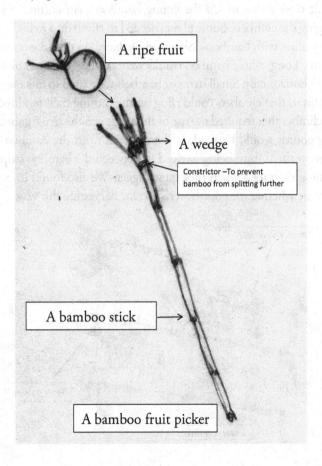

A ripe fruit

A wedge

Constrictor –To prevent bamboo from splitting further

A bamboo stick

A bamboo fruit picker

Stakes for Climbers

Different parts of the bamboo could be used as stakes for vegetable climbers. We stripped the leaves off a branch, sharpened the thicker end of it, and we pushed it upright near a climber. We cut huge bamboo stems to size—about six to eight feet long—then split them. One had to be very careful when splitting them, as the split edges could be quite sharp. Each strip was as broad as two to four centimetres. Bamboos are resilient plants. The green stem with the buds intact could grow easily when it came in contact with moisture. If the bamboo strips were not dried, buds from those stakes of green split bamboo would sometimes sprout from the nodes. If that happened, the farmer would have a difficult time trying to kill the young bamboo stem cuttings without damaging the climbers. Some plants needed to climb on a trellis. We also made trellises with bamboos. Short, whole bamboo trunks were used as columns. Long, whole bamboo trunks were used to join one column to another horizontally. Small strips of bamboo were used to line the top of the trellis so that climbers could cling on them using their tendrils. One good climber that required the use of the trellis was the snake gourd. The young gourds would be made to hang down from the bamboo strips to prevent them from being wedged in between the bamboo strips and becoming deformed when they grew bigger. We also found it easier to determine whether the gourds were ripe for harvesting this way.

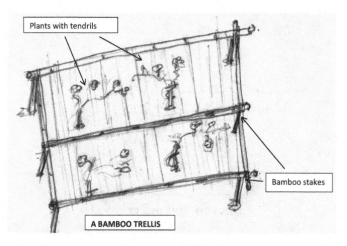

Plants with tendrils

Bamboo stakes

A BAMBOO TRELLIS

Bamboo as Carrying Poles

Stout bamboo stems were also made into carrying poles. A good carrying pole was one that could withstand the mass of a load as well as be able to bounce with the spring of the walker's step. Most important of all was that the carrier should feel comfortable when using it.

Bamboo Poles as Clotheslines

To date, the slender bamboo poles for hanging clothes to dry have still not met their substitute. Today's bamboo poles are covered by a coloured plastic sheath to make them more attractive. The bamboo poles that we used were their natural colour.

Other Uses of Bamboo

To drive poultry such as chicken or ducks to their designated areas, a slender bamboo stick was used. It was slim, supple, very light and did not easily snap.

I have previously mentioned the stud breeder driving his boar with a rope tied around its neck. He would use a small bamboo stick to tap its body to direct it. A person unfamiliar with the activities of the village folks might have thought he was taking his pet for a walk.

Bamboo for Wrapping Food

Earlier I mentioned that the fifth day of the fifth moon of the lunar calendar was the *Tuan Wu Jie*, or the Rice Dumpling Festival. It was only during this period we could eat rice dumplings. Days before the festival, we had to go to a grove of very tall bamboo trees at the boundary between our land and Piah Teng's to pluck bamboo leaves. That species of bamboo had very thick trunks and the leaves were very broad. We plucked only those within reach. We did not cut down the whole tree, as the leaves higher up the trees were not as broad as those at the base. Then we had to dry them in a cool, dry place. We usually put them in a bamboo basket and hung the whole basket of leaves on a hook from the ceiling. When making rice dumplings, we took the leaves down to soak so that they would not break so easily. After preparing the filling for the dumplings, we sat down to fold the bamboo leaves into pyramid-shaped containers and then filled them. The larger leaves were reserved for fillings that were very rich, such as glutinous rice with mushrooms, pork, dried prawns and a piece of *buah keras*. The slender leaves were for common red bean dumplings. Then the bamboo leaves were folded to seal the fillings and tied with dried banana fibre. Some people tied their dumplings with a type of reed known as *kiam chow* in Hokkien (salty reed fibre), which was found in the swampy areas.

In the meantime, we had to prepare a makeshift stove by arranging a few bricks. An empty four-gallon cooking oil tin was put on the stove. The tin was then filled with water. After that, the bundles of dumplings were put into the tin to boil.

Bamboo Shoots as Food

On certain days, we would go around the bamboo groves to hunt for bamboo shoots with a *changkol* in hand. If we spotted one, we would dig it out very carefully. We would aim the blade sharply at the joint between the shoot and the underground stem. After digging, handling them was a challenge. On the sheaths were tiny, black hair-like spikes. These spikes could make the skin itch. So we would usually wear a long-sleeved shirt and long pants. When preparing those shoots to cook, the sheath would be carefully cut and put aside, taking care not to let the spikes come into contact with our bodies.

Bamboo for Other Household Utensils

If my dad were by chance to come upon some suitable odd bamboo stems, he would split them and shape them into chopsticks using a penknife. But of course, they could not be compared with the commercially produced ones. Those were smoother to the touch. Mugs and pencil holders were also shaped from those odd bamboo pieces.

Bamboo as Toys

Seeing that my neighbour, Ah Hee, had a bamboo flute, I too wanted one. So I cut a length of bamboo stem, bore a few holes on it, at equal distance, and a flute was made.

There were a few occasions our Malay neighbours used bamboo trunks as 'cannons', which made ear-splitting booming sounds. A small hole was cut a few centimetres away from the last node. All the rest of the nodes were dislodged to create a clear passage. Carbide was inserted into the small hole with a small amount of water. Just like with the carbide lamp, the reaction produced a gas. A lighted splinter would be placed over the small hole. When the gas passed out of the hole, it would be ignited, creating a loud *boom*.

Poles

Once I saw my friend Sahid burning coconut leaves in the open, and with the help of a few kampong folks, they were turning and bending a few long and slender bamboo poles over the flames. But they were not burning the bamboo poles. They were straightening and drying them so that they could make light, straight poles for harvesting coconuts. Now the cat was out of the bag. I had always wondered how these people got such straight poles. I learnt that bent bamboo stems could be straightened with the application of heat.

Firewood

Dried bamboo stems burnt very well, giving out very little smoke. So bamboo stems was one of our sources of firewood. But we had to be very careful not to use the whole stem. We needed to split them up. If we did not split them up, a small explosion could occur. The air in between the nodes would expand if heated and if the heat was intense; the sudden expansion would force the stem to break abruptly and with great force.

A, B, C and Other Things

Sometimes, from odd bits of bamboo, my grandma would split them and weave baskets and other containers. Mr Bong's wife was really adept at making bamboo baskets. After making a considerable number of pieces, Bong would carry them to the kampong to sell. In and around their house, there were so many bamboo pieces—some were split and some were not. Other pieces of bamboo were used as fences and gates.

Apart from the objects that we made ourselves, we also bought some other objects which were made of bamboo. One interesting thing that we acquired was the dual-purpose bamboo chair. When it was made to stand upright, it was a chair for an adult. When it was made to lie sideways, it was a chair for a toddler.

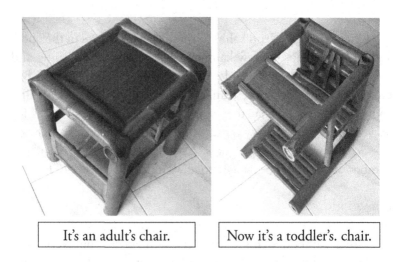

| It's an adult's chair. | Now it's a toddler's. chair. |

Another bamboo item that we bought was the chicken cage. It was conical and its base radius was about half a metre. If we wanted to make sure that the chickens did not wander about, we would put the cage over them. It could also be used as a trap for the chickens. If a chicken were too difficult to catch, we would just put some bait into a half-opened cage, prop it up with a stick that had a piece of string attached to it. When the bird was in the cage, we pulled the

326

string hard. The stick would dislodge from the cage and the cage would come down, trapping the chicken.

Whenever the kampong folks had any spring chickens to sell, they would contact the chicken dealer. He would come in the evening with his bamboo cages on his big gentleman's bike—two huge cages on the back carrier and a smaller one in front. He would catch all the chickens himself with the aid of a long, powerful torchlight. He held the chickens up by their legs and tied them with gunny strings in bundles of fives. They were then weighed using his *daching*. The weight was totalled and the amount was paid in cash. He then arranged the chickens carefully in the bamboo cages. The two huge cages were secured tightly at the rear carrier, while the small one was secured at the front to prevent the loaded bicycle from tipping backwards. He then pushed his load until it gathered speed and then mounted it and rode away. While riding in the dark lanes, he had to be on the lookout for two different kinds of waylayers—the robber and the corrupt policeman. The corrupt policeman would accuse him of stealing chickens and threaten to take him to the police station. He would then have to bribe the policeman with a few dollars.

Bamboo ladders

Rubber Trees (*Hevea braziliensis*)

It was Englishman Sir Henry Wickham who brought rubber seeds from the lower Amazon area of Brazil to Kew Gardens in London in 1875. However, the climate in England proved unsuitable for rubber trees. They were then sent to Singapore because the rubber trees needed a tropical climate. In Singapore, it was Henry Nicholas Ridley who propagated and experimented with rubber trees. In the 19th century, coffee trees in Southeast Asia suffered from a blight so they had to be destroyed. At that time in Europe, the motorcar industry needed rubber to make tyres. In order to meet the demand for rubber, the planters destroyed the coffee trees and replaced them with rubber trees.

At first, rubber trees were felled to get latex. It was Ridley who experimented and perfected the process of collecting latex by cutting the bark.

I did not know who planted the rubber trees in the estate we lived in. They were planted in between the coconut trees. The lower girth of each tree was so huge, quite unlike those we found in the Malayan rubber estates, which were so small in circumference. The height, I guess, must have been about 60 metres. I believe their huge size might be attributed to the open space and ample sunlight. The flowers were in bunches; so were the fruits. The flowers were small and yellow. I believe they were pollinated by insects. The unripe fruit was green and each fruit had three seeds in it. When the fruits were ripe, they dried up and turned brown. They then gave a very loud *crack* sound. The shell of the fruit split, throwing the seeds far, hitting leaves and anything else in their way and then landed on the ground with a smattering of *plops*. We children often carried a bamboo basket and collected the shells. They made very good firewood. We collected the seeds too, either to make toys or to play games with them.

"Ouch!" I yelled one day. The pain was excruciating. I examined my calf. There was a red spot, as if it had been scalded. Then one of my brothers walked away gleefully, holding a rubber seed.

My dad knew at once what had happened. One of my brothers had rubbed the rubber seed on our rough cement floor to make it hot then had immediately pressed it against my calf.

He was given a sound thrashing by my dad, of course. We had learnt a very painful lesson—friction produced heat. Caning also produced heat and could cause pain.

I always admired the leaves of the rubber tree. Each leaf had a long stalk, and at the end there were three large leaflets. Botanists termed the leaf formation as trifoliate. During the equivalent of winter here, the leaves turned yellow and then fell off. Sometimes, we thought the trees had died. But then, by the next month, new shoots and leaves would grow again.

One fine morning, Teow Swee and his sons brought in the rollers, which were machines for flattening rubber slaps, latex collecting cups, latex processing trays, acid and other paraphernalia to collect latex. Mr and Mrs Bong and a few others were trained to cut the bark of the rubber tree with a grooved knife. That knife could cut grooves on the bark of the tree up to a certain depth. If the cut was too deep and penetrated the woody trunk, it would damage the tree. For each tree, two grooves in the shape of a 'V' were made.

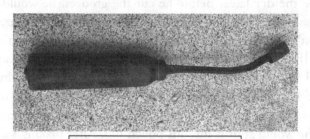

The rubber-tapping knife.

The white latex would flow down along the grooves into a small, V-shaped metal piece which had been temporarily inserted into the bark to channel the latex into a clay cup. The cup was supported by a steel wire holder. The tappers would start as early as 5 a.m.

Today, the process of rubber tapping is cast in concrete at the Botanic Gardens to educate future generations.

The tapper would sling a pouch, which contained his tapping knife, metal channels and clay cups. There was also a compartment to store the dry latex. Before he cut the grooves, he would make sure the dried latex of the previous day's flow had been removed. He would detach the dried latex, and it would stretch like a rubber band. If the dried latex strand were too long, he would wind it around his palm and then roll it into a ball and put it into his pouch. Then he would proceed to make fresh cuts on the bark. If there were water in the cup, he would empty it. If there were dried latex, he would stuff it into his pouch too. After making sure that everything was in order, he proceeded to the next tree. By the time he had finished tapping all the available trees, it would already be 8 a.m. After resting for an hour, Mr Bong and the other tappers would each carry a pail and start collecting the latex from the trees they had tapped earlier in the morning. After pouring out the latex from each cup, he had to use his finger to wipe the inside of the cup, so it was completely clear of latex. Then he returned the cup to the steel holder, just in case there was more latex dripping from the tree.

There were many rubber trees around our house. Those trees were not transplanted in neat rows like those in the Malayan rubber estates. They had grown quite naturally from seeds dispersed by splitting and had escaped our parent's *changkol*.

In the afternoon, sometimes we would go around the rubber trees to collect dried rubber latex strands and wind them into a ball, as I have mentioned earlier. A rubber latex ball was very heavy and bouncy. It could bounce several times higher than ordinary balls.

The liquid latex collected by the tappers was poured into measuring trays and a chemical was added so that it could coagulate. The trays of liquid latex were left for several hours. At about 5 p.m., Teow Swee's sons and daughters would remove the coagulated slabs of rubber and start flattening them into thin sheets with the rollers. These rolling machines were manually operated. I often went to help them turn the rollers. After each turn of the rubber slab, the roller gap was narrowed. The rubber slab that moved through the narrower gap would be stretched to become longer and broader as well as thinner. A slab of coagulated rubber taken out from a tray about 12 inches by eight inches by two inches could be flattened and lengthened to about 36 inches by 24 inches by 0.3 inches. The plain rubber sheet had to undergo yet another round of rollers—the final patterned one. One had to use great strength to roll the patterned rollers. I usually could not do it. After that, the rubber sheets were hung up to dry and then they were smoked. After that, they were visually graded and tied into bales and brought to the warehouse.

During those days when rubber tapping was carried out, my dad was careful not to destroy any rubber trees. Mr Bong would occasionally carry a sickle and a *changkol* and go to every rubber tree to clear the undergrowth and bushes so that it would be easier to work in the early hours of the morning.

After the bark had been cut all the way down to the base after many successive days of tapping, we would find that new bark would have formed over the areas where the tree had previously been. The new bark would be cut again to repeat the process of tapping.

Dried rubber wood was best used as firewood. Rubber wood has traces of latex, which caused it to burn easily. On some afternoons, our parents would ask us to collect firewood. Our first thought would be the dried rubber branches. We took with us a long bamboo pole with a steel hook at its end and a *parang*. We got the dried branches down from the trees with the hook and then chopped them. Then we arranged them into piles. Each pile was tied up with twisted lalang leaves and carried home on our shoulders.

One afternoon, we discovered that the rubber estate after Mr Kidd's farm (the present-day Bedok South Wet Market) had been turned into a sand quarry. A dam was built across a stream so a pond was created. Huge motor pumps were used to pump the water from the pond to loosen the sand from the hills. A group of workers had cut down the rubber trees and sawed the wood into logs using handsaws. Those saws were gigantic—about six to eight feet in length and the teeth were huge. For a child of ten like me, one look at the saw frightened me. Each of those giant saws had two handles, one on each side. Thus, sawing a log needed two men. After sawing the logs, they put them neatly in piles. A man carrying an axe would then split the logs. The axe that he handled was so different from ours. Ours was very sharp; the cutting edge was about 15 degrees. But the man who split the wood had an axe, which was very blunt. The cutting edge could have been about 60 degrees. After observing him for a while, I realised that a sharp axe was good only for cutting or chopping wood. A blunt axe was very suitable for splitting wood, as the splitting angle was wider and therefore acted like a wedge. The further one drove the axe into the wood, the wider the wood would split. The man seemed to enjoy splitting the wood with ease.

When a rubber tree was felled on Mr Kidd's farm, the kampong folks, my mum and I would rush forward to hack the branches off with our *parangs* and chopping knives. My mum would chop the branches, and I would gather them into a heap. Within minutes, the felled tree was denuded so only the trunk and thick branches were left. After that, we took our time to strip off the leaves and tie them in bundles using lalang. Before twisting the lalang leaves together into ropes, we would smash the root, stems and hard stalks on to a stone or a sturdy trunk to make them soft so that they could be worked easily. While tying them up, we would jovially recount how we struggled to get a certain branch, and how we managed to obtain a ready cut branch from someone, and how we had lost a choice branch to someone else. Then we would enjoy ourselves laughing. I would carry the first bundle on my shoulder home, while my mum kept watch over the rest of our branches. Then I would ask my dad and siblings to help us carry home the rest.

The trunk and thick branches were reserved for the contractor who would split them and sell them as firewood or make them into matchsticks.

When the water pumps on Mr Kidd's farm had washed away the soil, exposing the roots of the felled trees, we would rush forward to cut them. We were prepared to get ourselves soaked in the water, especially when the weather was hot. It was really fun to play in the gushing water that carried the sand down the slopes. We were not aware of the danger that we might fall and get injured. Maybe we were immune to the pain of cuts and injuries, so we did not fear getting more. If any one of us ever got a cut or an injury, our parents would slap us and then say that we were not careful. I had cuts and bruises all over my limbs. Each time I bruised or cut myself, I would bravely rub away the blood or wash it and utter, "Never mind. No pain," and then continue to play or work.

Today, there is rubber wood furniture. But in the 1950s, rubber wood furniture was frowned upon. We had heard of milk cases, wine cases and other boxes made out of rubber wood but not furniture. The reason was that rubber wood could split easily and it was a favourite of white ants.

With so many different materials around, especially bamboo, we felt we were very fortunate. We needed to purchase things only when they were really necessary. Those we could make ourselves, we would. Waste was therefore cut to a minimum.

Fauna

At other times, my dad encountered several types of snakes, such as cobras and pythons. Most of them were lying across sandy paths. I wondered why they did that. Most likely, they liked the warmth, as the grass could be quite chilly in the early morning. Most often, my dad would get hold of a sturdy bamboo stick and beat them. A few whacks on their heads would make them look like mincemeat. My dad always advised us to use a sturdy bamboo stick as it was supple. He had this maxim: "A snake is afraid of bamboo. Use it to kill if you need to." Furthermore, he said that a dead snake would have its tail still wriggling. That was true. Every time my dad killed one, I saw that the tail was still moving. He did not bother to whack the other parts, as he said that it was not necessary, as its head had died. Then he would hook the snake and throw it deep into the bushes. He was against burying a dead snake. I wondered why. Usually, in the rural areas, whenever a snake was killed, it was often thrown into the bushes or on to the road for motor vehicles to run over it. Often, I found snake bones fused with the tar on the road. Most likely, the other kampong folks had the same idea.

Another taboo for him was to allow an injured snake to escape. My grandma used to tell us this story. Once, a kind-hearted man felt sorry for hurting a snake. It was allowed to escape. Not long after, a huge stump had formed on the injured part of the snake. One night, the man was sleeping in his bed under a mosquito net. The snake slithered up the bed and entered through a small hole in the mosquito net. Unfortunately for the snake, the small hole on the net prevented the stump from completely going through. It was caught hanging just a few centimetres above the sleeping man.

The man's friend saw it when he came back early in the morning after working the night shift. Without waking or alarming him, he pulled him sideways from the bed and down to the floor with a loud thud. When the man woke up, he remembered the incident of allowing the snake to escape. He took a stout bamboo stick and struck at the snake, which was still hanging on the netting. It was believed that because of his kind-heartedness, the poisonous snake had failed to take revenge on him.

There was once a cobra that had entered our well and could not escape. It swam and hissed desperately, forward and backward in the water. We wanted to kill it with a bamboo pole, but it was able to dodge all the blows. It dived and surfaced, and wriggled left and right so swiftly. The distance between the person handling the pole and the surface of the water as well as the narrow well wall hampered the movements of the pole. Feeling frustrated, we left the long pole in the well. Immediately, the cobra wriggled up the pole and slithered away at lightning speed. We stared at each other for a few seconds. Fearing the cobra might have contaminated the water, we had to empty the well and wait for fresh spring water to fill it up.

In another incident, it was about one in the morning. In our chicken coop, we could hear the brief fluttering of hens followed by short yelps. We suspected that something was amiss. We looked high and low in the coop with our torchlight. The chickens were either sleeping on the rungs of the racks or on the floor. Everything looked fine. Then we went to sleep. The next morning, we found three mother hens dead and two missing. To our horror, a huge python about three metres long was seen coiled next to the dead hens. Too shocked to scream, we rushed to tell our parents.

"Oh! My heaven!" they shouted. They rushed forward, but it had already shifted its position to coil on a fallen bamboo trunk. We took out our catapults and shot it with steel nuts and whatever we could lay our hands on. But the hits proved to be of no threat to it. Light *poop* sounds were made as the projectiles bounced off harmlessly to the ground. One of us hurried to get the help of the rambutan estate owner, Ee Shi. He had a rifle. We hoped he could shoot it with his rifle. When he arrived, the python had already escaped.

There were other interesting encounters. One afternoon, I heard a distressed croaking, as if appealing for help, among water hyacinth. The frogs and other creatures seemed disturbed. There was a flurry of movement and then silence. Then I saw that a slender green snake had a small frog struggling in its mouth. At other times, small green snakes were sighted. We were told that they were harmless and we left them alone.

Monkeys

In the kampong, if anyone were to point and stare at anything, he would attract a curious crowd. Once a group of kampong folks were staring, pointing and shouting excitedly at something at the top of a coconut tree. Upon scrutinising it carefully, I saw a monkey sitting on a coconut frond. We seldom saw any wild monkeys around, but that one could have escaped from captivity. The kampong folks coaxed, cajoled, and shouted, but the creature seemed to be enjoying itself, making monkey faces at the people below and swinging from tree to tree until it went off to the neighbouring estate.

There were a few people in our estate who reared monkeys as pets. My neighbour once had one. He tied a chain round the neck of the animal and had it perched on his shoulder and went everywhere with it. Wherever he went, children were attracted to the monkey. They handed it food and should the monkey accept, they would go wild and go searching for more food. Others excitedly called to it, "Monkey! Monkey!" Some mimicked its actions. The whole crowd would roar with laughter, saying that the children looked like the monkey.

Skinning and Eating an Iguana

One afternoon, there was a visit from uncle Ah Tang, uncle Chew's brother. He occasionally visited us as in those days, friends and relatives were few but upon acquaintance, they became thick like flesh and bones. My dad and he were in the midst of a conversation, when suddenly, there was a commotion. We heard faintly that there was a funny creature. Everybody was rushing around and shouting, peering in every nook and corner under the bushes and in between fallen coconut trunks. Uncle Ah Tang joined in the fray, excitedly claiming that catching wild creatures was his favourite pastime. He disappeared under the bushes at the bank of a sluggish flowing stream. There was a sudden movement and the bushes shook violently. An excited voice was heard, "Got it!" Then out of the bushes came uncle Ah Tang with a creature struggling in his hand. There was a flurry of excitement. They came crowding to see the creature. He called it a 'four-legged snake'. Actually, it was an iguana.

Without wasting a second, he nailed the iguana on the coconut tree trunk with its belly facing out. He took out a sharp penknife and slid its underbelly. Blood flowed out. We could see the internal organs inside still moving. He cut out a greenish substance.

"It's the gall!" he exclaimed.

Suddenly, without uttering another word, he sped off—up the hills and down the valley several times until he was panting hard. Then, in between gasps of air, he swallowed the gall.

After having rested he said proudly, "Do you know why I did that just now? Well, that's the most effective way of making the best use of the efficacy of a snake gall. It makes a person immune against many ailments."

Like an expert, he peeled off the skin. Then he cut the reptile into bite-sized pieces and cooked a soup with it. He added a lot of ginger and a pinch of salt. I had a small bowl of soup and a piece of it. It tasted like chicken.

Rats

One late night, I woke up with a start. Our parents were digging and shining torches at a hole under the main post of the house in their bedroom. I quietly came in between them and they were surprised.

"Did you see any rats eating the copra in the hall? There is a trail of dung and the gunny sacks of copra are damaged, leaving bits all over." Mum was furiously poking a steel rod into the hole on the floor, at the same grumbling that they had to wake up early to go to the market the next day.

They were trying to get rid of the rats in the house. They had already dug quite a bit in the room. They saw several holes connected to the main one. To dig them up would entail destroying a considerable area of the floor. They poured water and DDT into the hole and even banged loudly on the floor, but to no avail.

Then mum boiled several kettles of water and poured them into the holes. Dad immediately sealed them up with cement. Well, that problem seemed to have been solved. There were no more complaints of rats eating our animal feed.

A traditional rat trap.
If a rat were trapped, we would push the whole trap with the rat in it into the pond to drown it.

Rat Traps

Rats were so elusive. They seldom came face to face with us. When they saw us coming, they would scamper away so fast and hide in nooks and corners of places we could not even imagine. We tried different ways of trapping them. One was using the rat trap as shown in the picture above. Another was the spring trap. The person setting a spring trap must be very mindful. He must think of the safety of himself and the people in the house, otherwise we would also be in danger. Rat glue was used too but it was expensive. Usually we failed to get the rats, but many other small animals like cockroaches, moths and house lizards were trapped instead. There were rat poisons, but after being poisoned, they would die in some obscure corner we could not identify until there was the smell of something decomposing. The smell of animals decomposing could be overpowering.

White Ants

One night, we were preparing to sleep. *"Ah Ma! Le thia! Le thia! Chi tau ooh ki kuai eh sieah!"* (translation from Hokkien: Grandma! Listen! Listen! There's a mysterious sound coming from inside here.) I exclaimed excitedly, pointing at the post behind the bed.

Grandma moved over and listened intently.

"Oh my gosh! White ants are attacking it," she said. "Don't worry, I'll deal with them tomorrow morning." We had an uneasy sleep that night.

The next morning, we knocked at the post. It seemed hollow. We gave it a gentle push. It gave way. We peeled off the outer layer. To our horror, white ants were scurrying about—some were trying to escape and some hurried to their hiding places deep in the wood. A few bit my hands. It was quite painful. I immediately brushed them off, killing them in the process. My dad replaced the pillar and painted DDT on it.

Coincidentally that day, we were cooking the pig's food. The infected pillar was immediately taken to the giant stove and used as firewood. The whole nest of white ants perished.

Centipedes

Once, I was trying to lift several planks that had been left lying on a heap for some time. Suddenly, I felt an excruciating pain in one of my fingers. I gave a loud yell, letting the planks come crashing down. A swelling immediately formed. There were two red marks on the swelling. My grandma examined it and said that a centipede had bitten me. We searched the whole heap of planks for the culprit but in vain. Centipedes are adaptable creatures that could move very fast and hide themselves in cracks and crevices of wood and concrete. Experts say that a sting from a centipede could last for a few hours but is not fatal. The pain in my fingers did last a few hours. My dad would give his advice—before putting your fingers or hands on anything, watch for dangers that might be lurking unseen.

Note:

Centipedes have been around in Singapore long before Raffles landed in 1819. Centipedes had been bothering the populace so much that Major General William Farquhar had to offer incentives for anyone who could bring dead centipedes to the government agencies.

Once, there was a strong wind blowing. The coconut trees swayed vigorously. As usual, we were up and about searching for fallen coconut fronds. Suddenly, a frond dropped in front of us. We rushed forward as a huge centipede, darkish red, about 15 centimetres long, scurried away from the leaflets. What a shock we had! We stared at each other wide-eyed and counted ourselves lucky not to have been bitten by it.

In those days, lorries transporting office workers were quite common. Such lorries were covered with canvas to protect the passengers from the weather. The seats were mere planks laid across the two side panels of the lorry. There was once a group of kampong folks gathered together, waiting for a lorry to transport them to a *wayang* performance at Somapah Road.

While waiting, my mum suddenly gave out a loud cry and grimaced in pain. She pressed a point on her forearm. Someone said she had been bitten by a centipede. Someone rubbed Eng Ann Tong Tiger medicated oil, a well-known brand, on to the wound. The pain did not abate. Others tried their favourite brands of medicated oil with them, but they still could not relieve her of her suffering.

From among the crowd, someone suggested, "Let's fight poison with poison!" He whipped out a matchstick from a box of matches, struck it and as it burnt, it made a sizzling sound. Immediately, he pressed the burning match head on the puncture marks on my mum's arm. She gave out a loud yell. After a few seconds, the pain was gone—leaving just a slight irritation on the part scalded by the match head. She could join the rest of the kampong folks to enjoy the evening's outing. Was it true that poison could counteract poison? Well, experts say that animal and plant poisons could be neutralised by heat. I thought the poison on my mum's arm was likely neutralised by the heat rather than the poisonous chemicals from the match head.

My grandma used to say that during the dry season, the poison from the centipede was at its most potent. She explained that in arid weather, the centipede had less moisture in its body and, as a result, the poison was more concentrated. A person or creature bitten by it suffered more then than if bitten during the wet season. She might be right, but could it be that during the dry season, there was a lack of food? So if there was a chance of hunting something, the hungry centipede might inject more venom?

Chameleons

Very often, we saw hideous creatures with frightening, thorny bodies. They moved among the fruit trees and bushes. When frightened, they puffed up their bodies, showing off their thorn-like hoods. One such creature was the chameleon. When they were on the tree trunks, their bodies took the colour of the trunks. When they were among the leaves, their bodies changed their colour to green.

A chameleon

The Cowherd

Quite often, we would see an Indian man with a piece of cloth wound round his head, carrying a sickle and a piece of rope. He would go to the bank of the stream, where there was abundant succulent grass growing. He then proceeded to cut the grass, tie it up in a bundle, heave the bundle on his head, and carry it away.

Sometimes, he drove his whole herd of bulls, cows, and calves along the road and then to the banks of streams to let them feed themselves. While walking along the road, the traffic would patiently wait for them to move aside and then slowly pass. I had witnessed several such occasions, but had never seen any impatient driver tooting his horn. Could it be they were afraid that the cattle might panic and run into their vehicle and damage it? Or were they more gracious than the drivers of today?

As the herd walked, they went splashing the road with their dung. There were some kampong folks who followed them, carrying pails and spades to collect the dung as fertiliser. We watched the herd of cows with a different objective. When we saw them coming, we would immediately run to them and act as a lookout. We did not want them near our vegetable farm. The cowherd, who carried a stick and dressed in a *dhoti,* would immediately come to the edge of our farm to prevent any of his charges from crossing over the boundary.

Two places near our constituency where I knew cows were reared were on the right of the Bedok schools (the present-day Man Fatt Chinese Temple) and at 6 Milestone (the present-day Sheng Siong Bedok). The roaming of cows along the road was banned due to pollution by their dung as well as the traffic obstruction they created.

Some Anecdotes Involving Cow Dung

In those days, whenever children stepped on anything sticky, parents were quick to refer it as stepping on cow dung. They could have stepped on any other sticky things however.

In the early days of the Singapore Armed Forces foot drill training, whenever the sergeant major called for attention (the command "*Sediya!*"), if he heard the different timings of footsteps on the parade square, he would refer to them as dung dropping from bulls.

After the banning of cow rearing in Singapore, cow dung was no longer used on new grass fields. Instead, human sludge was used. Whenever children asked the adults what the 'black substance' on the field was, the answer was always 'cow dung'. The parents were slow to realise that there were no more cows to produce dung.

Whenever a person stepped on dung, someone would say, "Dung brings you luck," to soothe his annoyance.

Music from the Bumblebee

Among the trees and undergrowth there were sounds of different pitches and volume. We young children were very curious as to where the sounds came from. One day, while playing among some old timber, we heard sounds coming from a piece of rotting wood. It was music to us. We put our ears on the wood to get a clearer sound. Then we saw a bumblebee come out of a hole at the side of the wood and fly away. In order to prevent more from escaping, I plugged the hole with my finger. "Ouch! I've gotten a sting!" I exclaimed. Luckily, it was not a bad one. The bumblebee is a huge, clumsy bee with a fat thorax and an abdomen with a yellow band around the thorax. It is different from the tiger head species, which had a slender thorax. We had learnt a very important lesson—never plug any holes in wood with bare fingers.

The Tiger Head Hive

One day, my dad came hurrying from the farm. He warned us not to play under the rubber tree nearby. There was a tiger head wasps' nest in it. In the village, the very words 'tiger head wasp' struck terror in their hearts. We were curious. We nervously walked towards it and very quietly scanned the tree. True enough, we saw a nest with orange stripes around it. We could feel goose pimples. We ran for our lives. That night, my dad got a basin of water. Then he hooded himself with an old singlet and put on a pair of long pants and a long-sleeved shirt. He carried an unlit firebrand. He waved mum and us children to stand at a safe distance. Gingerly, he put the basin of water under the nest. Then he lit the firebrand and set fire to the nest. Some of the wasps escaped, but some dived down into the basin of water. After the nest was destroyed, he quickly went to kill those struggling in the basin.

We had similar methods of destroying honeybees' hives, as we had been stung by honeybees before. Once a honeybee stung us, it left behind its two stings embedded on our skin; then it flew away to die. We would remove the two stings with a needle and then apply medicated oil on the puncture. After having burnt the nest and killed the bees, we knocked it down. The larvae were all roasted in their cells. While they were still hot, we pulled out the larvae and ate them. We also sucked the honey from the honeycomb.

We also experienced being stung by small bees found in fruits and bushes. The pain of those stings lasted for half an hour. We took them quite lightly.

Roasted Cockroaches

At night, we had to study in the hall, using candles and kerosene oil lamps as our light sources. There were kerosene lamps of different types and sizes for different purposes. The colourful reflectors had different designs. There was one with a painting of a cockerel crowing at a rising sun and one had a photograph of a Hong Kong actress. If we wanted it to be brighter, we would turn the wick to make it longer. The light attracted cockroaches. They flew about, disturbing us. The topic on cockroaches was brought up and discussed with our parents. We had heard that the dung of the cockroaches could be used to cure asthma. We also heard that cockroaches' heads could be roasted and eaten for good eyesight. Since the lamps attracted so many cockroaches, we decided to try roasting them. We caught the cockroaches, pulled off the heads by gripping the tough feelers, and then put them over the candle flames. While roasting, they exuded a particular smell like roasted meat. Then we ate them. When we tell this story to children of today, they squirm with horror.

This kerosene lamp has a photograph of a Hong Kong actress on its reflector

Other Creatures

We children were most curious when we came across any unusual creatures. We were usually ignorant of whether they could be harmful or not. When we came across an unknown creature, we would presume that it was the same as another creature we had seen that looked similar. The millipede was one of them. When we saw a millipede, we would exclaim that it was a centipede. However, upon closer examination, the millipede has more legs than a centipede. The millipede, when disturbed, would curl up and remain motionless. In wet places in and around the farm, we saw so many of them. We had never been bitten by a millipede. We learnt that it was an herbivore.

One creature that looked like a miniature iguana was the skink, a type of small lizard. When we encountered something like the skink, we would call it the iguana or the four-legged snake. It did not move very fast, but it could hide itself very well in the undergrowth.

Its diet included small creatures. It was prey for bigger carnivores like the cat. One day, my sister Hong Game got the shock of her life. Our cat was chewing a skink. Blood was streaming out of its mouth. Hong Game screamed and cried and was traumatised for hours.

We children were active and inquisitive all the time. We seldom took naps in the afternoon. If we were not playing under the coconut trees, we would be playing in the ponds catching water creatures. Once, I saw a long, brownish creature moving slowly in the pond. That creature looked like a snake. My dad said that it was an eel. It was found in the mud of the pond. The way it made its escape was very fast. It put its head in the mud, and then within seconds, its whole body disappeared into the mud. It was very difficult to catch with our bare hands, as it was covered with slime, which made it very slippery. We wet our hands and dabbed them on a patch of dry sand so the sand would stick. Then with our sandy hands, no matter how hard they struggled, they could not escape due to friction. The eels we caught made good meals for us.

Fresh Water Creatures

The rattan wicker baskets were good for carrying earth. They were also useful for catching fish, as water could drain out swiftly. When we spotted a water creature, the first thing we thought of was the wicker basket. On our farm, there were different types and sizes of wicker baskets. As children, we would choose the smallest size. Then we would plunge the basket in the spot where the creature was and immediately lift it up to let the water drain away. The creatures caught would be jumping and scurrying about, trying to escape. Some of them included the tortoise, snakehead (*haruan*), catfish, eel, perch, tilapia or Java fish or *ikan sampan, ikan belukar*, fighting fish, rainbow fish or guppy, and others like the dragonfly nymph, water spider, snails, diving beetles and water boatman.

Snakehead (*Haruan*)

After it rained, big fish like the snakehead would swim to the surface of the water and perform their acrobatics. They would jump about a metre high and then splash into the water again. Sometimes they landed in the neighbouring streams. My dad thought that the best time to hook a snakehead was after the rain. So he put a few baited hooks, fashioned from bamboo sticks, around the pond. The next day, several fish were caught. We had snakehead soup for dinner. The snakehead was a very hardy fish. It could survive the drought by hiding in wet mud. The Chinese believed that those who had undergone a surgical operation should eat the snakehead fish so that the wound would heal quickly. So whenever anybody underwent an operation, snakehead soup was prepared for the patient to consume.

The preparation of snakehead soup:

1. Put the live snakehead into a big salted vegetable jar of clean water for a few days. This lets them clean their systems before being cooked. The snakehead is a very powerful fish so the lids on the jars were weighed down with bricks to prevent them from jumping out.
2. To kill them, we put them into an empty jar and poured boiling water into it. Usually, we cooked the soup with a lot of ginger.

Another fish that we caught and ate was the catfish. To catch a catfish was a problem for those who were inexperienced. We had to approach it head on, push its head down with our second and third finger, making sure that the head was between them. Then, we pushed out the barbs from the bases, so that the right barb would jut out between the thumb and the index finger and the left one was between the third and fourth fingers. After that we gripped it tight, close to the palm. No matter how it struggled, we were safe from the barbs. To be jabbed by a barb was the last thing one would want. The pain was unbearable.

Normally, we stir-fried catfish with *sambal belacan.*

Perch could survive long periods out of water. We had seen these fish move out of the pond, wriggle along the bund, and go into the ditch. The perch had a lot of scales and we had trouble eating it.

Tilapia

This species of fish has caused a lot of confusion for many people. Sometimes, it is called the Java fish, and at other times, it is called the Japanese fish. Actually, this species of fresh water tilapia fish from Java was introduced by the Japanese during World War II, so it was quite accurate to call it either the Java fish or the Japanese fish.

Frogs and Toads

To catch a frog was not as easy as it was thought. Its body was covered in slime, which was very slippery. So we caught frogs in the same way as we did eels: we wet our hands and then dabbed it with sand.

Birds and Insects

Whether it was day or night, our place was never silent. Every now and then, there would be strange sounds coming from among the trees and bushes. They were either from the birds, the animals, the insects, or made by the breeze that rustled the leaves. During daylight, the mynahs would shriek, scream, cackle, whistle and fight noisily. Sometimes, they would fight so seriously that the whole flock simply dropped to the ground. After that, they picked themselves up and flew away. The kingfisher, with its blue body and long reddish beak, would sit atop a tree stump by the side of our pond to wait for fish to surface. Upon spotting one, it would swoop down and catch the fish with its beak. The white-headed bulbuls would be perpetually found in the string bushes eating the fruit and building their nests there. Like the mynahs, they could be very noisy.

The vast number of birds and insects made so much noise that someone who had never experienced country life could not sleep peacefully. One bird that could temporarily silence all the other birds was the eagle. As it was circling in the sky, all the birds would warn each other to hide and then there would be complete silence. The eagle would make its usual cry and then continue gliding. Sometimes it made a swift swoop downwards and a bird would be caught in its talons.

Nocturnal Sounds

At night, the nocturnal birds would appear and make their presence felt. Such birds were the nightjars, the owls and the nighthawks. At times, someone's dog would bark incessantly at a creature up in a tree, much to our annoyance.

During the day, the noises made by the insects were drowned out by other sounds. However, at night, the noises made by the insects were loud and most distinctive. Sometimes, we children would hear a sound other than those we normally heard. We would then ask our grandma what sound that was. She would snap, "Small children, just hear and don't ask." We knew what was in her mind, as she was a superstitious lady. She was thinking of unearthly creatures that roamed among the trees at night. Living in the countryside and among the tall trees, moving about at night could be a very challenging experience. A person could imagine all sorts of things in his mind. My grandma had this to say, "Set your heart firm, walk steadily straight on, don't run, and never turn your head to look backwards. No harm will come your way." These sayings were always religiously etched in our minds.

Habitats

We could identify different habitats in and around the area of our farm. They were the tree, the rotting log, the pond and the field, among others. In each habitat, there were different plant and animal populations in different communities.

The Grasshopper Catcher

One very unusual occupation that we seldom heard of was the grasshopper catcher. This man wore a tattered long-sleeved shirt and long pants and either a cap or a hat. Strapped round his waist was a cylindrical container made of fine green netting with a hole and a flap-door on top. He carried a small, netted hood with a long handle. He went about—usually on grassy patches—waving his little net about among the grass. The disturbed grasshoppers would jump, and he would hood the grasshopper. He would close in and press the hood with the grasshopper pinned underneath. With his free hand, he would lift the rim of the hood and take hold of the grasshopper. He then lifted the flap of his container and put the grasshopper in it. He sold the grasshoppers to the bird shops. That was his full-time job.

Glowing Creatures

Occasionally, we would find fireflies flying about. We would be in awe, wondering what those creatures were. Then we would trap them and observe them. Unable to find out how they could glow, we eventually released them.

My grandma told us a story about fireflies. Once there lived a very poor family. The members had to work very hard in the farm, earning a meagre amount to feed themselves. They had a very hard-working son. He helped his parents in the day and studied at night by candlelight. He found that burning candles to create light was a waste of money but what could he do? He needed the light to study.

One night, he went out of the house to ease himself. He found some lights moving about. He was curious. He discovered that the light was actually flying. He stretched his hands out to catch these moving lights and realised that what he had caught were actually insects. But these insects were different from others. They could glow. An idea came to him. He caught the insects and put them in a container. Because of the glow of the insects, he no longer needed to light any candles.

Once I squashed a very small, centipede-like creature under my bed. Then I blew out the kerosene lamp and lay on the bed. In the pitch darkness, I saw something glowing at the spot where I had killed the creature. I lit the lamp to look but there was nothing there except the bodily fluid of the creature. I blew out the lamp again and again but I could still see the glow. It was body fluid that glowed in the dark. How strange!

On the farm, we had encountered many other creatures, but to record them all would fill volumes.

Chapter 16
Our green fingers

My dad always said that farming was a very honourable occupation and he was proud of being a farmer. He told us that farming was revered by the ancient Emperor of China as the most highly regarded of all occupations, because farmers were the food producers. The *Chiu Gu Tor* (Chinese yearly lunar calendar or the literal translation from Hokkien 'Buffalo Chart)' was calculated with the farmers in mind. Without fail, yearly, dad had to get the 'Buffalo Chart' from our regular supplier of poultry food. The Buffalo Chart predicts the rainfall of the coming year, conversion of the solar years into the twelve zodiac signs, tells the fortune of each zodiac sign, the dates of each major festival, the calendar of the year etc.

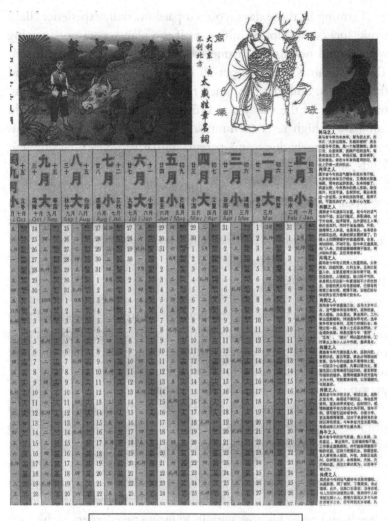

The *Chiu Gu Tor* (Buffalo Chart)

Water and sunlight play very important roles for plants to produce food. However, fertiliser is necessary for the plants to thrive. Those days, the fertiliser we prepared was very traditional. We did not bother about having to use much modern technology or waste precious energy. Everything we got from the farm was returned to the farm.

Farming in those days required passion, skill, experience, hard work, luck, and a lot of initiative. If the plants were not growing well, we did not simply blame the earth. The soil at the valley of Tanah Merah Kechil was not all humus. It comprised more sand than humus. Soil that contained mainly humus was a dark colour, but the soil of the valley was brown, which indicated that it did not have a high level of humus. The success of farming in this valley was largely due to my parents' initiative. They used different kinds of organic fertiliser. Dung from the pigs was collected and fermented. Human waste was purchased and decomposed in a cesspool. Rejected and rotten fish were bought and fermented in tanks. Dried ground prawns were used on more high-end vegetables such as kalian and lettuce to enhance their saleability.

Tuba Root

A plant which was highly useful but also deadly was the tuba root. We used this tropical shrub to make pesticide. Preparing tuba root solution demanded careful attention because the slightest mistake would lead to a fowl being handicapped or dying. The person preparing it could also be in danger.

My dad had sourced the tuba root from the market, from a neighbouring farm and from our own farm. To prepare it, he had to get a pounder or a hammer ready, as well as a sturdy pounding board, half a pail of water, and another pail of clean water for washing his hands. Gloves were not easily available in those days, so the preparation was made with bare hands. My dad would fold a handkerchief into a triangle and cover his nose with it, knotting two corners at the back of his head. The third corner was left loose, covering his mouth. He pounded the plant's stems and roots carefully, so that the sap would not splash about. The sap was milky and emitted a strong, pungent smell that could make one faint. Then he immersed the pounded stems and roots gingerly into the half pail of water. He would wash the sap from his hands frequently during the process. If he did not, the skin would itch and rashes would develop. If the sap got into the eyes, a person would go blind. After having carefully pounded all the plant parts, he would wash the pounder and the board thoroughly and store them away safely until the next time.

He would dilute the preparation and then, dip a crudely made brush of dried grass, into the pail and sprinkle this solution onto the plants. We would not harvest any of these vegetables for about ten days because my parents did not want to be accused of harming consumers by selling them tuba root-contaminated vegetables. My dad had a keen sense of morality. If anyone were to be harmed because of his greed or carelessness, his conscience would prick him for the rest of his life.

Note:
Tuba roots were used by the aborigines for killing fish. This method of fishing was highly undesirable and unethical, as the poison also killed or harmed every living creature in that area. People had even been known to commit suicide by drinking a tuba root preparation.

Pig Dung

Many people will likely squirm at the idea that animal waste and urine was used as fertiliser in those days. Many children even abstained from eating vegetables, as they did not understand how these waste products were processed before they could be used as fertiliser.

Piped water was not heard of in those days. Wells were dug to provide the water for cooking, washing, watering the plants and other activities. A well was dug in front of the pigsty. The water from this well was used to dilute the pigs' food as well as to bathe them and wash the pigsty. A pail was attached with a long string. To get water, the pail would be lowered into the well. A skilful tug on the string would make the pail upturn and fill with water. Then we would haul it up. A big concrete cesspool was constructed behind the pigsty. Dung from the pigs was dumped into the pool and left to decompose. The decomposed solids sank to the bottom. The liquid was used as fertiliser. Big watering cans were slung at the ends of a carrying pole and each can filled with the liquid fertiliser. Using the carrying pole, the two cans were brought to the vegetable beds. The watering cans were tilted with the their spouts aimed at the vegetables. This fertiliser from the cesspool behind the pigsty was hardly enough for the 50 or so beds of vegetables though. Furthermore, dung from pigs was not as fertile as chicken dung or human excreta. The pigs were fed a mixture of cooked water hyacinth, dried copra, and various small fish discarded by the fishermen. As a result, the smell from their dung and urine were not so overpowering.

Human Waste

Another cesspool was constructed at the end of the farm. That pool was used to contain the human excreta bought from a health worker (otherwise known as a night soil carrier), who collected this waste from bucket toilets in town. This pool exuded an overpowering smell and attracted a big swarm of houseflies. Dark brown casings of the pupae of the houseflies lay about in heaps at the sides of the pool. Maggots writhed in the dung. When we walked past, we heard the drone of houseflies that rose in swarms. However, they immediately settled down again once the danger was gone. The liquid fertiliser was scooped using a dipper fixed to a long bamboo pole. Two scoops—about 4 litres, would be mixed with a large watering can of water. Too high a concentration of fertiliser could retard the growth of the vegetables. Only plants in the growing stage needed fertiliser. Those about to be harvested must not be fertilised. Usually, one should not apply fertiliser or pesticide to plants ten days before harvesting. A strict farmers' code on fertilising was followed. My parents were very honest and cautious people. They would never do anything to harm anybody. Even if immediately after applying the fertiliser or pesticide, the price of vegetables should suddenly increase, they would never make a premature harvest just to earn a few dollars more as eating vegetables which had just been sprayed with pesticide would harm the unsuspecting consumers.

Burnt Earth Mounds

Besides these organic fertilisers, burnt earth was also used. To prepare a burnt earth mound, a patch away from the planting beds was prepared. Dried grass, weeds, dead vegetables and plants, and whatever other discarded organic material found on the farm were collected in a mound. Then dried earth was spread over the mound using a wicker basket. The mound could be three metres squared and one metre high. Then a dried lalang firebrand was used to light a fire all around the mound. Initially, the fires would burn ferociously and freely. But after the heat had reached the plant material under the layer of soil, the fire died down and the mound began to smoulder. When there was a slight breeze, part of the farm would be engulfed by the smoke, depending on which direction the wind was blowing. We— the people who were involved in specific chores such as ploughing the beds and watering the plants using the watering cans—could not abandon whatever we were doing and move away to another area when the smoke billowed in our direction, as we had to complete our chores before the day was out. We had to exercise controlled breathing until the wind changed direction. It was most uncomfortable for our lungs and eyes. The embers would continue to smoulder until the plant material was exhausted—usually after two dry days.

After the fire had died out, my grandma would upturn the ash and mix it with the earth above each mound with her long *changkol*. Then it was left there until it was needed as fertiliser.

To plant new crops, my parents used the *changkol* to dig holes the size and depth of a *changkol* of equal distance on a newly ploughed bed. Then, a small amount of burnt earth was put into each hole. Liquid fertiliser was poured over the burnt earth before the seeds were sown. My parents used this method for planting *kangkong, bayam* long beans, bitter gourd, brinjal, bottle gourd and hairy gourd.

My theories regarding burnt earth were that they enriched the soil with minerals and chemicals suitable for plants. Furthermore, eggs of pests and the seeds of weeds and grass were destroyed, thus saving the farmer's time in destroying pests and weeding the newly planted beds later.

My dad said that once in a while, plants needed to be smoked. Why, I did not know. I have seen workers in coconut estates make smoking mounds too. They claimed that the smoke would drive away beetles and insects that harm the trees. Today, if we were to do that, the Ministry of Environment will not hesitate to slap us with hefty fines for polluting the air.

Growing Vegetables

The plants were watered daily. Hardy plants like bitter leaves, *bayam*, brinjal, long beans, snake gourd (snake marrow), bitter gourd, hairy gourd, cucumber, chilli and tomato were watered once in the morning and once in the afternoon. Leafy plants like lettuce, *chye sim, pak choy, kailan, kang kong* and lettuce needed to be watered every three to four hours in the daytime. These vegetables had very big leaves and short stems and roots. Water evaporated faster through the big leaves. The farmers called them lowland crops whereas the hardy plants were called highland crops.

At first, we planted only the hardy highland crops such as chilli, ladies fingers, brinjal, papayas and bitter leaves. They have sturdy stems and long roots and do not need much water. All they needed was fertiliser. But when applying fertiliser, we had to be very careful. Fertiliser had to be placed in the middle of the space between four plants. If the fertiliser were applied directly on the plants, they would suffer retarded growth or wilt and die. The roots took some time to grow towards the fertiliser. By the time the roots reached the fertiliser, it would already be diluted.

A ladies' finger plant with buds.

On our farm, each and every member of the household had a role to play. I was delegated to fertilise and water the plants and weed and plough the empty plots. In the late afternoons, the boys of our family were to transplant the week-old young seedlings into neat rows from the nursery, then water them. The next morning, the newly transplanted seedlings needed constant watering and shading. The shading was mainly done by Hong Bian. It involved knocking V-shaped stakes into the ground across the beds at intervals. A sturdy stick was laid on the two V-shaped stakes. More stakes were driven in, depending on the length of the bed. Then, dry coconut leaves were placed on sticks shelter the newly transplanted seedlings. In the late afternoons, the dried coconut leaves were removed to let dew settle on the vegetables. This process was repeated for several days until the plants grew strong. Only then could fertiliser be added. If this was done before the plants could adjust to the transplant, they would either die or suffer retarded growth.

Every afternoon, mum and dad would gather the fruits and vegetables, wash and prepare them to be transported to the market the following day. Those vegetables gathered in the afternoons were the hardier ones such as the brinjals, papayas, long beans, chillies, bitter gourds, snake gourds, *bayam*, and *kang kong*, etc. Grandma would bring tea or coffee and biscuits for us in the afternoon. When the day's work was done, it would already be quite dark, about 7 p.m. Then we bathed at the wells.

My dad knew that crop rotation was important for the well-being of the plants and the soil. He had a fixed formula for rotating the crops. He never planted the same crop on the same spot twice. His reasoning was that the second crop might not be that healthy and would affect the harvest. He could have been right. When a different crop was planted, the pests and diseases of the former type of crop might not spread to the new crop and therefore could possibly be eradicated. Another reason was that the chemical compound in that soil might not be overtaxed by planting a new crop. New crops might take chemical compounds differently from the former.

My dad had discovered that cucumber tasted bitter when planted on the plot used to grow bitter gourd previously. I wonder whether the characteristics of plants are affected by planting them on plots used by other crops. Maybe agriculturists can unravel this.

A young cucumber plant

The long beans, hairy gourds, bitter gourds, and snake gourds were climbers. Usually, a large space was needed to plant the long bean plants. Weeds needed to be cleared off the plots. Then ploughing could start. After ploughing, small paths had to be created. These small paths were actually dugouts. Soil from the dugouts would be put onto the beds. I have read from research that the Chinese had been practising this method, as it allows the wind to flow through the beds smoothly without interfering with the growth of the plants, and at the same time, farmers can gain easy access to the plants. Seeds were not immediately sown on the beds after ploughing. I did not know why. My dad did not divulge the reason. I thought it was likely either to let the water drain from the soil or to sun the soil so that pests and diseases from the former crop could be eradicated. Next, little holes about the size of the *changkol* blade were dug about two feet apart. After that, footsteps had to be made on the holes. This was most likely done to compact the soil. Then liquid fertiliser, about half a scoop (about 500 ml), was poured on to each hole. Next, long bean seeds, which were either purchased from the market seed shops or obtained from previous crops, were sown four to a hole. We buried the seeds in half an inch of soil with a deft movement of our feet. The seeds were then watered twice a day—once in the morning and once in the afternoon. In three to four days, the shoots would have sprouted. But of course, the roots would have grown much earlier. During this period unwelcome visitors such as the birds, snails, moles and rats and caterpillars would try to make meals out of the young shoots. We children would go around everywhere to search for used milk tins, Milo tins, in fact, anything that would make sounds when shaken. My dad would tie several bundles with thick corrugated iron wire on a tall tree branch nearest to the beds. To build a scarecrow, he took two long sticks and tied it in the form of a cross. Then lalang grass was tied on the sticks to make it look like muscles and flesh. A round ball of lalang was put on top of the cross to represent the head. Then an old shirt was draped on the shoulders and an old hat was placed on the head. When the wind blew, the shirt would flutter and the birds would be frightened, but not for long. The birds were not easily fooled. After a period of time, they treated the scarecrows as any other inanimate objects around.

But what about the bundles of tins that were tied to the trees? Well, a long piece of rope was tied on each bundle. We would lead the other end of the rope to a shady spot under another tree and wait there. When the birds came, usually between 9 a.m. and 5 p.m., we would jerk the ropes so tins would make a lot of noise. The birds would fly away. Sometimes, when we were not on duty, the birds would come in large flocks, especially the mynahs. They came, fought among themselves, making a lot of cackling noises, and pecked at the seedlings. Of course, our dogs Black Mouth and Folded Ears also wanted to be a part of the action. They charged straight to the quarrelling birds without looking out for the young seedlings, trampling down some of them. If you shouted at them to get out, they obeyed instantly, but trampled another few on their way back. Dad would cry out his usual obscenities and carry out the repairs.

Every morning, before the sun rose, grandma (my grandpa passed away immediately after the war) would carry out an inspection of the seedlings for snails and caterpillars. The snails would bite off the stems. The caterpillars would graze on the leaves, leaving a trail of greenish slime. Grandma would catch the snails and smash them either on a stone or the back of a hoe. She squashed the caterpillars with her fingers. If we were free, we would be inspecting for pests too. At the end of each session, our fingers would be stained with the greenish slime of the pests. Then we would go to the pond to wash up. Do you know why we would inspect for these pests so early in the morning? The temperature was low and there was a lot of dew, which attracted these pests. When it was hot, they would go back to their hideouts. If pests wiped out a group of seedlings, we had to transplant seeds to fill that spot.

Weeding had to be carried out, or else, the weeds would compete with the long bean plants for space, sunlight, water and fertiliser. Grandma and all my siblings would routinely check for weeds. Then, we would pull out the weeds and put them into the wicker basket. When the basket was filled, we took them to an empty plot to dry. After drying, they could be used to make a burnt earth mound.

We needed to provide stakes for the climbers. The stakes were straight branches of trees or shrubs found in the undergrowth of the coconut estate. Sometimes, split bamboo stakes were used. Only dried bamboo stakes were used. If fresh ones were used, shoots would grow from the buds, creating problems for us. The leaves of the live bamboo would block out sunlight for the long beans plants. Furthermore, they competed for fertiliser. The job of planting the 6-foot long stakes to act as a support for the long bean plants was always done by dad. He had the strength and the skill to do it. If the stake was not pushed in sufficiently deep, it would fall. If the force was too great and the soil was too hard, the stake would break. One might injure oneself in this way. The stake must also not be pushed in too near the plant's roots. If the roots were damaged, the plants would either die or become retarded. The stake must also be pushed in at an angle, so that it would meet the opposite stake at a vertex, most probably to support each other. A piece of twined lalang grass was used as a rope to tie the two stakes together at the meeting point. Next, my dad needed help to retrieve some of the climbing stems that had gone astray onto the wrong stakes. We had to unwind them and then re-twine them on to the proper stakes. That had to be done all the time. Initially, we had to tie the shoot on to the stake with a lalang blade or banana fibre. In this way, the rows and rows of long bean plants looked very orderly. An orderly row of long bean plants was easier for us to water, as well as fertilise. Long bean plants are trifoliate. If the leaves were too many, we needed to prune them, usually two at once from each stalk. One needed experience to do that. It looked like only mum and grandma knew that. They knew which leaves to pluck. We children never did. They explained that if a group of long bean plants growing together had overcrowding leaves, the plants would not bear fruit as much. The plucked leaves were then soaked in water and then tied in bundles of ten. They were sold as vegetables.

The preparation of these long bean leaves for eating was not as easy as one might think. First, the main and branch veins of each leaf had to be removed as the veins were very fibrous. That was done by tearing out the leaf blades. Next, the leaf blades were soaked in water then shredded to fine bits by hand. They were then sieved. The water by then was greenish with chlorophyll. The shredded leaves were either fried with eggs or boiled with soup or noodles.

Long bean flowers had both male and female parts. The petals are usually light blue but that also depended on the species. The bumblebees loved to gather nectar among the flowers. After fertilisation, the petals dropped, leaving a small long bean and the sepal. Sparrows were especially fond of the young beans, so we always had to watch out for them. Caterpillars too could be found in abundance. In the early days, tuba root preparations were used as pesticide.

If the long bean plants were well cared for, they usually had long lives. The long beans would continue to fruit for a long time.

We got rid of them when the plants grew beyond our reach, usually when they reached about ten feet tall. They would also show signs of age and were not capable of producing healthy beans. The job of uprooting them fell upon the children. Each of us would use a sharp sickle to cut away the stems that twined around the supports. After the supports were cleared, they were carried to a centralised area near the tool shed. My dad would inspect each support, to see if they could be reused again. The rotted ones were used as firewood. The beds were cleared of weeds, ploughed and planted with another crop. It was not our practice to plant the same species as the one that has just been grown in that plot.

Cucumber

Preparation of beds to plant cucumber was quite similar to preparing for planting long beans. It involved the same hard work, such as ploughing, seeding, weeding and laying the supports. The difference lay in the plants. Cucumber plants had big, broad leaves and they climbed by the use of tendrils. Each plant had male and female flowers. The flowers are yellowish. The male flowers were easily distinguished from the female. Each male flower was attached to a very thin stalk. Each female flower had a very thick stalk, which would become a fruit when ripe. When fully grown, the stem could be quite big, as it needs to support the fruit. The average length of a fully-grown fruit is about 15 centimetres and is cylindrical in shape.

This plant too needs a lot of fertiliser. Grandma pruned only the old yellowish leaves as well as the stray branches. We especially loved to be on duty here because we could always get one of the cucumber fruit and eat it raw. Sometimes, they could be bitter. There was a way to avoid the bitter taste. We would cut a small slice off where the stalk was and then rub the two cut pieces together until white foam formed. Then, both pieces with the white foam were sliced off. I did not know how far it was true. I just did it. True enough, the cucumber tasted nice. Another explanation for its bitter taste was that it was planted in a plot in which we'd previously grown bitter gourd. Was it true? I did not know.

Brinjal

The method for germinating brinjal and bitter gourd was different from that for long bean plants. The brinjal and the bitter gourd seeds had to be sown in a nursery. A nursery bed (not necessarily very big—about a quarter of a standard bed) had to be prepared. Next, fertiliser was spread on the bed. Seeds were sown. A thin layer of loose earth was spread over the seeds. The nursery bed was watered twice a day. After about two weeks, the young seedlings were able to make food so they could be transplanted.

The seedlings were transplanted on prepared beds. The brinjal and bitter gourd seedlings were planted at an interval of about two feet. In between them, away from the seedlings, a depression was dug for the fertiliser. The brinjal plant would grow to a bush, as it had a short sturdy stem and many branches.

A brinjal plant is quite hardy but its fruits can easily be attacked by fruit flies. The fruit flies lay eggs inside the young fruit. Spraying pesticide could deter fruit flies. Brinjal also needed a lot of fertiliser to grow. Otherwise, the fruits would be stunted. They were small and hard. Good, healthy plants produced fruits which were big, soft, succulent and silky to the touch. An experienced person would know whether a fruit was fit to consume or not by merely touching it.

Bitter Gourd

The bitter gourd climbed by tendrils. The tendrils were the tough fibres that grew from the axle of the leaves. The stakes for the bitter gourd were different from those for the long beans. The stakes driven in near the plants were shorter and thinner. My dad had to add many twigs to enable the tendrils to entwine on them. The tendrils were curled like springs twining around the support. Once they curled onto it, it would be tough to detach them. When a slight breeze blew, the plants would sway in the wind with the curls of the tendrils relaxing and contracting. This prevented damage to the stems. The bitter gourd plants had separate male and female flowers.

The male flowers had long, thin stalks, but the female flowers of the bitter gourd had thick, ugly protuberances between the stalks and the flowers. At the end of the protuberances were the petals and the stigma. The yellowish flowers attracted honeybees to pollinate them. After fertilisation, the protuberances of the bitter gourd plants became bigger and longer, as well as developing deep, craggy surfaces. The petals wrinkled and dropped off. The moment when the bitter gourd plant produced fruit was the most crucial. Birds and a species of slender-bodied bees would attack the fruits. Once the fruits were attacked, they either rotted or became deformed. Our customers were always very fussy and they would not buy a deformed fruit. To prevent insects from attacking the tender, young fruits we had to bag them. We made the bags from old newspaper. It was our experience that the tender young fruits that were bagged often became damaged after a strong breeze because the breeze made the bags flutter. My mum had a very innovative idea. She bagged each fruit and pinned the fruit and the bag securely either on the stem or onto the support. Thus the damage to the fruits was minimal.

Making Bitter Gourd Bags

To prepare the bags, we had to purchase old newspapers, as we did not subscribe to any.

Method:

1. Cut a page of a standard newspaper into four pieces.
2. Fold each piece lengthwise, leaving an allowance of about two centimetres as a flap to glue and fold.
3. Starch the flap.
4. Fold the flap over and glue it at the opposite side.
5. Arrange the bags and let them dry in the sun.

Starch was made from tapioca flour. Here is how we made starch: First, boil some water. Get a tablespoonful of tapioca flour ready. Put the flour into a mug. Pour a little water (separate from the boiling water) in and stir until the flour dissolves. When the water is boiled, add the boiling water slowly into the mug of dissolved flour; at the same time, stir the mixture until it turns into a sticky colourless substance. Once the mixture turns colourless, stop adding hot water. Otherwise, the starch becomes too watery and the paper will not stick well.

Note:

Tapioca flour has different properties from wheat flour therefore wheat flour cannot be used as a substitute.

The pin was made from the mid-ribs of the coconut leaflets. This is how it was done:

Method:

1. Gather a newly fallen coconut leaf (worn-out leaves will not make good pins).
2. Strip the leaflets from the leaf. We need a parang to do this.
3. Get each leaflet and cut away the leaf blades with a sharp penknife.
4. Choose the sturdy mid-ribs and cut them into lengths of six centimetres.

When it was time to harvest, mum was adept at that. She would feel the fruit for its maturity. If she was not convinced by touching it, she would look through the underside of the bag. If the ridges were broad and succulent and the colour pale green, the bitter gourd was ready to be harvested. If the fruit turned soft and yellow, the fruit was overripe. She cut each mature fruit and gingerly lowered them into cane baskets. Next, she chose the best fruit, sliced them open down the middle, and removed the seeds. These seeds were for the next planting.

Snake Gourd

An unusual gourd we planted was the snake gourd. Today, it is difficult to find one in the stores. But in those days, it was quite commonly available. The snake gourd is long and slender. It is greenish white and with stripes of green. Once, my mum had the fright of her life. She was harvesting a gourd that hung from the trellis late one afternoon when she saw a particularly unusual fruit. She wanted to touch it but suddenly, it slithered away. She ran helter-skelter, dropping her harvested fruits and knife. With tears, she related her experience. We laughed but at the same time sympathised with her. No wonder the vegetable was known as snake gourd.

To plant a snake gourd, there must be sufficient space for the climber to climb. The intervals between each plant were great—about two metres. After sowing the seeds on a patch of fertiliser, we had to water the seeds twice a day. Then the shoots appeared. Because of the availability of fertiliser, soon each seedling grew into a healthy, lush plant. The snake gourd climber could grow very quickly. Soon, there was a need to install a support for each plant to climb using its tendrils. Before it became unmanageable, dad would get ready to build a huge trellis. He cut down some tall bamboo and left them to dry. They were sawn to pieces, each about two metres long. These were for the support. Smaller bamboos were used as beams. Small strips of bamboo were laid cross the beams. Soon, the plants would climb up the support and finally reach the top of the trellis. Then they would cling on to the strips of bamboo and creep along the surface. We had to constantly watch out for the fruits on the trellis above our heads. If the young fruits were spotted, we would make adjustments to them to hang down from the stalks. This would facilitate easier monitoring and harvesting later. If the young fruits were left to lie on the strips of bamboo, chances are they would be deformed. A fruit, when hanging on the stalk, looked fresh, and pristine. As usual, adding fertiliser and spraying of pesticide had to be done. A fruit attacked by insects, especially a small garden bee, would either rot or become deformed.

Tapioca

Tapioca needed soft, loamy soil to grow. It must not be too wet either. Tapioca grown on plots that were too wet tasted rather flat and felt pasty. Those grown on drier plots exuded a fragrant smell and were hard to the touch. Tapioca plants in fertile soil could grow up to a height of three to four metres. The roots were said to be as wide as an adult's thigh. I wondered how far that was true. If a plant had too many leaves, there would not have been too many swollen roots. Grandma would prune the older leaves and leave them on the plot to rot. Some people would pluck the very young leaves and cook them. My Malay neighbours loved them.

There were several species of tapioca. Two very pronounced species were the red and the white. The red species had red leaf stalks, young stems and even the bark of the roots. The white species had the same parts white-coloured. So at one glance, we could identify the species.

A plot of tapioca

Planting a plot of tapioca involves the following steps:

Method:

1. Preparation of the plot. The plot must be well ploughed. Use a *changkol* with a long blade about 30 centimetres in length and 20 centimetres wide. The ploughing must be deep. Any hard lumps of soil must be knocked loose using the head of the *changkol*. Any foreign objects such as dead stems, roots, and discarded tins must be taken away. Once ploughed, do not let anyone step on the plot. Make a path for servicing the plants as well as for draining the water when it rains.

2. Preparing the stem. Choose the healthiest stems. Make sure the buds are all intact. Use a sharp parang to cut the stem. Choose only the part away from the roots as well as away from the shoot. The middle part grows best. Each stem for planting must be only about 20 centimetres long (10 centimetres for burying into the soil and 10 centimetres exposed to the air). The stem will rot if it is buried too deep. Too many buds would grow if the exposed part were too long. The plant will be healthy if there are only one or two buds growing on a stem cutting.

   One must be careful when planting the stem. One must choose the correct side, which is the side with the bud facing up. If the wrong side is embedded, the plant has to make adjustments for the roots to grow downwards and the shoots upwards. It will take time. The stem has to be embedded at an angle of about 45 degrees. One likely reason is that if it is planted at an angle, the shoots will have more space to grow and get sunlight. If a stem were planted upright, the shoots would overshadow one another.

   If the planting of the stems is done in an orderly manner—in the same direction and at the same angle—the beds will look neat and pleasing to the eye. 'Even the plants are happy.' My grandma used to say.

Sweet Potatoes

"Grandma, why do you cut the sweet potato stems and leave them aside? They are withering."

"Well! You children don't know this. I'm starving them so they will produce more sweet potatoes."

I really did not understand why we needed to starve the stems. After a few days, she took all the stems to plant in a prepared plot. The stems took roots very quickly. At the same time shoots grew from the buds. With more fertiliser and watering, they grew luxuriously. Grandma would pluck the leaves and prepare a dish from them. To prepare the dish, first, she had to tear up the leaf blades and peel away the outer covering from the leaf stalks, which were quite fibrous. Then she broke the peeled stems into three centimetre lengths. My sister Siew Gim would fry them with *sambal belacan*. How heavenly the *sambal belacan* tasted!

The explanation for plucking the leaves of the sweet potato was the same as for plucking the long bean leaves. With fewer leaves, the plants would produce more sweet potato roots.

The sweet potato plant is a runner. It can run all over the beds if it is not controlled. Weak and unhealthy stems need to be removed. Healthy stems need to be redirected onto the beds, and not be allowed to grow wild. When the leaves looked a little weak, grandma would say, "It's time to harvest!"

With expert hands, dad would land his *changkol* on a precise spot and yank. The soil loosened. White roots could be seen. With a second swing of the *changkol*, the roots were totally exposed. They were promptly gathered and the *changkol* swung once again. Those actions were repeated until the whole bed was dug. Not many of the roots were damaged. It looked as if dad could see through the soil to locate the potato roots.

Kang Kong

Kang kong can be planted in four ways—by hydroponics, stem-cutting, from seeds and transplanting.

Hydroponics

When growing *kang kong* by hydroponics, the most important factor is water. The water must be fertile, cool and clear. After removing the leaves of the *kang kong* for cooking, we collected the stems. We spaced the stems at equal distances in the pond. If the conditions for growing *kang kong* were met, they would grow prolifically. We always had to be on the alert for grasshoppers, butterflies and moths. The grasshoppers would eat them. The moths and butterflies would lay eggs on the leaves and cause considerable damage. If there were frogs and toads, they would eat up those pests. That was part of the ecosystem. If frogs and toads were not present, we had no choice but to use pesticide.

Stem-cutting

The process of planting *kang kong* by stem-cutting was the same as planting sweet potatoes. Healthy stems were collected and starved. Then, they were planted on prepared beds. To get really healthy, succulent *kang kong*, water and fertiliser had to be applied constantly. The harvest was done by plucking away the side branches, leaving behind the main branch. The main branch could grow side branches again. That process could occur many times until the growth chemicals in the soil were exhausted. The indicator was that the new branch stems would get smaller and less healthy, even though there was sufficient fertiliser. Then, dad would gather every bit of the plants and feed them to the poultry. The plots were ploughed again, and a different crop planted.

Seed-sowing

The third method of planting *kang kong* was by sowing the seeds on the beds and letting them grow. The beds were prepared. Then fertiliser was splashed on them. Next, *kang kong* seeds were spread evenly on the beds. The beds were watered twice a day—once in the morning before the sun got too hot and once in the evening when the sun went down. *Kang kong* planted in this way would grow unevenly due to the spacing and sunlight. We did selective harvesting. The taller ones were harvested first. Then we waited for another few days for the second harvest. That continued until all of them were harvested.

Transplanting

The fourth method was transplanting. The seeds needed to be sown in the nursery. When the seedlings had grown to about four centimetres tall, they were transplanted in neat rows on prepared beds. They were then watered and fertiliser was applied. We continued to do that until they were about 30 to 40 centimetres tall; then we harvested them.

Different cooks prepared *kang kong* dishes differently. It was up to them to decide what they preferred. A cook that prepared *kang kong* cuttlefish would prefer to have *kang kong* grown by the hydroponics method, as *kang kong* grown by this method is bigger and juicier. For frying with *sambal belacan,* a cook would prefer smaller and sturdier *kang kong*. In restaurants, the *kang kong* dish was given very fanciful names to entice customers.

Bottle Gourd or *Labu Labu*

A very huge creeper that we planted was the bottle gourd or *labu labu*. In order to maximise its growth, more manure was required. With a significant amount of manure, it could grow to a great length. The leaves were huge like those of the yam plant. It bore separate male and female flowers on the same plant. Although it produced tendrils, my dad preferred to let it creep along the ground. Whenever a young fruit was found, my mum would try to remember its location. Every now and then, she would check on them for damage, growth retardation and sunlight exposure. If it were exposed to direct sunlight, she would try to protect it using dry leaves or newspapers. In a plot, there might be 20 plants creeping in all directions, fruiting in different places. We had to be very careful when walking through a plot of bottle gourds, as we might accidentally step on them and damage them. When each fruit was mature enough to be cooked, it could weigh 2 to 3 kilogrammes easily, but that was subject to the species and the amount of fertiliser used. At each planting, we would choose the best of the fruits to let it grow till it ripened. A ripe bottle gourd is whitish brown and is very hard. Then we would cut it open to retrieve its seeds for the next planting.

The Yam

When we talk about yam, we think about the kind used for making yam cake. That yam plant grows from an underground stem. Those that we see above ground are the leaf stalks and heart-shaped leaves. It is easy to grow. Dad would take an underground stem and cut it into quarters. He would dig a shallow depression in the soft garden soil with a *changkol* about 15 centimetres deep, plant each piece of the yam, and top the depression with soil. Then he would water it when needed and wait for it to grow.

True Yam

The true yam has swollen roots. It has a twining stem. The

The True Yam

heart-shaped leaves are slightly bigger than the leaves of long beans and are quite fleshy. One rather strange feature of this plant is that it twines in an anticlockwise direction. Other twining plants climb by twining clockwise. When it matures, small dark brown fruit-like objects can be seen hanging from the stem. These are not fruit. They are part of the plant's food storage system. When we were sick, our grandma used to buy these from uncle Kidd, a farmer who had a farm on a hill-slope at the other side of Tanah Merah Kechil, directly opposite Piah Teng's land. Now Bedok Court condominium is located there. Uncle Kidd used to plant a big plot of true yam. My grandma would teach my mum how to prepare the underground stems and then boil them. I suppose, when we were sick, we had no appetite, and it was just another ploy to make us eat. However, grandma had other reasons. She believed that the true yam had properties to cure the sickness we had.

Papayas

We reserved a plot specially for planting papayas. One day, my dad came home with a few choice papayas. They were huge, sweet, red and juicy. A brief survey among the people in the market told him the customers preferred this species. The small yellowish, strong-scented species (most likely the Hawaiian species) was not preferred, as the scent was described as being akin to chicken dung.

The papayas were cut and tasted by everyone in the family. Needless to say, we had never tasted such delicious fruit. The seeds were gathered and dried. A nursery was prepared and seeds were sown. When the young plants were about a foot tall, they were transplanted. For each plant, a large hole was dug, burnt earth and ash was buried, and it was planted. Every morning and evening, we had to water the papaya plants. My dad would inspect them, weed out unwanted plants around, and look for signs of healthy growth and disease. These plants grew fast, and within a few months, huge long fruits were produced. The trees were quite low—about five feet high. Care was taken not to damage the young fruit. When the young green fruit was scratched, a white sap would flow. That sap, when it came in contact with our skin, would make it itch. When it came into contact with our eyes, our eyes would itch and swell. Children were told not to go near the fruiting plants unless it was really necessary.

A tree laden with papaya

Then came the first fruit. Its skin was so smooth. The colour was a bright orange, and it looked like a huge mango. Everybody got to taste it. Subsequently, more fruits ripened. They were taken to the wholesalers, who purchased them in bulk. Later, a tall, lanky man came to gather the fruits himself. He brought a huge basket and helped himself to the fruit. I was shocked that he gathered even the unripe fruits. We normally gathered only ripe fruits. He explained that the so-called unripe fruit was actually 90 per cent ripe. The fruit would ripen after a few days. I disagreed. Fruits ripened that way would not be fresh. Fresh fruits were fruits that ripen on the trees.

Every few days, he would come to gather more fruit. As the trees grew taller, the fruits were beyond his reach. He expertly used a stick. By pushing the bottom of the fruit slightly, it would somersault, detach from its stalk and fall into his waiting hands. He seldom missed.

Dad would spray fertiliser at the base of each tree (away from the main root), clear the weeds, and prop up trees that were weighed down by abundant fruits with bamboo trunks. Branches would grow from the trunk of each tree. Then, the branch fruited as well. I was puzzled that the teachers in school, as well as textbooks, told us that papaya trees, as well as coconut trees, had no branches. I tried to argue, but I was greeted with annoyance.

On stormy days, the trees that had escaped being propped up by my dad fell like ninepins. Some of the branches with heavily laden fruit got ripped off. After the storm, we would gather the fallen fruit. The fruit that were about to be ripened were separated from the unripe ones. The unripe fruit were carried to the kampongs and sold to the kampong folks, who cooked them as vegetables. We also made peppered soup with them. Dad then busied himself clearing the fallen trunks and leaves as well as strengthening the props.

Sugarcane

Sugarcane has a fibrous root system, and therefore, the leaves have parallel veins. The sword-shaped leaves are very long and the leaf stalks always cling to the stem. On the edge of the leaves are very tiny hairs, which can cause the body to itch when touched. The sugarcane stores its food in the stem. It is an herbaceous plant. Its stem is not woody. The bark is hard but can be peeled. Today, the sugarcane juice we drink comes from crushed cane. In those days, we peeled the cane with our teeth. Then we bit it off piece by piece to chew and suck the juice. The dried fibre was then spat out.

We planted several species of sugarcane. The most common one was the light green species. There were also the purple cane and a species that had a very thin stem. If conditions were right, sugarcane could grow tall and healthy. My dad would preserve a set of two light green canes for Tien Kong's birthday celebrations.

The tall slender species was bland and hard and the bark was not easy to peel. We chopped them into lengths of about six inches, bundled them up, and sold it to people for making cooling drinks.

If sugarcane is planted in a large estate, then the spraying of pesticide and subsequent harvesting are done by machines. However, if they are planted only for personal consumption, care must be taken to prevent ants, spiders or other insects hiding in between the leaf stalks and the stem. If the leaves are dried, they must be removed. The stem will look very clean and healthy. When the stem changes its colour to a paler shade of green and has grown to a certain height, we can guess it will produce the sweetest juice. Very young or very old sugarcane did not produce very sweet juice.

Our experience tells us that on rainy days, sugarcanes do not produce sweet juice. This was true also for sugarcane that was planted in waterlogged areas. It could be that the sugar content in the plant is diluted.

Chilli

We planted several species of chilli. The most common species we planted was the chilli padi. It is called chilli padi because of its size. The Malay translation for chilli padi literally means rice grain chilli. It is small like a rice grain, but its spiciness is beyond description. This species thrives in well-drained soil. With proper watering and fertilising, it gives very good fruit. We harvested the fruit when it turned bright red. The birds, especially the bulbuls, are very fond of chilli padi.

Other than the chilli padi, we also grew the local chilli. It was not very spicy but when conditions were right, the fruit could grow to a size about the length and thickness of an adult finger. When it was ready to be harvested, the fruit turned bright red.

There is yet another species of chilli. The fruit never turned red. They remained green. If not harvested, they would rot and drop off. This species is used for making *archar* as well as preserved with salt and vinegar. The preserved chilli is meant to be a condiment. The Indians used to eat this green chilli raw with *vadai*. We planted other chilli species too but they were only for novelty and decoration.

From experience, we realised that plants that were very bushy seldom produced abundant fruit. We used to pluck the young leaves of bushy chilli plants and fry them with eggs.

Bayam

In my farm, we cultivated the ordinary *bayam* species—which could often be mistaken for spinach—the one found in the market.

We sowed the tiny seeds in a nursery. When the seedlings grew to about five centimetres, we transferred them to vegetable beds. With frequent watering, fertilising, and pest control, within two months before they flowered, we could harvest them. At that stage, the plants were tender and sweet.

There was a species that was shorter and which flowered very quickly. They were reddish and some greenish, and they grew almost everywhere—in fact, they grew so fast that they became an irritant. We called them *'bird bayam'*, as birds loved to eat them. We always added this to all other vegetables that we harvested. During our free time, we would go around the farm, collecting and bundling them. Then we would sell them for ten cents a bundle.

One of the *bayam* species

Then someone introduced another *bayam* species to us. It was very tall, with very big, dark green leaves. If there were enough nutrients, they could grow to about three metres tall. We seldom harvested this species to sell in the market, as it had a very strong 'veggie' smell, and the cooked leaves and the gravy turned dark green. We always harvested the tender ones for our own consumption. The rest that grew wild in the remote part of the farm was harvested. The leaves were cooked together with other ingredients for the pig and poultry. The stems were donated to Heong Lian See Temple on Koon Seng Road, where my grandma was a member, to be cooked as a vegetarian dish.

This species was known as Japanese *bayam*. Most likely, it had been introduced by the Japanese during World War II.

The Chai Chee Market

My grandma was a very thrifty lady. At times, in order to save a few cents, she would walk all the way from Changi 5 Milestone to Changi 8 Milestone. She had to walk past the Koon Hin timber yard, the Hainanese Cemetery, a green minaret mosque, the Chai Chee market, the copra processing factory, a couple of concrete bungalows, then she snaked her way past lalang grassland before turning into the Tanah Merah Kechil dirt track. Sometimes, she did her marketing at Chai Chee market before coming home. Chai Chee market was at 6 Milestone Changi. It was along a stretch of windy road with many attap houses built close together side by side. Chai Chee market was on a ridge of a hill. The villagers built the houses right down the steep slope to the valley below. In the morning, the bus stop in front of the noodle factory was always crowded, as that was the only major link to the towns and other villages. The entrance to the market was always crowded with bicycles, motorcycles, cars, and lorries. Coffee shops, bicycle shops, Chinese medical shops and provision shops flanked both sides of the narrow street. The street sign was hidden by some of the advertisement boards, so one had to be very observant to see it. The cluster of shops continued right to a *wayang* stage. On the left of the stage, the road continued as Peng Ann Road; it wound past Guan Hin timber yard and other shops before it tapered down into the valley. Peng Ghee Road started from Changi Road junction leading to the right side of the wayang stage and continued its way, flanked by more shops and coffee shops, to the Pin Ghee High School and forked out to the right. It ran past the right side of the school, the joss stick factory, and continued its way to Sungei Bedok. The left flank of Peng Ghee Road wound right down the slope to a tributary of Sungei Bedok, then up the hill to the houses in the coconut estate before continuing its way into kampong Kaki Bukit.

The hive of activity at the open-air Chai Chee market started as early as 5 a.m. The merchants, petty traders, cigarette smugglers, and stallholders were eager to display their wares. The unlicensed vegetable sellers, butchers, cake sellers, coffee bean hawkers, biscuit sellers and fishmongers stationed their wares right in the middle of the Chai Chee market, thus dividing the road into two flanks— Peng Ann Road on the left and the right, the Peng Ghee Road. Peak hours were from seven till eleven. Like any open-air market at that time, the customers jostled with the hawkers, competing with one another, trying to get the best price for the goods.

As far as I can remember, my grandma used to hang the farm produce at the ends of a carrying pole and hurry to Changi 8 Milestone (at the junction of Changi Road and Simpang Bedok Road), where there was a small open-air market. A group of vegetable and fruit buyers was there to purchase produce en bloc—big and small, tall and short, ripe and unripe—from the nearby farmers. But the amount paid per *kati* was usually unreasonably low. They knew that the farmers would not know how to dispose of their goods if they did not sell them. These buyers brought the produce over to markets in town and sold it to the retailers at a higher price. The retailers were allowed to select the better quality fruit and vegetables, of course. The rejects were either discarded or sold very cheaply.

On certain afternoons, my mum, who was quite enterprising, would pack long beans and *kang kong* in bundles, and we would go around the kampongs to sell them at 30 cents per pack. We would call at every house, as the houses were few and quite sparse. Sometimes, we would be chased by their dogs. The dogs within the fences would bark ferociously. Imagine that. One bark by a dog would trigger a chain reaction and soon almost every dog in the neighbourhood would join in the fray. We would return home only after we had finished selling all the vegetables.

Grandma's Stall at Chai Chee

From the journeys to the Chai Chee market, grandma learnt something. Why should we bring our produce to the wholesalers? We could sell them ourselves at Chai Chee market for greater profit. She started with long beans tied into bundles. Each was priced at 30 cents. Then bundled long bean leaves were added. Every morning, she could dispose of her wares. The last few bundles were bartered for either meat or fish. She became a regular vendor there. Then my dad and mum joined in. They did not bring the produce to the en bloc purchasers at Changi 8 Milestone any more. Every morning, they would rise as early as 5 a.m. to harvest the vegetables using torchlights to show the way. After harvesting, they had to wash the goods at the ponds. Then my mum would proceed first, as she had to walk along Tanah Merah Kechil Road and catch a bus at Changi Road 8 Milestone bus stop. My dad would pedal the load of vegetables all the way to Chai Chee Market. There, they displayed their wares on a makeshift platform on the ground. They had to compete with the others for a place. If one was late, then they had to display their goods at the tapered end between the Peng Ann Road and the Peng Ghee Road which could be quite narrow for both human and vehicular traffic.

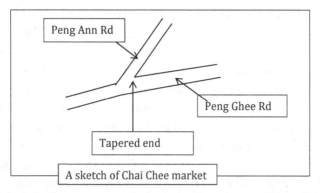

A sketch of Chai Chee market

My dad, after emptying the baskets of goods, would have breakfast and purchase some necessities before coming home. My mum would stay there to sell the goods. Life was not rosy, as she had to compete with so many vegetable sellers. It seemed that place had more vendors selling vegetables than others. No wonder it was called '*chai chee*' in Hokkien, which meant 'vegetable market'. There was one particular vendor, older than my mum, who had a knack for touting. Her goods were the first to finish. But one thing my mum had to admit. This woman's vegetables were the lowland types, such as the lettuce, *kailan*, *choy sum*, and *pak choy* and were greener and fresher. Ours were beans, gourds, bitter gourds, brinjals, ladies fingers, long beans, and potato leaves and leafy vegetable such as *bayam*, *kang kong* and *bitter leaves*.

Mum's Battle

"We can't take it lying down. We just can't sell anything until our rival sells hers. We have to do something." Mum came home at almost 1 p.m., hot and sweaty.

I had been to the market with her a few times. It was really very hot sitting in the sun waiting for customers, although she had her long-sleeved blouse and a wide-rimmed bamboo hat on.

The battle to compete for more value-added vegetables was on. My dad would go to the vegetable seed shops at Changi 10 Milestone. The seed shops were there because there was a large concentration of farms at New Village at Koh Sek Lim Road. The soft alluvial soil there was just the type of soil required for planting the lowland vegetables. One would be surprised to see rows and rows of neatly planted vegetables. It was there where one could get advice on fertiliser and pesticide from the government-owned Primary Production Department.

A vegetable bed

After buying the seeds, my mum would impatiently prepare the beds nearest to the ponds. *Choy sam* seeds were the first ones sown in the nursery. When the seeds sprouted, all of us were excited. We had never seen such seedlings before. We looked after them with more care than usual. When they were about four inches tall, we transplanted them. We had no knowledge of how to do it. We just dug a hole about one to two inches deep, put the roots in, and pressed the soil down. Then we watered them. Many died under the hot sun. With discussion and observation of other farmers, we persisted. We struck upon the idea that the young plants must be sheltered. We rested dried coconut leaves on stakes to shade them and we watered them at almost two-hour intervals on hot days with cool water. When newly planted plants started to grow, fertiliser from decomposed chicken dung was used. Sometimes, prawn dust was used. After that, the growth was fantastic. But caterpillars seemed interested in devouring them. We resorted to catching them and grinding them between our fingers. Surprisingly, a species of caterpillar lived in the soil. They came out to eat at night when it was cool and hid in the soil when it was hot. It was just not possible to comb the soil for caterpillars. We consulted the Primary Production Department. The officers came and recommended a certain pesticide. So spraying paraphernalia had to be purchased. My mum was eager to lay hands on this equipment and pesticide. The vegetables were then grown without the holes made by the caterpillars. But the end product was still not as good as our competitor's. The fault was in the soil. The soil in our farm had more sand than alluvium and was more acidic and the water we used was not cool enough. To solve the problems of acidic soil, we sought the advice of the Primary Production Department again and found that we had to add lime to the soil.

To neutralise acidic soil

My dad and I cycled to Changi 10 Milestone, turned into Somapah Road, cycled past the timber yard, the open air market, the coffee shops and food stalls, then into the Chinese village. We cycled past ponds, coconut estates, the Red Swastika School, then into a cluster of lime-processing yards. No one could miss the sight of those lime-processing yards, as the whole environment was white—the path, containers, trucks, machines, stores, and even the clothing of the workers. There were crates and crates of the finished product—whitewash to be sold to timber yards. The villagers bought these to dilute with water to whitewash their timber houses. The lime that we were buying was made of heated seashells. We bought these by the *kati*. We loaded them in bags and pedalled home. My dad poured the lime on a vacant plot and then sprinkled some water over the area. In the next instant, as if by magic, the temperature of the shells rose, a vapour was given off, and the shells crumpled into powder right before our eyes. We had never seen such a sight. Everyone in the farm crowded round to watch. The powder was then spread onto the empty bed. It was mixed thoroughly with the soil before the seedlings were transplanted into the bed.

Then we decided to dig deeper ponds. The stepping boards built to walk into the pond were lengthened. As usual, we balanced two watering cans, scooped cool water at the deeper end of the pond and watered the *choy sum*. We were busier than ever but were satisfied that the produce was as good as the others in the market. More varieties, such as *kailan*, *pak choy*, lettuce and celery were added to our farm. Their growth cycle was short and therefore the harvest was more frequent.

With the introduction of the lowland varieties, my mum had more customers and was busier and therefore happier. But the quality of our lowland vegetables still could not match the competitor's.

Herbs

While we paid a lot of attention to the planting of vegetables, as lovers of greens, herbaceous and medical plants were not ignored either. Herbs such as lemon grass, *centella asiatica* (with leaves that look like scallop shells), turmeric, *langkuas* (large ginger), and *plantago major* (local frog weed) were planted in beds.

When my parents lugged the vegetables off to Chai Chee market to sell, herbs and medicinal plants were not ignored.

Lemongrass

Dad watering the plants with a pair of water cans. The water cans were specially constructed.
Photographed by Lu Siang Hee

DDT Spraying

Once a month, the Public Health Division would send its health workers to look for mosquito larvae in the ponds and streams. Usually, a well-dressed man in white would carry a metre-long rod with a small, shallow plate attached to it. He would lower the plate into the water and scoop up some to examine for mosquito larvae. Sometimes, he took some samples of the larvae and put them into a small vial. The next day, someone dressed in a brown shirt and short pants, carrying a knapsack Indian pump would visit.

(Note: The knapsack container contained DDT. A pump and a spray came with the container.)

If the health worker wished to spray DDT onto a pond he would activate the spray by pulling a pump in his hand. He would then spray a pungent liquid onto the ponds and streams. My dad would usually drop whatever he was doing and rush to ask him to spare the ponds and watering holes where we fetched the water to water our plants. We did not mind him spraying the streams. If there were weeds along the banks, they would be killed together with whatever living creatures were in the water. The person was very understanding. He always acceded to my dad's requests. Sometimes, my dad was not there to remind him and he would spray the liquid in places that he suspected had mosquito larvae. However, he always gave our ponds a miss. We had several ponds. The main pond was a huge one—about a quarter of a football field in area. In it, there were different types of fresh water fish and water plants—both submerged and semi-submerged. With so many creatures inside the pond, I was sure the *mandor* (foreman) could not find any mosquito larva. In the smaller ponds, he made sure that there were fish inside.

"*Inche, minyak ini banyak berat lah. Boleh tolong tak?* (This oil is very heavy. Can you help?)" He appealed to my dad rather pitifully one day.

To lighten the load the health worker was carrying, my dad would bring him to the back of our house discreetly and transfer some of the liquid into his empty tin. My dad was a kind and considerate man. Seeing him working so hard to please the *mandor* and him, he gave the health worker a small token of appreciation for his cooperation. For that, he always borrowed this Hokkien phrase from the cement plasterer: "*Chit been buah piak, siang been keern.*" In literal translation, it is, "With one stroke of the cement spatula, both sides of the wall are smoothened." The liquid was of valuable use for us to get rid of white ants as well as any pests around the house and farm.

A man could carry this portable sprayer container (which could contain a few gallons of DDT) with ease.

Not long after that incident, I saw a very familiar person scooping up our pond water and examining it very closely. He was none other than the person who had often come to our farm to spray insecticide. He had been promoted to a *mandor* (foreman). I was sure the health authorities had recognised that he had done a good job at keeping the breeding of mosquitoes at bay while understanding the needs of the farmers to keep their plants and animals in the ponds and water holes alive.

As more and more plots of land were used in planting lowland vegetables, fewer and fewer highland varieties were planted. As our farming techniques improved, with the help of Primary Production Department officials, it was time to give up. The sad news came in 1962.

Leng Seng Land Ltd. had bought over all the land in the area for housing development. My parents cried. Where were we to get another plot like the one we had?

Chapter 17
Disasters

The Air Crash at Kallang Airport 1954

Not many aeroplanes flew in those days. Occasionally, the slow moving pre-war model of the twin winged fighter planes rattled above us. Sometimes, they did aerial acrobatic displays and we would marvel at them. One afternoon, I was on the ridge of the coconut estate. An aeroplane, very much bigger than the usual ones we saw, flew in a southwesterly direction from where I stood. Suddenly, there was loud explosion. Smoke billowed into the sky. I was too young to rush to the scene. My cousin, Hong Thong, who happened to be at my house, immediately hurried in the direction where the smoke was. He reached Kallang Airport. He claimed to have seen luggage and paper fly everywhere in the vicinity. There were even body parts, like little fingers, scattered on the ground. He said the stench of burning flesh drifting throughout the area. The smell was unbearable. What a sheer waste of human lives!

This happened on 13 March 1954 at Kallang Airport. The plane, a Lockheed 749A-7933 Constellation, belonged to British Overseas Airways and it was flying from Australia to London and had a stopover at Kallang Airport. At that time, it was carrying 40 passengers—31 passengers and nine crew members. The number of fatalities was 33 passengers and two crew members.

According to the official report, it crashed short of the runway, hit a wall, overturned and caught fire. Proper landing procedures were not followed by the pilot and pilot fatigue was to blame for the crash.

I was only eight years old then, but the sights and sounds of that disaster are deeply etched in my mind.

The Big Flood of 1954 and the Bedok Canal

It was the December holidays and I was eight years old. During that year, the rain was exceptionally heavy. It rained non-stop for days and nights. We lost count of the number of days it had been raining. The newspapers reported that New Village of Somapah Road was underwater. The flood victims might have been evacuated to higher ground at Changi 10 Milestone and other areas. I was too young to know. But one memory that is firmly etched in my mind was my trip to my primary school—Bedok Boys' School. I had never seen so many adults and children occupying our classrooms before. Some were sleeping, others were daydreaming. The mothers were either feeding their babies or hanging up their laundry on lines which were strung across the rooms. All of them had withdrawn faces of emptiness. When we went to the canteen, the sight was the same—more people cramped in the whole canteen.

That year, I was told the water had nearly reached the rooftops of most village huts, destroying almost everything the residents had. The victims had to wait for rescue boats to pick them up from the rooftops. When school reopened the following year, all the victims had already returned to their houses, leaving a grim reminder of what had happened a few weeks before. In the music room, there were still many baskets of donated clothing. My teacher announced that we could choose a few pieces of clothing to take home. I chose a few shirts, but was later chided by my mum. She said we were not flood victims, therefore we should let those less fortunate than us have them.

We learnt that the wooden bridge across the Bedok River had been washed away. Later, a very long, black, wooden bridge with railings at both sides was built to replace the one that was swept away. A huge excavating machine from the Public Works Department was seen every day deepening and widening the Bedok River. Today, it is known as the Bedok Canal.

The Bedok Canal today.

Note: A short history of the Bedok Canal.

When the government took over Paya Lebar to develop the Paya Lebar Airport in 1951, the farmers there were resettled along the banks of the Bedok River. These areas were known as New Village. The soil was most suitable for planting lowland vegetables such as kailan, choy sam, pak choy, lettuce, etc. However, it often flooded after a period of rain. In 1954, it rained incessantly. The farmers experienced the worst flood in their lives. The government then decided to solve the flooding problem by turning it into a canal. For years on end, I saw dredging machines dredging the river beds as well as widening the canal. A water barrage was built at Lembah Bedok to control water from the upper reaches of the Bedok River flowing unchecked into the flood plain of Koh Sek Lim. During heavy rainstorms the sluice gates at the barrage was narrowed to restrict the flow of water into the lower part of the canal. That caused the formation of a lake towards the area before the barrage. The flood problem was transferred from the lower reaches of Bedok River to that of the upper reaches. In the 70s, the hills beyond the upper reaches of Bedok River was moved to reclaim the sea off east coast. Sand from the hills too was mined for the Housing and Development Board causing a deep depression. Today it is the Bedok Reservoir. The land on both sides of the Bedok Canal (originally farms) were raised. The Sewerage Water Treatment Works was built followed by the Newater Plant.

The Area Around Koh Sek Lim

I had been to Kok Sek Lim to watch Chinese *wayang* performances organised by the temple there. Once I went with my dad to attend a political rally at the temple's permanent *wayang* stage. At other times, I helped my dad distribute temple offerings after their prayers to the members of the Seventh Moon Committee. My dad had to do that because he was the *'lor chu'* (executive member of the committee). To reach the temple at Koh Sek Lim, we had to walk into the village that was shaded by numerous rubber trees opposite the Bedok schools. There were also a few occasions I have described, just before the school holidays, when our teachers took us on long walks. After walking past the rubber estate, we came to a swamp which was overgrown with nipa palms. The track was made of mud from the swamp. Occasionally, we saw monkeys and squirrels among the palms. We also saw people harvesting the fruit of the palm. The palm in Malay was known as *attap*. Hence, the seeds of the nipa palm were called *attap chee*. *Attap chee* was commonly added to *chendol* and ice *kachang*. There were also people gathering the fronds of the palm trees. The leaflets of the fronds of the palm trees were very much bigger than coconut fronds so they were very suitable for making *attap* panes. An *attap* pane was about one metre in length. It was made of many folded palm leaflets stitched together using small lengths of split canes. The roof of an attap house was made of many rows of overlapping attap panes tied together on sloping stakes that were nailed onto the top beams of the house.

An Attap pane

Mudskippers were a common sight in the mud of the swamp. These fish have gills which can hold a pocket of water and extract air through it. They skipped and flicked their tails and moved swiftly into the muddy holes when they felt they were in danger. Their unusual eyes atop their heads made them look very queer indeed.

Before the big flood, Sungai Bedok was very narrow. A narrow wooden bridge with no railings was built across it. It was most frightening crossing the bridge. The water rose and ebbed with the tides. When the high tide was going out, the water under the bridge would flow very rapidly. We siblings felt as if the bridge was moving. We felt giddy and frightened. All of us walked very slowly, and when we were about to reach the other side, we sped up, heaving a sigh of relief when we reached the muddy bank on the other side.

Relocated lowland farmers from Paya Lebar were settled around Lembah Bedok (New Village). The sand quarries were found about two kilometres before the Bedok seacoast.

After the government took over the land at Koh Sek Lim in the 1970s, redevelopment took place. Today, the Bedok Sewerage Treatment and Newater Plant are there. Bedok Canal was widened and straightened. All bridges across it are in concrete. On the other side of the canal are industrial buildings and the MRT depot.

The Bedok Canal in the 1970s. In the 1950s and 1960s, the whole area comprised of vegetable farms.

Gunnysack and Gunny String

Today, we seldom see any gunnysack or gunny string around. In those days, they were commonly used. The word 'gunny' comes from the Sanskrit word *goni*. Gunny cloth was weaved from the fibre of the jute plant. The cloth could be dyed in different colours, but the texture could be quite coarse. The cloth was tough and very long lasting. We always purchased rice in huge gunnysacks. Each sack of rice was about 100 *katis,* which in those days, was just the right weight for a man to carry. On the sacks, words, numbers, and trademarks could be printed. I remember that a broad green line, about five centimetres thick, could be seen running from the middle of the rice sack's opening end to the rear. Anybody who was familiar with Thai rice knew what it contained. Other items such as corn, coffee beans, grains, copra, charcoal, salt, sawdust and sand were also packed in gunnysacks.

A gunnysack

In our home, there were several items that were related to the gunnysack. A steel hook the size of a man's palm with a short handle, known as wolverine's claw was used to hook a sack of materials. Because of its durability, the hook did little damage to the sack. My dad used to stitch the sacks together for the pigs in the pens on cold days. To stitch gunnysacks, a curved eight-inch needle (about 20 cm) with an eye of about 0.5 centimetres was used. The point was slightly flattened and the needle body was a solid metal rod. Gunny string would be run through the eye of the needle first.

Gunny cloth was also used as mats or rugs at the doorway. A gunny cloth could be used to line a wet, slippery floor to prevent anyone from slipping.

Farmers used to put their fowl or piglets into gunnysacks before transporting them to the market for sale. Unlike plastic bags, gunnysacks allowed for high breathability, therefore the animals would not suffocate.

We had also read about kidnapped children being placed in gunnysacks before being transported to hiding places to avoid being detected.

During our schools' sports days, there was an item called the 'sack race'. Each competitor would jump into a gunnysack and put each foot into each of the bottom corners. With both hands holding the sack tightly at the top corners, they raced to the finishing line. This race needed lots of practice. A skilful competitor could do it quite gracefully.

When castrating the boar, my dad used to drape a piece of gunny cloth over it before gripping its hind legs and wedging the squealing boar between his thighs. My grandma would then proceed to castrate it. The gunny cloth was to prevent the boar from accidentally biting him and also to make sure that he had a good grip on the boar.

Gunny string could be purchased in balls. Several strands of jute thread were braided into the string. If one wished to get a leaner string, he could undo the braids. If one wished to have a stronger string, he could braid several strings into one. My grandma was very skilful at braiding several gunny strings into one.

With so many gunnysacks around, we would stack them in a corner of the hall. A gunnysack collector would come by on his bicycle and sometimes in his lorry. He would count the number of sacks and pay us for them.

There were many other uses for gunnysacks, left to the ingenuity of their users.

My Bicycle Experiences

Sometimes when my father was ill, I, being the eldest boy in the family, would take over his duties. Changi Road, in those days, ran along the ridge of the hills. It was winding and undulating and filled with potholes. It had only two bitumen lanes which were slightly raised—one for each direction of traffic. To pedal a heavy load up and down the narrow winding road was not easy, especially for a child. Usually, to go uphill, I immediately dismounted and pushed the load. Sometimes, a huge vehicle would come too near me and I had to veer to the left, down the bitumen track and then to the sandy ground. To get back to the bitumen track was not easy. Once, I lost my balance. My front wheel could not get onto the track. It careened along it and the bicycle fell. I struggled to get the bicycle and the load up, but in vain. Luckily, one of the market's vegetable sellers who went the same way parked his load and helped me to my feet.

Once, I pedalled my load down a hill. I came to a wooden bridge (where the present-day Tanah Merah MRT station is). As I was struggling to pedal up to Changi Road, suddenly a few dogs came chasing after me. I was in a quandary. I lifted my legs as the bicycle moved on its own, at the same time shouting and staring at the dogs ferociously. The bicycle soon slowed down as it lost momentum. I dared not put down my legs to pedal it, as I feared they would become breakfast for the dogs. I lost my balance and then the bicycle, the load, and I fell with a loud crash. Upon hearing the loud commotion, the dogs took to their heels with their tails between their legs.

Cursing and swearing, I lifted the heavy load. After much struggling, the bicycle was up and I had to re-tie the load on to the carrier, as it had become loose. I suffered some bruises on my legs.

There was another incident. Every morning, my mum had to hurry to the bus stop at Changi Road junction to get to the Chai Chee market and I would pedal her there on my bicycle. I tried my best to get her to the bus stop as quickly as possible. I asked my mum to sit sideways on the horizontal bar of the bicycle frame. She placed her hands on the handlebar. I pedalled along. Then I descended a slope. While going down the slope, I tried to slow down by pressing on the brakes. Suddenly, there was a loud snapping sound. My mum and I were flung off the bicycle. I suffered abrasions on the face and legs and my mum had too. She felt a pain in her thigh. Luckily, there was a public standpipe nearby. We washed ourselves. With her injuries, she limped to the market. The site where the public stand pipe was is the present-day monsoon drain along Tanah Merah MRT station.

I picked up the broken bicycle and then walked home, feeling very guilty and sorry for my mum. The original fork of the bicycle was bent, so I had salvaged another fork from a discarded bicycle and replaced it, not knowing that the replacement fork had a hairline crack.

Because we lived in such a far-flung place, moving about without bicycles was very slow and inconvenient. Getting a motorised vehicle was out of the question. My dad owned several bicycles. In those days, one needed to get a licence to own a bicycle. Every bicycle had an enamel-coated licence plate screwed on at the rear mudguard. The earlier plate was green. Later, a red one was issued.

The enamel-coated plates were delicate. The enamel broke when hit, revealing the metal below and the numbers would be damaged. The latest version was the embossed aluminium licence plate before the registrar of vehicles decided to stop licensing bicycles.

The law stated that at night, every bicycle had to have a lighted lamp. Sometimes, my dad needed to go out at night so he filled the bicycle lamp with kerosene and lit it before riding off. I was fascinated with the lamp, as it was a cube shape and had a big, circular, transparent lens in front. On the left side was a red lens and on the right was a blue lens. Directly below the lenses were a few small ventilation holes. It was built like a hurricane lamp. Breezes would not blow out the flame. There was a spring on the holder to absorb the impact of bumps and vibrations. I did not see such lamps again for a long time until I came across one many years later, in 26 April 2009. Later, bicycle dynamo lamps became popular and the kerosene lamps slowly disappeared from bicycles.

A kerosene bicycle lamp from 50
years ago.

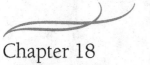

Chapter 18
The Boat-breaking Contract

In 1960, my uncle Yeo Koon Seng signed a contract with the British Naval Base to 'break' 100 wooden boats. The contract was to transport the boats to our house to recover all the metal and return this metal to the boatyard. They were huge—similar to the length and width of the bed of a three-tonne lorry. The outer shell of the boat was made of thick plywood—at least six to eight plies each. About 70 of the boats had three sides—left, right and rear—reinforced with steel frames. The fore was tapered with the bottom so that it had a streamlined body. The top of the fore and the rear were enclosed in plywood. The middle, which was about the length of one-third of the boat, was open. They were all painted jungle green. But nobody knew what these boats were for. There were no obvious signs that they were for the transportation of men. Neither were there signs they were for the transportation of goods or materials as the physical makeup of the boat did not allow it. There were stakes supporting the boat walls, making the storage of goods cumbersome.

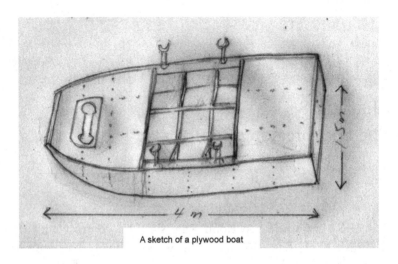

A sketch of a plywood boat

There were no signs or indications for a motor to be fixed. There were drainage holes and plugs for the draining of water as well as to prevent water from getting into the boat. There were some fixtures that indicated that oars were used. But there were no oars fixed to a single boat. However, there was a fixture at the top fore that allowed the boat to be towed.

The remaining 30 of them were cuboid boxes—all enclosed. The top part had three trap doors which could be locked from the outside. The four plywood walls were also reinforced with steel frames.

All the bottoms of the boats were made of plywood too but reinforced with three-centimetre by three-centimetre strips of wood at regular intervals from the fore to the aft.

I once went into one of the boats, as one of the lids of the manholes at the top was open. Suddenly, someone closed the lid. Inside, it was pitch dark. I could not breathe properly; I felt like I was going to faint after about a minute. My strength was draining away and I was shivering. I struggled to punch at the boat's roof and shout, but my punches were weak and hardly made any noise. I thought I was going to die inside without anybody knowing. Suddenly, the lid was opened. What a relief! One of the men nearby had been playing a prank on me.

The first few lorries that transported the boats to our house attracted a considerable number of curious kampong folks. Each lorry could transport two boats—one stacked upon the other. To unload the boats, the driver and the assistants used brute force to heave and push each boat off the lorry. While they were doing this, someone—I do not know who—was already thinking of how to make the job easier. A very strong rope was looped on to one of the sturdy fixtures of the boat on the bed of the lorry. The other end of the rope was tied round the base of a coconut tree. Then the lorry driver revved his engine hard. The lorry moved forward and the boats fell to the ground. There was a huge round of applause. Then someone suggested putting cylindrical logs on the bed of the lorry before loading the boats so that when unloading, the logs would serve as rollers, causing less strain on the lorry while also decreasing the risk of the assistant getting hurt. After that, this became the usual way to unload the boats. That was how people learned, by improving on an idea through practical experience. After all, necessity is the mother of invention.

My uncle gathered his gang of men mostly from Kampong Eunos, including one party from his cousin, Koon Hor. They stripped off every metallic part from the boats efficiently and stored them in a corner of our vacant chicken coop. There were two other groups working. Even Chew Eng Teng, my cousin, had a hand in it. A fee of $30 per boat was paid for recovering the metallic parts.

Every day, several groups of workers were busy. As a result, there was the sounds of knocking, chipping, unscrewing, scraping, tearing, searing, banging, dragging and other noises anyone could think of. At the end of the day, the metallic parts were returned to the vacant chicken coop, which by then was converted into a makeshift storehouse and office. Wages were paid and workers packed up and went home to their families.

My uncle and my dad would prepare to send the metallic parts to the headquarters. Screws, bolts, nuts, rivets and stray pieces of metal for repairing the damaged boats were not included. After all the hundred boats had their metal frame and parts removed, the wooden structures left were scattered over a wide area under the coconut trees. My family has fond memories of them. We children had so much fun playing hide-and-seek among them. On rainy days, rainwater would collect in some of the concave sides of the hulls. We were instructed either to knock holes through them to drain away the water or to upturn the parts to clear the water to prevent mosquito breeding.

The rivets that were used to attach the stakes to the bottom of each boat were made of copper. Each day, when we were free, we would prise away the rivets and store them in pails. Meanwhile, dad would make enquiries about the price of copper. When the price was right, he would transport the rivets to the scrap metal yard to sell.

Prising loose the rivets required skill and suitable tools such as hammers and steel chisels. To salvage a long strip of wood attached to the bottom of the boat, we must be very careful while chiselling the rivets. Each strip was about three centimetres by three centimetres and about 400 centimetres long. The strips were made from very hard and durable wood. We would reuse the strips as supports for climbing plants and to make fencing. The odds and ends were used as firewood. The plywood from the sides of the boat, which was mostly still in good condition, was used as fencing for pigsties as well as floorboards for the preparation of vegetables before sending them to the market.

In most of the boats, the screws used to attach the plywood were made of iron. Most of them had rusted away. However, in some of the boats, brass screws were used. They still seemed as good as new. We would unscrew and collect them. Sometimes, copper plates were used to cover up small damaged parts of the boat and then they were painted over. Whenever we discovered a patch that was painted over, we would try our best to scrape off the paint to find out if it was a piece of copper. If it were copper, we would feel excited and immediately set about removing it. A piece of one foot by one foot copper plate could be sold for quite a substantial amount of money. Sometimes, the work was hard. We needed to use brute strength to move each hull to search for such pieces, as the boat hulls were stacked one on top of another. Some of the copper plates were found resting at the bottom of the boat, making the chiselling job difficult. We needed to turn the hull over to make chiselling easier.

The boat-breaking contract really gave us another source of activity and income. When we moved to Chai Chee, we even transported some of the remnants of the boats there.

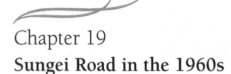

Chapter 19
Sungei Road in the 1960s

Whenever we needed any tools, my dad would take me to Sungei Road. In those days, it was called the Thieves Market or *Robinson Petang* in Malay. In literal translation, it means 'Afternoon Robinson's' and that was where cheap used goods could be purchased. The well-to-do did their shopping at Robinson's Department Store at Raffles Place. When one talked about shopping at Robinsons, the impression was that the person must be well off. The poor would say, "I did my shopping at Robinson *Petang*."

This bridge connects Arab Street to Weld Road across the Rochor Canal. In Hokkien it is *Kek Sng Kio*. Running parallel to Rochor Canal is Sungei Road. The name 'Sungei Road' is a misnomer. The Malay word 'sungei' means 'river'. It makes no sense to put the two words, one in English and one in Malay, together.
The Chinese speakers name the flea market after the bridge and the English speakers name it Sungei Road.

Another name for that area was *Kek Sng Kio*. In literal translation, it means 'Ice Work Bridge'. In the 1950s, the Singapore Ice Works located there supplied blocks of ice to the general public, as refrigerators were expensive and electricity had not reached most parts of Singapore. So people had to depend on the ice from the ice works to preserve their perishable goods as well as for consumption. The Singapore Ice Works was situated along the Rochor Canal. There was a bridge across the Rochor Canal leading to the ice works. So in the Hokkien dialect, it was called *Kek Sng Kio*.

The New Singapore Ice Works

It was said that anyone who found parts of their vehicles or other equipment missing, could find them being sold at Sungei Road.

There was once a watch repairer who was robbed of two expensive watches—one was already repaired and the other one was waiting for the arrival of parts. He was furious.

"My reputation is at stake. How am I going to convince my client that it was a genuine robbery?" he wailed. He went around alerting those known to be second-hand dealers at Sungei Road to watch for anyone who wished to sell the two particular brands of watches he had been robbed of. To impose criminal charges on the vendor in Sungei Road who didn't realise they were selling a stolen watch for robbery would be tricky, as the watch repairer had no proof of who the thief really was. Within a week, he recovered the watch that had some parts missing. The other one was not recovered. At least he could tell his client that he had done his best to recover the items.

In the 1950s, the houses around that area—Weld Road, Perak Road, Kelantan Road, Larut Road, Pitt Road and Sungei Road— were dilapidated. Rents were cheap and the goods there were cheaper than at other places. In the afternoons, road sweepers and scavengers, rags-and-bone men, second-hand goods dealers who dealt with seamen, tourists and even thieves, would ply their goods there. As their cost price was next to nothing, the items exchanged hands very cheaply. Furthermore, with so many vendors from so many different walks of life, some goods could be unique. People would go there for spare parts, new and second-hand goods, antiques, collectibles such as toys, watches, coins, stamps, currency notes, cameras, books—including banned and obscene books—cassette tapes, records, old clothing and shoes, redundant materials and precious

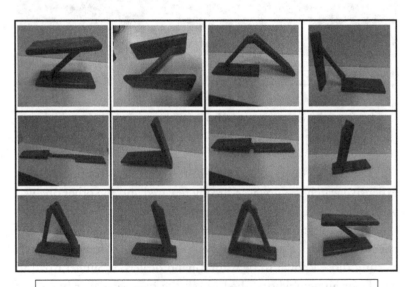

The wooden contraption.
Nobody seems to know what this contraption is used for.

stones. Sometimes, things you had never thought of were on sale there.

At other times I could hear the vendor and the prospective buyers arguing about what a machine was really used for. Once I saw a wooden contraption. It came in three parts and had movable joints. I tried to figure it out but to no avail. Was it a toy? Was it a machine? Nobody could tell me what it was!

There were also a row of shops selling used containers of all shapes and sizes. They could make them or alter them in whatever way one wished.

To sell something, one could spread out a ground sheet or simply display the wares on the bare ground by the side of the road. Spaces were awarded on a first-come-first-served basis. No rent was charged. Dealers, buyers and bargain hunters would examine the things on display and if they were interested in an item, bargaining would commence. However, it was important to know that goods, once they changed hands, could not be returned and they did not come with a guarantee. However, the vendors would usually be willing to buy it back at a price lower than what you had originally purchased it for.

My dad would spend the whole afternoon going from shop to shop and stall to stall to examine suitable tools we needed. I was surprised that some of the things on display there were discarded items such as used exercise books, torn textbooks and rusty tools and nails. After purchasing what we needed, we proceeded to have a meal of *laksa*. At 30 cents a bowl, it was worth it. We thought it was the best *laksa* in Singapore. We washed it down with an aromatic coffee. The *laksa* and coffee combination proved to be a hit with the customers as they complemented each other.

At the end of the day, we proceeded home satisfied that we had gotten most of the things we wanted at a price we could find nowhere else.

Camera vendor, Ah Lim, at Sungei Road in 1970

Chapter 20
Time to Say Good-bye

Pirate Taxis

In the kampongs, car owners who saw familiar faces going the same route deep into the kampong would stop and offer them a lift. If there were a need for transport in an emergency, a car owner, if he were free, would render his help readily. My grandma and mum had very good experiences and were grateful to those who had helped them on those occasions.

There were groups of car owners who ferried schoolchildren to school for a fee. Schoolchildren were packed like sardines in their Ford Austins, Morris Minors and Cambridges. After sending their school charges off, they were free to use their vehicles to earn extra money in other ways. They plied regular bus routes and charged double the fares. They picked up and dropped off passengers along the way at any place requested.

The bus fare for an adult from Tanah Merah Kechil to Chai Chee Market was ten cents. The pirate taxi charged 20 cents. My mum found it quite convenient to come home by a pirate taxi, as it saved her the trouble of lugging her heavy rattan basket of purchases up and down the bus. Furthermore, pirate taxis, having a full load of only four or five passengers, moved faster than a bus. Once a passenger had been picked up, the driver would rev his engine and speed all the way until requested to stop or to pick up another passenger. If he found the car too stuffy because of the full load of passengers, he would fix a cardboard piece to the small, triangular window of the front door to divert some of the air outside to himself. Those days, air-conditioned cars were hard to come by.

Commuters found this mode of transport so convenient that it became a habit. In certain places where taking and changing buses was inconvenient, pirate taxis came in handy and cheaper too. For example, students who wanted to go to Teacher's Training College from Capitol Theatre had to rush and be crushed with the other commuters during peak hours. These buses would also not send them right into the campus. All the students needed to do was to get into a pirate taxi and wait until they got a full load of four passengers then off they went right into the campus, saving them time and inconvenience.

Because of pirate taxis, regular yellow and black taxi operators had their income reduced, as they had to obey the Registry of Vehicles' (ROV) rules, pay higher taxes and insurance premiums and undergo vehicle inspections. Their concerns were raised and the ROV had to come down hard on the pirates.

In the early 1970s, pirate taxi operators were slowly phased out. To ferry schoolchildren, special SCH number plates were introduced. Those caught pirating would have their cars confiscated and have to pay heavy fines and face jail terms.

In the days when pirate taxis still plied their trade, uncle Yeo Koon Seng, who owned a Hillman, sometimes picked up passengers to supplement his income. Uncle Koon Seng, my dad's elder brother, was a housing contractor. He had ten children. They all lived in Kampong Eunos. As I have mentioned, in the 1960s, the demand for low cost housing was so great that the pond and pigsties that my grandma built were all converted into attap houses and rented out. At that time, because of the Rent Control Act, the rental collected was minimal. With so many mouths to feed, uncle Koon Seng's income from his housing contracting works and rental was barely enough. So he had to moonshine as a pirate taxi driver.

One fateful day in 1966, after driving, he came home to lie down on his canvas bed to take a nap. Sadly, it was his last. To my siblings and I, he was always the amiable *Ah Pek* (uncle). Whenever, my grandma was ill, he would put down whatever he was doing and rush her to the clinic in his old, trusted Hillman. He will always be remembered as kind gentleman who had the welfare of others at heart.

The Portable Canvas Bed

The canvas bed was a very convenient piece of foldable, portable furniture. It was durable and there was no fear of it being damaged as the canvas could be easily replaced.

The canvas bed is a simple piece of furniture seldom seen nowadays. It was very popular during those days. The village houses were cramped and lacked ventilation. Children were many. There was practically no place in the bed for an adult to sleep with the children. So the father would say, "I'll sleep on the canvas bed."

The canvas bed was cheap. It was easy to construct and was foldable. It was comfortable and cool as there was airflow all round. After having a good night's sleep, one just folded it and tucked it in some obscure corner of the house.

The canvas needed to be changed consistently but that also depended on how it was used. If one were to jump up and down on the canvas bed, that would surely shorten its life. To change the canvas was easy. Just get a new canvas cloth the same size as the old one, some one-inch nails and two split rattans. Nail the split rattan over the edge of the top frame of the canvas. Test the replacement canvas. The job could be done in a jiffy.

The Singing of *Majulah Singapura* and the Collecting of FDCs

Until the early 1960s, we never had a radio. My grandma had to go to madam Ong Ka's house to listen to her favourite Hokkien stories or opera performances. Many Malay families in the kampong had radios. They often turned up the volume and as a result, the programmes could be heard by many families. From what the disc jockeys said and from the sound of the music, we could guess what each programme was about and the time it started and ended. The programmes also served as a timing device as we did not have a clock.

As I have also mentioned, we heard the news from the school's public address system and we heard stories, songs and opera performances from Rediffusion at Kampong Eunos (known as Lian Teng Hng) when we visited our uncle. We watched live *wayang* performances. Our main source of information about the outside world was either the *Nanyang Siang Pau* or *Sin Chew Jit Poh* newspapers, which my dad occasionally bought from the Chai Chee open-air market.

On 30 May 1959, we were very interested to know the results of the general elections. It was the first election in which all the seats were determined by the voters, according to the new Constitution of Singapore of 1959. In previous elections, some seats would be chosen by Singapore's colonial rulers. We went to madam Ong Ka's house to listen with her son Ah Hee, who had a small transistor radio. He had to connect a wire from the attap roof down to the aerial of the radio. The reception was not good, so we had to strain our ears to hear what was being announced. While waiting for votes to be counted, traditional music was played. From 10 p.m. onward, the results from one constituency then another streamed in. The result for the Changi constituency was announced: Mr Teo Hock Guan was returned as a Member of Parliament. We were jubilant. We waited until all the results were announced. The People's Action Party was given the mandate to rule Singapore after it won 43 seats out of 51 in the Legislative Assembly. After that, our affairs with the radio were temporarily halted, as we could not afford the time for leisure.

I first heard of the *Majulah Singapura* being sung from Hong Tong, my cousin. He learnt it at the community centre at Kampong Eunos and Rediffusion. It was one day in December 1959 that Hong Tong arrived at our house with the national anthem song sheet in the form of a card. He read the Malay version and also looked at the Chinese translation. Then he tried to sing it. We aped it. Usually, we sang it out of tune and the lyrics went haywire. We laughed then we repeated it all over again. That was the first time I heard the national anthem. When school reopened, we sang it more often and the symbolism of the state flag and the crest was explained to us.

Our *Yang di-Pertuan Negara* (head of state), Tun Yusoff bin Ishak, was introduced to us and we had to commit his name to memory. Goodbye to Sir Robert Black, Sir William Goode and Tun Lim Yew Hock. 'God Save the Queen' was never sung again.

"Have you got the first day cover?" Yew Gin asked me on the morning of 2 June 1959.

"What's first day cover?" I asked, feeling rather puzzled, as I had never heard or seen one.

"Yesterday, there was a set of new stamps issued. The first day cover is the special envelope on which the new set is pasted and stamped with the date of the first day of issue. It was reported in the *Straits Times*," he said.

I was never exposed to reading the newspapers. It was in secondary 1 that my English teachers wanted each of us to contribute a news item from the papers. I bought it only for the school project. The other news was not seriously read or reflected upon, as I was too ignorant to understand what was reported. Since that day, after Yew Jin told me about the First Day Cover, I began to take more of an interest in reading the newspapers. The beginning of a new hobby unfolded—the collection of modern Singapore stamps and First Day covers.

Dryburgh English School

In December 1958, on the noticeboard next to the Bedok Boys' School Principal's office, were pinned the results of our Secondary School Entrance Examinations and the secondary schools we were posted to. Quite a number from our class were posted to Dryburgh English School.

My grandma knew where that school was. She had friends from the *Heong Lian See* Temple at Koon Seng Road selling sweet black rice gruel and *laksa* at the canteen. When the school reopened on January 1959, my uncle Yeo Koon Seng took grandma and I there in his old Hillman. I remember it was raining that afternoon. We alighted at the gate. Many other boys and their parents were already there. We went to the hall and our names were called. I was in the same class as Chua Boon Seng. My other two friends, Lim Ban Lim (Richard) and Tok Thiam Chye (Robert) were together in the neighbouring class. The list of books we had to buy was written on the board. It was a long list. We had to copy it painstakingly on a piece of paper. A few titles that I could remember was *Correct Your English*, *General Mathematics Volume 2* by Durrell, *The World*, *General Physical Geography*, *General Physics*, *St Luke and Acts of the Apostles*, *Landmark in the Land of Christianity*, *Chemistry*, *Biology*, *An Anthology of Poetry* and *The Lost World*. Soon it was recess time. We went to the canteen. It was at the rear of the school building. My grandma was there waiting for me. She introduced me to her contemporaries who were canteen vendors—Kor Por (who had the same surname as us, Yeo) and Ee Por (who shared the same surname as grandma, Koh). Whenever I bought food from them, they would give me a double portion, much to the envy of my classmates.

Quite often we had been sending gifts of vegetables to the Heong Lian See Temple where these two ladies lived. So out of gratitude for keeping an eye on me in school as well as being her close friends, from then on, my grandma asked me to convey gifts of vegetables from our farm to them often. Being an obedient boy, I did so. But I felt rather awkward as I needed to lug my books to school too.

The two ladies were not our only acquaintances in the school. I noticed the *char kway teow* vendor from Chai Chee, the market where my mum plied her business.

The double-storey school building was quite old—repainted with many layers of paint. The blocks were named Lim Theng Heap Wing and Har Par Hall. The blackboard was actually cement slabs painted over with black paint. I thought that was queer. My idea of a board was a huge piece of wood.

Every afternoon, the entrance to the school was crowded with hawkers selling ice water, *kachang puteh*, toys, *tikam-tikam* and ice cream, among many other items. It was made worse when students had to make a gamble with one of the hawkers. The hawker first pulled out a coloured stick from a small brass container. The player had to pull out from that same container a stick with the same colour. If he pulled out one that matched the hawker's, he won a mega-sized ice cream without having to pay for it. If he lost, his money would be forfeited.

We had to squeeze our way into the gate and also be on the lookout for cars, bicycles and trishaws. The large compound was shared with the Choon Guan Public School and the Presbyterian church. Across the road was the annexe of Choon Guan Public School. One could just imagine the crowd during the change of sessions from both schools at the same time.

During the morning session, our school had a different name and a different principal from the afternoon session. In the morning session, it was called Presbyterian Boys' School and was headed by Mr Gay Wan Guay. During the afternoon session, it was called Dryburgh English School and was headed by Mr Sia Kah Hui. Perhaps it was the norm in those days to have different school names and different principals for each session.

415

Every day, we had to assemble at the Har Par Hall, sing some hymns and say prayers before going to class. In class, most of the pupils were from the primary school in the same building. Most of them knew each other and behaved as if they knew the place better. Most of them communicated with each other using a mixture of Malay and English. In fact, they were Peranakans. One very particular incident that irked me was this:

One day, out of the blue someone came to me and said rather loudly, "Eee, Devil!" That attracted many of the others around.

"If the principal were to know about it, you will surely be sacked!" shouted another.

I was shocked. I did not know what I had done to cause them to shout like that. They began pointing at the back of my shirt. My hair stood on end. Why? Was there a devil behind me? Then I realised that they were pointing at the red imprint at the base of my collar. I have mentioned how, every year on Goddess Kuanyin's birthday, my grandma would gather some clothing belonging to everyone in the family to get them blessed and imprinted at the temple. That shirt happened to be among them.

The whole crowd turned, trying to look at the imprint. More cried, "Devil! Devil!" I felt so horrid that I cringed and backed against the wall. I had never been treated like that.

I went to temples to pray, participate in their activities and drink their holy water. I heard the priests and priestesses prayed for world peace, harmonious living, prosperity and happiness in the family. I had never known that they were *devils*. I also feared that should the principal come to know about it, I would be expelled! The whole world came tumbling down on me. I had no extra shirt and there was no way to cover the imprint. When class was dismissed, I had to run as fast as I could to take a bus home.

At home, I told my grandma about it. I was assured that Kuanyin was no devil. "Let Kuanyin deal with those who taunted you!" she said calmly.

Why had the whole group reacted in such a way? I realised that since they were young, it had been ingrained into them that all non-Christians were devils. They were not particularly restrained and had no problem blurting it out. Every week, we had a period of RK or religious knowledge. But it was not knowledge of all religions. It was about Christianity. We studied the New Testament, especially St. Luke, St. Mark, St. Matthew and the Acts of the Apostles. In fact, the subject should have been named Christian knowledge and not religious knowledge. Before school, there were senior boys carrying Bibles, preaching to us about the religion they were practising. They showed evidence that the events that happened in the Bible were actually true. They quoted offhand from chapters and verses in the books, regarding what Jesus said and did. There were other groups distributing flyers with Christian messages. There were also Bible meetings at the music room in the attic, during which hymns were sung, speeches were given and prayers were said. There was also a middle-aged man selling Christian literature at one corner of the hall.

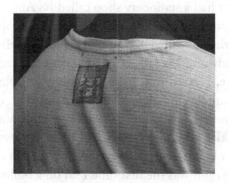

A sample of a temple imprint
on a shirt.

Every year, for a few days at a stretch, everyone had to attend talks at the Presbyterian church at the far end of the school compound. The pastor would talk about his experience as a non-Christian and how he was converted and later, how he came across the sufferings of non-Christians and how he convinced them that a Christian way of life was better. During prayers, the pastor would ask us to raise our hands if we wanted to accept Christ as our Saviour. At first, there were none. Then more and more did. After the sessions, those who raised their hands were asked to stay behind. They were told that they were new Christians and had to abide by Christian laws. In those days, a great majority of the students' parents were non-Christians. How these young Christians were able to blend into the ways of their parents and live harmoniously was a mystery. Perhaps problems of disharmony in the families and in the society resulted because of the conversions and preaching. Perhaps that prompted the Singapore government to introduce the Maintenance of Religious Harmony Act in 1992.

Some of those classmates I had a longer relationship with were Poh Yew Jin, Kaniantra and Das, as we were in the same class throughout our secondary school days. We used to do projects together as well as go on outings, but we never discussed religion. Furthermore, Yew Jin's house was just round the corner at Joo Chiat Road. His aunt had a stationery shop called FS Ang. I used to park my bicycle along the five-foot way outside her shop. There were a few times when I visited Yew Jin at his house. His mother was a very kind lady and his father was English-educated and worked in town. Once, I asked him to help me buy an Olivetti portable typewriter. Kaninantra's father had a pharmacy called Chery. Perhaps his mother was Chinese. I was not sure, but he was very fluent in Hokkien, although he looked Indian. Das was Indian. His father owned a bullock cart. I sat on his bullock cart one day along Koon Seng Road. It was the first time I sat on a bullock cart.

You may be wondering why I cycled to school. It was because the buses were always crowded, there were traffic jams and I had to walk from school at Koon Seng Road along Tembeling Road to East Coast Road and vice versa. Our sports field was at Lorong J Telok Kurau. We had to walk the whole length of Koon Seng Road, cut through Still Road, through Lorong J then cross Telok Kurau Road and go through Lorong J on the left of Telok Kurau. The field was quite near the Siglap Canal. Whenever we had sports practice, we wasted so much time walking the long distance. After practising for a short while, it was time to go home. From the field, we walked back to Telok Kurau and then to East Coast Road to take a bus to Bedok. Then I had to walk along the whole stretch of Jalan Haji

Salam, through the kampong, to reach my house. My parents saw how late I arrived home every evening—almost 8 p.m. There must have been much discussion about my predicament.

After the cross-country run, a certificate would be awarded.

This one was signed by Principal Siah Kah Hui and Sports Secretary Edward Fung.

Bus Journeys

One of the greatest nightmares in my life was to take a bus from Tembeling Junction to East Coast Road between 6.30 p.m. to 7 p.m. By that time, all the schools functioning in the afternoon session would have been dismissed. The buses picked the students up from Chung Cheng High, Tanjong Katong Girls', Tanjong Katong Tech, Kuo Chuan Girls', and St. Hilda's. When they reached that junction, they were already packed to their capacity. In those days, packed to

419

capacity could mean there was no space even to cling on to the door handles and put one foot on the last steps of the entrance or exit of the bus. We had our schoolbags to worry about too.

Most of the time, we managed to catch a foothold on the last step of the entrance or exit and cling onto the handles or the safety bars. Should we slip or the door handles give way, it would have been fatal. There were instances when passengers slipped and fell and were dragged on by the bus. The bus drivers were usually quick to stop before the passengers were pinned by the rear wheels.

To prevent passengers from clutching on to the stem of the exterior mirror, one of the drivers wound barbed wire around it. It was declared an illegal fitting by the registrar of vehicles after members of the public complained.

Therefore, the three of us, Lim Ban Lee, Toh Thiam Chye and I, decided to cycle to school. They used the lighter roadsters. Ban Lee had a Rudge and Thiam Chye had a China-made Forever. I used my dad's heavy-duty goods bicycle, which had a huge carrier at the rear. Attached was a red, round enamel number plate: Singapore 259353. It rattled loudly on uneven roads. If all the bicycles there were cars, mine was a lorry. It was a giant among dwarfs. Ng Choon Bee had a similar bike but without the carrier and the heavy-duty stand. My parents must have understood what suffering I had undergone.

My Raleigh Bike

One Sunday morning, my cousin Hong Tong cycled to my house. He was on a brand new Raleigh bicycle. The red aluminium number plate was: Singapore 289383. My dad said that it was for me. Tears rolled down my eyes. I was so happy. Immediately, I took a rag to clean it. The dynamo and lamp were of the Miller brand. The lamp was bright and sparkling in the sunlight. To prevent dust from getting on to it, I wrapped the lamp with a handkerchief. From that day onward, I cycled to school on the new bicycle. I parked it at the bicycle rack together with the other bicycles behind the Haw Par Hall.

The Little Red Cliff

One day, I found my precious lamp ripped off. No one could understand how sad I was. Stealing bicycle parts was very common in that school. One day, Thiam Chye's friend's lamp was also stolen. We marched straight to Mr Sia Kah Hui, the principal. A suspect was named, but he remained a suspect. Nothing was recovered.

On Sports Day, I raced with my Raleigh roadster in the bicycle race event. For the first few laps, I did not do badly. But somehow, halfway through, I felt that it was getting tough on the uneven tracks of the cow grass field. There were intermittent patches of sand too. One rider after another overtook me. Of course, there wasn't any chance of a roadster competing with racing bikes.

This battered Raleigh has braved all kinds of weather, terrain, neglect and abuse for more than 50 years. Now I'll try best to spruce it up to its former glory.

Have you ever ridden at the same speed as the rain cloud? Well, on several occasions, I did. From Tanah Merah Kechil to Koon Seng Road was about eight kilometres. The sky looked sunny. As I was cycling, it began to drizzle. I thought I could beat the drizzle as the sun was shining. The road ahead was dry. So I sped on. To my surprise, the speed of the rain clouds was almost the same as mine. I was constantly pelted by the rain. When I reached school, I was drenched, while those in school were as dry as bone. Those who saw

421

me laughed their hearts out. Well, I had no extra change of clothes with me, so I had to sit under the fan to dry.

The Six-day Week

When Singapore gained self-government in 1959, it emphasised science and mathematics education as the most important. So in the third term of the school year, we had to go to school on Saturdays. Every one of us was taken by surprise. Obviously, we did not read the newspaper, as the majority of us did not subscribe to it. We bought the newspapers only as and when somebody told us there was important news. Well, we overheard what the teachers said. The six-day week in school was not very welcome.

Assistant Librarian

I, together with Tong Kim Long, was appointed the assistant librarian at school. Each of us was given a school badge with the words 'Asst. Librarian' above the standard one. Fewer than ten students in the whole school's cohort were given this special badge. We were really proud of that. The teacher-librarian was Mr Loo Soo Ching, the Chinese language teacher. The library was not particularly impressive. A lot of old books—mainly fiction, were shelved in a few standard bookshelves. Few people visited it. Occasionally, the student leaders used it for meetings. There was a constant supply of free magazines, such as *Press Release* and *The Mirror*, published by the Ministry of Culture. The school subscribed to *Readers' Digest*. The students could get a copy at a discount from the office while stocks lasted.

Our duties were to see to the cleanliness and order of the library. We filed the magazines, repaired torn books and sometimes serviced and catalogued new books. Whoever wished to borrow any books, we serviced them. Each book could be borrowed for two weeks. A date stamp on the due date slip inside the book cover indicated the date when the book had to be returned. We reported for library duty every day one hour ahead of school assembly time.

At the end of secondary school, one of the statements in our testimonial was: "So and so was so responsible that he was given the role of an assistant librarian."

Climbing Mount Faber

In 1960, I remember we did a project on an expedition to Mount Faber. We started at Kampong Radin Mas in Telok Blangah. It was a small kampong at the foot of Mount Faber. According to legend, the place came to be known when Princess Radin Mas took refuge there with her father, who was the crown prince. Her uncle, who was the sultan, had murdered her mother. When Radin Mas died, she was buried nearby. Her shrine is still there. The kampong had to give way for the building of a road up Mount Faber in 2001.

We found a tiny track up Mount Faber. It was a trying journey, as if trekking through virgin jungle. We had to ward off spider webs, get through the undergrowth, and at the same time watch out for snakes and insects. We stopped at the World War II bunkers and examined the trash somebody had left behind. The rancid smell of vegetation was omnipresent. After a brief rest, we continued the climb. Finally, we reached the summit. We let out a huge sigh of relief. We enjoyed the greenery of the area as well the forested island of Pulau Blakang Mati. The flame atop one of the chimneys of Pulau Bukum was burning. We were wondering why. We scanned the other islands and the coasts, the city areas and then the kampong below. The attap houses were hidden among tall, swaying coconut trees. All these details were jotted down in our notebooks. We walked along the sandy path of the narrow ridge. The sandy path was most likely created by the constant pounding of feet by adventurers like us. We descended from the ridge by the path that led to Pasir Panjang. That was quite an experience.

Tracing the Singapore River

Another project we had to do was to trace the Singapore River to its source. We started from Anderson Bridge, crossed the old

Cavenagh Bridge, went along the ever busy and crowded Singapore River, ambled with the lunchtime crowd while enjoying the aroma of the food cooked by stallholders, at the same time taking care not to brush the legs of the low stools provided for the clients.

Hawker food stalls by the banks of the Singapore River
Photo: Yeo Hong Eng's collection

After that, we emerged from the hawker centre. It was a different scene—*twakohs* with their black eyes and red eyebrows were chugging away. Others swished along with attendants using a long pole to jab at the bottom of the river and push hard to make the boat move forward. We had to dodge coolies and their loads coming up from the narrow gangplanks which swayed and sagged under their burdens. Upon reaching the waiting lorry, their colleagues help them to unload the cargo from their shoulders and deposit it on the lorry bed. Others used cranes to lift bales from boats that anchored along the riverbanks. There were men in their short pants and singlets carrying notebooks and pencils checking the goods as well recording the number of trips each coolie made. Some, with their pencils tucked behind their ears, looked for missing bales. We walked along the never-ending stretch of double-storey warehouses and offices. The people were always busy rushing, pushing carts of goods, shouting instructions and ferrying drinks and food, while the lorries moved and groaned under full loads of goods. Stray dogs added to the excitement and bustle of the riverbanks. When we had reached Elgin Bridge, we realised that we had already crossed the belly of the river—the busiest part of the river with the boat quays on both banks. Then we crossed the Coleman Bridge, went over to North Boat Quay, the Read Bridge, the Ord Bridge, then to Pulo Saigon. By then, the river had narrowed considerably. It had become a stream with bushes and occasional sightings of carcasses of animals on its banks. It was no longer passable for river traffic. We traced it to a hill in Queenstown. At that time, bulldozers had removed the debris of the attap houses. They were flattening the hills to build a housing estate. Perhaps those were the most enjoyable times of my years in secondary school.

We siblings in those days had very few chances of going on picnics or to places of interest in Singapore, as our parents were always so busy. There were a few instances when our classmates grouped together and we went on our own to places such as Haw Par Villa, Bedok and the Changi beaches.

An outing with classmates to Haw Par Villa. I am second from the left, in the first row.

I was once invited to Yew Jin's cousin's house to fly kites. I remember it was at Woo Mun Chew Road. There was a sandy lane which led to the double-storey zinc and wood house. To me, it was imposing, as my home was only an attap house. We had a great time flying our little square kites.

There was an occasion when a few of my close friends, Poh Yew Jin, Kaniantra and Das, visited my family's farm. They were very surprised at the size of the farm and the produce we had. They took to the guava trees like fish to water, clambering up its trunk and branches. They were so excited that they could literally pluck the fruits and eat them, but they found the scent from the pigsty overpowering.

In 1961, when I was in Secondary Three, we had to choose the subjects we were good at. We were then streamed into the pure science class, the general science class and the arts class. I was put into the arts class. That was my most tumultuous year. The teachers were willing to teach, but the boys were rowdy, always shouting and talking among themselves. Furthermore, the pupils were obsessed with the nonsensical phrase '*Ah Kiong*'. Every day, conversations would end up with this phrase '*Ah Kiong*'. It was a fad. So it was '*Ah Kiong*' here and '*Ah Kiong*' there, '*Ah Kiong*' never ending. The teachers would be very angry. They could not stand the rowdiness in the class.

There was a science teacher, Mr Law. It just so happened that the science topic he was teaching was Boyle's Law. The students made fun of his name and the topic. He gave up after several lessons. A new science teacher took over. The more vocal students had the cheek to complain that they did not know what the former teacher had been teaching. After a few lessons, the new teacher gave up too. There was hardly any discipline in class. They distracted the teacher by asking questions on things other than the topic she was teaching. The pupils who were serious were powerless, as they were in the minority. As a result, there was a length of time when our class went without a science teacher. Teachers from other classes stood in. There was one particular teacher from the pure science class. Knowing the notoriety of most of the pupils from my class, he came in, shouted angrily at us to do our work, then sat in the chair and put his feet on the teacher's table, enjoying his paperback novel.

Finally, a no-nonsense science teacher, Mrs Singh, arrived. Not a squeak was heard from the rowdy group and there was peace at last.

The Chinese teacher, Mr Loo Soo Ching, had problems with the Peranakan pupils. They were totally not interested in learning Chinese. They spoke to each other in *pasar* Malay. We did the simpler Chinese, as we had very little Chinese language background. When the behaviour of the Peranakan students became intolerable, the teacher got the most notorious of the lot to stand at the chalkboard. However, when the teacher was not looking, he played with the chalk duster and sent the chalk dust flying all over the front of the classroom. The teacher could do nothing but send him out.

The art teacher was Mr Koh Choon Hong. He was the strictest of all the teachers then. We had never seen him smile. During his periods, he would walk in at a measured pace and stand at the front doorway. We all stood up immediately and greeted him. Then we were told to sit. He meant business and all of us had to sit down at once. They branded him Bulldog Koh. His words always carried weight. He spoke loudly and clearly and only once. For the collection of fees, he would fix a date. On that day, all fees, in the exact amount, had to be on the desk. He would give us work to do and while doing our work, he walked to our desks to collect the fees. He did that even for the Cambridge examination fees, which was no small amount for the poor families in those days. There was no second collection. If one did not bring one's fees, he would roar, "Go and steal, go and rob!" By hook or by crook, that poor student had to get it that day.

He had a special liking for me. Whenever he needed vegetables for his still life painting lessons, he would ask me to bring some from home. I would select the choice plants for him. My parents would help me pack them carefully in thick brown paper bags meant for packing powdered cement. Then, I carefully tied them on the rear carrier of my bicycle and sold it to him at a big discount.

There was a mathematics teacher who seldom explained how one could get a problem right. He would select a few problems from the textbook and we had to work on them. While doing so, he paced up and down the room, mumbled to himself and shook his head a little. When it came to marking, regardless of whether we did them right or wrong, there were always ticks. Halfway through the year, that teacher left. He probably retired. A new teacher arrived. He was very strict. Whenever he talked, his eyes were not focused on us. Should he wish to speak to anyone, his finger would be pointing at the student but his eyes were staring elsewhere. On hindsight, I think that most likely, he had a squint eye. All of us behaved ourselves regardless of whether he was looking at us or not. We learnt a lot at his class. He was none other than Mr Bose.

Form Three in 1961 with Mr Bose, our form teacher. I am standing in the second row, the second person on the right.

There was one occasion when our history and bible knowledge teacher was very irritated with our class monitor. I did not know what happened but suddenly there was a commotion. He gave the boy a hard slap on his cheek. There was bad blood between the teacher and student after that.

There was a group of boys who had always been a thorn in my flesh or maybe I had always been a thorn in theirs. We never saw eye to eye. There was a boy named Koh Kian Lock who was much taller and bigger than me. I did not know what made me angry with him. I scolded and cursed him. It must have touched a nerve and he gave me a punch in the mouth. I suffered a cut lip. I wanted to fight back, but then I knew that the consequences of fighting back were not worth it. I knew he later regretted what he did because he tried to be nice to me after that.

Black-and-white pornographic materials circulating among the pupils were plentiful. I wondered how these pupils got them. Every day, pupils would be discreetly discussing and exchanging them. Smoking was also rampant in the hard-core group. Every day before school, they would congregate at the *mamak* shop opposite the rear gate to smoke cigarettes at five cents per stick.

Have you ever heard of marking essay-type answers using a ruler? Well, one particular teacher marked our geography papers by measuring its length. The longer the essay one wrote, the better the marks. Those who wrote long essays, regardless of whether they were relevant to the question or not, got better marks. That gave some students ideas during examinations. Their writing scripts were unusually large and they wrote on alternate lines. Some even wrote on only one side of the paper. As a result, there were constant requests for writing paper from the invigilators. Can you imagine that?

Still, back then, no students in Singapore ever protested to the school management about their choice in appointing the principal. But it happened at Presbyterian Boys' school. One morning, several ministry officials appeared in school. They had a very intense discussion. I soon found out about what. It was reported in *Student World*, a monthly students' magazine, that the students of Presbyterian Boys' were not happy when the management wanted Mr Sia Kah Hui of Dryburgh English School to be their head. The Boys' Brigade band, in full uniform, played in protest and refused to enter their classrooms. Some even carried placards declaring: 'We want Gay. We want Gay', referring to their principal, Mr Gay Wan Guay. Who were they to influence the decisions of the management? Their protests came to nought. Mr Sia Kah Hui became their principal.

During the 1959 general elections, that school, Presbyterian Boys', made another mark in history. Their principal, Mr Gay Wan Guay, stood as a candidate in the Joo Chiat Constituency on a Liberal Socialist Party ticket. Every few minutes, his supporters would drive past our school with the loudspeakers blaring songs in praise of him. However, he was defeated.

Many years later in 1980, Mr Sia Kah Hui, the former principal of Dryburgh English School, stood as a candidate for general election on a PAP ticket in Paya Lebar. He won uncontested.

In 1961, there was yet another round of name changing of the school from Presbyterian Boys' to Nee Soon Presbyterian Secondary School. Our new exercise books were stamped with the new school name while the old name was deleted. There were so many decisions made by the management such that the educators lost their focus— the education of their charges. In the end, the school did not come to be known as Nee Soon Presbyterian for long. After I left the school in 1962, there was further merging and the name changed yet again. In the late 1980s, it became Kuo Chuan Presbyterian Secondary School. The land was acquired by the government and the school was relocated to Bishan. Now Haig Girls' School occupies the site of my former secondary school.

On 25 May 1961, our form teacher made an appeal to St John's Ambulance members to volunteer in aid of the Bukit Ho Swee fire. We heard that it was very serious, but after the news, it was soon forgotten. Most likely, we were too young to realise the gravity and also, nobody took the lead to organise a team of volunteers.

The trauma I experienced at the beginning of 1959 has never left me. Since I left that school in 1962, I have never stepped in that place again. I gained nothing. I lost my self-confidence and self-respect. On the day of the Cambridge School Certificate results, I stood dumbfounded for a long time along the school's corridor. My teacher Mr Bose understood my state of mind. He said, "You can join the LGPD (*Lembaga Gerakan Pelajaran Dewasa*), if you want to," he said, referring to the Adult Education Board.

Group photo after a project in 1962

A Chinese New Year visit to Robert Tok's house in 1962

Tok Thiam Chye and Lim Ban Lee were never in the same class as me after Primary 1 at Bedok Boys'. My grandma knew Ban Lee's parents and Thiam Chye was a close friend of Ban Lee. That was how we were acquainted. At Dryburgh, we were in different classes too, but we had many opportunities to get together such as Chinese

New Year and weekend free film screenings at the Reformative Training Centre at Jalan Lembah Bedok, because it was convenient to cycle to each other's places. Lim Ban Lee was at a kampong at Bedok 8½ Milestone, whereas Tok Thiam Chye lived at the bank of Bedok Canal, opposite the Yu Nerng School. We drifted apart slightly when we entered adulthood, as each of us had a different outlook on life.

Dark Clouds

In 1963, the year when Singapore, together with Sabah and Sarawak joined Malaysia, dark clouds loomed over our heads. Leng Seng Land, a real estate developer, bought over the whole area of Kampong Tanah Merah Kechil (the present day Limau Estate) which stretched from the perimeter of the Bedok School grounds to Tanah Merah Kechil Road, to develop the area into a private housing estate. Our joy and happiness turned to shock, despair, and helplessness. The worst hit was our parents. Every night, they hugged each other and cried, "Where to get another piece of land to provide for the future of our six children, ourselves and mother?" My dad approached many organisations for help. The first to look into our case was the Country People's Association. Several people from the association visited us, asked a few questions, and took down our particulars. They nailed a small plaque on the top right-hand corner of the doorpost before they left. Mr Soh Heng Chye from the People's Action Party paid us a visit too. He promised to look into our problems.

Yeo Chye Peng, a distant relative, was also consulted. After much discussion, he said the compensation should include loss of income, capital outlay, expenses for the search of a new location, the capital investment for the new location. He said we should demand $15,000. The next day, this was conveyed to the site manager.

After a week, the site manager came back to us. He said that a sum of $6,000 had been allocated for us. After much deliberation, we finally accepted it. We had to go to his office at Bonham Building in Finalyson Green to collect the cheque. I accompanied my dad. It was a small office. The cheque was ready. A clerk checked my dad's identity card before he signed on the dotted line on a sheet of paper. We were given a certain amount of time to pack up. We went home feeling very down.

From that day onwards, every day we made enquiries for a new farming site. We went to inspect any sites that friends recommended—Mata Ikan, Padang Terbakar, Ulu Bedok— but all in vain. Then we met my uncle, Yeo Koon Seng, whose daughter-in-law's relative owned a piece of land at Peng Ghee Road, Kampong Chai Chee.

For the next few months after that, our normal lives were disrupted. We had to wind things down at Tanah Merah Kechil and set up our farm on the virgin premises of Peng Ghee Road.

Hong Teck was studying at Sin Min Public School along East Coast Road, a Chinese school where many of our neighbours and relatives were enrolled. Gan Teck Ann, the son of Gan Cheng Huat, was teaching English there. It was converted from a big bungalow situated on the top of the cliff. To reach the school one either had to walk up a long steep flight of steps or go around a gradual slope via Parbury Avenue. My dad thought the distance from Sin Min, where we attended school, to our new home would be too inconvenient. There were two options—to get a transfer either to Yeu Nerng School or Pin Ghee High School. After much deliberation with the principal and neighbours, my dad decided that sending Hong Teck to Yeu Nerng School was a better option. The two reasons were that there was a pirate taxi ferrying children from Peng Ghee to Yeu Nerng School and the school had a better track record. Almost every year, it had a 100 per cent pass rate for the Primary School Leaving Examinations. Hong Hup remained at Bedok Boys' School, but he had to share a pirate taxi to get there. Hong Bian and I relied on our bicycles, so we had no problems with transport.

So many incidents occurred that year. We had practically no time to concentrate on our studies. After the disastrous results for my 'O' Level Cambridge Examination in 1962, I was advised by my teacher, Mr Bose, to enroll in the Lembaga Gerakan Pelajaran Dewasa (Adult Education Board) at Tanjong Katong Girls' School

Centre for night classes. That suited me. During the day, I could help my parents set up the new premises.

My dad had to sell the pigs and fowl prematurely. Minimal farm work was done. In the afternoons, we had to carry our knives, *changkol* and other farming implements on our bicycles to our new premises to clear the virgin plot of land of vegetation. My uncle Koon Seng was the contractor. He went to the land office to prepare what was necessary so our house could be built. After the house was up, every weekend, Hong Huat would borrow his employer's lorry to transport whatever was needed from our farm to Peng Ghee Road. By the end of 1963, the move was complete. A new chapter of our lives had begun in a new environment. This time, it was in a Chinese village. I would face a new beginning and a new life.

The Little Red Cliff: Kampong Life in Singapore from 1946-1963

Yeo Hong Eng
wwwyeohongeng.blogspot.com
yeohongeng@yahoo.com.sg

The author has contributed parts of the events in the book to the following:

1. *'Foodage' programme on OKTO Channel Singapore in 2011.*
2. *'The Day I Say My Pledge' on Channel News Asia in 2013.*
3. *'Memento' on OKTO Channel in 2013.*
4. *'A Day in the 80s' Opening of Toa Payoh MRT Station on National Geographic Channel 2013.*
5. *'Treasure Hunt" on Channel News Asia 2014*
6. *"Days of Rage—1964 Racial Riot" on Channel News Asia 2014.*
7. *Audio and Visual Social Studies supplementary materials for the Ministry of Education of Singapore 2013*
8. *'There was A Time on Media Corp Channel 5 2013*
9. *'Campaigns' on OKTO Channel June 2014.*

Watch out for the next book: Kampong Chai Chee (1964-1974)